Contents

Into the Wilderness

This is a 'how-to' book, an instructional volume intent on showing you how to move and live in wild country safely and in comfort. Much of the book is concerned with the items needed to do this and how to use them; factual stuff leavened with a little bias and opinion but down-to-earth and functional nevertheless. Even so, some explanation as to why it's worth trying to convey this information is, I think, required.

But capturing the essence of backpacking in words—the joy of walking through the ever-changing, ever-constant natural world, the magic of waking to sunlight glinting on a mist-wreathed lake, the excitement of striding through a mountain storm—is very difficult. At heart I feel it is impossible to describe these things to the uninitiated, the baffled disbeliever. How can one talk to them of the liberating sense of living in the moment, of being free of always thinking of tomorrow, of the almost painful delight in the exquisite beauty of a transient cloud, a tiny flower in an ocean of rock, a butterfly's wing, of the awe engendered by a mountain vista stretching unbroken beyond the power of sight, of the fragile moment of identity when you stare deeply into a wild animal's eyes and just for a second connect? But then it is not for those people that this book is written. Those interested in my thoughts on backpacking will already be responsive to the real world outside our modern technological shell.

But why backpack? Why forgo the comforts of home or hotel for a night out under a flimsy sheet of nylon? Many people walk in the wilds but seek a return to civilisation at night. To my mind this is only experiencing part of what the wilderness has to offer; it is akin to dipping your toe in the water instead of succumbing to the refreshing and invigorating shock of immersion. Only by living in the wilderness 24 hours a day, day after day, do I gain the indefinable feeling of rightness, of being *with* instead of against the earth that provides the deepest sense of contentment with life that I have found.

Now I'm aware that all this sounds quite nebulous, verging on the mystical even, but I make no apology for that. We are, I think, too prone to value only that which we can define and explain in hard logical terms and that which can be given a cash value. Yet the world, the natural self-regulating earth, does not run on these lines; it cannot be quantified and calculated and summed up. Every attempt to do so produces another unknown, another mystery just beyond our grasp. And this pleases me. I am content not to comprehend fully the value wilderness living has for me as I suspect that—like chasing the ends of rainbows—trying to do so would be a fruitless task and one that if ever realised, would only result in disappointment.

The heart of backpacking lies in the concept of the journey, the desire to explore the world beyond the known of everyday life and in doing so to explore the self. Until comparatively recently all journeys were like this because the realm of daily life extended very little further than one's home town. Now though, with today's modern communications and mass transport, most so-called journeys are merely the mechanical moving of bodies efficiently from

The Backpacker's Handbook

CHRIS TOWNSEND

 The Oxford Illustrated Press

ISBN 1 85509 200 X

Published by:
The Oxford Illustrated Press,
Haynes Publishing Group, Sparkford,
Nr. Yeovil, Somerset BA22 7JJ, England

Printed in England by:
J.H. Haynes & Co Limited,
Sparkford, Nr. Yeovil, Somerset

British Library Cataloguing in Publication Data:
A Catalogue record for this book is available from the British Library:

Library of Congress Catalog Card Number:
91-72667

Acknowledgements

There are far too many people who have added to my store of knowledge and assisted on my walks to thank them all personally here but there are some I feel I must single out.

When I began backpacking in the early 1970s Eric Gurney and the members of the Backpackers Club helped guide my first steps with advice and companionship. Club weekends are still good places to learn basic skills. I generally avoid formal instruction preferring to learn by trial and error but I did decide that some initial teaching was necessary when I took up ski touring and for getting me started my thanks to ski instructor, mountaineer and *Great Outdoors* magazine editor Cameron McNeish.

Since I started writing various people have encouraged me and helped me believe I had something worth saying, most recently and in particular John Traynor.

Although I more often than not travel solo I have learnt much from the many companions I have shared trails and camp sites with over the years and have many valued memories of our treks. My thanks to Denise Thorn, Fran Townsend, Kris Gravette, Graham Huntington, Alain Kahan, Mark Edgington, Chris & Janet Ainsworth, Andy Hicks, Scott Steiner, Larry Lake, Dave Rehbehn, Wayne Fuiten, Ron Ellis, Todd Seniff, Clyde Soles, Tim Daniels, Steve Twaites, Al Micklethwaite, Alex Lawrence and all the others I've shared the wilderness with.

Many equipment makers and designers have assisted me generously over the years with both advice and equipment. My thanks in particular to Gordon Conyers of Craghoppers, Harald Milz of Akzo (the makers of Sympatex), Paul Howcroft founder and once the inspiration of Rohan, Mike Parsons and the staff of Karrimor, Peter Lockey and the staff of Berghaus, Hamish Hamilton of Buffalo, Peter Hutchinson of Mountain Equipment, Rab Carrington of Rab Down Equipment, Nick Stevens of Survival Aids, Nick Brown of Nikwax, Derrick Draper of Outdoor Pursuits Services, Alan Waugh and Ken Rawlinson of Phoenix Mountaineering, Tony Wale of Silva, Ben and Marion Wintringham of Wintergear, Morgan J. Connolly of Cascade Designs, Chris Brasher of Brasher Boots, Nigel Gifford of Camera Care Systems, Tony Howard of Troll, Jim White of Vango, Bob Gorton of The North Face, John Skelton, once of Ski & Climb, the staff of Highland Guides, Dr. John Keighley, Tony Pearson and Huw Kingston.

The book was written in a beautiful house in the Scottish Highlands in a study looking out across Strathspey to the Cairngorm mountains. The house isn't mine and I owe many thanks to its owners Denise Thorn and Mike Walsh and their children Rowena and Hazel for allowing me such a peaceful haven to work in and for putting up with having an obsessive backpacker wandering about their home constantly muttering about stove boiling times and tent weights and other arcane subjects.

one place to another, the process being so sanitised and safe as to preclude any sense of adventure or personal involvement. Only when I shoulder my pack and step into the wilderness do I feel a journey is really beginning even if I've travelled half way round the world to get to the start.

A journey requires a beginning and an end even though what it is about is actually what happens between those two points. I learnt this when I once set out into the mountains of north-west Scotland with no plan and no idea of where I would go. The weather was good, the scenery spectacular and the camp sites pleasant, yet after only a few days I began to feel a vague sense of dissatisfaction and after a week I abandoned the trip. Without a purpose to my wanderings I had no incentive to keep moving, nothing to give shape to the trip, nothing to define its limits. Even on day walks I always set myself a goal, whether it is a summit to reach, a lake to visit or a certain distance to cover. Though this appears to be imposing those blinkers I rejected above, part of me finds it necessary. Once I have an overall aim for a walk I can concentrate on the day-by-day, hour-by-hour, minute-by-minute details which is what it is really about.

Walking is the only way to really see a place, to really grasp what it's like, really to experience it in all its aspects. This applies even to cities but much, much more to mountains and deserts, forests and meadows. Seen from a car or a train or even a 'scenic viewpoint' these are only pretty pictures, postcard images for the surface of the mind, quickly forgotten until the snaps come back from the processors. By walking through a landscape you enter into it, experience it with every one of your five senses, learn how it works and why it is as it is, and become, for a time, a part of it. And once you stay out overnight and entrust your sleeping self to its care a deeper bond is forged and perhaps, fleetingly and at the edge of the mind, you begin to grasp that we are not *apart* from the earth but *part* of the earth.

This process of exploration of the relationship between the self and the natural world is one that grows and expands as you become more experienced and more confident in wilderness wandering—at least that is my experience. It does not, I suspect, have limits although it reflects perhaps our need to return to our most basic roots of all, when our most distant ancestors were nomadic hunter-gatherers.

Not that I would suggest or contemplate even for a second returning to such a state. I do think though that we have gone too far the other way, too far towards a belief that we are superior to nature, that it exists purely for us to control, tame and exploit. To say this is becoming almost commonplace but while the new awareness is to be applauded, too often, the words are mouthed by those for whom they are only words—i.e., cynical politicians who are more interested in the short-term vote than in the environment.

Backpacking provides a unique insight into nature, a unique opportunity for experiencing the reality of the natural world. If it has any validity apart from providing a satisfying personal experience (good enough in itself of course) it lies, I think, in this. For at a time when the balance of nature itself is threatened—when we seem intent on destroying our only life-support system—backpackers in particular should understand that we have to change our ways in relation to nature; to acknowledge that our interests are the same. If we don't, then worrying about the preservation of acres of wilderness for backpackers to wander in will become quite irrelevant.

This, however, is a manual on backpacking, not a green polemic, so I will restrain myself from saying more, other than that backpackers above all people should be involved in bodies like the Sierra Club, the Scottish Wild Land Group, the John Muir Trust and other groups trying to preserve our still-beautiful world.

Before plunging into the detail of equipment and technique though, I'd like to look at the idea of wilderness, a magic word redolent of mountain and forest, of untamed nature, of a wild beauty. First, prosaically, a definition.

A wilderness, in contrast with those areas where man and his own works dominate the landscape, is hereby recognized as an area where the earth and its community of life are untrammeled by man, where man himself is a visitor who does not remain . . . .
(1964 US Wilderness Act)

According to a Sierra Club survey at least a third of the earth's land surface, more than 48 million km²/18 million sq. miles, is still wilderness, and untouched by human development. And that is only taking into account areas of over 4000km²/1500 sq miles, which excludes many regions. The survey also omitted areas where there was any human signature, from the western deserts of the USA (overgrazing by livestock) to most of Iceland (too many four-wheel drive tracks), that others would still regard as wilderness.

Many areas backpackers visit don't fit these descriptions. In Europe in particular, wilderness areas are small, and if defined in terms of never having been touched by human hand, virtually non-existent. But if there is enough land to walk into and set up a camp and then walk on with that freeing of the spirit that comes when you escape the constraints of modern living then, to me at least, that constitutes wilderness, in spirit if not by definition.

All wilderness, from the vast expanse of Antarctica—the only continent in the Sierra Club survey considered 100 per cent pristine—to the small pockets still existing in even the most heavily industrialised countries, needs defending. The Sierra Club survey also points out that only 3 per cent of wilderness will be protected by the end of the century, a pitifully small amount. To know that there are places that can only be reached on foot, that require an effort and a commitment to visit, is vitally important. It will be a sad day if the last such spot ever succumbs to the paved road, and the hollow stare of the detached tourist.

But wilderness also needs defending from those who love it. Damaging practices and the sheer weight of numbers are turning many popular areas into worn-out remnants of their former selves. Traditionally wilderness travellers lived off the land for shelter as well as for food, building lean-tos and teepees, cutting boughs for mattresses and logs for tables and chairs. Recently such practices have become more popular, even in countries such as Britain with very little wild land left and even fewer forests, as a result of the promotion of 'survival' games. However these days such an approach is irresponsible even in remote areas of the world. There is too little wilderness left and every scar diminishes what remains.

Even with modern equipment backpackers have more impact on the land than daywalkers and therefore more responsibilities. No-trace camping techniques must be the norm if any wild country is to survive and these practices apply to little-visited areas as well as popular ones. Throughout this book there is an emphasis on these techniques, for there are only two solutions to the problems of wilderness visitors degrading the areas they profess to respect: one is self-regulation, the practice of minimum impact techniques by all; the other is the imposition of regulation from outside. This already occurs in many national parks world-wide. In some, mainly in North America, wilderness camping is allowed only on specified sites, in others, such as several in the Alps, wild camping is forbidden altogether, and people are required to stay in mountain huts. Such restrictions are anathema to the spirit of freedom inherent in backpacking but they will become the norm, and rightly so, unless backpackers learn to leave the wilderness untouched.

The Load on Your Back: Choosing & Using Equipment

The aspect of backpacking that puts off so many people, is the fact that you have to carry everything you need for days, maybe even weeks on your back. The resulting load looks to the uninitiated, backbreakingly heavy, heavy enough in fact to take all the joy out of walking, all the pleasure from a day in the mountains. Now I am not a masochist. I don't like pain, I don't like aching shoulders, sore hips and trail-pounded blistered feet. Nor do I like being wet or cold. So after suffering all those in my first few attempts at backpacking I began to take a keen interest in equipment and I learnt that you don't have to go through agony to go backpacking.

Whilst experience and technique have a large part to play, no amount of skill will make an inadequate pack carry a 25-kg/55-lb load comfortably, or a leaking rain jacket waterproof. The right equipment can make the difference between a successful trip you want to repeat and a hellish nightmare that will make you shudder every time you see a rucksack. This is no exaggeration. I've met walkers who back away at the mention of the word backpacking, muttering about their one attempt on the Pennine Way (a trail that seems to attract people without the skills to enjoy it) and how their backs ached, their knees gave way, their tents leaked and they suffered for weeks afterwards. It doesn't have to be like that.

My initial interest in equipment was born from a couple of soakings on the hills that ended in descents in the dark and near hypothermia, and from lugging a heavy cotton tent that leaked at the merest hint of rain around the English Lake District in a pack that resembled a medieval torture rack. Not that I ever carried such a tent up any hills—reaching a valley camp site from a bus stop was exhausting enough. I used this equipment through ignorance. I simply didn't know anything better existed.

Two experiences showed me that it was possible to be more comfortable. The first was when an American hiker expressed horror at the sight of my huge pack frame. 'No hipbelt?' he exclaimed. 'What's a hipbelt?' I replied. He handed me his pack, an even bigger one than mine. I put it on and tightened up the hipbelt. The weight of the pack seemed to melt away. Ever since I've viewed the hipbelt as the key feature of any pack designed for heavy loads.

The other occasion was on a farm camp site where I was using a wooden-poled cotton ridge tent that weighed a ton. Sitting outside this neither wind nor waterproof monstrosity I watched a walker with a moderate-sized pack come down from the mountains and unpack and pitch a tiny green nylon tent. The next morning he packed everything up, shouldered his pack and headed, effortlessly it seemed, back into the hills. To say I was impressed is an understatement. The realisation that it was possible to backpack in comfort led me to visit outdoor shops, write away for equipment catalogues and indeed read books about backpacking.

Later on I worked for a time in an equipment shop and started writing reviews of gear for outdoor magazines. I've been doing this since the late 1970s and thus have a fairly detailed knowledge of what's available and, more importantly as individual styles and names come and go, what to look for in equipment. My interest in gear may seem to give it a greater importance than it deserves. After all, it's only a tool. Backpacking is not about having the latest tent or trying out the new guaranteed-to-keep-you-comfortable-in-all-weather-conditions clothing system. However, knowing enough about equipment to select the stuff that really works and won't let you down means that when you're out there in the wilderness you don't need to think about your gear. You can take it for granted and get on with what you really came for— which is experiencing the natural world in all its glory. Worrying about whether it will rain because you don't trust your waterproofs to keep you dry or what you will do if it's very cold at night because of your threadbare sleeping bag, will come between you and the environment, and may even become the dominant factor in your walk. In some circumstances, inadequate gear could even threaten your life. So it's worth taking your time choosing equipment. It'll be with you for many a mile and on many a night and if it doesn't live up to expectations your experience of backpacking will, to say the least, be an unpleasant one. Of course if you find an item that works as near to perfect as you can imagine for your style of backpacking then stick to it and forget about the alternatives until it needs replacing.

THE WEIGHT FACTOR

Three major factors govern choice of gear: performance, durability and weight. The first is simple; an item must do what is required of it. A waterproof must keep out the rain, a stove must bring water to the boil. How long it goes on doing so efficiently is a measure of its durability. But it's easy to make items that perform well and last for ages. The problem for backpackers is the weight of such gear and much time is spent by equipment designers trying to produce stuff that will perform well, last a long time and yet weighs very little. For when you're carrying everything on your back, weight matters a great deal. More time is probably spent by backpackers trying to reduce the weight of their packs than on all other aspects of trip planning combined. And such time is usually well spent. A 1-kg saving in weight means another day's food can be carried. The difference between a 15-kg/33-lb pack and a 20-kg/44-lb one is considerable, especially near the end of a long hard day.

Equipment available currently can be divided into two categories: standard and lightweight. The first is where compromises have been made between weight and durability to produce gear that is light enough to carry but strong enough to last for years of average use and also for the duration of a long multi-month expedition. It's what most people use most of the time. With this equipment I find that in summer, a load for a week-long solo trip, without food but including fuel, maps, boots and clothing, weighs around 12kg/26lb. Extra items for a much longer trip that may run into autumn or even winter, push this up to around 16kg/35lb. (see Appendix One for a complete list). If you're travelling with a group, shared camping and cooking equipment will knock a little off this, whilst the need for specialist gear for winter conditions will push it up. After talking to other people these weights don't seem far off the norm.

Events such as mountain marathons where you have to run/walk long distances off-trail, over rugged terrain, carrying all you need for a couple of days, have spawned a complete range of gear where weight is the prime factor. I've done such marathons where my partner and I have carried no more than 6kg/13lb each and survived the most awful stormy weather. Survived is the key word though. I wouldn't like to use such gear for weeks on end, appealing though the lack of weight is, and anyway much ultralight equipment wouldn't last if it is used day in, day out.

There are crossovers between the two categories naturally. On mountain marathons, with just one night spent camping, I've used the same tent for two that I use solo on longer trips. And ultra-lightweight waterproofs, some of which barely merit the name waterproof, are fine for trips to areas where constant heavy rain

The author and his gear plus food for ten days at Fort Selkirk on the Yukon River during a three-month walk through Canada's Yukon Territory.

is unlikely and they'll spend most of their time in the pack. So specialist equipment shouldn't be rejected out of hand. Some of it could help to lighten your load. The more durable items have moreover started to become standard gear, as we shall see.

Weight is subjective too. When you set out on a deep-into-the-wilderness venture carrying a 32-kg/70-lb pack containing two weeks' supplies, the 18-kg/40-lb load you emerge with feels amazingly light. Set off cold with 18kg/40lb for a weekend and the burden will seem unbearable. There are limits of course. I once carried a load of over 50kg/110lb (including snowshoes, ice axe, crampons and 23 days' food) through the snowbound High Sierras in California. I couldn't lift my pack but had to sit down, slide my arms though the shoulder straps and then roll forward on to all fours before slowly standing up. Carrying such a weight was not fun and I was exhausted by the end of every 20-km/12 mile day. I wouldn't do it again. Since then I have started on sections of long treks with 36kg/79lb in my pack and found that too much

for real enjoyment. Only after the first week do such loads come down to bearable proportions. My aim is never to carry more than 32kg/70lb on any trip and preferably not that much; 28kg/62lb I find quite manageable, however, as long as my pack is up to supporting the load and that's really the most I think it's possible to carry and still enjoy a walk.

I start a trip on the assumption that if I think I need something I'll take it. If the total weight then seems too much I'll try and work out what I can do without. When you're packing it's a bit late to decide you could do with a lighter tent or sleeping bag though, which is why your original choice of gear is so important. In every case when selecting gear, if the only difference between two items is the weight, then I go for the lighter one. Whilst it's obviously with the big items (tent, sleeping bag, pack, stove, etc.) that weight builds up, every gram counts and it all has to be carried. I like to know the weight of *everything* I consider carrying—down to the smallest item. A set of scales is essential for this. I use kitchen ones that measure to the nearest gram. If you can't decide between two items and the store doesn't have scales, it might be worth taking your own along. Catalogue weights are often inaccurate.

CHECKLISTS

For any walk you have to decide exactly what to take and here I find a checklist essential (see Appendix One). No walk is the same and I doubt whether I've ever taken exactly the same gear on more than one trip. When, where and for how long you go determines what you need to carry. To decide which items are needed you need to know about the weather and any special factors that apply to the area (do you need cord for bearbagging food, insect repellent, an ice axe?). I like to feel I can cope with the most extreme weather I am likely to encounter at the time of year I'm going. If I can do so then I should have no problems coping with 'average' conditions. I work from a basic list of all my gear, making a specific list for every walk. As every item has been weighed I can then work out just how much basic gear I'll be carrying. By adding on food at the rate of 1kg/2.2lb per day plus the weight of my camera gear, I then know just what the total load is. Usually at that point I go over the list again to see if anything can be left out or replaced with a lighter alternative (for major trips that will last many months I do this obsessively over and over again). Once you can judge fairly well what you need for a trip however you'll probably find, as I now do, that your first list rarely needs more than tinkering with.

CHOOSING AND BUYING

The highly competitive nature of the outdoor equipment market means that styles and names change rapidly. Companies come and go, brand names are taken over, new materials emerge. Some of the changes are cosmetic only, some involve breakthroughs in design. No book can be up-to-date with new developments. What a book can do, as I hope this one does, is give general guidelines about choosing equipment and point out features to look for. For the latest information on equipment though you need to turn to four sources: the specialist shops, the mail order companies, manufacturers and importers, and outdoor magazines.

If you can find a good equipment shop with staff who use the stuff regularly and know what they're talking about, cultivate it. Such a shop will be in touch with what's happening and will be able to keep you informed as well as give good advice. You may not live near a specialist shop, however, or the shop may not be particularly helpful. Moreover, even the best retailer only stocks a fraction of what is available. So you may need to look at other sources.

One alternative to the high street shop is mail order, and there are now a number of reputable companies who produce regular informative catalogues often featuring 'own brand' items not available elsewhere as well as comparison charts of equipment. Companies I've bought gear from and found reliable, and who also produce excellent catalogues, are Field & Trek, Survival Aids, and Cotswold Camping in the UK, and REI in the USA (see Appendix Three for addresses). They'll all supply overseas customers. Just watch the exchange rate!

Company catalogues and brochures are worth writing for and often give a lot of information on materials and uses as well as on specific products. All will tell you their product is the best, however, and some, particularly those from British companies sad to say, lack essential details such as weights.

For a more detached viewpoint consult the outdoor magazines. Most run regular gear reviews and tests, often going into great detail. They also carry news of the latest gear and advertisements from most of the big names plus many smaller companies whose products you may never find in a shop or mail order catalogue.

In Britain four magazines I consult regularly are *Trail Walker*, *The Great Outdoors*, *Climber & Hillwalker* and *High* (see Appendix Three for addresses). The first two are the ones with most material on backpacking, the last two having a slant towards rock climbing and mountaineering.

In the USA the leading specialist magazine for many years has been *Backpacker* which has improved markedly under new owners Rodale after something of a decline in the mid-1980s. *Outside*, although covering a wide field, often has features of interest to backpackers. In Canada the same applies to *Explore* (see Appendix for addresses).

QUALITY

Where gear is made is no longer a relevant factor. Outdoor companies are international and you can buy the best gear worldwide. Much high-quality equipment from reputable companies is made in the Far East, which was once known only for budget items and several American companies have factories in Europe. You may want to buy gear made in your home country for patriotic reasons, but you don't need to do so to ensure good quality.

What you should do is check carefully and thoroughly every bit of gear you buy. However reputable the company and however careful the quality control there's always the occasional faulty item that slips through. It is better to discover that your tent door zip jams when half closed or that the poppers fall off your jacket the first time you put it on (one of the commoner faults in my experience) at home than far from anywhere in a raging blizzard. Make sure everything works. Check too that stitching is neat and unbroken and the ends of lines are finished properly. With filled garments and sleeping bags you can't see what the work is like inside but if the outside is put together well, chances are so is the interior. On garments and tents with taped seams check that the tapes are flat and run in straight lines. Attention to such details should ensure that you pick up any manufacturing defects before they cause problems out in the wilds.

COST

Buy the best you can afford. In a blizzard on a mountain top the money saved on a cheap jacket is meaningless. Its performance is crucial. Your life might depend on it. At the same time this doesn't mean that you need to buy the most expensive items or that you shouldn't go out if you can't afford top-of-the-range gear. There are huge price differences in many areas, especially clothing where high prices often mean the latest styles, colours and fabrics rather than better performance. Indeed the most expensive garments are often too complex and heavy for the backpacker, who will be better off with simpler, more basic and cheaper designs. Depending where you go there are critical items of gear in whose choice money should be no object but other items where spending a great deal—or indeed anything—is unnecessary. The limitations of your gear might restrict you in terms of where and when you can go but should never stop you going out at all. And if it's a choice between a new tent or a warm jacket and a few

days or a week in the wilderness, get on out there!

COLOUR

Everything from packs to sleeping bags and even boots comes in bright colours these days so I am dealing with the subject here so that I don't need to repeat myself for each type of gear.

When I began backpacking the choice of colour for most items was between various shades of green, brown and blue. Waterproof jackets and tents were also available in orange or red 'for safety reasons'. This caused some controversy, with many objections to the lines of orange-clad day walkers to be seen on the British hills. However those mutterings were mild compared with the reaction of some people to the explosion of brilliant colours and multi-hued equipment that started in the 1980s and which shows no sign of abating. 'Visual pollution' is the cry of those who seek a return to the green clad hillgoers of yore.

I have to say that my views on this are unclear, not to say confused. For a decade and more I was very much in favour of being inconspicuous. Indeed at one time a group of backpacking friends and I acquired the nickname 'the green cagoule brigade' because that was what we all wore. Two factors have caused this view to be moderated. The first was the upsurge of interest in 'survivalism' (not to be confused with general survival techniques, though the two unfortunately overlap a little) and the use of the hills and forests for pseudo-military activities. I don't go into the wilds in order to pretend I'm in the SAS or the Marines and I don't want to be associated with those that do. Green and brown clothing does imply such an allegiance (four of us were once mistaken for soldiers when skiing in the Alps because of our olive green windproof clothing). I now prefer to wear at least one item that doesn't look as if it is military surplus.

However the main factor has been photography. On the Pacific Crest Trail in 1982 I wore dark blue and green clothing and used a sludge brown tent. In my photographs of that trip I usually look like a black smudge whilst the tent blends neatly into the trees. A bright garment, especially a red one, can give a splash of colour that makes a photograph.

At the same time however I don't like seeing brightly coloured tents dominating the view in a mountain cirque so I've come to a compromise of sorts whereby I still prefer fairly dull colours for my tent (though these may be pale shades) but always like to carry at least one item of reasonably bright clothing. I don't however, go for the glaring multi-coloured garments that are available though I've used one or two that have been supplied as test items. Subdued, pale shades can stand out well in photographs without signalling to everyone else that you're around. As for the safety argument, I always have at least one if not two orange or red stuff-sacs in my pack which could be used to signal my whereabouts if necessary.

LABORATORY TESTING

Many manufacturers spend a great deal of time and money subjecting their equipment and fabrics to laboratory tests, the results of which often pop up in catalogues and advertisements. There are tests for everything from the water-proofness of a fabric to the wind resistance capabilities of a tent. Different manufacturers often don't use the same ones so comparing results can be difficult. Moreover, although such tests can provide a pointer as to how a garment will work in the outdoors they in no way guarantee a particular level of performance and anyway gear often works differently for different people. This especially applies to warm clothing and sleeping bags. What keeps one person nice and cosy may not be enough to stop someone else shivering. Read and note laboratory test results by all means but don't assume that the perfect-sounding item will perform exactly the same way in the real world.

FINAL THOUGHTS

The next chapters cover the intricacies of equipment and how to use it. Technical details of gear and information on techniques are interwoven rather than dealt with separately as no equipment, however good, is of any use if you don't know what to do with it. An experienced backpacker can function more efficiently and safely with a minimum of basic gear than a novice with the latest hi-tech designs. The views are my own and experienced backpackers will undoubtedly find much to disagree with. Those who don't have the experience yet to have strong views (prejudices?) of their own should note that I am only describing what works for me and that there are other valid and efficient ways of operating. Take what I have to say as a guide but, please, not as a rule. I've named names, so to speak, as it's easier to illustrate details that way. Much of the equipment I describe is that which I've used and which has worked well for me. No one can try out even a fraction of what is available though and there is a lot of other gear which is as good as that I've selected. I've mentioned items which I know of by reputation or from friends whose judgement I respect, but there are some which will be missed out completely. I make no claim to being objective. This is a subjective book, and nowhere is it more so than in the equipment and technique chapters. In the process of putting my thoughts on paper I've reassessed my views about gear, which in some cases has resulted in a complete reappraisal of my beliefs on the subject. New ideas and bits of gear have appeared during the writing of the book and these have been incorporated, with a note on their newness. Development is ongoing so this book will be out of date before it is published with regard to certain items. However the general principles outlined here will hold true I'm sure, and, the reason for describing specific items is to illustrate those principles. Remember though that the reasons for going backpacking are timeless, what gear you use being in this sense totally irrelevant.

A Note on Weights and Measures
Items I've used I've weighed myself so the weights quoted may differ from those provided by manufacturers. Elsewhere catalogue weights have been used when available. Although it may be clumsy, I've given both metric and imperial measurements; because of the state of confusion regarding the replacement of the latter by the former in both the USA and the UK (Canada seems to have managed it better), some equipment makers use one, some the other, some both. Where I've given only one, it isn't because I grew fed up with doing the conversion, but because there is actually an accepted standard, as for example with skis and ice axes which are always measured in centimetres.

Footwear & Wilderness Travel

More backpacking trips are probably ruined by sore feet than by all other causes combined. Pounded by the ground below and the weight of you and your pack above, your feet receive harsher treatment than any other part of your body. Whilst feet are marvellously complex, being flexible and tough at the same time, they need care and protection if they are to carry you and your load for mile after mile through the wilderness in comfort. This comfort is provided in the main by your footwear.

There are many accessories that make walking easier and safer—from staffs to socks and, for snow travel, ice axe, crampons, snowshoes and skis. It can be argued that using either of the last two doesn't constitute walking. They do however greatly aid travel in deep snow especially when carrying a heavy pack so I have included them here.

BOOTS and SHOES

The Function of Footwear

Before going into the details of boot materials, construction and design, it's worth considering what backpacking footwear is meant to do. The essentials are to protect the foot and ankle against bruising and damage from rocks and the ground, to give support to the foot and ankle and to provide good grip on slippery, steep and wet terrain whilst at the same time being comfortable to wear for many hours and many miles. Secondary considerations are to keep the feet warm and dry. Protection and support for the upper foot and ankle is given by a close but not too tight fit that stops the foot from twisting in the boot but which has enough 'give' to allow the foot to expand as it swells during the day and an outer that is tough enough to resist penetration by sharp objects and which has enough stiffening at the ankle, heel and toe to prevent injury from rocks and stones. Note that the ankle is held in place by a stiff lower heel counter and not simply a high boot. Some running shoes give more support to the ankle than some boots. Protection for the sole of the foot is provided by layers of material in the boot sole that cushion it against hard ground and that are stiff enough laterally to minimise the twisting of the foot when traversing steep ground but soft enough to allow a natural toe-to-heel flex. Good grip is given by the pattern cut out of the hard rubber of the outer sole. The best grips not only give security on rough terrain but also minimise damage to the ground surface. Top-quality leather is fairly water resistant but only boots with 'breathable' membrane inserts can be considered waterproof and how long they stay so is open to question. Plastic boots are waterproof (as are rubber ones) but lead to hot, sweaty feet. There are better ways to keep your feet dry than fully waterproof boots.

The Fit

Choosing boots is not something to rush; they'll be with you every step of the way. If they aren't right, you'll suffer and suffer badly. Nothing is worse than boots that hurt your feet. In the following pages I go into great detail about types of boots and shoes, construction methods, materials and more. All of these are points to consider when buying footwear, but they are immaterial compared with one crucial factor: the fit. A pair of the most modern, hi-tech, waterproof, breathable, unbelievably expensive boots are worse than useless if they don't fit your feet. As everyone's feet are a different shape fit is more than just a question of finding the right size. For that reason it is unwise to set your heart on a particular model before you go shopping, however seductive the ad's prose.

Time is needed when purchasing footwear. It's best to allow several hours for the job and to try to visit a shop at a quiet time and not on a busy Saturday afternoon. Feet swell during the day so it is best to try on new footwear later rather than earlier. Take with you, if you can, the socks you intend wearing with the boots. If you can't, most shops provide thick socks to wear whilst trying on boots. Your normal shoe size should be used only as a guide. Sizes vary from maker to maker and there are three different sizing systems on the market (British, European and American—see chart) just to make matters more confusing. As a shop may stock boots made in Britain, the USA, Italy, South Korea, Czechoslovakia, Sweden and other countries you can't expect consistency in sizing. Make sure that you to try on both boots. Everyone's feet vary, perhaps by as much as half a size. If there is a big difference make sure it is the larger foot that has the best fit. An extra sock or insole can pad out a slightly large boot, but nothing can be done for one that is too small.

Fitting light- and medium-weight boots and shoes is quite easy as they conform quickly to the feet and generally stay the same shape in use, especially if made of nylon/suede material. Heavier boots are stiffer and therefore tend to feel uncomfortable when first worn, which makes finding a good fit in the shop harder. Yet because they are so unforgiving, a good fit is essential even though they also stretch (in width, but not in length) and mould to your feet. So more care is needed when fitting traditional and heavy leather boots.

With any boot, what you are looking for is a snug but not too tight fit. Length is the first point to check. If your toes touch the end of the boot whilst leaving no space at the heel, then it's too small. With your foot slid forward in an unlaced boot there should just be room for a finger to be inserted between the boot and your heel. If you can't do this the boots are too short, and will cause bruised and painful toes, especially on long downhills. If there is room for more than one finger the boots are too big. When the boots are laced up your heel shouldn't move up and down by more than a centimetre when you walk. Nor should it move from side to side. If it does the chances are you'll get blisters and the boots will not provide support on rough terrain.

Boots should be wide enough for you to wriggle your toes easily in them but not so wide that your feet can slide about. In the USA many boots come in different width fittings, which makes finding the right width easier. In the UK, unfortunately, this is not so. As someone who has very broad feet I have had great difficulty in finding boots that fit. The Brasher models fit

Boot Size Comparison Table

14

me, as they only come in a wide fitting whilst a few Scarpa models and most Vasque and Merrell ones are available in several widths, as are New Balance running shoes. But that's it. Asolo make different width fittings but none is available in the UK at the time of writing. Insoles make a difference to the width—take them out for a larger boot, put in thicker ones for a closer fit. Realising the potential of this Vasque have produced a series of lightweight boots called the Clarion range featuring a choice of three footbeds in different widths. Vasque call this the Variable Fit System. I haven't used them but it seems a good idea—though I doubt whether it can provide as wide a range of width fittings as boots made on different width lasts, which is something Vasque also do.

Once you have found boots that seem to be roughly the right length and width you should walk around the shop in them, going up and down any stairs there may be. Note any pressure points or feelings of discomfort. On a long walk these will be magnified. The uppers should be spacious enough not to press too hard on the feet but snug enough with the laces tightened up for your foot not to move in them. Check in particular the base of the tongue, a common place for boots to rub. Only part with your money when you're happy that you have the best fit possible. Then take the boots home and wear them around the house to check the fit further. Good shops should exchange boots that haven't been waxed or worn outside if you decide that they don't fit after all.

A made-to-measure service for those who really can't find an off-the-shelf pair that fit is offered by Swedish bootmakers Lundhags or through their agents Survival Aids (see Appendix Three for details). I've had boots made for me by this company. Working off a sketched outline of my feet which I sent them, they produced a well-fitting pair of their 1500-g/3-lb Mountaineer boots which I immediately took on a two-week walk in the Pyrénées. They proved very comfortable and I had no problems with sore spots or blisters, though unfortunately the lack of a heel counter (to be added in future models) made them unsuitable for off-trail travel. In the USA Peter Limmer & Sons offer a similar service (see Appendix Three). There are probably other companies which offer the same service, though I've not come across any. Your local outdoor shop may know. You can also draw an outline of your feet if you have to buy boots by mail order—most companies have clear instructions for obtaining the right size—but nothing beats trying on a variety of boots in a shop.

Breaking In

Gone, thankfully, are the days when boots had to be worn for many short, gentle strolls before you dared risk your feet in them on a real walk. With lightweight boots you can set off on a 30-km/18-mile walk the day you buy them and suffer not a blister. With medium-weight models a short breaking-in period is advisable though not essential. Only if you have particularly tender feet do you need to wear boots for any length of time before setting off on a major trek, unless you're wearing heavyweight boots which do need a considerable breaking in period—which I don't recommend.

Lightweight/Heavyweight

Until the early 1980s virtually all boots were what we now call heavyweight with leather inners and outers, leather midsoles, steel shanks and heavily lugged rubber soles. A typical pair weighed around 2kg/$4\frac{1}{2}$lb for a size 43 and took dozens if not hundreds of miles of walking to break in. Lighter boots were available but were neither very supportive nor very durable.

The introduction of lightweight leathers, synthetic fabrics and running-shoe derived features at the start of the 1980s led to a revolution in walking footwear that has completely changed what we wear in the wilderness. Most backpackers were won over, though some stayed—and still stay—loyal to the old heavyweights. Even these have been made more comfortable, however, by the use of new design features. My conversion came nearly 2400km/1500 miles into my walk from Mexico to Canada along the Pacific Crest Trail. My traditional boots had been giving me hot, sore feet on long forested sections of trail, so when the time came to have them resoled I threw caution to the winds and replaced them instead with a pair of the new fabric/suede walking shoes, the Asolo Approach, so-called because they were designed for the approach marches of Himalayan climbing expeditions whose members had taken to wearing running shoes rather than boots. They were less than half the weight of my boots. The staff in the shop where I bought the shoes were horrified on hearing I intended backpacking over 1600km/1000 miles in them and only sold them to me on condition that I understood that they weren't recommending them. My feet, released from their stiff leather prisons, rejoiced and my daily mileage went up. The shoes, although full of holes by the end, gave all the support and grip that the boots had done, with vastly increased comfort. I was so impressed that I have never worn traditional footwear since.

Shaped footbeds, shock-absorbing midsoles, curved lasts and softer materials have all made footwear more comfortable and even traditional-style boots now have many of these features. That lighter footwear is less tiring to wear seems to me to be indisputable. The general estimate is that every 450g/1lb on your feet equals $2\frac{1}{4}$kg/5lb on your back. So wearing 1kg/2.2lb rather than 2kg/4.4lb boots is like removing $4\frac{1}{2}$kg/10lb from your pack. On a long day that makes a big difference to your comfort and degree of tiredness.

The question is though, how light can footwear be before it no longer provides adequate support and protection? —especially when you are carrying a heavy pack. Personally I find the lightest footwear the best in all but the most rugged or snowbound terrain though I am very aware that many people feel such footwear can be dangerous. Indeed on an Ultimate Challenge Coast-to-Coast walk across the Scottish Highlands I was berated on the summit of Mount Keen by a very experienced mountaineer and backpacker for the lightweight boots I was wearing! Clearly this is a contentious subject and what works for one person may not do so for another. My suggestion is to go for the lightest footwear in which you feel secure in the type of country you generally frequent. Only you can decide how light that is.

Please note that when boot weights are referred to below it is for a man's size 43 (British 9, US $9\frac{1}{2}$) as this is my size. Obviously boots several sizes larger or smaller than this will weigh proportionately more or less.

Materials and Construction

Boots are complex creations and there are many ways of making them and many different materials are used. Which you choose depends on when and where you'll use your boots—not to mention personal preference. It's perfectly possible however to buy and use boots without knowing whether they have graded flex nylon midsoles or EVA wedges or are Blake sewn. There are many good boots available today and if you buy a pair that fit well from a shop where the assistants know what they are talking about and can point you in the right direction you won't go far wrong. But for those who want to know more here's some technical details interspersed with a few subjective views.

Uppers—Leather: Leather is still the main outer material for quality boots, though synthetics have taken over for midsoles and linings and nylon/suede outer boots do have their uses. When I began backpacking, finding out what sort of leather boots were made from was quite easy as there were only a few types. The key was always to find out whether leather was full/top-grain or split-grain as the former, the outer layer of the cow's hide, is tougher and more waterproof than a split which has had the outer layer removed. Split-grain leather is often coated with polyurethane or PVC to make it more water resistant and more attractive to look at, though this shiny layer wears off fairly quickly. It is still useful, when judging the quality of a boot, to know whether the leather is top- or split-grain, but many manufacturers no longer divulge this information. Instead there are a vast number of fancy names for leather, few of them meaning much. If the boots looks good you usually have to take it on trust that the leather is good quality, a leap of faith that can be assisted by the reputation of the manufacturer. Anfibio, Crochetta and Gallusser are some of the names of quality leather worth looking out for. The one type of leather that is different to the rest is the one which has been tanned in a new way (tanning is the chemical and mechanical process by which the animal hide is turned into leather) that renders it more water repellent and quicker drying when it gets wet. Again this goes under various names, such as Hydrostop 12 (HS12), Hydrobloc and Aqua-Stop, which are added as prefixes to the base leather type (e.g. HS12 Calf). I've used this type of leather and found that it is more water repellent and quicker drying than conventional leathers, especially when new, but I wouldn't use it as the main criterion when choosing boots.

Suede is the inside half of a split leather and has a rough rather than a smooth surface. (Some top-grain leather boots have the rough, inner surface facing outwards, though most have

A selection of footwear. From the left New Balance 575 running shoes; Brasher Hillmaster lightweight boots and Vasque Summit mediumweight boots.

the smooth side doing so. 'Rough-out' leathers are easily distinguishable from suede by their thickness and solidity.) Suede is used to strengthen the wear points of synthetic footwear and to make very lightweight boots such as the 900-g/2-lb Brasher Boots. Although it is not as durable, supportive or water resistant as top-grain leather or the best splits, good-quality suede is still worth considering for lightweight footwear.

There was a trend against leather in the early 1980s because of its association with heavyweight traditional boots. In wet areas such as the British hills, however, walkers soon found that synthetic boots were nowhere near as water resistant as leather ones and leather soon regained its popularity. Owing to changes in outsoles, midsoles and linings and the introduction of high-quality lightweight leathers, there are now leather boots as light as any synthetic ones. Weight is no longer a reason for rejecting leather. Reasons for choosing leather are that it outlasts other upper materials, it keeps your feet dry longer and absorbs and then passes through moisture (sweat) quickly and efficiently. It is also flexible and comfortable to wear. For most purposes leather is still the material to choose.

Uppers—Nylon/Suede: The first new light-weights aped the nylon/suede design of the running shoes they were based on. Many such boots are still around and they work well when used on good trails and in dry conditions. The problems one encounters with them are to do with their design rather than the materials. The necessity for many seams means that they are vulnerable to abrasion and thus not suitable for use in rough, rocky terrain where boot uppers take a hammering. I found this out the hard way by wearing a pair for scrambling and walking on the incredibly rough and sharp gabbro rock of the Cuillin Hills on the Isle of Skye. After two weeks the boots were in shreds, virtually every seam having been ripped open. Waterproofness is not a strong point with nylon/suede boots either, unless they have a 'breathable' membrane insert. This is due again to the seams and the fact that grit and dirt can penetrate the nylon areas much more easily than it can leather; membranes do not last as long as they do in leather boots. This is the case whether the synthetic part of the boot is a lightweight nylon or the much tougher Cordura material.

Why consider these boots at all then? They are cooler than most leather ones for hot-weather use, they need little or no breaking in and they are very comfortable. All these factors apply to the lightest leather boots as well however, and I have to say that given the choice between leather and nylon/suede boots of the same weight I would go for leather every time.

Uppers—Plastic: Plastic has taken over for mountaineering and downhill ski boots; it is better than leather at providing the rigidity, waterproofness and warmth such pursuits require. Walking boot uppers need to be flexible however and also moisture-vapour permeable so that sweat can escape. I've tried walking in both plastic ski mountaineering and plastic climbing boots and it is an experience to be avoided. I have never had such sore and blistered heels, nor such aching feet. The rigid soles and outer shells mean such boots work against rather than with your feet. For backpacking they are totally unsuitable. Few plastic walking boots are available. Those that are have soft, flexible plastic over the front of the boot to allow for a walking gait and a synthetic liner to absorb sweat. I've only tried one pair, an early Dolomite model; I found them more comfortable than I expected but after a 40-km/25-mile day walk in freezing conditions, my feet were soaked in sweat and far too hot. That walk was on reasonably gentle terrain but I still noticed that the boots didn't support my feet in the way that leather ones do. It seems that plastic can either be supportive or flexible but unlike leather, not both. My experience with these boots also left me wondering how they would feel in warmer conditions and how they could be dried out on a backpacking trip (although some later models do have removeable linings). All in all, I couldn't see enough value in such boots to try them again. However, those who suffer from wet feet or whose concern for animal welfare precludes the use of leather footwear might well find plastic boots to be the answer. Dolomite make a walker's model, as do Koflach and a few other companies.

Uppers—Heel Counters and Toe Boxes: Heels need to be held in place and prevented from twisting and toes need protecting from rocks and anything else you may stub them against. A heel counter is a stiff piece of material, usually synthetic though sometimes leather, built into the rear of a boot that cups the heel and holds it in place. I regard heel counters as essential. Although you can't see them they can always be felt under the leather of the boot heel and they are always worth checking for. A soft, sloppy heel without a counter won't support the ankle however high the boot. Toe boxes are made from similar material inserted in the front of a boot. Alternatively protection may be provided simply by a thick rubber rand round the boot toe. If you intend crossing rocky terrain a full toe box is to be preferred as it protects the tops of the toes as well as the ends.

Linings and Padding: Traditionally linings were made from soft leather—as they still are in some boots. However, lighter, less absorbent, harder-wearing, quicker-drying, moisture-wicking and non-rotting synthetics are taking over. The main one is Cambrelle though there are others such as Sportee (found in Vasque boots). I find these new linings vastly superior to leather ones.

Many boots have thin layers of foam padding between the lining and the outer, usually just round the ankle and upper tongue areas but occasionally throughout the boot. Whilst padding does provide more cushioning for the foot it also makes boots warmer, something to be avoided for footwear used in hot weather. Foam also absorbs water and is slow-drying. I prefer boots with a minimum of padding in them, relying on socks for warmth.

Sock Liners: Many boots now have moisture-vapour-permeable membranes such as Gore-tex and Sympatex added between the lining and the outer. These certainly make the boots waterproof when they are new—but how long they last is a matter of great debate—some people swear by them—rather more swear at them! My experience with such liners suggests that they last longest in boots with the fewest seams and in boots with leather rather than nylon/suede outers and that Sympatex is the most durable material. I'm not convinced though that they add enough to the performance of a boot to be worth either seeking out or paying extra for. A good boot should long outlast the best sock liner. There are better methods of keeping water out of your boots.

The Tongue: Sewn-in, gusseted tongues with light padding inside are the most comfortable and the most water resistant. They are found on most boots. The only disadvantage I've found to this type of tongue is when walking in snow which can collect in the gussets and then soak into the boot if gaiters aren't worn. Better for snow, though not found on many boots, is the design that has two flaps of leather, basically extensions of the upper, that fold over the inner tongue, which may or may not be sewn in. These flaps are often held in place by small velcro tabs. On high ankled and stiff leather boots the tongue may be hinged so that it flexes easily.

Lacing: There are several methods for lacing up boots, using D-rings, hooks and eyelets. D-rings may be plastic and sewn to the upper (the norm on shoes and ultra-lightweight boots) or metal and attached to a swivel clip riveted to the upper. The easiest to use is a combination of several rows of D-rings above the base of the tongue followed by several rows of hooks at the top. With this system you can fully open the boot when putting it on by unhooking the laces at the top, yet quickly tighten them up. This may seem a trivial matter but I assure you, from my own experience, that it's not when you're trying to don a half-frozen boot that won't bend whilst wearing thick mitts in a small tent with a blizzard raging outside. Some systems have the lowest hook set below the others, which is claimed to help keep the laces tight. I can't say I've found that it makes any difference however. Boots with just D-rings involve far more fiddling with the laces and are harder to tighten precisely. Old-style eyelets are uncommon on boots now, though they are found more often on running shoes. Although the most awkward system to use, eyelets are the least susceptible to breakage.

Laces are usually made from braided nylon, which very rarely breaks—though it may wear through from abrasion after much usage. Round laces seem to last longer than flat ones though there isn't much in it. I used to carry spare laces but it's years since I did so and years since I had a lace snap, even on really long walks. If or when one does I'll replace it with a length of the nylon cord I always carry.

Scree Collars: Many boots have one or more rolls of foam-padded soft leather or synthetic material at the cuff designed to keep out stones, grass seeds, mud and other debris. I find that for this to work the boots have to be laced up so tightly that they restrict the movement of the ankle. Scree collars don't seem to cause any problems though so their presence or absence can be ignored when choosing a boot.

Seams: The traditional wisdom has always been the fewer seams the better, on the basis that seams mean weak points where water can enter and which can abrade, causing the boot

to drop to bits. One-piece leather boots with seams only at the heel and round the tongue will prove the most durable and water resistant, continues the conventional view. I find, on consideration, that I agree with it. I've used quite a few pairs of synthetic/suede boots and ones made from several pieces of leather and have found that their life expectancy is determined by how long the seams remain intact. Side seams are the ones that usually split first, a failure that can be held off though not prevented by coating them heavily with something like Sno-Seal's Welt Seal. This also decreases the likelihood of seams leaking.

I don't only choose one-piece leather boots, however, as there are many excellent ones, especially in the lightweight category, which are made from several bits of material. With lightweights the state of the boots in general is usually such by the time the seams split that they should be discarded anyway. However I have come round to the view that for long treks, especially in winter conditions, I prefer one-piece leather boots. This follows my walk along the length of the Canadian Rockies on which I used two pairs of sectional leather boots. They were different makes but each eventually split at the side seams after around 1200km/750 miles of walking. I believe that only a one-piece leather boot would have lasted the whole walk.

Insoles and Midsoles—Stiffness and Lateral Stability: The boot sole must support the foot and protect it from the ground. For walking it needs to have the right flex to enable a natural gait to be maintained whilst providing the stiffness needed to deal with rugged terrain. Immediately under the foot most boots and shoes now have an insole or footbed which has a curved foot shape and which can be removed for drying and replaced when worn out. Footbeds support the foot better than a flat insole and provide a bit of cushioning. If more is required they can be replaced with thicker, more padded ones using neoprene rubber or Sorbothane, both shock-absorbing materials. A few boots, such as some Salewa models, come with Sorbothane footbeds and some companies like Brasher advise replacing the standard footbed with a Sorbothane one for heavy-duty use. Note though that Sorbothane footbeds are heavy, adding some 150g/5oz to the weight of a pair of boots.

Perhaps the best insole of all, though extremely expensive, is one that is custom-made, as this fits the foot exactly, cupping each toe plus the ball of your foot. Originally introduced for alpine ski boots, custom-made insoles are now offered for walking and running footwear and many shops have the facilities for making them. This takes some time as the material has to be heat moulded to the shape of your feet. I had a pair made during my Canadian Rockies walk when the insoles that came with my first pair of boots gave me blisters; I found they prevented any movement of my feet inside the boots, thus minimising further blistering. Whether they were worth the money (they just lasted the rest of the walk, a distance of around 2000km/1250 miles), I'm not sure but I intend having some more made so that I can form a definite opinion.

Under the footbed lies the midsole or soles. Fibre-board is common in running shoes and the lightest, most flexible boots. However many of the best boots now feature stiff plastic or nylon midsoles that are graded for flex according to the size of the boot. This means that smaller-sized boots have the same stiffness as average and larger boots. With other forms of stiffening, small boots are often too stiff and large ones too bendy. The traditional form of stiffening is a half- or three-quarter- length steel shank, only a centimetre or so wide, running forward from the heel to give solidity to the rear of the foot and providing lateral stability and support for the arch whilst allowing the front of the foot to flex when walking. Full length shanks are for rigid mountaineering boots and not for walking boots. Some boots combine a steel shank with a flexible synthetic midsole, though that doesn't seem necessary to me.

Found in many boots is a third midsole consisting of a shock-absorbing material such as EVA. This appears as a tapered wedge under the heel, very similar to that of the running shoes from which it is derived. These midsoles really do absorb shock and I always look for one in a boot unless it has a dual-density outsole. The difference such a wedge makes to how your feet feel at the end of a long day is quite startling. The main purpose of such midsoles is to protect against heel strike, the point of impact when your heel hits the ground at each step. This jars the knees and lower back as well as the feet. On a long day out I do find my legs and feet become more sore when I am wearing boots without a shock-absorbing layer than they do when I wear a pair with one, so I for

one am convinced that such layers or equivalents do work.

As an alternative to the EVA wedge a few boots, notably some Asolo models, feature a layer of Sorbothane in the heel between the midsole and outsole.

Outsole: The traditional Vibram carbon rubber lugsole, although still around, has been joined by many others in recent years with Skywalk being one of the commoner ones. I've tried several styles and found there isn't really much to choose between them. Any pattern of studs, bars and other shapes seems to grip well on most terrain. There has been some concern about the damage that heavily lugged soles do to soft ground and there are soles around that claim to minimise this by not collecting debris in the tread. I've found that studded soles seem to work best in this respect but I feel that unless your walking will be done on gentle trails only, grip is the most important aspect of outsoles and should not be compromised, especially if steep, rugged terrain is to be traversed. Mountain rescue teams in Britain regularly report accidents caused by slips due to inadequate footwear.

Many of the new soles, including some from Vibram, are made from a dual-density rubber with a soft upper layer for shock absorption and a hard rubber outer for durability. I've used boots with this type of sole and find it a good alternative to the EVA-style wedge.

In terms of durability heavier soles with a deeper tread will long outlast lighter ones. It's hard to give mileages, however, as wear depends on the type of surface walked on—tarmac wears out soles fastest, followed by rocks and scree. On soft forest duff soles will last forever. I have found on long walks that lightweight studded soles (as found on Asolo Approach and Brasher footwear) last between 1300 and 1600km/800–1000 miles, and the traditional Vibram Montagna at least 2000km/1250 miles.

Whilst there is little controversy over sole patterns the design of heels has created much discussion, some of it heated. Indeed certain designs have been blamed for fatal accidents. The debate is over the lack of a forward heel bar under the instep, together with the rounded heel design of running-shoe-derived outsoles, and how these features perform when descending steep slopes, especially wet grass ones. Traditional soles have a deep bar at the front of the heel and a square-cut rear edge making it, say its supporters, very safe in descent. With the newer sole designs, they say, you can't dig in the back of the heel for grip nor use the front edge of the heel to halt slips. Instead the sloped heel designs make slipping more likely. This criticism has had enough effect for some makers to add deep serrations to their sloping heels to add grip and to replace the forward edge.

After much experimentation with the different soles, as well as observation of other walkers, I've come to the conclusion that it all depends on how you walk downhill! If you descend using the back or sides of the boot heel for support then you are more likely to slip in a boot with a smooth sloping heel than one with a serrated sloping or square-cut one. However if you descend as I do, with your boots pointing downhill and placed flat on the ground and your weight over your feet, the style of the heel is irrelevant. I've descended long steep slopes of very slippery vegetation in smooth, sloping heeled footwear without slipping and without feeling insecure. Just before writing this passage I was out in the English Lake District with a group of walkers, all of them experienced and wearing a variety of boots. Towards the end of our walk we descended a steep, wet, grassy slope. Many people slipped and fell over, some several times. Comparing them with those who kept their feet I noticed that the walkers who slipped had their boots angled across the slope and were descending using the edges of the sole. Those who kept their feet were coming down in the way I have described. To keep your feet flat on a steep slope like this you need flexible footwear. If you use the sole edges and the heel for support a stiffer boot works better and some form of serration or a square-cut heel is needed.

It is claimed by companies who use them that rounded heels minimise heel strike by allowing a more gradual roll on to the sole instead of the jarring point of impact that occurs when the edge of a square-cut heel hits the ground. I can see the logic of this argument but I can't say I've noticed any difference between the two types of heel in practice. The presence of a shock-absorbing layer in the sole seems to me to be far more important for reducing heel strike.

Rands: The most likely place for water penetration in a boot is at the crucial junction between the sole and the upper. Some boots have a rubber rand running right round this join to protect it whilst others have just toe or toe and heel rands or bumpers. Rands do work, especially on lightweight boots where the thinner materials are more vulnerable to damage. On heavier boots although they help prevent water ingress they aren't really necessary.

The Last: All footwear is built round a rough approximation of a human foot known as the last. This varies in shape according to the bootmaker's view of what a foot looks like and is sometimes designated 'European', 'British' or 'American'. Ignore such descriptions. What matters is finding boots that fit your feet. The nationality of the last is irrelevant to this. In the 1980s the 'sprung' or anatomic last was introduced. This is a last which has a curved sole to mimic the forward flex of the foot when walking. Boots produced on such a last, as many now are, have what is often called a rocker sole that gives no resistance to the forward roll of the foot but in fact helps it with what Scarpa, who use it on their Trionic boots, call 'increased toe spring'. The first boots I used that were built on such a last were Brasher lightweights. I was amazed at the extra comfort the curved sole gave. They really did seem to make walking easier. Years of wearing such boots have reinforced this feeling, especially as I have also used boots built on the old-style straight last during the same period. A curved sole is now a feature I look for in boots. As well as Brasher and Scarpa other bootmakers who use anatomic lasts include Vasque, Lundhags, Hanwag, Terrain and DB Mountainsport. It's such a major improvement in boot comfort that I expect other manufacturers to follow speedily.

Women's feet are generally narrower as well as smaller than men's and there are now boots produced on lasts designed for women. In the USA, unlike Europe, women's boots are sized differently. This means that most boots in the USA come in a woman's fit whilst only a few so far do so in Europe, where Scarpa, Zamberlan and Terrain are among the few companies who make models specially for women. Of course men with small, narrow feet may find women's boots fit them best, just as women with larger, wider feet may prefer men's boots.

Construction: Joining the sole to the uppers is the critical part of boot manufacture. If that connection fails the boots fall apart. Stitching used to be the only way of constructing boots but this method is now only used in a few traditional models, usually designed for mountaineering or Nordic ski touring rather than walking. The commonest stitched construction is the Norwegian welt in which the upper is turned out from the boot then sewn to a leather midsole with two rows of stitching. These are visible and exposed and can be protected by daubing with Sno-Seal Welt-Seal or something similar.

Most boots these days have the uppers heat-bonded to the sole to give a strong waterproof seal. Some are also Blake- or Littleway-stitched which is to say the uppers are turned inwards and then stitched to a midsole to which the outsole is bonded. Unlike the Norwegian welt, these construction methods cannot be checked but have to be taken on trust. Only once have I had a bonded sole fail on me and that was many years ago. On that occasion after only 400km/250 miles the sole started to peel away from the boot at the toe. I was on a long trek and far from a repair shop so I patched the boots up with glue from my repair kit almost every night and nursed them through another 800km/500 miles. I wouldn't like to repeat the experience.

Types of Footwear
Now that the revolution in footwear has settled down, categories have emerged based on design, materials and weight.

Running/Approach Shoes: Shoes designed for off-road or fell running make good lightweight backpacking footwear. Similar but slightly sturdier are the walking shoes made by many boot companies. Design features are suede/synthetic fabric uppers, shock-absorbing midsoles, shaped removable footbeds and strong heel counters. The biggest problem with such footwear is the complete lack of waterproofness so I wouldn't recommend them for wet weather or boggy terrain. In rocky country care is needed too as they don't protect the ankles against knocks and on running shoes the toes aren't hardened—though those designed for walking usually have toe boxes. Also a lack of lateral stiffness means they aren't supportive enough for off-trail travel on rugged terrain—though some walking shoes do have graded nylon midsoles and even half-length metal shanks, features worth seeking out if you want to use such footwear for cross-country walking in dry country such as the deserts of the south-western USA. For good trails in dry terrain non-stiffened shoes are excellent and a good alternative to the lightweight boots described below. Be careful though to avoid road-running shoes whose soles may not have the tread needed to grip properly on rough, wet ground.

A typical example that I've walked long distances in, including more than a third of my Continental Divide walk down the Rocky Mountains from Canada to Mexico, is the New Balance M575 running shoe which weighs 720g/25oz for a pair of size 43s. The carbon-rubber outsole has a good tread and is very hardwearing and the hard heel counter makes the shoes very stable. In terms of comfort they are superior to any boot and the shock-absorbing midsoles make them ideal for long treks on unforgiving surfaces such as tarmac or compacted earth. Because of their lightness I often carry a pair as camp footwear and for stream crossings. Most running-shoe companies make similar models. I came to the 575 because New Balance offer different width fittings, the widest of which, the 4E, fits even my feet. Whilst the 575 remains my first choice in shoes I've recently bought a pair of the same company's Trailbusters which are the same weight but which have a studded sole that grips even better on wet ground and steep, loose slopes, though the ankle support is not quite as good as with the M575.

Other running shoes that look good for backpacking come from Reebok, Nike, Ron Hill, Hi-Tec, Walsh (who specialise in fell-running shoes which, unfortunately, are too narrow for me) and Adidas (who offer different width fittings in North America but not Britain). There are undoubtedly more. Walking shoes for backcountry use (not to be confused with shoes for 'fitness walking', a peculiar activity taking place on roads and other unsavoury places) come from Nike, Berghaus, Zamberlan, Vasque, Hi-Tec, Mountain Equipment—(I've used their Zanskar and it's a good alternative to a running shoe if you want more lateral stability)—Lundhags, Junior Sport, Asolo (whose Approach shoes I can recommend having walked 1600km/1000 miles of the Pacific Crest Trail in them), Gronell, Terrain, Daisy Roots, Trezeta and most other boot companies.

The Lightweights: This category of boots weighs between 900 and 1350g/2–3lb. This includes most synthetic/suede boots and a few leather

A selection of soles. Clockwise from top left Vasque Skywalk Dolomite, Scarpa Skywalk Trionic, Vibram Telemark XC Ski, Brasher Lightweight, New Balance 575, New Balance Trailbuster.

ones, most notably three Brasher Boot models. The advantages of these boots lie in the instant comfort they provide as well as the weight. However, except for those featuring sock liners they aren't very waterproof and the seams make them vulnerable to abrasion. In fact only the higher ankle really makes them very different from the shoes described above and they have many of the same design features, with the addition of rands—either full or just at the toe and heel—cushioned linings, sewn-in tongues and, on some models, graded flexible midsoles and half-length shanks.

My favourite boot comes into this category—the Brasher Hillmaster. At 1070g/2lb 6oz, it's one of the lightest all-leather boots available. Built on a curved last the Hillmaster features an EVA midsole, removable footbed, proofed nylon lining, hook and D-ring lacing, padded sewn-in tongue, all round rubber rand and studded, cleated sole. The leather uppers are sec-

tional rather than in one piece. The fit is wide and I find these boots immensely comfortable and suitable for all but the most rugged terrain. The curved last really puts a spring in my step and pushes me forward, and on really long days my feet feel less tired in the Brashers than in any other footwear except running shoes. Waterproofing is reasonable and when wet they do dry quickly. The only disadvantages are the lack of any lateral stiffness, which makes them unsuitable though not unusable for long cross-country treks, and their short life. I wore a pair for the second 1300km/800 miles of my Canadian Rockies walk and by the end they were worn out, with holes appearing in the uppers. However this was a tough, mostly off-trail trek and the boots were soaked for days on end. I doubt if any other footwear this light would have lasted as long. I have a pair I've worn on shorter, easier treks and given more care to, which look as though they should last longer. The original Brasher Boots in suede don't give quite as much support to the feet as the Hillmasters though they are even lighter at 900grams/2lb and just as comfortable. If you don't venture off good trails they are ideal and again they can be used in more rugged country. I used a pair on a two-week summer walk in the eastern Pyrénées where I did a fair bit of scrambling and traversing steep scree and boulder fields and found the boots adequate though a bit more care was required in placing my feet than would have been the case with a heavier, stiffer pair.

There are a fair number of high-quality leather boots available in this category: Zamberlan, Berghaus, Vasque, Merrell, High Country, Daisy Roots and Junior Sport are some of the companies which offer models. There are also however a number of inexpensive lightweight leather boots around with few of the features of the quality models. From looking at these I doubt whether they would last long or provide much support on rough ground or protection in wet weather. Synthetic/suede boots exist in their thousands, those with good reputations come from Asolo (one of the first with this type of boot), Nike, New Balance, DB Mountainsport, Vasque, Hi-Tec, Merrell, Tecnica, Gronell, Hanwag, Dachstein, Dolomite, Junior Sport and many more.

Medium-weight Boots—The Backpacking Standard: Weighing between 1350 and 1800g/3–4lb these are the boots most suited to year-round backpacking in most areas. They provide the best combination of the best qualities of traditional boots (durability and support) with the best qualities of the new designs (instant and long-term comfort) yet available. They are mostly leather boots—many one-piece, though there are some nylon/suede models. Nearly all have some form of stiffening in the sole, either graded nylon midsoles or half-length shanks or both, and heavier models will often take a crampon for walking on hard snow and ice. Generally medium-weight boots will cope with off-trail travel in the most rugged terrain and in any weather. The best feature one-piece top-grain leather, synthetic linings, padded sewn-in tongues, heel counters, toe boxes, footbeds, and shock absorbing midsoles or dual-density outsoles, and are made on curved lasts.

Because of the extra weight and extra solidity of the materials, the fit of medium-weight boots is more crucial than with lightweights and a short breaking-in period is advisable with those at the heavier end of this category. I only found a pair of boots of this type that fitted me properly, after the first draft of this book was written (Vasque Summits, see below for details), which is one reason why I've pushed the Brasher Hillmasters beyond their intended limits (see 'Lightweights' section above). In the offing though are Brasher Mountain Boots which might well prove the ideal ones in this category. I'm looking forward to trying a pair. I can wear many medium-weight boots for day walks over moderate distances with a light pack but as soon as I stay out several days and carry a heavy load I find nearly all of them too tight—which results in painful, often blistered, feet and a shortened trip. On my Canadian Rockies walk I wore Hanwag Cross boots for the first 1300km/800 miles. They weigh 1500g/3¼lb, are built on a curved last and have a Sympatex sock liner and EVA midsole plus the other features listed above. They proved comfortable but did not have the lateral stability I would like from a boot of this weight nor did they last long, the seams splitting towards the end of their usage. Also to achieve a correct width fitting I wore a size too large which I think was the probable cause of the heel blisters I suffered in the first two weeks of the walk. Only in waterproofing were they superior to the third lighter and more comfortable Brasher Hillmasters I wore on the second

half of the trek.

However, in the autumn of 1989 Vasque boots, well known in North America, appeared in Britain for the first time and I obtained a pair of the Summit model in a wide fit. The Summits weigh 1600g/3½lb, are made of one-piece water-repellent Pervanger leather with a Goretex sock liner and built on a curved last. Other features are sewn-in padded tongue, heel counter, toe box, Sportee lining, graded polyethylene midsole with steel shank, footbed, toe rand and dual-density Skywalk sole. Vasque describe the Summit as suitable for 'serious backpacking and mountain climbing with heavy pack in extremely rough, rocky and wet terrain' and as needing a short break-in time. A few short trips showed that the boots fitted well, provided good lateral support, and kept out water. Knowing that most of the walking would be cross-country in rugged terrain I took the Summits on my Yukon Wilderness walk. After 1600km/1000 miles of bog, scree, boulder, forest, snowfield and dirt road, I knew these boots lived up to the claims made for them. I suffered no blisters and only had sore feet after long 32-km/20-mile days on hard-packed dirt roads or paved highways in very hot weather. The boots survived the trip well with the uppers intact and the soles not needing replacement. The only real wear is inside where the linings have worn through at the heel.

For those who don't have my fitting problems there is a large choice in this category and good-looking boots also come from Daisy Roots, Terrain, DB Mountainsport, Zamberlan, Gronell, Danner Mountain, Merrell, Salewa, Asolo, Raichle, Hanwag, High Country, Dolomite, Junior Sport and Trezeta, to name but a few.

Heavyweight and Traditional: Having almost disappeared in the early 1980s with the success of the new lightweights for walking and plastic footwear for mountaineering, heavyweight (1800g/4lb and upwards) boots have enjoyed something of a comeback. This happened after people discovered that in that nebulous area where walking merges with climbing and crampons are worn for long periods or narrow rock ledges are traversed, light- and medium-weight footwear is a little too soft and bendy whilst plastic boots are too rigid. This type of low-grade mountaineering, the sort carried out on easy alpine snow ascents in summer and the steeper Scottish hills in winter, is what these boots were originally designed for many years ago. Traditional designs with leather midsoles, full-length or three-quarter-length steel shanks, thick one-piece uppers, Vibram Montagna soles and Norwegian stitching are still available from companies such as Dolomite, Gronell, DB Mountainsport, Raichle, Hanwag, Vasque, Merrell and others. The same companies, along with Scarpa, Asolo, Zamberlan, Junior Sport and others also make heavyweight boots whose armour-like qualities have been mitigated by some of the features of the newer lighter-weight designs such as graded nylon midsoles, footbeds, synthetic linings, curved soles and shock-absorbing heel inserts.

Whether purely traditional or modified, these boots have solid, unforgiving uppers and rigid or very stiff soles. They require a considerable breaking-in period and weigh heavily on the feet. I find them uncomfortable and tiring to walk in and haven't worn a pair for many years. For backpacking I think they are too heavy and stiff unless your walking really does venture into serious mountaineering. If it does then your activities are outside the scope of this book. For myself I find the little snow and ice climbing that I do when backpacking (rarely above Scottish Grade 1 for those who understand these things) can be accomplished using medium-weight boots which will take articulated crampons and which are far more comfortable to walk in on easier terrain. If I want to climb more difficult slopes I won't be backpacking and I'll wear plastic boots. On steep, rocky terrain where scrambling and easy climbing may be required I find medium-weight and indeed lightweight boots perfectly adequate. But if you really do prefer a stiff, heavy boot this category is the one to choose from.

Specialist footwear

Very few backpackers will require any footwear not included in the categories above except perhaps for Nordic ski-touring boots. These are generally of traditional design with one-piece leather uppers, Norwegian welt construction, half- to three-quarter-length steel shanks and leather midsoles. The outsole has a squared-off toe containing a metal plate with three holes drilled in it for locating the binding plus a tread for grip when walking. The Vibram Telemark is a good-quality sole I've skied many miles on. Nordic touring boots must have lateral rigidity

to stop them twisting off the ski during turns but forward flex for easy gliding. With the renaissance in Nordic skiing has come a wealth of footwear, not all suitable for backcountry touring. Make sure that you buy boots designed for this and not the similar but stiffer ones made for telemarking on downhill pistes or the lightweight general or in-track touring boots which aren't robust enough for backpacking on skis. The latter are also unsuitable if you have to carry your skis for long periods which, believe me, happens all too often, as they have smooth, synthetic soles rather than lugs. Good boots come from Asolo, Meindl, Gronell, Junior Sport, Merrell and Scarpa amongst others. I use the Anfibio leather Asolo Snowfields which weigh 1890g/4lb 2oz and are a good compromise between flexibility for moving on the flat and uphill and rigidity for downhill turns. They have proved very durable.

For walking in marshy areas such as those found in many parts of Scandinavia, northern Canada and the eastern USA high-topped rubber, rubber/leather and insulated leather footwear, often with felt or wool liners for winter use, from companies such as Lundhags, Nokia, Sorel and Timberland, are popular amongst anglers and hunters and some walkers. Such boots may keep your feet drier than anything else but how comfortable or supportive they are for walking with a heavy pack is another matter. Without ever having used a pair my view is that they don't appear suitable for backpacking. However if you habitually cross country where you have to slosh or even wade over miles of boggy country, these boots might well be ideal.

Care and Repair

Although most boots are fairly tough, proper care is needed to ensure that they last as long as possible. All mud and dirt should be washed off after use. If it is left to dry on the boots it will also dry out the leather, causing it to harden and, if you're unlucky, also to crack. A stiff brush helps to remove mud from seams, stitching and inaccessible places like tongue gussets. Too much heat is even worse at causing leather to harden and split and isn't very good for nylon either, so wet boots should never be left to dry in a hot place such as next to a car heater, a house radiator or a camp fire. Even midday sunshine can be too warm and if you stay in a mountain hut or hostel with a drying room during a long trek, you should keep your boots out of there as well. Boot leather (and this includes the suede reinforcements on synthetic models) should never become too hot to touch. Boots should be left in a dry but cool place to dry out slowly, with the insoles removed and the tongue fully open. If they are really sodden, they can be stuffed with newspaper to help the drying process. The problem with drying boots slowly is that it really can take a long time—several days at least for medium-weight leather boots. As I write I have a pair of boots drying in the corner of the room that were last worn two days ago and which I hope to wear for a three-day trek in a couple of days' time—if, that is, they dry out in time.

This problem becomes greater on long treks when drying boots, that may have been sodden for several days, over a camp fire becomes very tempting. And I for one occasionally succumb. During the second half of my Canadian Rockies walk, when the route was mostly cross-country and in wet terrain and I had wet boots by the end of most days, I often helped my boots to dry by standing them a little too close to my camp fire. The penalty for this was to walk the last snowy few weeks wearing boots with cracks in the uppers and the soles peeling off at the toes.

When dry, boots need treating to restore their suppleness and a degree of water resistance. Synthetic and suede footwear can be sprayed with proofing compounds such as Nikwax Texnik, Grangersol's G-Sport, Scotchguard and other similar sprays and paint-on compounds. Don't expect miracles though. This type of footwear is inherently lacking in waterproofness. What treating it will do, is limit the amount of water it will absorb and thus the time it takes to dry.

Leather boots are a different matter. Proper treatment can increase water resistance and will certainly prolong the life of a pair of boots by keeping the leather supple. What constitutes proper treatment depends in part on the type of leather. Most manufacturers will recommend a certain wax or oil, often their own brand. Use this by all means but there are probably others as good or better and often easier to obtain. Virtually all leather boots are now chrome-tanned rather than oil-tanned and require dressing with wax rather than oil. Liquids such as Mars Oil and Neat's Foot Oil can over-soften leather and

I would only recommend them for leather that has been allowed to dry out and harden and which needs softening, or perhaps for cuffs and scree collars if they are rubbing. Overall though I avoid such products, except for Liquid Nikwax, the one I prefer, which I use as the first coating on new boots.

For regular treatment a wax is required and there are many on the market. Not so long ago, in Britain at least, dubbin was the only specialist treatment available. This greasy substance was rumoured to rot stitching and it certainly over-softened leather if applied too liberally. Improvement came with the introduction of Nikwax, a tougher proofing that lasted longer and didn't ruin the leather or the stitching. Now Nikwax, G-Wax, Biwell, Sno-Seal, Mars Oil Wax Polish and others all have their adherents, whilst companies like Vasque, Zamberlan, Daisy Roots (whose name Wax Lyrical appeals to me though I've never used it) and Timberland have their own products. Makers suggest that you don't wax boots made from some of the specially tanned leathers like HS12 until they are scuffed, as they won't absorb wax before then (although they will absorb Liquid Nikwax, which I recommend as an initial coating). I've not found a wax that is vastly superior to any other and at least one boot company believes that ordinary shoe polish is just as good. I usually use Nikwax which I find as good as if not better than anything else.

Boots should be waxed the evening before use (and before long-term storage) to allow the wax to penetrate. I was in the middle of the last sentence when the phone rang and by coincidence it was Nick Brown, the man behind Nikwax. I used the opportunity to ask him about treating boots. He pointed out that over-treatment is bad for boots whatever the type of wax; several thin coats are more effective than one thick one. With Nikwax, heavy coats are not needed anyway, he says, as each coating reinforces the last to build up a layer of protection, the wax curing to form a flexible coating. Although a rag can be used it's best to apply wax with the fingers, as the warmth helps to melt it and improve penetration.

Whatever wax you use, a few hours' walking through dew-wet grass or melting snow is all it takes for most boots to become wet, so don't expect long-term waterproofing. However, properly waxed boots will dry out more quickly and absorb less moisture. Unwaxed boots soak up water like a sponge. I think of waxing as caring for the leather and extending the life of the boots rather than as waterproofing them. On the same theme, I treat seams and stitching with Liquid Nikwax when the boots are new and then apply a welt-seal such as that from Grangers or Sno-Seal. It doesn't stay on forever, but it protects seams for a little while and helps to stop them leaking.

On walks lasting more than a few weeks I carry wax—either a tube of Biwell or Sno-Seal (more convenient) or else a tin of Nikwax (more effective), wrapped in a cloth and stored in a plastic bag. Whenever my boots become dry enough to be waxed I do so.

The uppers of lightweight boots often wear out at the same time as their soles so although resoling is possible it's hardly worth it. Top-quality ones can be worth repairing, though, and I know people who have successfully had running shoes resoled. Medium-weight boots should last the life of at least two soles and heavyweight boots even more (I had a pair that was on their fourth sole when the new lightweights came along and swept them from use). The key is to have boots resoled before the midsole becomes worn, as replacing this can be very expensive. EVA-type wedges usually need replacing along with the soles. For safety reasons you shouldn't let soles wear down too much anyway.

Most outdoor shops will accept boots for repair and send them to either a local cobbler or a national repair shop. In Britain one company dominates the boot-repair business and that is Shoecare of Preston, who are recommended by most major bootmakers. They offer a comprehensive service including repairs to boot uppers and a wide choice of soles, so you can try out a different pattern if you like or, have a dual-density sole put on a boot that lacked a shock-absorbing mid sole, as a friend of mine has done. I've had boots resoled by Shoecare and can vouch for the quality of their work.

SOCKS

Too many people spend a great deal of time choosing boots and then don't think about their socks, just buying whatever the shop has to offer. Until I started thinking about writing this book, I was one of them. Yet socks are important. They cushion the foot, prevent abrasion from the boots, wick away moisture and keep the feet at the right temperature. For a decade and more I used loopstitch wool socks because that was what the outdoor shops sold. On coming to write about socks I asked myself why I wore this type and I came up with no answer other than convenience. Yet when I asked myself if they gave me what I wanted from socks the answer was that they didn't. So I began to look at what socks are available apart from loopstitch models and to try out different styles to see what really worked.

I can see why I—and most other walkers, at least in Britain—use loopstitch socks. With their fluffy loop pile inners they look very comfortable and warm, far nicer than the old knitted Ragg socks we used to wear. On the first day out they feel wonderful, and if you can wash them properly after every day's use they last fairly well. However, on a backpacking trip you can't wash your socks every day. Indeed on a long trip where you can only afford the weight of three or four pairs you may end up wearing socks for several days, maybe even weeks, at a time. After a few days' constant wear, loopstitch socks matt down into a hard sweaty mass under the foot, and rinsing them out in cold stream water does little to restore that initial fluffiness. In fact I've found that even repeated machine washings won't revive them. Such socks then provide little insulation or comfort underfoot and I tend to relegate them to the spares shelf, which is now crammed full of dozens of pairs of loopstitch socks that have had perhaps only two weeks' use. I cannot now understand how I could have been so blind as not to notice what was happening.

Instead of loopstitch socks I've gone back to wearing the flecked grey Ragg ones that are still standard in the USA. In Britain I've found it hard to obtain non-loopstitch socks. An investigation of several shops eventually produced some Star 50 per cent wool/50 per cent nylon ones (calf-length, 100g/3½oz) in just one of them. Then I learnt that Sport Montagna bring in the Norwegian Ryla-Sport 70/20/10 wool/rayon/nylon Olaraggen socks (calf-length, 110g/4oz; knee-length, 185g/6½oz). Janus socks, which I remember from years ago, I could not find anywhere so I bought some by mail order from REI in Seattle, who call them Long Wearing Socks (calf-length, 120g/4¼oz). These are made from 100 per cent wool and are also

Norwegian. For comparison a standard pair of 70/30 wool/nylon loopstitch calf-length socks weigh 110g/4oz so there's nothing in the weight.

I have found Ragg socks to be vastly superior to loopstitch ones and I have taken both on two week long treks and worn them for the same number of days each to check this. I found that the more open structure of the Ragg socks meant that they didn't matt up so much and that when rinsed out in cold water they came up almost as good as new. Of the different types I've tried, the Star ones proved a little too warm in summer weather, probably because of the high proportion of nylon in them, and being thinner they didn't provide as much cushioning as the Olaraggen or Janus ones. The Janus ones are the warmest, especially when wet, which makes them good for winter, though again they are a little hot for summer use. All three types have had far more wear than loopstitch socks get before I decide they're too matted and they look as though they'll last a while yet. I've come to the conclusion that for backpacking loopstitch socks are not worth it.

Wool is the accepted material for socks whatever the style because socks need to cushion the foot, keep it warm in winter yet cool in summer, absorb and wick away sweat and be warm when wet—all of which wool will do. Nylon is often added as a reinforcement at the heel and toe. I wouldn't buy a Ragg sock that was less than 50 per cent wool however and 70 per cent or more is better. Despite this, I also tried non-wool socks in my reassessment, namely stretchy 85 per cent Orlon/15 per cent nylon loopstitch Thorlo-Pad Hiking Socks (calf-length, 90g/3oz). These are claimed to make your feet feel more comfortable than any other sock by virtue of their complex construction, which involves thicker sections under the heel and round the front of the foot. I've found them adequate though a bit hot in summer weather. They don't matt down as much as wool loopstitch socks and they wash out in cold water better too. However they do become saturated with sweat quicker than any wool sock and they feel cooler than wool when they do so. Overall I prefer Ragg socks as I find wool still the best material but for anyone allergic to wool the Thorlo-Pad socks would be a good choice. If you do try a pair make sure you get the Hiking Socks and not the Trekking Socks (which contain wool—see below), the lighter Walking Socks or any of the sportswear series.

There are similar synthetic socks to the Thorlo-Pads around, such as Lakeland Pro Socks, whilst another alternative to wool socks for those allergic to wool would be one of the many thick polypropylene socks available. I've tried REI's Polypropylene Hiking Socks (85g/3oz), which have an inner loopstitch layer of polypro and an outer of wool (actual breakdown: 60 per cent polypro, 25 per cent wool, 15 per cent nylon), and found they work quite well though they do need washing every day or two. Again there are similar socks around.

Thorlo-Pad also make socks which are similar in design to the Hiking Socks, but which contain wool. These are called Trekking Socks and consist of 45 per cent acrylic, 38 per cent wool, 9 per cent stretch nylon, 6 per cent hollow-core polyester and 2 per cent spandex. They are calf-length and weigh 110g/4oz. Discovering them in a shop just before I left for Canada, I bought a pair to use on my Yukon Wilderness walk. I found them very comfortable and hardwearing and softer underfoot when walking on hard surfaces than the Ragg socks I also wore. This was due to a loopstitch construction which didn't matt down until after several days' wear and which fluffed up again when washed. They were cool when wet however and slow-drying despite the low wool content. I liked the stretch uppers, which don't sag after several days wear as the Ragg ones do. I'll probably use the socks again and may even buy another pair, though I can't say that my feet feel better in them than in the Ragg socks, as the advertisements claim they will (or your money back!). However they are the only socks I would consider other than Ragg ones for long treks.

Whatever type of socks you wear you should make sure that they fit well and that there are no loose threads, knots of material or harsh stitching that might cause blisters and sore spots. With long trousers or shorts I like calf-length socks that I can turn down over my boot tops to keep out stones and grit. With breeches (knickers in America) knee-length stockings are needed. Check that the breeches can be tightened down over them at the knee or you'll find a cold gap appearing. I usually only wear breeches in winter, when I also wear gaiters, so not being able to turn the sock over my boots doesn't matter.

How many pairs of socks you should wear is a matter of much debate amongst walkers. I was originally taught to wear two thick pairs but abandoned this years ago because of my wide feet. I simply can't find boots I can fit my feet plus two pairs of thick socks into. I now generally wear one thick pair, summer and winter. The other approach is to wear a thick pair with a pair of thin liner socks. The idea is that the liners help to reduce friction and remove sweat. Cotton liners are useless because they absorb sweat and then take ages to dry, cooling your feet whilst they do so. Cotton socks also ruck up and are liable to cause blisters. The best materials are the same as those suited for wearing next to the skin on the rest of the body— that is silk, thin wool or a synthetic wicking material like polypropylene or Capilene. I've tried silk liner socks and polypropylene ones (30g/1oz each per pair, both from Survival Aids). I have an inkling that they work but because they need rinsing out almost every day I've given up wearing them and gone back to just one pair of thick socks. They are nice for sleeping in, however.

If you really want to try to keep your feet dry, Gore-tex socks are available. I've used two types, W.L. Gore's own Seels (400g/14oz) and Berghaus's Gore-tex Socks (350g/12oz). Both are calf-length and have taped seams but whilst the Seels are open at the top and made from non-stretch material the Socks have an elasticated cuff and are made from stretchy fabric. When Seels first appeared in Britain review pairs were duly given to all the gear reviewers writing for the outdoor press at the time, myself included. Over the next few months an amazingly consistent series of reviews appeared. Every tester, again including myself, found that the Seels worked well and kept the feet dry when new but fell apart at the seams after about two weeks' use. I didn't find them very comfortable either as their bulk meant that I could only wear a thin sock under them and I missed the cushioning effect of thick wool. I've only worn the Berghaus Socks on nine days so far. Compared with Seels the close-fitting cuff, which keeps moisture and debris out, is a big advantage. I've worn the Socks in knee-deep snow without gaiters on and found the cuffs kept my inner socks dry. Being stretchy and thinner than the Seels they are more comfortable and I can just squeeze them on over a medium-weight

sock. I've tried them over just silk liners and they did keep my feet dry and warm but I missed the comfort of thick socks and my feet were sore after a day's walk. Over the Thorlo-Pad socks they are more comfortable. If they prove durable I might use them on treks in thawing snow and through dependably wet terrain but I'm not convinced of their value for general backpacking, especially as they are very expensive. Good gaiters and perhaps Gore-tex or Sympatex-lined boots are probably better and in an emergency plastic bags are surprisingly effective.

On long trips I carry three pairs of socks and try to change them every couple of days though I have worn a pair for as long as ten days. I always like to keep one pair dry for camp wear unless I'm carrying booties or pile socks for that purpose. On the 23-day snowbound High Sierra section of the Pacific Crest Trail walk where my socks and boots became soaked every day I wore two pairs, alternating them daily with the previous day's wet pair hung on the pack to dry. If possible though I like to rinse socks out in water taken from a stream or lake (a cooking pot makes a makeshift washbowl) every couple of days. They can be hung out on a line to dry in camp or just draped over a rock or branch. Wool takes time to dry though so it's often necessary to hang them on the back of the pack to finish the process the next day. Now that I've changed to different socks I don't know how long a pair will last, though I have pairs in good condition that have had several months' wear, including Olaraggen and Janus Ragg socks and Thorlo-Pad Trekking Socks (one pair of each) that were used on the three- month Yukon walk and are still in good condition. With loopstitch ones on long walks I often wore them until they were in holes, which meant two or three months of use. By then they had long lost any cushioning effect. Ragg socks I think will prove better.

At home socks should be either hand washed or put through the wool cycle on a washing machine and then line-dried. Non-detergent washing powders remove less of the wool's natural oils. I use Ecover and also add TX.10 in place of fabric conditioner.

GAITERS
Neither breathable membrane sock liners nor Gore-tex socks will keep your boots, socks and feet dry for long in deep snow, boggy terrain or heavy rain. Once water or snow rises above

ankle level or rain starts to run down your over-trousers then you need gaiters to keep it out. These waterproof coverings for the lower leg come in various styles. The lightest and simplest are short gaiters, often called stop tous or anklets. These are around 20cm/8in high and are worn to prevent stones and bits of grass entering the boot. I've tried a nylon pair but found them too hot because, I suspect, they prevented moisture-vapour escaping out of the boot tops. I haven't bothered with them for years.

Knee-length gaiters are the standard design and come in two types, those that only cover the upper boot and those that cover it all. Both types have full-length zips running down the back, side or front of each gaiter. Ones with front zips are easier to put on but it's essential that such a zip has a velcro flap over it to prevent it leaking. The lower edge of a gaiter is elasticated or randed so that it grips the boot and there is a further elasticated section round the ankle. A drawcord pulls the gaiter in below the knee. I don't like gaiters much and only wear them when the alternative is wet, cold feet, which I like even less. Generally I only ever consider carrying gaiters when deep snow is likely to be encountered and even then they often stay in the pack.

The exception is on ski tours, when I wear gaiters all day. The ones I use then are Berghaus Yeti gaiters which cover the whole boot, gripping the lower edge with a tight-fitting rubber rand that also runs under the instep in a thick band. With these gaiters on, your boots remain dry and unscuffed for days on end, though if you ski through much melting snow or wade rivers you will eventually get wet. No other gaiters come close in terms of performance. The front zip means you can put on and lace up boots without removing them so I fit Yetis to my touring boots at the start of the ski season and don't remove them until the end. I have two pairs, an old pair with a proofed nylon lower section and a cotton canvas leg that weigh 500g/17oz and a Trionic Yeti pair in Strata Gore-tex weighing 340g/12oz. Both work well though the canvas/nylon ones are going to outlast the Gore-tex ones, which are showing signs of wear at the ankles. However although the Trionic Yetis are still available, the canvas ones have gone for good. They have been replaced by hard-wearing and waterproof but non-breathable nylon in a version designed for plastic mountaineering boots that is too big in the forefoot to fit well on walking or Nordic skiing boots. This is a pity, as the canvas ones are tough, comfortable and can be reproofed. The alternative to the Gore-tex Yeti Trionics is proofed nylon ones, much cheaper but rather hot and prone to condensation. Whilst I would rather have canvas I'd choose Gore-tex before proofed nylon.

Although they are meant for Scarpa Trionic footwear Trionic Yetis will fit Nordic backcountry ski-touring boots and some medium-weight walking boots. There is a third kind of Yeti gaiter though, the Yeti Attak, which will only fit boots with Trionic Attak soles as it has an additional cross-strap that fits into a groove on the boot sole. There is also an insulated Yeti Expedition gaiter made of nylon and Gore-tex and filled with Berghaus's White Heat polyester filling designed for rigid plastic boots and bitterly cold weather. For general backpacking the Yeti Trionic is the one to consider. They come in six different sizes so check that the ones you buy will fit your boots. Don't however believe sales people who tell you the gaiters will only fit Trionic boots. It's not true! Although the rands on Yeti gaiters can be replaced I find that they wear out so quickly on rocky or rooty terrain that I only use Yeti gaiters for skiing or walking in snow. For that though there is nothing better. Other brands of gaiters that cover the whole boot exist but I've seen none that match the Yetis.

Ordinary gaiters also come in proofed nylon, Gore-tex and cotton canvas and again despite the extra weight I prefer the canvas ones—though I don't wear such gaiters very often. Gore-tex ones that I've tried have worn out very quickly, even when the lower section has been made from proofed nylon. Sympatex ones, when they eventually appear—as they undoubtedly will—may prove more durable. On these gaiters an adjustable cord, strap or wire runs under the instep. When tightened it holds the gaiter in place. In my experience such instep straps always fray and eventually break so it's important that they can easily be replaced with a piece of paracord or string from the repair kit. Look for brass eyelets on the gaiter's edge to thread the cord through rather than fancy buckles which only work with the original strap. The gaiters I use most for walking are an ex-hire pair I bought in Creede in southern Colorado on the

Continental Divide walk, when early season snow in the San Juan mountains caught me unawares. They have proofed nylon lower sections, light canvas uppers, a rear zip, are made by Outdoor Products and weigh 220g/7¾oz. They're all right, but I'm not over-enthusiastic about them.

CAMPWEAR

On most long treks I carry running shoes as spare footwear both for the trail and for camp use. On trips lasting a week or less I often don't bother with spare outdoor footwear, especially if it looks as though the weather will be making me spend my evenings in a tent. However on long treks I find it essential to be able to change my footwear in the evening and my feet feel such relief when I do so that I think it must be good for them. It is certainly good for my morale to don clean socks and light, cool running shoes on my hot, sore feet after a hard day. To back up the running shoes and to wear in the tent I always ensure I have a pair of dry, clean socks with me—thick wool ones in cold weather, often just silk liners in summer.

If I know the weather on a trip is going to be very cold and snowy and I don't want to spend all evening in the tent, or if I'm planning on using huts or bothies I carry insulated booties. Booties are very warm, and the thought of pulling them on at the end of the day is blissful when one is struggling on with wet, cold feet on a bitter winter's day. They are however lethal to walk in on anything but flat ground. Climbing down a bank to fetch water from a stream or pond in them can seem like a major

expedition. Booties are available with both down and synthetic filling. I prefer the synthetic ones as I don't have to worry about getting them wet when wandering round in the snow. The choice isn't large as they are a somewhat specialist item. If you're going to wander round camp in them, booties must have a closed-cell insole, preferably sewn in, to insulate them from the ground. The ones I have are REI Polarguard Booties, which weigh 320g/11¼oz for the large size and have packcloth soles, closed-cell foam insoles, nylon outers, a warm polyester/cotton/nylon lining and a front drawcord. (Current versions are Polarguard/Thinsulate insulated, have Cordura soles and weigh slightly less at 311g/11oz). Down-filled ones include RAB Down Equipment's Down Boots which are zipped and have a showerproof, breathable outer of RAB'S own Shelter material (300g/10½oz) and Sierra Design's Hot Shooties with a 56g/2oz down fill, closed-cell foam insoles, leather outsoles and velcro closures (250g/9oz).

On winter trips, where I'm planning on spending most if not all my time in camp in the tent (and probably in the sleeping bag) I often carry pile socks rather than wool ones as tent wear, as they are warmer. The ones I have, and one of the few on the market (Buffalo make some which I haven't seen), are Helly Hansen fibre-pile Boot Liners. Mine just reach the ankle and weigh 100g/3½oz, but the current catalogue pictures show calf-length ones which must weigh a little more. The name suggests that they could be worn in boots but I wouldn't like to try doing so as they're non-absorbent. They're great for sleeping in however and nice to wear in the tent

Walking staffs. Above: Tracks Chief of Staffs. Below: Leki Lightwalk. Both are shown in their collapsed form.   3.4

when you aren't in the sleeping bag. As they are socks not booties and don't have proper soles they can't be worn outside. However a solution to this—which I haven't tried as I've only recently come across it—could be Outdoor Research's Modular Mukluks and Moonlite Pile Sox. The Mukluks are made from Gore-tex and Cordura, have removable closed-cell insoles and reach up to the knee. The pile socks are also removable. Weight is not given in the Field & Trek Catalogue, the only place I've seen them, but it can't be more than a pair of booties, to which these could be an alternative. Of course for short excursions outside the tent you could just pull stuffsacs or plastic bags over your pile socks or even don your boots again if the snow's not too deep.

A THIRD LEG

The walking stick or staff is not an item of gear many backpackers ever consider using, yet for me it has become as essential as a sleeping bag or a pair of boots. It was not always so, and I backpacked for a decade and more without ever thinking of using a staff. Then I started using Nordic skis in winter and spring and discovered that when I had to carry the skis on my pack my balance was helped by continuing to use the poles. Even so, it was a few more years before I started using a staff regularly—though I did begin picking up stout sticks for use on steep climbs and stream fords. The realisation that having a staff with me all the time would be very useful came on a week-long walk in Iceland in early summer when I didn't take one and when there were no sticks to pick up, as Iceland is virtually treeless. Shifting and slippery pebble and gravel beds mixed with large areas of soft thawing snow plus deep, snow-melt-filled rivers made for a difficult walk on which a staff would have made all the difference. Without one I was constantly off balance, slipping and stumbling along.

Indeed the main reasons for carrying a staff are for balance on rough terrain and as a third leg for river crossings. Even with the heaviest load I can cross steep scree slopes, negotiate boulder fields and traverse tussocky moorland with confidence if I'm using one. But I have discovered it has far more uses than these. On level ground and good trails it helps maintain a walking rhythm. On boggy ground and when crossing snow it can be used to probe for hidden rocks and deep spots as well as for support. Bushes, barbed wire, stinging plants and other obstructions can be held out of the way with it. Perhaps most useful of all it saves energy. All the time whilst walking I am convinced it takes some of the weight off my feet, particularly when I lean heavily on it when climbing steep slopes. The German mountaineering equipment company Edelrid say that according to 'mountain doctor' Gottfried Neureuther 'each placement of the ski pole takes between 5 and 8kg weight off the lower part of the body, which is equivalent to a total of 13 tons during a one hour walk on flat ground and an amazing 34 tons total load reduction when walking downhill'. Edelrid recommend the use of two poles rather than one.

My staff also has other, less medical, uses. When I stop to look at the view or the clouds or the wildlife I can use it to lean on, again taking the weight off my feet. During stops it turns my pack into a backrest. Then in camp it can act as a pole for turning a flysheet door into an awning, tieing a washing line to or supporting a tarp if I am using one. It also helps in retrieving bear-bagged food where necessary.

I have tried without much success to convert others to using a staff. People generally seem to interpret my using one as a sign that I'm getting old. However on a two-week trek in the Pyrénées undertaken whilst this book was being written, I managed to persuade one of my companions to borrow my staff after he wrenched his shoulder and was finding walking with a pack painful. I pointed out to him that by using the staff in the hand opposite his sore shoulder he would lower that shoulder and take some of the weight off it (this is a reason for not always holding the staff in the same hand—if you do you may end each day with an aching shoulder). Mark did this and was impressed enough with the result to buy a cheap ashwood staff when we reached Gavarnie a couple of days later. Because he praised the staff so highly my other companion Alain bought one as well. Both ended the walk convinced of the value of them.

The obvious material for a staff is wood and it's quite easy to find a suitable piece in any woodland. As long as it's reasonably straight, solid enough and at least elbow height (so that it can be held with the lower arm at right angles to the body, the most comfortable position) any strong stick will do. Most tourist shops in popular mountain areas sell wooden staffs, usually at very low prices unless you want a fancy carved and varnished shepherd's crook. However such staffs have the big disadvantage of not being easily transportable. You can't put them in the pack and they would have to travel as separate items of luggage on a plane. Faced with transporting them home from the Pyrenees by train and ferry my companions left theirs behind. And, as I found in Iceland, you can't always buy or find a staff when you reach an area.

The answer to this problem is the adjustable staff. Made from aluminium and modelled on collapsible ski-poles these are lighter and stronger than wooden sticks and can be carried in or on the pack. Many alpine ski-pole companies make them, having noted that skiers in the Alps often use their poles when walking in the summer. The one I've used most is the Swiss-made Leki Light-Walk, a gold-coloured, three-section aluminium staff weighing 200g/7oz that has a wood handle rounded at the top, a nylon wrist strap and a strong carbide tip. The three sections slide into each other and lock in place by twisting a plastic collar. The stick adjusts from 51 to 107cm/20–42in in length. For someone of my height (172cm/5ft 8in) this is just long enough though it might be a little short for anyone taller than me. I took the Light-Walk on my Canadian Rockies trek and it served all the functions of a staff admirably. Unfortunately I left it behind after nearly 2000km/1250 miles of walking. I missed it so much that I replaced it with an aspen pole taken from an abandoned hunter's camp. I now have another Light-Walk but I discovered from using the aspen pole that it lacks one feature I'd like. The aspen pole came almost to eye level and had a flat top and I found it made an excellent if crude monopod for supporting the camera when taking pictures of animals that appeared and disappeared so quickly there was no time to set up my tripod. The Light-Walk is shorter and it is impossible to balance a camera on its rounded handle. It is useless, in other words, as a monopod.

Searching for something better I had a look at purpose-designed monopods but didn't find one I thought would stand up to the rough usage a walking stick receives. Then in the REI catalogue I found the Chief of Staffs walking stick with hardened steel point and a removable rubber foot, an adjustable length of 84–145cm/33–57in, a weight of 450g/1lb and, wonder of wonders, a universal tripod mount hidden under the wooden handle. This looked as though it combined all the good points of the Light-Walk with those of a monopod. I used it on my Yukon Wilderness walk, which was nearly all cross-country in very rough terrain with many creek crossings, and found it ideal. The foam-padded handle is very comfortable though it was full of holes by the end of the walk (it's easily replaced) and the extra length over the Light-Walk is welcome as I can use it at elbow height. Fully extended, it makes an excellent centre pole for a tarp. The only problem is the collapsed size, too long to fit in all but the largest packs, though it can be strapped alongside a full Gregory Cassin without sticking out.

The Chief of Staffs is made by Cascade Designs, who also make four other staffs though none of them are adjustable. The most useful looks to be the Mountain Guide as it breaks down into three sections for carrying and is available in heights of 122cm/48in, 132cm/52cm and 142cms/56in.

If you're a skier one of your ski poles, especially an old one or the one left over when you break one, will make a perfectly functional staff if you don't need a collapsible one. After all, the Light-Walk is only a modified ski stick. Leki Trekker Poles (adjustable from 61 to 152cm/24–60in) come in pairs (510g/18oz the two) and have alpine ski-pole grips. With baskets on they'd be ski poles. Edelrid do in fact offer 'walking-hiking' telescopic poles with baskets and ski-pole handles. The weight is 525g/18½oz a pair.

ICE AXE

Whenever you are likely to encounter slopes of hard snow and ice you should carry an ice axe. Winter is the obvious time to expect such terrain but snow patches can linger well into spring and even summer after a hard winter. I often don't pack my ice axe away until June and I have had to seek out an alternative route as late as September in the Pyrenees when a steel-hard bank of old snow blocked the trail to a high pass. In the British hills many if not most accidents to walkers in winter are caused by slips on icy ground. An ice axe could have prevented many of these.

Whilst it is very useful for balance in soft snow, a staff or ski pole is not adequate when crossing steep, hard packed snow or ice. On such surfaces a slip can easily become a rapidly accelerating slide. The only way of stopping such a fall is by a method known as self-arrest, which requires an ice axe. This book is not the place—nor am I enough of an expert—to go into the details of this procedure. For instruction see a mountaineering text book. *Mountaineering: The Freedom of the Hills,* edited by Ed Peters (The Mountaineers) and *Mountaincraft and Leadership* by Eric Langmuir (Scottish Sports Council/Mountainwalking Leader Training Board) are both useful sources for all aspects of snow travel other than skiing, as well as ice axe use. However I'm not at all convinced that self-arrest can be learnt from a written description. Really you need either to take a general snow- and ice-skills course at an outdoor centre or have an experienced friend show you the technique. Practice is essential as in a real fall you have to react immediately and automatically. And you must be able to stop yourself whether you fall with your head downhill or on your back so practise in those positions too. When you are on slopes where you may have to self-arrest if you slip, it's best to carry the axe with the pick pointing backwards so that it's in the right position for self-arrest. On easier slopes I prefer to walk with the pick pointing forward so that if I stumble I don't impale myself on it.

Other uses of an ice axe are to cut steps in ice and snow too hard to kick your boot into (though wearing crampons makes this unnecessary—see below) and to use instead of a staff for balance when walking on snow. If you do slip on a snow slope thrusting the axe shaft into the snow can often prevent a slide starting. A staff can also be used for this but of course it cannot be used for self-arrest if it fails to hold you. Other uses I've found for an ice axe, which a staff will not do, include pulling pegs out of frozen ground or hard-packed snow, chopping holes in frozen streams or ponds to get water, chipping ice off rocks I want to stand on without slipping when fording streams, and digging toilet holes.

There are many complicated—not to say bizarre—styles of ice axe available, most of them designed for those who wish to climb frozen waterfalls and iced-up vertical cliffs. All the backpacker needs is a simple traditional ice axe,

usually described as a 'walking' or 'general mountaineering' axe. The head of the axe should have a wide adze, which is useful for cutting steps and possibly for self-arrest in softish snow, and a gently curved pick. Two-piece heads are perfectly adequate for walking use. The shaft material can be aluminium alloy, reinforced fibre-glass or wood, the first being the lightest. Wrist loops are useful and worth attaching if your axe doesn't come with one. Length is a matter of debate, the conventional wisdom being to choose an axe whose spike is a centimetre or so off the ground when the axe is held by the side. However my advice is to go for an axe five centimetres or so longer than this if you intend using it as a staff on easy ground as well and ten or more centimetres less if you carry a staff or ski pole for the gentler terrain. I now mostly do the latter and carry a 55cm axe rather than the 70cm I always used to take. Weights run from 500 to 800g/18–28oz and makes to look for include Salewa, Stubai, SMC, Mountain Technology, Simond, REI, Camp, Grivel and Chouinard.

The axe I currently use is a ten-year-old 720-g/25-oz 55-cm fibre-glass-shafted Stubai model, originally bought for climbing rather than backpacking. This has replaced a 70-cm Simond one that did the whole length of the Pacific Crest Trail but whose pick eventually broke when it was used for changing a car wheel on the way back from a ski-mountaineering trip to the Alps. If we'd had the right tools I'd probably still be using it. As it is I'm thinking of changing to a Mountain Technology Snowhopper model, mainly for its weight of just 500g/17oz, but also because it has a broad adze which my Stubai one lacks. There are plenty of other models.

Ice axes are dangerous implements and care should be taken in their use and carriage. Rubber protectors are available for head and spike and should be used when transporting the axe to and from the mountains, especially if you are travelling by public transport. Indeed you may not be allowed in a vehicle without covering your axe in this way.

CRAMPONS

If conditions warrant carrying an ice axe then crampons will probably be useful as well. These metal spikes strap or clamp on to the soles of your boots and enable you to cross ice and hard snow without slipping. I find I rarely use them but when I do they are essential, so I also rarely leave them at home. Articulated crampons—that is ones that are hinged in the middle—can be fitted to most medium-weight boots for walking purposes. Rigid crampons are for climbers. The number of points a crampon has doesn't really matter for walkers; eight- ten- or twelve-point models are all available. I do find points that angle out from the front of the boot useful for climbing steep slopes, as you can then use the toe of the boot. So I would recommend crampons with these rather than the ones with only vertical points which are often offered to walkers. To fasten them to most walking boots straps are needed as ski-type bindings, which are found on crampons designed for serious climbing, can't be used on boots without a prominent welt. The best straps are neoprene ones as these won't freeze. Fitting crampons to boots is a complicated business if you've never done it before and finding the right size can be difficult, so I would advise novices to take their boots into the shop when purchasing crampons and ensure that the staff show you how they fit and how to do up the straps.

I have a pair of Salewa 12-point articulated crampons that weigh 900g/2lb, but I am thinking of changing to a lighter pair as a number of these have come on the market since I bought mine. In particular I'm considering getting some eight point Grivel Vallée Blanche Walker crampons that weigh just 600g/21oz and are designed for walking boots. As my crampons spend far more time in my pack than on my feet I want them to weigh as little as possible. As well as Salewa and Grivel, good general-purpose crampons are available from Stubai, SMC, Gab and Camp. Like ice axes, crampons are potentially dangerous and rubber protectors should cover the spikes when they're not in use if you carry them strapped outside your pack. I find the tangled rubber strands of crampon point protectors a nuisance and long ago abandoned using them, preferring instead to carry my crampons inside the pack in a side pocket with a side zip bought specially for the purpose.

Walking in crampons needs practice as it involves a different gait to walking without them, and on steep slopes special techniques are required. The basis of these is always to keep the foot flat on the snow or ice so that all the points bite, though on really steep slopes you can kick just the front points into the snow and walk up on your toes. I find that the least tiring way to climb moderately steep ground is to front-point with one foot whilst keeping the other flat on the ground, alternating the feet as they start to ache. For more information on crampon use see a mountaineering manual.

SKIS AND SNOWSHOES

Walking through snow more than ankle deep can be quite difficult. Once you sink in to your shins and deeper it becomes an exhausting and very slow method of progress, aptly known as 'postholing'. A few kilometres a day can be more than enough. The answer, as the Scandinavians found out some 4000 years ago, is to strap something to your feet that spreads your weight and allows you to float on the surface of the snow rather than sink in it. After years of plodding through the wet snows of the British hills I discovered this for myself in the mountains of southern California on my Pacific Crest Trail walk, when I travelled with three Americans who were using snowshoes. These were a revelation and I bought a pair in preparation for the crossing of the snowbound High Sierras. On this section two of the party swapped their snowshoes for Nordic skis and another secret of snow travel was revealed as they swooped down snowfields and glided through the forest leaving the two of us on snowshoes to plod along in their wake.

This is not to say that snowshoes don't have their uses. In thick forests they are more manoeuvrable than skis and the largest ones will keep you on the surface of deep powdery snow into which the widest of skis will sink. Also you can use them with your ordinary walking boots. Old-style wooden snowshoes are still available but need careful maintenance. Better are the more durable modern aluminium-framed ones with pivoting foot straps for use on steep slopes. The ones I used in the Sierras were Sherpa Featherweight Sno-Claw models that weighed a little over 1½kg/3.3lb with straps. The Sno-Claw is a serrated edge that fits under the boot for grip on icy slopes. I found it worked well on moderate slopes. On steep ones I changed to real crampons. Walking in snowshoes is hard work and not fast but it's far easier than walking in deep snow without them. Mine were left behind in the USA as they proved too large to mail back to Britain and I've never used any since. Smaller, less adequate but cheaper and lighter-looking models appear in catalogues from time to time. If you're really interested in pursuing this subject though the book to consult is Gene Prater's *Snowshoeing* (The Mountaineers).

The reason for abandoning snowshoes after just one, albeit three-week-long, trial was that the skiers in our party pulled way ahead time after time. Snowshoeing, it seemed to me, was a functional if tedious way to travel in the snow. Skiing looked fun. During a crossing of the High Sierras in May with a 45-kg/100-lb pack was not the time to learn how to ski however. The next winter I took a Nordic ski course in the Scottish Highlands, learnt the rudiments and, although no more than an average skier, have since been on ski backpacking trips every winter in places as far afield as the Vanoise Alps, the Norwegian mountains and the Canadian Rockies. It is, in my view, the only way to travel snowbound wildernesses.

Skiing is a complex subject and there are many types of ski. Out immediately for backpacking purposes are alpine or downhill skis. These are for lift-served skiing only or else for ultra-steep mountain descents. Even with special alpine ski mountaineering bindings and boots, progress on the flat and uphill is painfully slow and the weight of the gear tiring. Anyway, you won't be coming down the sort of descents you need such gear for carrying a winter backpacking load.

Nordic backcountry or mountain touring skis are the ones best suited to ski backpacking. As with boots, avoid the heavyweight skis designed for lift-served telemark skiing and the lightweight ones designed for cut-track and low-level touring with light packs. For carrying a heavy load and breaking trail in all manner of snow from deep powder to breakable crust mountain skis with metal edges are needed. These are narrower at the waist than at the tip and tail. For heavy-duty touring look for at least 10mm of sidecut as it's called. Typical dimensions are 63-54-58 (shovel, waist, tail). More sidecut is fine, less isn't. The length should equal your height plus 20cm. Such skis will weigh from 2 to 3kg/4½–6½lbs. My favourite pair are Asnes Nansen Mountain skis which have a 20mm sidecut and weigh 2.7kg/6lb. Other good makes are Fischer, Karhu, Tua and Rossignol. Whatever the skis, you need strong bindings such as the

Rottefella Super Telemark to clip your boots into as they'll have to undergo the stresses of your bodyweight plus a heavy pack.

This isn't the place to go into the details of ski technique or the mysteries of waxing. You should know though that only moderate skill is required to get about the wilderness on ski and that the enjoyment of ski touring far outweighs the effort required. Taking a course at a Nordic ski school as I did is a good idea for complete beginners. General details of Nordic equipment and technique can be found in *Cross-Country Skiing* by Ned Gillette and John Dostal (The Mountaineers/Diadem), and more specific ones on wilderness touring in *Backcountry Skiing* by Lito Tejades-Flores (Sierra Club Books). For equipment *Cross-Country Ski Gear* by Michael Brady (The Mountaineers) is pretty comprehensive.

Poles are essential with skis and a great help with snowshoes. Lightweight fibre-glass ones break easily. I'd recommend a metal pair. I like adjustable ones (long for the flat, shorter for uphill, shortest for downhill). There are many sorts available. My Leki Lawisonds weigh 625g/22oz.

FOOT CARE

Keeping your feet in good condition is a necessity if you are not to suffer when out walking. In particular toenails should be kept cut short and square; long nails will bruise, cut into the toes on either side and cause incredible pain on descents. Feet should be kept clean of course but remember always to dry them well to avoid softening the skin too much. Some people praise various skin-hardening methods such as dousing the feet in rubbing alcohol or methylated spirits prior to or even during long treks. I've never tried these but do go barefoot around the house and outside, weather and sartorial requirements permitting, as much as possible. This toughens the feet beautifully. By going barefoot and wearing sandals without socks I usually manage to achieve really hard feet by the end of the summer, just in time to swathe them in socks and soften them up again over the winter!

When on a walk it's important to stop and attend to any sign of a sore spot, covering the suspect area to prevent further rubbing. Failure to do so immediately may result in a blister. However it's easy to preach this, not so easy to practice it. All too often I ignore warning signs, telling myself that I'll have a look when I next stop. Then when I do, I find a nice plump blister. How to treat blisters is an arcane subject and the remedies and cures are legion. What is common to all is that the blister must be covered to prevent infection and to cushion it against further rubbing. It can be covered with ordinary plaster, moleskin, micropore tape or a more specialised material such as Spenco Second Skin, the treatment I currently favour. This is a gel that is placed over a sore spot or blister and then held in place by a piece of sticky tape or plaster. Second Skin is a slimy substance, difficult to hold and you have to remove backing film from both sides before use and store it in an airtight foil bag, but it works far better than anything else I've tried at both preventing blisters forming and stopping already-formed blisters hurting. Spenco do a Blister Kit consisting of a plastic wallet containing instructions, Second Skin in resealable bag, adhesive tape and some foam padding for really painful blisters (15g/½oz). I prefer to buy Second Skin on its own for long walks, however, as you don't get much in the kit (six 3-mm squares) and I never seem to use the foam pads. In whatever form, Second Skin lives in my first aid kit.

Some experts advise against bursting a blister before covering it, which is fine if you're not intending to walk for a few days (in fact, if this is the case you're better not covering the blister at all, as it will heal more quickly in the open air). If you are continuing to walk after a blister forms, however, then you'll have to burst it in order to minimise the pain. To do so I sterilise a needle in a match flame, pierce the blister at one edge then roll the needle over the blister until all the fluid has drained out. A piece of tissue (from the toilet roll if necessary) is useful to absorb the liquid and wipe the area dry. With large blisters several holes may be needed before all the fluid can be expelled. I know from painful experience that however long it takes, the blister must be fully drained before being dressed. Otherwise your first steps when you start walking again will hurt so much you'll have to stop again. Antiseptic wipes can be used to clean the area though Second Skin seems to do this well by itself.

Blisters are caused by friction and, if you can, it's best to try to find and remove the cause, which may be a tiny speck of grit that has entered the boot or a rough sock seam that can be trimmed. Often though there is no obvious cause and you just have to hope that covering the blister will solve the problem. Mysteriously, boots which have never given problems before can one day cause a blister yet be fine again on future trips. However, I would suspect boots that repeatedly cause sore spots. Either they don't fit properly or something inside needs smoothing down. I once suffered bad blisters from a pair of boots that seemed to fit properly. Although I couldn't work out how they were doing it the cause was the footbeds, for when I changed them the blisters healed and I suffered no more.

I like to remove my boots and socks several times during the day, as long as the weather allows for this, in order to let my feet cool down and air. Pouring cold water over them provides even more relief on really hot days. Some people also like to apply foot powder to help keep their feet dry. I carried some on one walk to see if using it made any difference. As it didn't seem to, I've not carried any since.

Carrying the Load:
The Pack

The heart of the backpacker's equipment is the pack. Tents, boots, stoves and waterproofs may all at various times and in various places be unnecessary. Your pack is always with you. It must hold everything you need for safe and comfortable wilderness travel over many days whilst being as little of a burden as possible. To do this a pack must be far more than the bag with shoulder straps that is adequate for day walks. Ever since aluminium frames and hipbelts were introduced in the 1940s and 1950s designers have tried to make carrying heavy loads as comfortable as possible. Internal and external frames, adjustable back systems, sternum straps, top tension straps, side tension straps, triple-density padded hipbelts, lumbar pads—the modern pack suspension system is a complex structure that requires care in selection and fitting. Time should be taken in finding the pack that fits you best, which may well not be the one that suits someone else. If you get the fit wrong you will suffer and suffer badly. In terms of comfort, only your boots are as important as your pack.

TYPES OF PACK

Walk into any outdoor equipment shop and you will be confronted by a vast array of packs. Sorting out which ones are suitable for backpacking is quite simple. Deciding which of those is the one for your sort of backpacking is a much more difficult matter.

Day and Running Packs

Small packs designed for day walks can be discounted immediately, though there are similar packs designed for the runner or ultralightweight fanatic who is prepared to compromise comfort and durability for lightness and low bulk and who is probably not going to be out for more than a night or two at a time. These packs are made from ultralightweight nylon and weigh around 300g/11oz, so light that I have on occasion carried one to take on side trips away from camp, using it as a stuffsac inside the main pack the rest of the time. Features are minimal—at most lightly padded backs, shoulder straps and hip belts plus a chest strap; capacities for backpacking are minute at around 30 litres/1830cu.in. I have used mine, the Rock & Run Ridgerunner, on two-day mountain marathons but such events don't bear much relation to general backpacking and most backpackers can ignore this category. If you are interested, if only to see how small a pack some people can fit their overnight gear into when they have to, similar packs come from Karrimor and Troll. Many people on such events just use an ordinary day sack.

Climbing and Trekking Packs

Next up in size are packs that are generally in the 30–60 litre/1830–3660cu.in. capacity range though a few can hold as much as 80 litres/4880cu.in. Designed for alpine climbing and skiing or hut-to-hut trekking, these packs usually come with padded backs and shoulder straps. A few have removable foam pads for extra support. Karrimor's Fformat, used in their Alpiniste packs, has metal struts built in as well. Waistbelts may be padded but are often just simple webbing. Back lengths are fixed, though the larger ones may come in a couple of sizes. The only difference between the two is that trekking packs have fixed side pockets and climbing packs don't. The more sophisticated ones, meant for mountaineering expeditions, have some of the features of internal-frame packs and could be used for short backpacking trips in good weather. The advantages of these packs are light weight, simple design (little to go wrong) and excellent stability, which is why they are popular with climbers and skiers. Most pack-makers have several packs in this range so the choice is large. I have a 58-litre/3540-cu.in. Pod Alpine Sac with padded back and shoulder straps and a lid pocket that I use for hut-to-hut ski touring. It is quite comfortable with loads of up to 14kg/30lb but the lightly padded hip fins and the lack of a frame mean that it won't carry heavier loads anything like as well as a pack designed to do so. If I only backpacked occasionally in summer I might well make it do. As it is even on short trips with a light load I prefer a fully specified backpacking pack.

Backpacking Packs

The next category is the one containing packs purpose-designed for carrying heavy loads. They are sophisticated, complex, expensive and marvellous. Without them I for one would find backpacking a much more arduous and less pleasant activity. This category subdivides into two suspension systems based on their frames, and about which there is much heated argument, each side having its dedicated proponents.

First came the welded tubular aluminium alloy external frame, its ladder-like appearance common on trails throughout the world in the 1950s, 1960s and 1970s. It's a simple, strong and functional design, good for carrying heavy loads along smooth trails but unstable when used in rougher, steeper terrain. Capacities are enormous as it's easy to lash extra items to the frame.

Just as the external frame seemed to be on the way out, new designs have appeared, featuring alloy frames with extreme curvature and flexible synthetic frames, designed to match the internal frames' bodyhugging fit, to give the old standby a new lease of life.

Mountaineers who wanted packs in which they could carry heavy loads comfortably but which retained the stability of the frameless alpine sack achieved their goal by inserting flexible flat metal bars down the back of the latter. Thus, in the late 1960s, was born the internal frame. Development of the design has been rapid since then, though the frames themselves have remained very basic, and now most backpackers choose packs with internal frames. Ranging in size from 50 to 174 litres/ 3050–10,620cu in. in capacity they will cater for just about any sort of backpacking from summer weekend strolls to six-month expeditions. They require careful fitting, as well as adjustment whilst walking, but for those prepared to take the time for this, they are an excellent choice.

Travel Packs

These developed out of internal-frame packs as the growing number of people travelling the world by plane, train, bus and thumb (and occasionally legs) realised that internal-frame packs were easier to carry and fit in vehicles than external frame ones. Large travel packs have the same suspension systems and capacities and are about the same weight as internal-frame ones. The smaller ones have just shoulder straps and hipbelts. On both, the harness can be zipped away behind a panel when you don't need it or don't want to risk the suspicion that packs bring from some officials and in some countries. In particular though, covering the harness protects it from the delicate touch of airport baggage handlers. With the harness hidden, travel packs look like soft luggage with their handles, zip-round compartments and front pockets, and they can be used like suitcases when packing and unpacking. How well they work for backpacking I don't know but the general consensus seems to be that whilst they'll do for the occasional overnight trip, they don't compare with real internal-frame packs for more serious trips. The larger ones with internal frames would probably prove adequate for long treks with moderate loads (18kg/40lb or so) if you don't mind the zip-round opening.

SUSPENSION SYSTEMS

When you choose a pack the suspension system is the feature that needs most attention, as it is this that actually supports the load and is the part of the pack in direct contact with you. A top-quality, properly fitted suspension system will allow you to carry heavy loads comfortably and in balance. An inadequate or badly fitted one will cause you great pain.

The Hipbelt

The back and shoulders are not designed for bearing heavy loads for long. Indeed the spine is easily injured, as it is compressed when carrying a heavy load, hence the prevalence of back problems. If you carry a load on your shoulders you have to bend forwards to counteract the backward pull of the load, which is both uncomfortable and bad for the back whilst the pressure on the sensitive nerves and muscles of the shoulders soon causes them to ache and go numb.

The solution is to carry the load on the hips, a far stronger part of the body and one designed to bear weight. The key to doing this is the hipbelt, by far the most important part of any pack system designed for carrying heavy loads, and the part of the pack I always examine first. A well-fitting, well-padded hipbelt transfers most of the weight (at least 75 per cent) from the shoulders and back to the much stronger hips, allowing the backpacker to stand upright and carry a load in comfort for hours at a time. If you put on a heavily loaded pack, take the weight on your shoulders and then walk a few yards, you'll be convinced you can't carry it any distance. Do up the hipbelt tightly and you'll feel the weight melt away. The difference is astonishing. Suddenly you feel you can stride out for hours.

Introduced in the 1950s the first hipbelts were unpadded and made of webbing. Today's affairs are complex multi-layered creations of foam, plastic and even graphite. A good hipbelt should be well padded, with two or more layers of foam, and at least a centimetre thick. The inner layer should be soft so that it moulds to your hips and absorbs shock whilst the outer layer needs to be stiff so that the belt doesn't distort under the weight of a heavy load. Some companies such as Karrimor, Kelty and The North Face have a third outer layer of polypropylene or polyethylene in the belts on their largest packs to minimise any twisting under a heavy load. Gregory go one further and have carbon fibre panels which flex easily round your hips

but are completely rigid from top to bottom.

As well as being thickly padded, a hipbelt should also be at least 10cm/4in deep where it passes over the hips, narrowing in towards the buckle. Conically cut belts are less likely to slip down over the hips than straight-cut ones, but this isn't something to worry about as almost all belts are conically cut on top-quality packs. Continuous wrap-around belts perform better with the heaviest loads than simple fins sewn on to the side of the pack in my experience. Most top models have these, though it may not be apparent in packs such as the Berghaus Cyclops II, where the belt webbing passes inside the heavily padded back. To provide support for the small of your back, the lower section of the pack back should be well padded. This can be a direct continuation of the hipbelt as in most external frame packs, a special lumbar pad as in most internal frames, or part of a completely padded back as in packs like the Cyclops II series.

Belts that are only attached to the frame or the lumbar pad at or near the small of the back need side tension straps to prevent the pack from swaying when you walk. These straps pull the edges of the pack in round the hips and greatly increase the stability. Most internal-frame packs have them. Also appearing on a few models (like some from Dana Design and Mountainsmith) are diagonal compression straps that run downwards across the side of the pack to the hipbelt, the idea being to pull the load on to the latter. I've never used a pack with such straps but reports suggest that they also help with stability.

Most hipbelts are nylon-covered inside and out, often with Cordura or something similar, which is adequate but can mean that they slip slightly when worn over smooth synthetic clothing, a problem that worsens as the load becomes heavier. Some companies use high-friction fabrics with names such as Tuff-grip (Lowe and Lipke) and Gription Mesh (Gregory), which work better.

The buckles on most belts are the three-pronged Fastex ones. These are tough and easy enough to use but I do find that they have a tendency to slip. The buckles where the two halves overlap, trapping the webbing between them, are more secure. Versions of these are used by Berghaus, Karrimor and Kelty. There's not much difference, however, and both sorts can be quickly released with one hand if necessary. I wouldn't like to try and do so in a real emergency though, as I fear the buckle might jam, and also that the few seconds needed to release it could be crucial. If I think I may need to jettison my pack in a hurry, as when fording a deep or swiftly-flowing creek, I undo the belt beforehand.

Size is important with hipbelts. The widest part of the belt should fit over the hipbone as that is where much of the weight of the load will concentrate, and there should be enough webbing left either side of the buckle after the belt has been tightened to allow for weight-loss and tauter stomach muscles on a long trek, and also for adjusting over different thicknesses of clothing. Most packs come with permanently attached hipbelts so the size has to be checked when you buy them. Packs that come in two or three sizes often have different-sized belts to go with each size on the basis that the taller you are the bigger your waistline. This means for example that whilst The North Face's large-size Inca Trail pack fits my long back the hipbelt is too big for my 83-cm/33-in waist, so I have had to change down to the slightly smaller standard-size pack. Companies which make packs with removable belts may offer a choice of two or three sizes as do Gregory, Kelty and others. Thus my large-size Gregory Cassin is fitted with a medium-size hipbelt. Obviously such modular systems are the best way to achieve the optimum fit, especially if you're not an 'average' size. Some one-size belts, such as those on VauDe Tergoflex packs, can be adjusted for an individual fit, the latter whilst the pack is on the back by means of a plastic ratchet system with pull loops on the outside top edge of each side of the belt. The resulting tight fit tips the belt in at the top, which helps prevent slippage.

How big a belt you need depends on the weight you intend carrying. I've found that moderately padded belts like those found on Karrimor and Berghaus packs will carry loads of up to 22–23kg/48–50lb well. However heavier loads cause them to compress too much and press painfully on the hip bone or start to twist out of shape, making it difficult to take most of the load on the hips. For really big loads the best belt I've used on an internal-frame pack is the one on my Gregory Cassin which consists of an outer layer of rigid plastic backed by high-density foam, two middle layers of softer foam and an inner lining of Gription Mesh. The new Gregory belt referred to above with added carbon fibre panels is meant to be even better. In external-frame packs the best belt I've found is that on the Lowe Holoflex which is made of extra thick bi-laminated foam with a Tuff-grip lining. What distinguishes these belts from most others is the vertical rigidity, the thickness of the foam, the width over the hips and the lining material.

Shoulder Straps

Most of the time the shoulder straps do little more than stop the pack from falling off your back. However for those times when you have to carry all or some of the weight on your shoulders (river crossings when you've undone the hipbelt for safety, rock scrambles and downhill ski runs where for optimum balance you've fully tightened all the straps to split the weight between shoulders and hips) these straps need to be foam-filled and tapered to prevent the padding slipping. This is now the standard design on most good packs. Many straps are curved too so that they run neatly under the arms without twisting. For fit the key thing to look for is the distance between the shoulder straps at the top. In most packs this is fixed and designed to be correct for the 'average' person. VauDe packs are among the few on which the width of the shoulder straps can be adjusted. If you have narrow shoulders or a broad neck you might find that not all shoulder straps fit comfortably. As women normally have narrower shoulders than men and the 'average' size is that of an 'average' man there are women's packs available from many companies (Karrimor, Berghaus, Lowe, The North Face and Kelty to name a few). They have the shoulder straps closer together than on men's packs. If you're a man with narrow shoulders these might be worth looking at.

Top Tension Straps

Packs designed for moderate to heavy loads (15kg/33lbs plus) should have top tension straps (sometimes called stabiliser, load-balancing or lift straps, or something similar) running from the top of the shoulder straps to the pack. These straps pull the load in over your shoulders to increase stability and also lift the shoulder straps off the sensitive nerves around the collarbone, transferring the weight to the much tougher shoulder blades. By loosening or tightening the straps, which can be done whilst walking, you can shift the weight of the pack between the hips and the shoulders and find the most comfortable position for the terrain you're on.

Sternum Straps

Most shoulder straps have webbing sewn down the front in a 'daisy-chain' fashion. (On Gregory packs this webbing is sewn to a larger nylon 'load control panel' that is stitched to the shoulder straps only at the top and bottom in order to spread the weight of the load and hold all stitching and thus minimise stress on the foam.) On many large packs sternum or chest straps are threaded through this webbing. These straps pull the shoulder straps into the chest and help to further stabilise the pack. I don't use them all the time but find them useful when skiing or scrambling and for varying the pressure points of a heavy load during a long ascent. Most are simple webbing straps but some have stretchy sections to prevent over-tightening. Avoid those that are fully elasticated, as they can't be tightened at all, and are basically useless. If your pack doesn't have them as standard sternum straps can be bought separately.

Frames

To hold the load steady and help transfer the weight from the shoulders to the hips some form of stiffening is needed in the back of the pack. For loads of less than 12–14kg/26–31lb a simple foam padded back is adequate but once the weight goes above this a more rigid system is needed. Packs have been made in which the gear packed inside provided this rigidity but these required so much care in packing that they proved too awkward to use and they have all but disappeared. All packs designed for heavy loads now have frames.

There are two types: the external, on which the packbag is hung, and the internal which fits into the back of the pack and is often completely integrated into it and hidden from view. There has been a lot of debate over which is best. In terms of sales internal frames appear to have won the argument and there are now more of them available than there are external frames— though the latter still have a following, especially amongst those who walk mainly on trails in forested and gentle terrain.

The debate is about which frame best supports a heavy load and which is the most stable on rough ground. The answers used to be externals for the first and internals for the second. Confusingly however the best internals will now carry heavy loads as well as the best externals whilst the best externals are now as stable as the best internals. Which should you go for then? For most loads in most places I would choose an internal frame. They're more stable than all but a few externals, easier to carry around when you're not on the trail, less prone to damage and perfectly comfortable with medium-weight loads, that is ones running from 14 to 20kg/31–to 44lb. Once you go above that weight then pack choice becomes more critical anyway, as only the very best of either camp will handle really heavy loads properly. Before my Canadian Rockies walk I would have said that internals won hands down with the Gregory Cassin being the best heavy load carrier I'd used. However on that Canadian walk I used a Lowe Holoflex Frame Pack and found it carried 30–40kg/66–88lb at least as well as the Gregory. So I have to admit I am in a state of indecision regarding large packs at present. What you can be sure of is that the very best packs, whether externally or internally framed, will handle heavy loads in a way that wasn't possible not so many years ago.

An argument for using external frames is that because they stand away from the back they allow sweat to dissipate, unlike internal frame packs which hug the body. In my experience if I work hard whilst carrying a heavy load I end up with a sweaty back whatever the type of frame.

External frames: The external frame has been around since the early 1950s and is still popular in Scandinavia and North America, though it has all but disappeared from the British hills and the Alps and Pyrenees. However new forms of external frame introduced at the end of the 1980s may well see a revival in its popularity. The traditional version is made of tubular aluminium alloy in an H-shape consisting of two curved vertical bars to which a number of crossbars are welded. Kelty introduced such frames in the 1950s and still make them in a barely altered form in their Tioga series. These nonadjustable frames come in three sizes and have padded shoulder straps and hipbelts plus backbands and frame extensions. Other versions

A range of carrying systems. From the left VauDe Tergoflex, Gregory Cassin, The North Face Inca Trail, Lowe Wedge Adjustment and the fixed back of the Pod Alpine.

include those from Fjallraven and Bergens in Europe and Camp Trails and REI in the USA. External frames are easy to fit and the weight transfers directly through the rigid frame to your hips—they are thus a vast improvement on unframed packs. Because of their rigidity it is easy to carry the load high above the head, keeping it close to the centre of gravity.

Such frames have big disadvantages, however, which is why they are no longer so popular. The main problem is to do with balance and stability. Because of their rigidity, external frames do not move with you. On steep downhills and when crossing rough ground they feel jerky and unstable. On good paths this doesn't matter but for off-trail travel it can make walking really difficult and even unsafe. Other disadvantages are that external-frame packs are bulkier than internal ones, making them awkward to travel with on planes or buses or in cars and difficult to stow in small tents. They are also more susceptible to damage, especially on aircraft. All this has meant that I haven't used a traditional external frame since the early 1980s and can't see myself doing so ever again.

The internal frame has been the focus of most attempts to solve the problems of external frames, but the design has thrown up a number of problems of its own. In particular it has proved difficult, though not impossible, to build an internal frame that will comfortably carry really heavy loads—ones above, say, 25kg/55lb. Some pack makers, instead of trying to build internals with all the advantages of externals and none of the disadvantages have turned this on its head and tried to build externals with all the advantages of internals and none of the disadvantages. Two ways of doing this have been tried; by modification of the alloy frame and by using flexible plastic instead of rigid alloy. Kelty have done the first with their Radial Frames which have an exaggerated S-curve to hold the frame closer to the body and a three-layer hipbelt and lumbar pad with a polyethylene plastic outer attached to a back band in a manner intended to allow independent movement between it and the pack and thus 'allow your hips to roll naturally with your stride, reducing the wobble in your pack'. Norwegian pack-makers Bergens have a similar frame whilst Swedish neighbours Fjallraven's external Gyro frames have forward projections that ride over the hips and a swivel attachment for the hipbelt permitting independent movement that again is claimed to give good balance on rough terrain. Instead of using welded joints Jansport's frame has crossbars attached to the side bars by flexible joints, which, it is claimed, allows it to twist and flex with body movement.

Not having used any of these frames I can't

43

comment on how effective they are. My only experience is with the North Face Back Magic aluminium alloy external-frame pack whose hip-belt is attached to the frame by a flexible plastic joint that allows independent movement of the belt. I carried one of these for the last 1600km/1000 miles of the Pacific Crest Trail and found it better than a conventional external frame, though still nothing like as stable as a good internal. However the Bergens one has been used by Nordic ski expeditioner Guy Sheridan on long ski tours in the Yukon and Himalayas and other places with loads of around 22kg/48lb (as told in his *Tales of a Cross Country Skier*, Oxford Illustrated Press), and he praises it highly. As skiing with a pack is the best test of stability, this design at least would appear to work. It seems that the key to giving better balance with a rigid alloy external frame is the freedom of movement of the belt in relation to the pack plus an increased curvature of the frame to more closely mould it to the body (something the Back Magic lacks).

It is with plastic frames, though, that I think the future for external frames lies. Oddly enough one of the first companies to introduce such a frame for very heavy loads was Lowe, the originators of the internal frame, who had never made an external frame before. In doing so they seem to be admitting that there is a limit to the capabilities of internal frames. In 1988 I used a Lowe Holoflex Frame Pack for all but 350km/220 miles of my 2500-km/1500-mile walk along the Canadian Rockies. I carried loads ranging from 30 to 40kg/66–88lb and found the pack superbly comfortable and extremely stable on very rough terrain. It really does combine the best properties of external and internal frames. The frame itself is moulded from hollow synthetic Zytel material which is flexible, enabling it to move with you. A complex hipbelt attachment called the Veraflex Waistbelt Support isolates the frame from the movement of your hips by means of a plastic joint whose range of movement can be adjusted. Above the heavily padded hipbelt is a padded 'posture pad'. The harness also has top and side tension straps and a sternum strap. The back length can be adjusted by pushing down on the yoke to which the shoulder straps are attached, moving it into another slot on the central vertical frame bar and pulling up to snap it into place. Unfortunately the cost of making the

Holoflex, coupled with some initial manufacturing problems (my Veraflex system snapped off the frame near the end of the Rockies walk) and the low numbers of consumers requiring such an expensive and complex system, has caused Lowe to cease production of this superb pack.

Similar in concept to the Holoflex is the Tergoflex system from the German company VauDe. Again this has a flexible synthetic external frame with an adjustable back length plus a three-layer adjustable hipbelt which can be fine-tuned around the hips whilst being worn. I obtained a Tergoflex Skagen to try out whilst writing this book and have so far used it for one four-day trek with a 22½-kg/50-lb load. I found it handled this weight well and was very stable on rough and steep terrain. However, short trials of a few hours with 32-kg/70-lb-plus loads caused the height-adjustable hipbelt to slip and painful pressure points to develop on my hips so I wouldn't recommend this system for very heavy loads and long treks. I shall continue to use the Skagen for lighter loads and shorter treks, though, as it is very comfortable. As this book goes to print however, VauDe have just launched a new stronger and thicker hip belt. *Internal Frames*: Nearly all internal frames consist of two malleable flat aluminium alloy bars running the length of the back of the pack. They hardly vary from the original internal frame first introduced in the late 1960s by Lowe Alpine Systems as an answer to the problems of the instability of the external frame pack on rugged terrain and the inability of the frameless sack to carry a heavy load comfortably. The bars or stays of an internal frame are usually parallel, though in some designs they taper in a little towards the top of the pack. They are also usually unconnected, though Berghaus ones are linked at the top and Mountainsmith ones in the centre by crossbars. Internal frames are light and easily bent to the shape of the user's back, allowing a body-hugging fit that gives excellent stability as the pack moves with the back rather than independently, as external frames do. As well as those makers already mentioned, parallel-bar frames appear in packs from Karrimor, The North Face, Gregory, Kelty, Lipke, REI, and others. Generally the stays are only slightly curved when new and you have to bend them to the shape of your back; not a difficult task. A few packs like the North Face Inca Trail and Burma Road models come with pre-bent frames. These look fairly similar in shape to those on packs I've worn for many miles, though they can still be bent further to adapt to your particular back shape.

Variations on the theme have appeared, most using a single flexible plastic sheet covering the whole of the back, sometimes with reinforcing stays as well. This is not a new idea–I can remember packs with ABS plastic backs produced by the Irish wing of Camp Trails in the 1970s, whose strength was tested by dropping the packs, fully loaded, out of helicopters (or so they claimed)! Current versions come from Mountain Tools, Dana Designs (with central aluminium stay and carbon-fibre stays at the edges) and Osprey (plus two aluminium stays). Also different is VauDe's Tergnomic SH frame as it is an internal version of the flexible plastic external Tergoflex frame described above.

During the 1980s Gregory packs became established as having one of the best—some would say the best—internal frame systems for heavy load carrying, a view that I share, after extensive use of the Cassin pack. On the latest Gregory packs the alloy stays have been changed for graphite ones which twist laterally as well as longitudinally and thus adapt to every movement of the back. The stays are fastened to the two graphite panels that form the outer layer of the hipbelt. These panels bend in one direction but are rigid in the other, the idea being to stop vertical flexing between the belt and the frame. The result is claimed to be 'the most structurally sound internal-frame pack on the market' and to 'completely eliminate waist-belt slippage'. I've not tried this latest Gregory suspension system but it has been enthusiastically reviewed in *Backpacker* magazine, and if my experience of Gregory's previous design is anything to go by it should be worth a long look.

Pads and Padding

As well as a padded hipbelt and lumbar pad, some packs have other areas of padding. On most the shoulder straps run far enough down the back to protect the shoulder blades, though Karrimor have added scapular pads to do this on their SA Backs. On some packs the whole back is padded except for the central adjustable section; this is rather excessive, as much of it is never actually in direct contact with the back. Removable mesh-covered foam pads that velcro on to the back of the pack above the lumbar pad come as standard on some packs including Lowe WA and some Gregory ones. Lowe call theirs a posture pad, Gregory, a breathable desert panel. I've used a Lowe pack with one and a Gregory without and can't say that I've noticed very much difference either to my posture or to how sweaty my back becomes.

External-frame packs need some form of band or pad to hold the frame off the back. Traditional alloy frames usually just have a wide band of cord-tensioned nylon for this but the newer plastic ones have detachable foam-filled pads which I find more comfortable, though hotter, and better at keeping the pack close to the back.

FITTING THE PACK

Modern packs are so complex that you can't just sling them on your back and walk away. Instead they have to be fitted and it is important that this should be done properly. A badly fitting pack will prove unstable, uncomfortable and in the long run so painful and inefficient that it may well put you off backpacking for good.

It's a waste to buy an expensive pack and then not use what you have paid for. If you really don't want to take the time to fit a pack properly and then to adjust it as necessary whilst walking, you could choose a traditional external-frame pack or else a fixed back length frameless model, as these need the least attention to the fit. With heavy loads and on rough terrain, though, these packs just don't compare in comfort with more sophisticated models.

The new external frame packs like the Lowe Holoflex and VauDe Tergoflex need to be fitted in much the same way as internal-frame ones, so the description below applies in essence to both. The key measurement for fitting a pack is the distance between the top of your shoulders and your upper hip bone. This is because the hipbelt should ride with its upper edge two or three centimetres above the hipbone so that the weight is borne by the broadest, strongest part of the hips when the shoulder straps are in their correct position. The most common and most precise way of achieving a good fit is with an adjustable harness, whereby the shoulder straps can be moved up and down the back of the pack to vary the distance between them and the hipbelt. On Berghaus Laser packs it is the hipbelt that moves whilst on VauDe packs both shoulder straps and hipbelt are adjustable. Hipbelt adjustments are limited in range and mean that the position of the base of the pack in relation to your body is also moved. I can't see any advantages of such a system over an adjustable shoulder yoke one and several disadvantages. The change in the position of the pack relative to the hipbelt is the main disadvantage, as this causes the load to press on the backside when the back length is shortened and to ride too high on the back when it is lengthened. Both interfere with the stability and comfort of a load.

Lowe were first with an adjustable shoulder harness, with their much-copied Parallux system whereby the shoulder straps are fitted into slots in a webbing column sewn down the centre of the pack back. The North Face also employ velcro in their version, with a strap that wraps round on itself. These are all fiddly systems to use; easier are the much more recent stepless ones where a locking slider, screw or similar device can be used to slide the shoulder straps up and down the central column. Examples are the Lowe Wedge Adjustment (WA) System and the VauDe Tergonomic System. Even simpler are the systems where the shoulder straps are attached to a stiffened plastic yoke which slides up and down the stays as on Karrimor's Self-Adjust (SA) System and Kelty's Fast Track Suspension System. These can be adjusted whilst wearing the pack by simply pulling on two straps attached to the base of the plate. Gregory packs have a plastic adjustment ladder into which the shoulder harness slots. There are several other systems. Whichever you choose, once you've found the right length for your back you can forget about it.

Obviously any system has a limited range over which it can be adjusted and at either end of this range a pack may not carry as well as it does if adjusted to a position nearer the middle. To overcome this, many packs (Gregory, Lowe, The North Face, Dana Designs, Lipke, Mountain Tools and Osprey) come in two or three sizes whilst others, fewer in number (Karrimor, The North Face, Berghaus), offer packs in shorter back lengths than the standard and with different shaped-harnesses for women.

Initially then you need to find the pack size within whose adjustment range you can obtain a good fit. This can be done by checking the height for which the pack is intended, according to the manufacturer. You should be wary, however. I have a long back and find packs meant for people taller than me fit perfectly. In a shop of course, you can soon see if this is so. A further check is to load the pack with at least 15kg/33lbs of gear (most shops will have items available for this) and loosen all the straps. All packs come with fitting instructions, some more detailed than others. Gregory has by far the best of the ones I've seen. Instructions differ according to the specifications of the suspension system of course, but there are some general principles which I'll attempt to outline here.

Some makers advise removing the stays of internal frames and bending them to the shape of your back before you start fitting the pack, but I've never been able to do this successfully and pre-bent stays are the very devil to reinsert in their sleeves. Whether you attempt this or not, the next stage is to put the pack on and do up the hipbelt until it is carrying all the weight and the upper edge rides a couple of centimetres or so above the top of your hip bone. Next pull in the hipbelt side tension straps. Then tighten up the shoulder straps and pull in the top tension straps. These should leave the shoulder straps at a point roughly level with your collar bone and at an angle of between 20 and 45 degrees. If the angle is smaller than that the harness needs lengthening; if it is larger it needs shortening. The aim is to achieve a back length whereby most of the pack weight can ride on the hips and the pack hugs the back to provide stability. Too short a back length and the weight will pull back and down on the shoulders; too long and whilst the weight will be on the hips the top of the pack will be unstable and will sway from side to side when you walk. Once you find the right back length most of your fitting problems are over.

You know when you've found the right length by the way the pack carries when you walk around. It should feel snug and-body hugging, almost as if it's been stuck to you. If it feels awkward or uncomfortable keep adjusting until you get it right or until you decide that this particular pack will never fit you. Once I think I have the best fit I can obtain with an internal-frame pack I usually bend over and stretch the pack on my back so that the frame can start to mould to my shape, a process that is usually complete after the first day's walk. Finally you can make sure the sternum strap is in its correct position, just above the part of your chest that expands most when you breathe in. If it's not, unthread it from the webbing and move it.

Minute adjustments to the harness are necessary every time you use the pack. Loosening the top tension straps then tightening the shoulder straps and retightening the top tension straps hugs the pack to the body for maximum stability, but it also shifts some of the load on to the shoulders. It's necessary for steep descents or when skiing or crossing rough ground–anywhere in short where balance is essential. For straightforward ascents and walking on the flat the shoulder and top tensions straps can be slackened off a touch to let all the weight drop on to the hips, after which the top tension straps should be tightened a little again until you can just slide a finger between the shoulder and the shoulder straps. And every time you put on the pack you have to loosen the side tension straps then tighten them up after you've done up the hipbelt, otherwise the latter won't grip properly. Whilst on the move, whenever the pack doesn't feel quite right or you can feel a pressure point developing you can adjust the straps to shift the balance of the load slightly until it feels right again. I do this frequently during the day, almost without being aware that I'm doing it.

Traditional external frames usually come in two or three sizes, and a precise fit is not essential. You simply choose the one that comes closest to your back length. A few internal-frame models come with fixed back lengths in different sizes, most notably the Berghaus Cyclops II packs. With these you have to find the right size in the shop by trying on loaded packs. If you're lucky enough to find one that fits well it will of course carry as well as an adjustable harness, with the advantage that there is less to go wrong. If the fit isn't exact, however, it is impossible to make the fine adjustments you can make with an adjustable back system. In that case an adjustable back would be better, especially if loads of over 22–23kg/48–50lbs are to be carried, as for them the best fit possible is needed.

PACKBAGS

Compared with all the intricacies of back systems, packbag design is fairly straightforward, especially as the choice is a purely personal one—the type of packbag you have has little effect on the comfort of your pack when it's on your back. How many pockets, compartments and external attachment points you choose to have depends on how you like to pack, and the bulkiness of your gear. Tidy folk like packs with plenty of pockets and at least two compartments so that they can carefully organise their gear. Those of a less neat disposition tend to go for large single-compartment monsters into which everything can be quickly shoved.

There are a couple of points to look for, however, with regard to the way a packbag will carry. To minimise stooping and to maintain balance, the load needs to be as close to your centre of gravity as possible. This is achieved by keeping it near to your back and as high up as is feasible without reducing stability. Whilst the suspension system is the key to this, it can be helped by a packbag that extends upwards and perhaps out at the sides but not away from the back. For this reason I would avoid packs with large rear pockets.

Internal frame packs come of course as an integral unit. The frame may be embedded in a foam-padded pack back, encased in sleeves or just attached at the top and bottom. Whatever the method the frame and pack work together and cannot be used separately. With external frames there are various ways of attaching the packbag, including drawcords (Lowe Holoflex), velcro (VauDe Tergoflex) and clevis pins/split rings (most traditional designs and the Kelty Radials). One frame can be used for several different-sized packbags, although I know of no backpacker who does this.

Size

How large a packbag is necessary is a matter of some controversy amongst backpackers. From what I've read of other people's views I'm in somewhat of a minority here as I come down firmly on the side of big is best, preferring those packs that *Backpacker* Magazine has called load monsters. I like to pack everything, including my insulating mat when possible, inside the pack, and I like to know I can cram everything in quickly and easily in the dark in a storm after the tent has just blow down if necessary. Those in favour of small packs say that a large pack means a heavy pack, as you'll always fill it up. This clearly applies only to the weak-willed! Packs in the 90–130-litre/5500–8000-cu in range suit me fine for long treks and winter expeditions, ones of 70–80 litres/4300–4900cu in for weekend and week-long summer treks. If I had only one pack I'd always choose the largest model. Note though that different manufacturers have different ideas of what a litre is so one maker's 100-litre/6100-cu in pack may be smaller than another's 75litre/4575-cu in model! The largest packs I've heard about though never seen are the North Face Snow Leopard HC at 144 litres/8800cu in and the Mountainsmith St. Elias at a vast 174 litres/10,620cu in. The latter might even be too big for me.

One advantage of internal-frame packs is that they usually have compression straps on the sides or the front that can be pulled in to hold the load close to the back when the pack isn't full. Traditional-frame packs lack these, though they do appear on new-style ones like the Kelty Radial, Lowe Holoflex and VauDe Tergoflex. Some packs have main bodies that can be increased in capacity by undoing vertical zips, a feature of the Karrimor Condors. The North Face Chameleon has side lacing that serves the same purpose. Makers often give such packs a variable capacity such as 60–100 litres/3660–6100cu in (Condor with side pockets) or 50–125 litres/3050–7625cu in (Chameleon). The maximum volume is what is of interest here.

External-frame packbags that run the length of the frame tend to be large, like the 94-litre/5735-cu in Kelty Expedition Tioga (large size) or the 105-litre/6400-cu in Lowe Holoflex. However although three-quarter-length bags like Kelty's Classic Tioga may only have a capacity of 68 litres/4130cu in (large size), extra gear (sleeping mat, tent, sleeping bag, etc.) can be strapped onto the frame under the packbag without in any way affecting the way the pack carries and if necessary even more gear can be lashed on top of the packbag. Start strapping extra gear under or on top of an internal-frame pack, though, and you very quickly ruin its balance and comfortable fit. So for carrying loads of differing size a three-quarter-length packbag on an external frame is as versatile as an internal frame one with compression straps. And if you want to carry a really awkward load you can remove the packbag from an external frame and replace it with whatever you wish to carry.

Compartments

Most large packs come with lower zip-fastened compartments, though ones with just one huge compartment are still available. I used to prefer the latter as I found lower compartments too small and the access zips too short. However over the years compartments have grown in size and zips now run right round the packbag or else curve down to the lower edges, providing easy entry. I now find that I prefer two-compartment sacks therefore, as they give me better access to my load. As the section of material separating the two compartments is held in place by a zip or drawcord on most packs and can be removed if a single compartment packbag is wanted, I can see no reason for not having the option. Few pack makers offer packs with more than two compartments, something which I suspect would make packing quite difficult. However, the largest Gregory Genesis packs (Atlas and Nova) have the main compartment divided vertically into three in order, say the company, 'to simplify organisation'. Maybe, but I have my doubts. Luckily the dividers are removable.

Lids & Closures

You need to be able to cinch down the lid of your pack easily (i.e. during a blizzard) both to keep the contents in and to prevent them moving inside the pack. Most packbags have large lids, sometimes with elasticated edges for a closer fit, that close with two straps fastened by quick-release buckles. These are easy to operate and a great improvement over the cord-and-toggle fastening still found on some external-frame packs.

A way to vary the capacity of the packbag is to have a floating lid that attaches to the back of the pack by straps and which can be extended upwards to cope with large loads but which can still be tightened down over a small one. A less effective way of doing the same thing is to have a lid that extends by releasing straps but which is still sewn on to the back of the packbag. The problem with this last design is that when the lid is fully extended it tends to restrict head movement, fails to cover the load and makes access to the lid pocket difficult.

Most detachable lids contain large pockets (up to 20 litres/1260cu in) and can be used as bumbags or even small daysacks by rearranging the straps or using ones provided for that purpose. I've found them useful for carrying odds and ends (film, hat, gloves, binoculars, etc.) for short strolls away from camp. In combination with the bumbag I always have with me on long trips, I've even used a detachable pack lid, worn as a daysack, for long day treks away from camp, managing to pack in waterproofs, warm clothing and other essentials.

The lower compartments of sacks are always closed by zips. Buckled straps may protect the zip from too much pressure and reduce the likelihood of it bursting. This has never happened to me, but I still like zips to be fairly chunky, whether they are toothed or coil. Lightweight zips, whether protected by straps or not, worry me. Zips often have lengths of material threaded through the pullers to make opening them easier when you're wearing gloves or have cold, numb fingers. I find these so useful that I always fit them if they don't come as standard. Any short, thin piece of cord can be used. I've heard they can snag on bushes and tree branches but I've never found this a problem even when bushwhacking through thick vegetation. There are other things that always snag first!

Top compartments usually close with two drawcords, one around the main body of the pack that holds the load in and one on the lighter-weight extension that covers the load completely when pulled in. Access is thus via the top only and items packed low down or at the bottom in the top compartment cannot be reached easily. One way to improve access is to have vertical or diagonal zip entry to the main compartment, as is found on many of the largest packbags.

Not so long ago there were many packs available with zip-round front panels for suitcase-type loading, which gave access to the whole of the packbag. For backpacking there were problems though, as they had to be laid down to pack and unpack—not a good idea in the rain and on muddy or snow-covered ground. A less than full load couldn't be pulled in tight either and would move around in the pack as you walked. Such designs are now found mainly in packs designed for general travel rather than backpacking, though Jansport still use them for their external-frame packbags and Gregory offer the Apollo in their Genesis range with a zip-round upper compartment, side tension straps for stabilising the load and a lower zip-round compartment.

A modified version of the panel-loading design is found in the largest VauDe pack, the Tergoflex Skagen, which has a zip-round panel at the front of the main compartment for ease of access to the contents but also a lid and two-strap closure as well, a combination that seems sensible.

Pockets

Pockets increase the capacity of a pack and are also useful for packing small, easily mislaid items and those that may be needed during the day. Lid pockets are to be found on virtually all packs other than traditional external-frame models. The best are large and have either curved zips or zips that run round the sides. Some models have a second flat pocket in the lid as well for storing documents, money and the like, which may have either an external or an internal zip. Lid pockets are always zip-fastened and as with lower compartment zips I like to have lengths of cord tied to each zip puller for ease of opening.

So-called backpacking or trekking packs usually come with fixed side pockets, usually one though sometimes two and, rarely, three on each side. Packs designated as expedition or mountaineering models never have fixed side pockets as these can get in the way when climbing. Although I usually use side pockets I prefer the latter design as it means that I can remove the pockets when I want to reduce the capacity of the sack or when I want to use it for skiing or scrambling, when side pockets are a nuisance. Detachable pockets attach to the compression straps or occasionally to special plastic strips as on the Karrimor Condors and add 10–20 litres/610–1220cu in per pair to the pack's capacity and around 200–300g/7–10 oz to the weight. Some side pockets have backs stiffened with a synthetic plate which makes them slightly easier to pack but also slightly heavier. Gregory also offer a 10-litre/610-cu in double pocket that can be attached to the back of many of their packs including the Cassin. The latter with such a pocket attached plus two side pockets has a massive 135-litre/8240-cu in capacity.

An alternative to the detachable pocket is the integral pleated side pocket with side zip entry which can be folded flat when not needed. Packs featuring these include the Lowe Specialist, the Berghaus Pulsar 60BC Plus, and the North Face Chameleon and Inca Trail models. I've used the last pack and have found the pleated pockets quite useful, though not as roomy as detachable ones. Overall I think I prefer detachable pockets.

Straps & Patches

Side compression straps can be used for attaching skis and other long items (walking sticks, tripods, tent poles, foam pads, etc.) as well as pockets. Packbags usually also come with one or two sets of straps for ice axes plus straps and maybe a reinforced panel for crampons on the lid. If straps don't come with the pack there are usually several patches provided to thread your own through. Such exterior fastenings are useful, though many packs come with far too many. You can always cut off those you'll never use.

Materials

All modern packs are made from varieties of polyurethane or silicone elastomer-proofed nylons and polyesters, cotton canvas having disappeared from the scene. These fabrics are hard-wearing, light, non-absorbent and flexible. Texturised nylons made from a bulked filament to give a durable, abrasion-resistant fabric are often used for the bases of packs, sometimes with a layer of lighter nylon inside. On some packs they are used for the whole packbag. The commonest name is Cordura, though a few companies have their own texturised fabrics such as Karrimor with KS100e and Berghaus with Ardura. Packcloth is a smoother, lighter nylon that is often used for the main body of the sack. Again some companies have their own versions of this, like Lowe with Tri-Shield, whilst others use their own similar polyester fabrics like Karrimor with KS100t. I've used most of these materials and they are all strong and long-lasting so I don't pay too much attention to the materials a packbag is made of when selecting a pack.

Whilst most of these materials are fairly waterproof when new, the coating that makes them so is usually soon abraded and scratched and anyway the seams, of which there are many on a packbag, will leak in heavy rain even if oversewn with tape. Some makers advise coating the seams with sealant to proof them but the thought of what this would involve fills me with such horror that I've never attempted it. Instead I rely on liners and covers to keep the contents of the pack dry.

WEIGHT

The pack is the one item of gear whose weight I don't consider to be of major significance. For big loads I've found that a heavy pack with a sophisticated suspension system is more comfortable than a lighter-weight one with a more basic design, despite the extra kilos carried. Even with loads below 15kg/33lbs which a simple pack will handle quite well, I prefer a heavier pack, finding it more comfortable.

External- and internal-frame models run to around the same weight for similar-capacity packs. In externals the traditional 90-litre/5500-cu in Kelty Expedition Tioga weighs 2.85kg/6$\frac{1}{4}$lbs (large size) whilst the 105-litre/6400cu in Lowe Holoflex weighs 3$\frac{1}{2}$kg/7$\frac{3}{4}$lb and the VauDe Tergoflex Skagen 2.9kg/6$\frac{1}{4}$lb. With internals the 90 litre/5500 cu.in. North Face Inca Trail weighs 2$\frac{1}{2}$kg/5$\frac{1}{2}$lbs (medium size), the 115-litre/7010 cu.in. Gregory Cassin (large size) 3kg/6$\frac{1}{2}$lbs, the 100-litre/6100-cu.in. Karrimor Condor 2.7kg/6lb and the 100-litre/6100-cu.in Berghaus Cyclops II Atlas 2.9kg/6lbs. Smaller packs run a little lighter but not much. Extra pockets add a little more weight, depending on size and design.

DURABILITY

Top-quality packs are very tough but I haven't found one yet that will last out a walk of several months. I've suffered broken internal frames, snapped shoulder straps and ripped-out hipbelts on long treks. On my first solo walk in 1976 along the Pennine Way the hipbelt tore off my new traditional external-frame pack after just 320km/200 miles. The longest a pack has lasted for is 3250km/2000 miles and 4$\frac{1}{2}$ months. This was a Karrimor Condor with a load averaging 30–32kg/66–70lb. My Gregory Cassin was used on the three-month Yukon walk with a similar load when it was five years old and had already been on several two-week treks. It survived the trek intact, apart from the top of one frame stay sleeve which ripped out. A bandage of duck tape held the stay in place for the rest of the walk. Such usage of course represents years if not decades of backpacking for those who go out for several weekends a month and perhaps a couple of two- or three-week trips a year, as most people do.

My pack failure experience is matched by other long-distance walkers. The other three people I know who did all or most of the Pacific Crest Trail the same year as me also all broke at least one pack. It seems that after months of constant use and harsh treatment something is bound to fail, which is hardly surprising when you consider how complex a modern pack is and how much there is to go wrong.

Crude repairs can be made but I find I'm loathe to continue backpacking in remote country with a pack that has begun to show signs of wearing out, at least not before it's had a factory overhaul. After having to replace broken packs at great expense in both time and money on both my Pacific Crest Trail and Continental Divide walks I set off in 1988 on the Canadian Rockies walk with a spare pack ready and waiting. On that occasion I replaced my pack early on because it didn't prove up to carrying the weight. The replacement pack broke two weeks before the end of the trek and I had to nurse it, bandaged with tape, to the finish. Perhaps I'm unlucky or particularly rough with packs but I shall certainly ensure that I always have a spare pack for future lengthy ventures and I would advise anyone else to do the same.

MODELS, CHOICES AND IDEALS

There are many good packs on the market that combine various of the features discussed above. My ideal one would have a suspension system that enabled me to carry 35kg/77lb as though it were 15/33 and was superbly stable when skiing and crossing steep, rough ground. Internal or external frame? I'm not really bothered! I would then want a packbag with a capacity of at least 100 litres/6100cu in, two compartments, detachable side pockets, an extendable, detachable lid with a large pocket and straps for ice axes and skis. It would also see me through a 4800-km/3000-mile six-month walk without anything breaking! Whilst everyone would want such a miraculous suspension system and such durability, some people might want only some or indeed none of the other features. I backpack regularly with friends who don't like side pockets or lower compartments and others who never use skis or ice axes. An American trail companion swears that traditional external frames carry heavy loads best despite having used Gregory and Lowe packs for snow travel, where he concedes internals are better for balance. Another prefers a fixed-back Berghaus Cyclops pack and pours scorn on adjustable systems.

The packs that I've used that come closest

The Berghaus Cyclops 11 back.

to my ideal are the Gregory Cassin and the Lowe Holoflex. Both have packbags with all the features listed above plus superb suspension systems that allow me to carry huge loads in relative comfort if not with quite the ease I dream about. It may well be that the new Gregory back system comes even closer to my dream.

Not far behind is the Karrimor Condor 60–100 which comes complete with a pair of detachable side pockets which have a capacity of 10 litres/610cu in each. Combined with full-length vertical zips that allow the main pack to be closed down in volume, these pockets enable the Condor to vary from a very neat 60-litre/3660-cu in pack for short and fair-weather trips to a roomy 100 litres/6100cu in for extended ventures and winter treks. The SA adjustment system is one of the simplest and easiest to use but the pack is let down by the hip-belt which flattens out too much and bruises the hips under really heavy loads (over 22kg/48lb). Karrimor have developed a better belt however, which will be on the market before this book is published on the new Condor Aurora pack. This should make it a serious contender as a pack for really massive loads and long trips.

PACKING

The main principles of packing are that heavy items should be high up and close to your back in order to keep the load close to your centre of gravity and enable you to maintain an upright stance, and that items that may be needed during the day should be easily accessible. These principles often conflict. A third requirement is always to know where everything is. This requirement takes on particular importance once you've had to turn the contents of your pack out into the mud in a desperate frenzy, so that you can find the insect repellent as swarms of midges devour you.

I normally use a packbag with side pockets, lid pocket and lower compartment, so my packing is based on this. I don't like anything except winter hardware (ice axe and skis) strapped on the outside, though I may fasten a closed-cell sleeping mat there if I'm using one instead of a Therm-a-Rest mattress, which is rare. Usually though everything goes inside. Most items are also packed in stuffsacs to help with organisation and to keep items that go together in the same place. The first thing to go into the lower compartment is the sleeping bag in an oversize stuffsac inside a pack liner (see below), so that it can fill out the corners and enable the pack, if it is an internal-frame one, to wrap around the hips. Next are my spare clothes in another stuffsac and my waterproofs. The latter pad out any unfilled spaces and are accessible for use if it rains (for the purposes of this description I'm assuming a sunny day on which I'm wearing shorts and tee-shirt). If I'm carrying a bivi bag of any sort this goes in the lower compartment too. I slide tent poles down one side of the upper compartment next to my back and through the cutaway corner of the lower compartment floor if they're long enough to make that necessary. Down the back of the pack goes my Therm-a-Rest mattress, folded into three. It's protected there from abrasion and anything piercing the pack (an unlikely occurrence but I'm very protective of my Therm-a-Rest) and it also ensures that hard objects can't protrude into my back. In the bottom of the top compartment I put pans and stove, with fuel car-

tridges if I'm using them, and small items like candles, boot wax and the repair kit. My food bag or bags go on top of these and towards the back of the pack, as they're heavy. I have of course already removed my lunch and trail snacks for the day. In front of the food bags goes the tent, separated into two stuffsacs, and my camp footwear. At the top of the pack I put books, spare maps, my second camera if I'm carrying one and, if there's room, the windshirt or warm top I've been wearing whilst packing to ward off the early-morning chill. If I can't fit this in the top of the pack I squeeze it into the lower compartment.

The lid pocket is filled, in whatever order they come to hand, with hat, headover, gloves, mitts, writing materials in their nylon pouch, tube of sunscreen, camera accessories bag, insect repellent, thermometer and any small items that have escaped packing elsewhere. One side pocket holds water containers and food for the day, the other fuel bottles if I'm using a white gas or alcohol stove, plus tent pegs, head lamp and first-aid kit. Any items that may not have fitted into the lid pocket or that I've overlooked also go in a side pocket.

In the bumbag round my waist (see below) I carry the relevant map, compass, mini-binoculars, camera lenses, dark glasses and perhaps gloves and hat if I think I'll need them. My camera in its padded case is slung across my body on a padded strap.

Then once I've shouldered the pack, tightened up the straps and picked up my staff I'm ready for the day's walk.

PUTTING ON THE PACK

This action, repeated many times daily, requires a great deal of energy. With most loads the easiest way to do it is by lifting the pack on to one hip by the shoulder strap or the loop of nylon that adorns the top of the pack back on nearly all models, putting the arm on that side through the shoulder strap then swinging the pack onto the back. With loads below 12–14kg/25–30lb you can simply swing the pack straight on to the back.

There comes a point with heavy loads, around the 25-kg/55-lb mark, where I find I'm swinging the pack on to my bent knee rather than my hip and then from a stooped position slowly shifting rather than swinging the load on to my back. It is with such loads that I become aware of just how much energy putting on the pack requires, so I always try to find a rock or bank to rest the pack on when I stop so that I can simply back out of and into the harness. Failing such a shelf—and they don't occur very often—I may sit down, put my arms through the shoulder straps and then slowly stand up if I feel I haven't the energy to heave the pack onto my back. If there's no other support my staff holds the pack up whilst I do this. I also try to take the pack on and off less often when it's that heavy, keeping items I need for the day in my bumbag and looking for something to rest the load against when I stop rather than removing it.

THE PACK OFF THE BACK

In camp I keep the pack in the tent if it's dry, if I'm not in bear country and if there's room. More often though I leave it outside with the pack cover on to protect it against precipitation. Items I don't need overnight are left inside it whether it's in or out of the tent.

During rest-stops the pack may act as a seat if the ground is cold or wet. One big advantage of using an external frame is that it can be used as a back rest by propping it up with the staff, its rigidity keeps it from twisting out of position and falling over as happens with most flexible internal-frame packs. So comfortable do I find this back-rest that I've tried to make an internal-frame pack perform the same function, and I have had a measure of success with a Gregory Cassin and my Chief of Staffs by wedging the latter into the pack's hand loop. Unexpected collapses owing to the pack slipping sideways still occur frequently, however.

CARE

All I do after a trip is empty the pack, shake out any debris that may have accumulated inside and then hang it up to dry if it's at all wet. You can try to remove stains with soap or other cleanser but I regard such marks as adding to the character of the pack and I'm also wary of damaging or weakening the fabric in any way.

Before a trip I check that all the zips are working. I also make sure that there are no signs of any stitching failure if I didn't do so the last time I used the pack.

ACCESSORIES

Liners and Covers

No pack, whatever the claims made for the fabric, is waterproof. Water will trickle in through the zips, wick along drawcords and seep through the seams, and when the proofing has worn off it will come straight through the fabric. The answer is to cocoon those items that must be kept dry (any down-filled gear, maps, books, etc.) in fully waterproof sac liners. Stuffsacs alone are not enough as they are rarely very waterproof. I place a cover over the pack in really heavy rain, as a back-up to the liners.

I don't use a large liner that fills the pack because quite often there are wet items in the pack (such as the tent flysheet and waterproofs) that I want to separate from other items. Instead I like to place my sleeping bag in its stuffsac inside a proofed liner. I used to use the cheap and light thick plastic bags that outdoor shops sell but I became frustrated with the speed at which they tear (after at most a couple of day's use, unless you're lucky) and concerned at the wastage of throwing so many away. For a number of years now I have used Field & Trek neoprene-coated Rucsac Liners which have taped seams. They come in 50- and 70-litre/3050- and 4275-cu in sizes. There are also small ones for pockets which I've never bothered with. I wrap my sleeping bag and any water-vulnerable clothing in the 50-litre liner and stow it at the base of my pack. It weighs 110g/4oz and has proved remarkably tough. It was used throughout my Canadian Rockies and Yukon walks and is still in use and still waterproof. There don't seem to be many other non-plastic pack liners around; two of the few I've located are made by The North Face and Karrimor.

I also use a Field & Trek Rucsac Cover. It too is made of neoprene-coated nylon and it weighs 200grams/7oz. It has an elasticated outer edge that enables it to cover a wide range of pack shapes and sizes and prevents it taking flight in high winds. I also use it to cover the pack when the latter is left outside the tent overnight. Many pack-makers, including Gregory, Lowe, Kelty and Fjallraven, make similar covers. The only time I don't take the liner is when I'm carrying skis or ice axe on the pack.

Bumbags

With a really heavy pack access to all the little

odds and ends that are needed during a day's walk can be difficult, especially if all you're wearing is shorts and a tee-shirt. Taking off the pack every time you need to check the map, apply sunscreen, nibble some trail mix or scan the route ahead through your binoculars is simply too much of a chore and requires far too much energy. The result used to be that I failed to do these things, preferring to wonder if I was really on the right route, risk sunburn and feel hungry rather than to be constantly removing and reshouldering the pack. However for many years now I have worn a bumbag (also known as a fanny pack or waist pack) the wrong way round, with all these items and more in it. There is a wide variety available ranging from ultralight simple ones of thin nylon to complex models complete with compartments and pockets and even padded hipbelts. Which you choose depends on how much you carry in it and how often you use it on side trips. Capacities run up to as much as 15 litres/915cu in.

The bumbag I've used most is the 110-g/4-oz Rock & Run Hipsac, which is just one refinement removed from the most basic design, that refinement being side compression straps that allow me to pull it tight over any size of load and prevent any movement. Otherwise the polyurethane-proofed nylon Hipsac is a one-compartment zip-closed bag of around 5 litres/300cu in capacity with a simple waist strap. I used one on the Continental Divide walk which just survived the full 4800km/3000 miles and six months of that trip, finishing it with a zip that kept bursting open and only ragged remnants of the proofing. But it did the job and I took another Hipsac on the Canadian Rockies walk—that one is still in service. On the Yukon walk though I used an 8½-litre/520-cu in Pod Hip Sac that has a padded base, zipped front pocket, zipped main compartment, two compressions straps, padded hipbelt with side tension straps and a grab handle. The material is Cordura and the weight a hefty 300g/10½oz. I have found that it will comfortably carry heavier items than the Rock & Run bag such as camera lenses. The padded base gives such items more protection too. For these reasons it has become my first choice. At first I worried that the wide padded belt and large Fastex buckle would feel uncomfortable under my pack but this hasn't happened.

There are many other bumbags available; some such as the Berghaus Blitz, Kelty MG Convertible and REI Convertible Fanny/Day Pack have small day packs rolled into them. More standard ones come from The North Face, Caribou, Mountainsmith, Kelty and no doubt a host more. If you want a really large one Gregory's Rumper Room has a 14.7-litre/895-cu in capacity with a weight of 740g/26oz and the same hipbelt as a traditional internal-frame Gregory back system.

Belt and Shoulder Pouches

Most pack makers and many other outdoor companies offer small zipped pouches and wallets designed to be fitted on to the pack hipbelt or shoulder straps. I've tried these and find that they impede putting on and taking off the pack. I prefer a separate bumbag for carrying small, frequently needed items, as outlined above. However there are plenty of small pouches around if you're interested, with capacities of a few litres and weights of around 100g/4oz.

Keeping Warm & Dry: Dressing for the Wilderness

When the clouds roll in, the wind begins to pick up and the first raindrops fall, you need to know that your clothing will protect you from the coming storm. If it fails to do so you may, at the very least, have to stop and make camp early, crawling soggily into your tent and staying there until the skies clear. At the worst you could find yourself in danger from hypothermia, a cooling down of the body that kills unprepared hikers every year. Whilst keeping you warm and dry in wind and rain is its prime purpose, clothing must also keep you warm in camp when the temperature falls below freezing, and keep you cool when the sun shines. Care needs to be taken in choosing clothes which do all of this and are also lightweight and low in bulk for carrying in the pack. Before looking at different items in detail, it's useful to have some understanding of how the human body works when exercising and what this means for one's choice of clothes.

Heat Loss and Heat Production
The human body is designed for a tropical climate and soon ceases to function if it falls more than a couple of degrees below 37 °C/98.4 °F. In non-tropical climates we need clothing to keep the body at that temperature as the heat it produces is lost to the cooler air. The purpose of clothing is to maintain a balance between heat loss and heat production so that we feel neither hot nor cold. Doing so whilst sitting still in a calm dry atmosphere is easy, regardless of the temperature. Doing so over a period of time during which we alternate sitting still with varying degrees of exercise in a wide range of air temperatures and in wind, rain and snow is much more difficult especially as the active body pumps out masses of heat and moisture which has to be dispersed but ceases to do so the moment exercise stops.

The body loses heat in four ways. Understanding these is important as they determine what clothing has to do to keep the body's temperature at an equilibrium.

Convection is the transfer of heat from the body to the air and is the major cause of heat loss. It occurs whenever the air is cooler than the body, which is most of the time. In still air, heat loss by convection is very slow but once the air begins to move over the skin and through your clothing it can whip warmth away at an amazing rate. To prevent heat loss by convection in windy weather, clothing must cut out the flow of air over the skin which means it must be windproof.

Conduction is the transfer of heat from one surface to another. All materials conduct heat but some do so better than others. Air is a bad conductor of heat so the best protection against conductive heat loss is clothing that traps and holds air in its fibres. Indeed, still air is what keeps you warm; all fabrics do is keep it in place. Water however is a good conductor of heat so if all your layers of clothing are soaked you will cool down rapidly. This means that clothing has to keep you dry. Keeping rain and snow out is not difficult in itself; the problem is that clothing must also allow perspiration to be transmitted to the outer air, a process known as 'breathability' or moisture-vapour transmission.

Evaporation: Preventing moisture entering a garment from outside whilst letting it escape from inside is the most difficult task clothing has to perform. The reason it is necessary is to prevent heat loss by evaporation. This occurs because heat is required to turn perspiration into vapour and remove it from the surface of the skin. During vigorous exercise the body can give off as much as a litre of liquid an hour. If this moisture stays on the skin a great deal of heat is needed to evaporate it so clothing must transport it away quickly. As important as wearing breathable materials through which moisture vapour can pass is wearing garments that can be ventilated easily, especially at the neck.

Radiation is the passing of heat directly between two objects without warming the intervening space. It is the way the sun heats the earth (and ourselves on hot clear days). As a direct pathway is required for it to occur, wearing clothes and especially clothing that is tightly woven and smooth surfaced, solves most of that problem.

THE LAYER SYSTEM

As if keeping out rain whilst expelling sweat and trapping heat whilst preventing the body becoming too hot were not enough, clothing for walkers must also be lightweight, durable, low in bulk, quick-drying, easy to care for and must work in all weather conditions. The usual solution is to wear several light layers of clothing on the torso and arms (the legs require less protection) which can be adjusted to suit the prevailing conditions and the level of activity, rather than one thick garment. The layer system is versatile and efficient if used properly which means constantly opening and closing zips and cuff fastenings and at times stopping to remove or put on layers. It applies mainly to the upper body, though I now find I use layers on my legs, hands and head in really severe conditions.

A typical layer system consists of an inner layer of thin material to remove moisture from the skin, a thicker mid-layer to trap air and provide insulation and an outer shell layer to keep off wind and rain whilst, ideally, allowing perspiration to pass through. The mid- and outer layers may involve more than one garment—how many depends on the temperatures you expect to encounter. A basic three-layer system consists of thin underwear, a pile, fleece or wool top and a breathable waterproof shell. To this may be added a synthetic, wool or cotton shirt or sweater to go immediately over underwear, a windproof shell to go over the warmwear in windy but dry conditions and a down or synthetic insulation-filled garment for wearing in camp and during rest stops in really cold weather. If wet cold is expected, the latter may be replaced by a second pile or fleece jacket. So on trips where a wide range of weather conditions could be expected the layer system might be thin underwear, medium-weight shirt, warm top, windproof top, waterproof top and insulated top—six layers rather than three.

How many layers you take on a particular trek depends on the conditions expected. I like to take clothing that should keep me warm in the worst weather that is likely whilst I am walking and do the same in combination with my tent and sleeping bag when I'm resting. If I'm in doubt as to what is enough I sometimes take a light insulated vest or an even lighter vapour-barrier suit as an extra just in case. This method seems to work as it's many years since I last found my clothing inadequate for a trip—though I came close to it in 1986 when I spent a week battling through the high winds, lashing rain and melting snow of an Icelandic June. I had with me a synthetic thermal tee-shirt, a thin synthetic thermal shirt, a light insulated sweater, a single-layer windshirt and a breathable waterproof jacket, and I was barely warm enough when walking, though part of the reason for that was that the shell layer failed to cope with the wet cold conditions and I was permanently damp. Luckily I'd taken a vapour barrier suit as back-up so I was able to stay warm in camp, but I would have liked a thicker warm layer as well.

There are alternative clothing systems which dispute the prevailing wisdom and claim that the layer system and breathable garments don't work. These are discussed in detail later. Briefly they involve replacing the layers with a single garment (the Buffalo Double-P System), and using a waterproof vapour-barrier lining to prevent moisture from leaving the skin instead of removing it as quickly as possible. First, though, let's look at the conventional three-layer approach.

1: The Inner Layer

Although often described as 'thermal' underwear the aim of this layer is to keep the skin dry rather than warm. If the moisture given off by the body is removed quickly from the surface of the skin it's easy for your outer layers to keep you warm. Conversely if the layer of clothing next to your skin becomes saturated and dries slowly then it will be very difficult for your other clothes to keep you warm, however good they may be. No fabric, whatever the claims made for it, is warm when wet. Whilst you are on the move, keeping warm is not too much of a problem even if your inner layers are damp, as long as your outer layer keeps out rain and wind and your mid-layer provides enough warmth. However once you stop, wet undergarments will chill you rapidly especially if you've been exercising hard. And it's often at such times, after a climb to a pass or a summit, that we do want to stop, both for a rest and to contemplate the view we've worked so hard to see. Once you stop your heat output drops rapidly, yet it is heat that is required to dry out wet underwear. So not only are its warmth-trapping properties impaired because there is less air in its fibres and more water—which as we've seen conducts heat much more rapidly than air—but a wet inner layer also draws heat from the body in order that the moisture can evaporate. The result is known as after-exercise chill. The wetter the clothing the longer such chill lasts and the colder and more uncomfortable you will be. Because it is the one that deals with after-exercise chill, the inner layer is very important—as is the outer layer. What goes in between these layers matters far less and this is where compromises can be made if necessary.

The material to avoid is cotton. However pleasant it may be to wear in everyday life, for backpacking it is useless as it absorbs moisture very quickly and in great quantities. It then takes a long time to dry, using up a massive amount of your body heat in the process and making you feel cold and wet. To make matters worse, damp cotton also clings to the skin, preventing a dry layer of insulating air from forming. I haven't worn cotton underwear for years now, not even on trips in sunny weather when some people like to wear light cotton or cotton-mix tops. I find a short-sleeved wicking synthetic fabric top works as well as cotton in the heat and enables me to carry one garment instead of two. In the discussion of inner-layer fabrics that follows, remember that although I recommend some materials and am not so polite about others, they are all far superior to cotton.

There are two ways in which fabrics remove body moisture. They either transport or 'wick' it away from the skin and into the air, or the next layer of clothing, or absorb it deep into their fibres to leave a dry surface next to the skin before more slowly passing it out the other side. The first is done by specially developed synthetic materials, the second by traditional natural ones.

In selecting fabrics though, there are other needs to consider as well as keeping the skin dry. You may have to wear garments for days or even weeks without washing them or even taking them off, so they must go on working for a long time and, ideally, not smell too much when they're dirty. Weight and bulk are hardly important for once, as none of these fabrics weigh much. Some of the synthetics come in heavier weights for colder conditions but the ones I've tried don't wick moisture or dry as fast as the lightest weights and are better suited for mid-wear rather than underwear. They will therefore be considered under that heading. Prices are quite low, certainly when compared with mid- and outer-wear garments, with natural fibres costing more than synthetics. Silk is the most expensive, costing well over twice as much as the cheapest synthetic.

Designs in all materials are usually simple, consisting in most ranges of short- and long-sleeved crew-neck tops, long-sleeved zipped neck tops and long pants. Synthetic briefs and underpants are available too and I usually carry a pair, though I tend to wear my shorts, which have a built-in brief, instead. I like short-sleeved tee-shirt designs for summer use and long-sleeved zip neck ones for colder weather. Close-fitting garments help in trapping air and wicking moisture quickly and also allow mid layers to fit easily over them. Long pants in particular need to have a snug fit. There's nothing worse than having baggy long-johns sagging down inside your other layers where you can't easily get at them. Elasticated waists are essential for keeping them up. Wrist and ankle cuffs need to grip well too to stop them riding up under other garments. Thin materials minimise moisture absorption. If they're stretchy as well that makes them more comfortable. Seams should be flat-sewn and not raised, to avoid rubbing and abrasion. Colours are usually dark, probably because dirt and stains show up less, even though light ones reflect heat better when worn on their own in warm weather and also radiate heat much more slowly when worn under other garments. It probably pays to seek out white and pale-coloured garments. Laundering instructions need to be checked too. On long treks I like to throw all my clothes in a launderette washing machine when I reach a town and then tumble-dry them. Items that require special care as many underwear fabrics do, are a real pain at such times.

Choosing a wicking synthetic fabric can be particularly difficult because of the large number of varieties available, many with fancy names and all claiming to work best. However only a few base fabrics actually exist, all derived from petrochemicals. Whatever the fabric, I've found that open-knit garments absorb less moisture, wick faster and dry more quickly than close-weave ones.The main choices are between polypropylene (polypro for short), treated polyester and chlorofibre (PVC).

Polypro is the lightest and thinnest of these fabrics. It was also the first available, courtesy of Helly-Hansen and their Lifa Super range, and for a time dominated the market. Polypro garments are available from a host of specialist manufacturers and, at a lower price, from many department stores, often under a trade name such as Meraklon or Montefibre. Polypro won't absorb moisture but quickly wicks it along its fibres and out into the air or the next layer. If you are wet with sweat when you stop exercising it dries on the body so fast that after-exercise chill is negligible. However on the negative side polypro stinks to high heaven after a day or so's wear, a stench that can be hard to get rid of as the material doesn't like heat and shrinks in hot washes and tumble driers. Apart from the smell, if you don't wash it every couple of days it ceases to work properly, leaving the skin feeling clammy and cold after exercise. So on even a week-long trek you either have to carry several garments or rinse one out regularly and learn to live with the smell of stale sweat.

This was true of all polypro and was the reason why other fabrics were growing in popularity until 1988 when Helly-Hansen introduced a new variety they call Prolite. This has a softer less 'plastic', feel than the early polypro and can also be washed at 95 °C/203 °F, a heat that soon rids it of noxious aromas. Prolite Polypro comes in two types: thin, close-woven Lifa Super and slightly thicker Lifa Super Net, which as the name suggests has an open-mesh constuction designed, say the company, 'specially for medium- to high-activity levels over a long period'. Although I haven't yet taken it on a long trek I've used a crew-neck long-sleeved Lifa Net top (the only design available—mesh constructions don't lend themselves to high necks) on several two- and three-day trips plus several day walks and short runs without washing it. Although it smells faintly musty I can bear to have it in the same room I sleep in, something I wouldn't do with the old polypro after even one day's wear. It still wicks moisture efficiently and, I suspect, faster than standard polypro. Lifa Net is also very stretchy, which makes it comfortable and non-restrictive to wear. At 150g/5oz the top weighs the same as a standard one, as do the long-johns at $100g/3\frac{1}{2}oz$. The colour is mid-blue (standard Lifa Super is available in white).

Polyester repels water and has a low wicking ability. However it can be treated chemically so that the surface absorbs water whilst the core still repels it, the result being that moisture spreads itself over the material and quickly dries. Patagonia's Capilene was the first treated polyester to appear, soon to be followed by others including Thermax, whose fibres have a hollow core to improve insulation, and Malden Mills' Polartek, the specifications of which seem to be identical to those of Capilene even down to the anti-bacterial treatment both have to prevent them smelling. Treated polyester garments are available from many companies with more joining in by the minute. Some have their own brands, like Berghaus with their Active Comfort Layer (ACL) and The North Face who seem to have two—Thermalene in Europe and Next-to-Skin in North America though it could be the same material under two different names. New at the time of writing is Akzo's Sportant Fresh, available in Craghoppers garments.

The advantage of treated polyester over all polypro other than Helly-Hansen Lifa is that it can be washed and dried at relatively high temperatures. I've tried Capilene which works well, certainly as well as polypro, and goes on working for days and weeks at a time. It also takes a week or so before it really reeks rather than a day or two, though when it does it's nearly as bad as polypro. At 180g/6oz my Lightweight Capilene Zip T-Neck is slightly heavier than a similar polypro one but not enough to make any difference.

Even better, however, is a new polyester fabric, Akzo's Sportant Fresh. I was supplied with a test set of short-sleeved top (100g/3½oz) and long-johns (125g/4½oz) made up in this material by Craghoppers for my Yukon walk, and I found it hard wearing, comfortable and very efficient. I wore the top every day of the three-month walk, both as a tee-shirt in hot weather and as an inner layer in cold, and found it both cool in the heat and warm when it was chilly. Twice I wore it for three weeks at a time without washing it and at the end of those periods it still wicked moisture quickly, felt comfortable and hardly smelt at all. It is now my first choice in thermal underwear fabrics. The trousers I found worked just as well both as warmwear under polycotton trousers and for wicking moisture under rain trousers. Craghoppers launched a range of clothing in Sportant Fresh in late 1990 and I expect other companies will have clothing available in the material by the time this book is published.

Chlorofibre is made of polyvinyl chloride (PVC) and like polypro and treated polyester absorbs little water and wicks well. However it cannot bear even the approach of heat, shrinking to doll's size if put in a more than lukewarm wash or draped over a hot radiator. The best-known brand is Damart, famous (or rather infamous) for their mail-order catalogues which drop though the letter box at an almost daily rate once they have your name and address. They call their chlorofibre Thermolactyl. Rhovyl is another brand name. Other users include Peter Storm and North Cape. Chlorofibre is comfortable and efficient—it's the washing problems that stop me using it. I once washed a set of Damart tops and bottoms in a machine set on a cool wash during a long walk and they shrank to half-size leaving me with 17 days of snow travel to do with no thermal underwear. Chlorofibre isn't as bad as polypro (nothing is) but it still smells after a few days' wear. For strength it's usually blended with nylon or polyester in an 80/20 mix but there is a type mixed with a natural material called Modal in a 70/30 ratio about which I've heard several good reports. Makers of Rhovyl Chlorofibre/Modal garments include North Cape, Lowe and Ami Chaud. It's lighter than the standard chlorofibre (a top of which weighs around 200g/7oz) and is treated so that it doesn't smell after prolonged wear.

As well as the big three there are other synthetic underwear fabrics around. *ICI Tactel* nylon, which usually appears in shell garments, is used by the company Sub Zero for underwear and is claimed to have the same characteristics as the better-known synthetics. I haven't used it but reports I've heard suggest it works well. *Dunova* is a porous acrylic made by Bayer, which was, until Sportant Fresh appeared, the best material for underwear for the backpacker in my view. I've used Rohan 100 per cent mesh Dunova Cool-T tops (100g/3½oz) on most of my long walks, once wearing one for 23 days without it being washed; at the end it still worked perfectly and barely smelt. Indeed on reaching a town I wore it to a meal in a restaurant before washing either it or myself and no-one complained! Because each fibre is hollow with a sponge-like inner, Dunova absorbs moisture as well as wicking it and never feels cold when it's wet as the layer actually in contact with the skin is always dry. It thus combines the best properties of both synthetic and natural fabrics. However there is one big problem with Dunova—you can't get hold of it. One hundred per cent Dunova hasn't been available since Rohan stopped making garments from it in the early 1980s. The 65 per cent Dunova/35 per cent cotton mix in a plain weave that Rohan currently offer is a travesty of the real thing, absorbing far more water, taking a long time to dry and feeling cold when wet. I'm lucky enough to have a small stock of Cool-Ts but it's dwindling fast.

Wool, the traditional material for thermal underwear, is not as popular now as it once was, yet it still has much to recommend it. Rather than rapidly wicking moisture, wool works more slowly, absorbing it into its fibres to leave a dry surface against the skin. Wool can absorb up to 35 per cent of its weight in water before it feels wet and cold, so after-exercise chill is not a problem unless you've been working really hard—certainly harder than any backpacker can normally manage with a heavy pack. I've worn wool next to the skin for winter ski tours and not overloaded it. On those tours I've also worn the same shirt for a fortnight with no odour problem. Wool's only limitation is its warmth which makes it a cold-weather-only material. I find that above about 15 °C/60 °F it's far too hot to wear and I don't usually take it if I'm expecting temperatures to be above 10 °C/50 °F. But for winter and the cold, wool works fine. It's not heavy either. I have a Best crew-neck wool top that weighs 200g/7oz, only a little more than a synthetic one. What puts many people off wool though is its reputation for being itchy. I used to think this after wearing thin wool sweaters bought from department stores next to the skin when I started backpacking, and I said as much in a number of magazine articles, one of which brought a swift response from a maker of wool underwear. Very fine wool that's designed to be worn next to the skin doesn't itch, he said. To prove it John Skelton sent me a set of his K2 underwear (now sadly unavailable), which I still have and still use, and I had to admit that I was wrong. I wasn't allergic to wool and the material meant for underwear didn't itch.

Silk is the other natural material used in outdoor underwear. It too can absorb moisture, up to 30 per cent of its own weight, without feeling damp and so feels warm when wet, but its best attribute is its feel, which is truly luxurious. It's light too, a long-sleeved top weighing just 100g/3½oz. I wore a silk top (from Survival Aids) on a two-week walk across the Scottish Highlands and at the end the smell was negligible and it still kept me warm and dry. It looked terrible though, being badly stained with sweat and dirt. I found that on stopping after strenuous exercise it would feel cold and clammy for a few minutes, but would then feel warm again. However the big problem with silk—and what would stop me taking it on a major trek—is the care needed. It has to be hand-washed and dried flat. It doesn't dry quickly either so it won't dry overnight in camp unless it's very warm.

There are various mixed-material garments available, most with a synthetic inner for wicking and a wool outer for warmth, like Helly-Hansen's Thermal Wool. I've never used any of these so my comments are based firmly on conjecture but I would rather have two garments that can be used separately than one that is meant to perform two functions. The outdoor writer—and a regular hill companion of mine—Graham Huntington has however used Thermal Wool tops and bottoms in winter and gives them high praise.

2: The Mid-layer

This is the layer that traps air in its fibres and keeps you warm. As well as doing this though, mid-layer clothing has to deal with body moisture passed into it from the inner layer, so like that layer it needs either to wick that moisture away or else to absorb it without losing too much of its insulation value. Mid-layer clothing can be divided into two types: that which will be worn when walking and that which is purely for wearing in camp and during halts. Into the first category come thermal shirts, piles and fleeces and the light micro-fibre-filled garments. In warm weather one or two garments of this type may be all you need. Once temperatures start to fall though, I also carry something from the second category which consists of down- and synthetic-filled garments. A typical selection for any trip other than a high-summer one in a warm climate would be medium-weight shirt, pile top and down jacket.

Mid-wear clothing comes in every design imaginable with shirts, sweaters, smocks, anoraks and jackets all available. Garments that open down the front at least a little way are easier to ventilate than polo- or crew-neck sweater ones. This is important as ventilation is the best way of getting rid of excess heat and preventing clothing becoming damp with sweat. Far more moisture vapour can escape out of an open neck than can wick through a material. Conversely I like high collars as they keep the neck warm and help to keep heat in. I used not to like over-the-head designs at all, fearing that I would overheat too easily when wearing one, but having tried a few I've realised that as long as you can open up the top 20cm/8in or 25cm/10in you can cool off when necessary. The pack's hipbelt prevents you opening up garments fully anyway. As over-the-head tops tend to be lighter than open-fronted ones I find that I now use them more often than not.

Shirts: Synthetic Thermal: For years I stopped carrying shirts, relying on a pile or fleece top for warmth. However after a number of trips on which I was slightly too cool without my pile jacket on but rather too warm when wearing it I started taking a light shirt, usually made from thermal underwear material, as well. You can of course just wear two layers of thin thermal material but most thermal underwear garments are offered in several weights and the thicker ones make better second layers. I often use either my K2 zipped wool shirt or an Expedition Weight Capilene zip T-neck top for this in cool weather. At weights of 260g/9oz and 280g/10oz respectively, they add little to the load if they end up in the pack. My favourite shirt though is another Rohan garment, but again one that is no longer available. The T Major is made from a treated polyester Rohan called Driline (not to be confused with another wicking fabric of the same name developed by W.L.Gore) and constructed of two layers, a mesh inner and a solid-weave outer. The latter doesn't cover the shoulders, armpits, the lower half of the sleeves or the sides to allow for fast wicking of moisture and good ventilation. The T Major has a stud-fastened neck and wrist cuffs and a highly useful zipped kangaroo pouch type pocket on the chest. The design is far superior to any other outdoor shirt I've seen. The T Major weighs 220g/7¾oz and can be worn for weeks on end without being washed. As Rohan seem to have abandoned the design I've been hoping that someone else will produce something similar. Happily, it looks as though someone will. On my Yukon walk I took a Craghoppers sweater made from a heavy version of the Sportant Fresh polyester that weighs 280g/10oz as mid-wear and found it worked well and was very warm. As I write, Craghoppers are about to launch a shirt in the material that could well become my favourite. I'm looking forward to trying it.

Shirts: Wool and Cotton: The traditional alternative to a thermal shirt is a conventional wool or cotton one. The former I find too bulky and heavy as well as too warm for what I want from a shirt, which is to be cooler and lighter than my main warm garments. Cotton I don't like because of what happens when it gets wet, though for mid-wear I'm not sure there's as much logic behind this view as I originally thought there was. I took a brushed chamois cotton shirt of the sort that appears under many labels (mine was from Survival Aids) on a two-week trek to remind myself of just how cotton shirts perform. Worn over a silk inner layer I found it very comfortable and quite warm, and despite some wet and windy weather, it never became more than slightly damp when it was worn under a breathable shell. I suspect that this was partly because the silk inner took up much of my sweat, and that with a synthetic inner layer it would have become damper. I haven't taken it on a trip since then though because at 500g/17½oz it is heavier than a much warmer fleece or pile top and twice the weight of my other shirts.

Pile and Fleece: These fabrics are marvellous! They can be regarded as the synthetic equivalent of animal fur and work in much the same way. Pile and fleece insulate well and wick moisture quickly, as well as being light in weight, incredibly hard-wearing, almost non-absorbent, warm when wet as the surface next to the skin dries quickly, and quick-drying. These properties make them ideal for outdoor clothing. I now always carry a pile top and have done so on almost every trip since discovering pile in the 1970s. When thin microfibre insulations came along I used them instead of pile for a time but found that they don't provide the almost instant warmth of pile and don't perform as well in cold wet weather as they absorb more moisture and dry more slowly. Neither do they last as long or cover the same wide temperature range. What using them taught me was just how good pile is.

There are many different types of pile and fleece and which is which is unclear, as some fabrics are called pile by one maker and fleece by another. Generally pile describes a loosely knit fabric with a furry surface and fleece one that is tightly knitted and has a smooth finish. As pile came first and fleece is really a variety of it, for the sake of tidiness and brevity I'll use pile to mean both fabrics in the discussion ahead. Most pile is made from polyester though a few types are made from nylon. Neither material has any advantages over the other. Polypropylene and acrylic piles can be found, but neither has ever become popular.

Worn over a synthetic wicking inner layer and under a breathable waterproof shell a pile top will keep you warm in just about any weather whilst you are on the move. They are most effective though in wet cold conditions, exactly those times when other warmwear doesn't work so well. A pile top can wick moisture as fast as synthetic underwear and so will quickly pull sweat through its fibres. I've often found at the end of a day of wet, windy weather that the outer of my pile jacket is quite damp but that the inner layer is dry. If you feel cold nothing will warm you up so fast as a pile top put on next to the skin, even if it's damp.

As with everything there are a few drawbacks, albeit minor ones. Most pile garments are not windproof, which means that windproof layers are needed over them in even a cool breeze. An advantage of the fleece types is that although they won't keep out a strong wind their tighter construction makes them wind-resistant enough to deal with a breeze. However, although it is a disadvantage at times, this lack of wind resistance does mean that pile garments can be worn over a wide temperature range; without a shell when it's warm or calm and with one when it's cold or windy. Shelled pile clothing is available but doesn't have the versatility needed for backpacking use. Such garments are heavier and bulkier than uncovered ones and you can't wear the two layers separately as is often necessary. The only other disadvantage of pile clothing is that it doesn't compress very well and so takes up a fair amount of room in the pack, far more than a down jacket for example.

Pile comes in different weights and in single and double versions—i.e. either one or both sides has a raised or plush surface to trap air. With use, little balls of fluff appear on the outside of single piles, making them look scruffy; this is known as pilling. It can be partly prevented by coating the outside of the fabric with resin or other material, but this makes garments stiff and even bulkier and adds weight. The best answer to pilling for those bothered by it—and I am not—is either to use a double-pile fabric as these don't pill, or else to put the smooth side, which is the one that pills, inside so that it is out of sight. All pile fabrics are usable in a wide range of temperatures but obviously the lighter and single ones aren't as warm as the heavier and double ones.

Pile garments need to be close-fitting to trap warm air efficiently and wick moisture away quickly. As they are prone to the bellows effect by which cold air is sucked in at the bottom of the garment, replacing the warm air, the hem should be elasticated, have a drawcord or be designed to tuck into your pants. Wrist cuffs

keep the warmth in best if they are close-fitting, as do neck closures. The broad stretchy ribbing found on the cuffs and hem of many pile tops works well at keeping in warm air but is prone to absorb moisture and then feel cold and take a long time to dry. Better is the non-absorbent and quick-drying stretch Lycra now found on many garments. I used to think, without much evidence, that this was a serious problem, and indeed said so in several magazine articles, advising readers against any clothing with rib-knit cuffs and hem. However after the rib-knit cuffs on my pile top got wet during a day out in wet cold Scottish November weather I found that whilst I noticed an occasional touch of cold they didn't really cause much of a problem. This makes me inclined to think that I've over-exaggerated the need to worry about this.

Pile garments are mostly hip-length, which is just about right as it means they don't ride up under your pack hipbelt. A high collar will help keep your neck warm. Pockets are useful, especially lower hand-warmer ones, for around camp and at rest-stops. Unlined pockets are warmer and lighter than lined ones which also add a tiny smidgeon of weight and absorb moisture. A few pile tops have hoods but these aren't necessary. A hat will do as well and restricts head movement and vision less. My preference in overall design is for either over-the-head tops with studded neck closures and chest and hand-warmer pockets or plain zip-fronted jackets with lower pockets. Fancier designs are unnecessarily complex for backpacking and simply add more weight.

Pile was first used in clothing by Helly-Hansen of Norway and tested in that country's wet, cold climate, for which it proved ideal. It soon became popular in Britain, another country with wet, cold weather, and throughout the 1970s British climbers and walkers on jaunts abroad could be identified by their navy-blue nylon fibre-pile Helly tops. Apart from a few design modifications and a choice of colours, these garments are still available and they are as good as any of the newer fabrics in terms of performance. They are somewhat cheaper too and their durability is proven. I have two Helly-Hansen jackets, one over a decade old, the other three years younger and a veteran of the Pacific Crest Trail. The older one is a single-pile Leisure Jacket with full-length zip, knitted cuffs and hem, high collar and side pockets. It weighs 580g/20oz. The other is a double-pile Field Jacket, again with full-length zip, high collar and side pockets, though these are zipped. However, instead of ribbing it has an extended back and a non-elasticated hem intended to be tucked into long pants in severe cold. The cuffs are long and non-stretchy too. They cover the upper part of the hands and have slits for the thumbs to hold them in place. The weight is 600g/21oz. Both these garments work well. The Field Jacket, unsurprisingly, is the warmer of the two. Being double-pile it hasn't pilled, unlike the Leisure Jacket, the outer of which is a mass of fluff.

Since the mid-1980s though I haven't used these jackets much because the newer pile fabrics that have become available provide the same performance for less weight. They also look smarter, don't pill and are available in bright, cheerful colours, (not that you'll get me to admit that this could possibly affect my choice!). Patagonia were the first to introduce new fabrics with their polyester Synchilla double pile which first appeared in 1983. This is a very thick material, somewhat warmer than Helly's double pile, that has since become more generally available, under the name Polarplus, in garments from a host of manufacturers. It's made by Malden Mills of Massachusetts, one of the leading developers of pile fabrics. I find Polarplus fine for really cold winter conditions but too warm for general use, though it could be carried instead of a filled garment as an extra warm layer in wet cold weather. Weights for garments run in the 450–850-g/16–30-oz range. That it's been a success can be seen by the fact that Helly-Hansen have introduced garments in their own double polyester fabric called Propile, which sounds as though it performs much like Polarplus.

My preference is for Polarplus's thinner single-pile relation Polarlite which provides about half the warmth and is less than two-thirds the weight and thickness. I have a North Cape Polarlite Smock with stud-fastened collar, two zipped hand-warmer pockets and rib-knit cuffs and hem. It weighs 410g/14oz and provides all the warmth I need when worn over a thermal layer and under a shell jacket on a cold rainy day. In summer it's all I need to keep warm, in winter when I usually wear the Smock all day I carry another warm garment for when I stop. With Polarlite the furry surface is on the outside so pilling occurs inside the jacket where it cannot be seen. I've been using the Smock regularly for over a year and it shows little sign of wear. Many companies now offer garments made from Polarlite—a welcome development, as in my view it's one of the most versatile pile fabrics around. A double-pile version called Polarlite II is being introduced which is somewhere between Polarlite and Polarplus in terms of weight and warmth and some makers are changing to this. Personally I don't need a warmer Polarlite and hope that the first version will continue to be available.

Both Polarplus and Polarlite are sometimes called fleece but I think of fleece as a smooth-surfaced fabric and these furry materials as pile. There are several true fleece fabrics on the market in various weights. The heavier, thicker ones like Malden Mills' Polarfleece I find too warm, especially as to their denser weave means that they function over a narrower temperature range than pile so it's easy to overheat in them. Most of these heavy fleeces have been replaced by Polarplus and similar piles anyway. Thin fleeces though are an alternative to Polarlite and have the big advantage of being wind-resistant owing to their tight non-stretch construction. Mountain Equipment have been the main proponents of these fabrics with their Ultrafleece. I have an Ultrafleece Pullover with stud-fastened collar, zipped chest and hand-warmer pockets and lycra cuffs and hem and a weight of just 350g/12oz. It has seen much usage including the second and colder half of the Canadian Rockies walk. After two years it looks as good as new and still performs excellently.

My favourite lightweight fabric, though, is the recently introduced Sportant Fleece from Akzo, a Craghoppers zip-fronted jacket in which I used on the Yukon walk. This garment was made from a lightweight single-sided material with the furry side as the exterior so it doesn't pill. There are thicker double-sided versions too that I haven't tried. The jacket I used performed superbly, proving hard-wearing, comfortable (it's slightly stretchy) and warmer for its weight (510g/18oz) than other fabrics I've tried. It has lightly elasticated cuffs and hem and two zipped hand-warmer pockets plus a high collar. As with the Akzo thermal underwear fabric Craghoppers will have a range of Sportant Fleece clothing on the market by the time this book is published and I expect other companies will be using the fabric by then too.

There aren't many other thin piles and fleeces around; most makers have gone for the Malden Mills fabrics. One used by the very small but innovative British company Bivvybug is Superfleece which they make up into a top called the Tor Shirt. This features a layer of windproof polycotton over the chest and collar, two map-size zipped chest pockets, a three-quarter-length front zip, a high collar and stud fastened adjustable cuffs. It has no elastication at the hem but is designed to be tucked into trousers. The weight is 310g/11oz and the performance is similar to Ultrafleece. I've used the Tor Shirt on a couple of short winter trips and am quite impressed as the addition of the polycotton means you can wear it in much stronger winds than Ultrafleece without needing to put a shell jacket on. Another fleece is Sub Zero's ICI Tactel Superfleece jacket, the material of which is fairly thick and advertised as 'three times as windproof as Polarplus', which doesn't mean much as the latter isn't windproof at all—three times nothing is still nothing. However Superfleece has been used for dog-sledging in the Arctic, a singularly cold activity, by outdoor writer Dick Sale and he rates its wind resistance highly.

Other piles and fleeces around include very stretchy ones for ease of movement. I've not used the latter myself but reports suggest that by cutting out dead air space stretch piles are warmer, weight for weight, than any others. Every outdoor shop and mail-order catalogue features a host of pile tops. My choices are for the thinner varieties like Sportant Fresh, Polarlite, Ultrafleece and Superfleece, but almost any pile can be recommended and I'd choose even the most basic polyester pile garment over anything else for warmwear.

Wool: Because I use pile and fleece almost exclusively for warmwear it's years since I carried a wool sweater or heavyweight wool shirt. In fact it's years since I owned one as I prefer pile for everyday wear too. I can see no point in carrying a garment which is heavier than pile/fleece for the same insulation, which absorbs moisture to make it even heavier, which takes ages to dry, which requires careful looking after and which isn't as durable. However there are people who like wool shirts and sweaters and there is plenty of choice in every clothing shop. And if you have wool sweaters in your wardrobe anyway you might as well wear them for backpacking and spend your money on good-quality inner and outer layers where specialist fabrics are more necessary. You can always replace them with pile garments when they wear out.

Insulated clothing: In winter, or places and weather where a pile/fleece garment won't keep you warm on its own, you need a second insulating layer. I carry one on any trip on which I think I'm likely to wear my pile/fleece top whilst walking, so that I can have extra warmth at rest-stops and in camp, and also on any walk in bear country, where I cook and eat outside without the warmth and shelter of my tent and sleeping bag. This garment could be a second, perhaps thicker, pile one but I find the bulk too great given that there are warmer items that pack up much smaller. Moreover, pile isn't windproof, a feature I require of a garment that will be worn as my outer layer much of the time. Instead I prefer filled, especially down-filled, clothing, as this is warmer and less bulky when packed than pile and is windproof. If the need for a second layer seems marginal or weight is pressing, I carry a sleeveless top, as it is the torso that needs keeping warm most. I did this on both the Pacific Crest Trail and the Continental Divide walks, backing up my main warmwear with down- and microfibre-filled vests respectively. These were just enough to keep me warm when the temperature fell way below freezing, as it did occasionally on both walks. Generally though I carry a full jacket as one doesn't weigh much more than a vest, and provides much more warmth.

Waterfowl down is the lightest, warmest insulation there is despite all attempts to create a synthetic that works as well. Garments filled with down pack up incredibly small and provide much more warmth weight for weight than pile. This makes them too hot for wearing when walking but ideal when resting. Down is also very durable. Its only drawback is that it must be kept dry as it loses all its insulation when wet and takes a very long time to dry out unless you can hang it out in a hot sun or put it in a tumble-drier. As it will absorb vast amounts of water a sodden down garment is very heavy to carry as well. Concern about down's vulnerability to wetting led me to choose synthetic alternatives for many years despite the extra weight, lower insulation value and shorter lifespan. However, since I've never had a filled garment get really wet, I've now reverted to down as my first choice for a second layer of insulation. As I only wear it in camp or at rest-stops in freezing temperatures, keeping it dry isn't actually much of a problem.

For backpacking purposes a lightweight down jacket or sweater of simple design is all that is required. Ones with complex constructions, heavy breathable waterproof shells and vast amounts of fill are for Himalayan mountaineers and polar explorers. Garments suitable for backpacking don't need to contain more than 180–250g/6–9oz of down or weigh more than 650g/23oz (preferably less). Lightweight nylon is adequate for the shell and seams can be sewn-through. A hood isn't necessary, though a detachable one can be useful in really cold weather. My favourite down garment is the RAB Kinder sweater with a 180-g/6-oz fill and a total weight of 480g/17oz. This is an over-the-head style garment with a long front zip, a short side zip at the hem to make it easy to put on and a large front hand-warmer pocket. The seams are sewn-through and there is no hood. The outer shell is made from RAB's hydrophilic coated Shelter Pertex nylon, which is shower-proof and breathable. I find the Kinder all I need for backpacking even in the coldest conditions when worn over a pile top. Even lighter are down vests which can weigh as little as 300g/10½oz, with fills of around 100–125g/3½-4½oz of down. Most makers of downwear offer one lightweight model and perhaps a vest amongst their many expedition-weight ones. Apart from RAB, makers of good lightweight down jackets include Mountain Equipment, Patagonia, The North Face, Marmot and REI. For a more thorough look at down and the construction of down-filled items see the section on sleeping bags.

For those nervous of garments that cease to function if they become wet and those allergic to feathers, there are plenty of high-loft (that is down-imitating) polyester-filled jackets available. Although cold when wet like every other material, despite what manufacturers claim, they do dry quite quickly and so perform better in the wet than down. There are few weighing less than 900g/2lb however and most are over that weight. Packed, they are bulkier than pile garments and over twice the size of down ones.

The lightest I've found is Field & Trek's Quallofil-filled Arete II Jacket at 700g/25oz, a weight achieved only because the garment barely reaches below the waist. It is still a practical garment, being very warm and windproof and packing up to about the size of a pile top. Apart from the Arete though, I'd rather carry a second pile jacket than one of these tops. Synthetic-filled vests, of which there are several available, make more sense, as they weigh between 450 and 700g/16-25oz. If you are interested in these fills, look for brand names like Quallofil, Hollofil and Polarguard, more details of which are given in the sleeping bag section.

The above fills expand like down when uncompressed to produce thick and warm-looking jackets. Alternatives to them are the thin microfibre insulations which have come to dominate synthetic-filled clothing, especially alpine skiwear, because of their slim looks and lack of restrictiveness. First in the field were 3M with Thinsulate, since when there have been a mass of others of which Neidharts Isodry is one of the best known. Many clothing makers have their own names for fills so there are quite a few around. They're made from very fine polyester and polypropylene fibres that are able to trap more air for a given thickness than anything else including down, enabling warm garments to be made that are not bulky to wear. This does not reduce their packed bulk or their weight though, so they are less useful than might at first appear. Garments that provide equivalent warmth to a light down jacket are heavy, running to well over 900g/2lb, and are as bulky when packed as equivalent high-loft-insulated jackets. As most microfibre-filled tops are like this they can be discounted for backpacking.

The best use of these fills to my mind is as an alternative to pile clothing. Microfibre-filled tops equal in warmth to medium-weight pile jackets weigh a manageable 700g/25oz or so. There are few garments like this available though, the only one I know of being the Insuflex-filled Rohan Olfio, a pullover top which weighs 700g/25oz and which I've used a great deal, especially on ski tours where the fact that it has a windproof polycotton outer is a great boon. However I would prefer a zip-fronted design and one with a higher collar and without the Olfio's uninsulated side pleats which let out heat. Unable to find such a garment on the market I persuaded Craghoppers to line one of their polycotton windproof Trail Jackets with Isodry and remove the hood. I took the resulting 740-g/26-oz jacket on my Canadian Rockies walk as my main warmwear, supplementing it with an Ultrafleece sweater for the second half of the trek. Worn over two thin thermal layers the jacket kept me warm sitting outside in temperatures down to −5 °C/24 °F and finished the whole three and a half months in good condition. Craghoppers never put it into production however, feeling that there wouldn't be a large enough market for such a jacket. This is a pity as lightweight microfibre-filled tops do provide a viable windproof alternative to pile and are useful to carry as second warmwear garments. Even lightweight microfibre-filled vests are becoming hard to find. My original Rohan Wild Vest weighs 450g/16oz and has an Insuflex fill, but the current version weighs 625g/22oz, more than a down jacket, and has a thicker Insusoft fill. At that weight it's not worth considering.

3: The Outer Layer

Keeping out wind, rain and snow is the most important task your clothing has to perform. It doesn't matter how good your other garments are if the layer that does this fails, as wet clothing exposed to the wind will chill you quickly whatever material it's made from. I've had a waterproof garment suddenly stop keeping out rain during a storm in the mountains and know just how fast you go from feeling warm if windswept to shivering with cold and on the verge of hypothermia. I now take great care in selecting my shell clothing.

There are two types of shell garment: ones that are windproof but not waterproof and ones that are both. The latter are essential, the former useful but optional. Despite what is sometimes said, any fabric that is waterproof is also windproof. A material that won't allow wind-driven rain through certainly won't let wind on its own in. Reports of certain types of waterproof fabric not being very windproof are based on a misunderstanding. If a garment feels chilly in windy weather it is easy to put that down to a lack of wind resistance. There are several reasons why you might feel cold under a waterproof garment as we shall see, but letting in the wind isn't one of them.

Breathable Fabrics: The moisture vapour given off by your body must eventually reach your outer layer. If it can't then escape it will condense on the inner surface of your waterproofs and eventually soak back into your other clothes. The solution to the condensation problem is to wear fabrics that will allow water vapour to pass through whilst keeping the rain out. These are known as moisture-vapour-permeable (MVP) or breathable fabrics. Many but not all waterproofs are now made from breathable fabrics. However this was not always the case. Until Gore-tex (see below) came along in the late 1970s the choice was between being wet from rain or being wet from sweat unless you only went out when it was sunny. As the first was far more unpleasant and potentially dangerous than the second, the standard wear in wet weather was a non-breathable waterproof.

Since the advent of Gore-tex a host of waterproof fabrics which claim to transmit moisture vapour have appeared. How well any of them work we'll see later but first let's look at the theory behind them. Such fabrics work through a pressure differential between the air inside the jacket and that outside. The warmer air is the more water vapour it can absorb. As the air next to the skin is almost always warmer than the air outside your garments it contains more water vapour. This is so even when it's raining. The further away from your skin the air is the cooler it is and the less water vapour it can hold. This is why condensation forms on the inside of a non-breathable fabric as this cooler air becomes saturated with vapour that cannot escape. Water vapour can pass through a breathable fabric though as long as the outside air is cooler than that inside and therefore holds less water vapour. Because of the way they work breathable garments need to be close-fitting to keep the air inside as warm as possible, as this enables the fabric to transmit moisture more effectively. However, ventilating them when possible by opening the front, lowering the hood and undoing wrist fastenings is still the quickest and most efficient way to let moisture out.

Breathable fabrics aren't perfect of course, and they won't work in all conditions: there is a limit to the amount of moisture even the best of them can transmit in a given time. This means that when you sweat hard while climbing a steep slope you won't stay bone dry under a breathable jacket nor will you do so in continuous heavy rain, despite makers' claims. When the outside of any garment is running with water, breathability is reduced and condensation forms. In a non-breathable garment however, condensation continues to form until you take it off so you stay wet even after it's stopped raining. With the best breathables, once your output of energy slows down and you produce less moisture any dampness will dry out through the fabric. The same happens after heavy rain.

In very cold conditions, especially if it's also windy, condensation may form on the inside of an outer garment. It might even freeze, creating a layer of ice. This seems to occur whether the garment transmits water vapour or not. What happens is that the point where air becomes saturated with water vapour, called the dew-point, occurs inside the clothing in freezing temperatures as the air farthest away from the body is very cold, as is the outer garment itself. And as we've seen when the temperature of the air drops it holds less moisture. I've found this to be particularly a problem if a windproof layer is worn under the outer garment, because, I guess, warm air is trapped inside the windproof layer leaving the air between the two shell layers very cold. This happens with windproof non-waterproof garments that transmit water vapour far faster than the best breathable waterproofs too. On a ski tour in still air in a temperature of −7 °C/20 °F in Finnish Lapland one spring I wore a microfibre-insulated top with a polycotton outer under a polycotton jacket. After a few hours' skiing I stopped to find a sheet of ice lining my outer jacket. I removed this and found I stayed just as warm, and no more ice or condensation formed. The best thing to wear under a shell garment when it's really cold seems to be a pile top, as then the air stays warmer throughout the clothing layers. Certainly I've had less problems with condensation forming and freezing when I've worn this combination.

There are two categories of breathable materials: coatings and laminates. The first are layers of waterproofing, usually but not always polyurethane, applied to a base fabric, usually a type of nylon. The second type is a sandwich of materials, the key layer of which is a very thin waterproof breathable membrane. Both coatings and laminates work in one of two ways—microporous and hydrophilic. *Microporous* fabrics are so called because they are full of billions of tiny holes which are far smaller than raindrops but much larger than moisture-vapour molecules, making them impervious to the first whilst allowing the second to pass through. *Hydrophilic* fabrics work in a more complex and much harder to understand way unless you're a chemist. I for one am unclear exactly what happens but the explanation is that the active layer (the coating or laminate), although non-porous and therefore completely waterproof, has chains of water-loving (hence 'hydrophilic') molecules in it along which water vapour is conducted.

Coated fabrics are legion with new ones appearing all the time, though many of these are not in fact different to the others but the same ones with a new name. Microporous ones include Entrant (the first on the scene), Cyclone, Helly-Tech, Ultrex and Patagonia's H2NO Storm. Hydrophilic ones include Witcoflex, Cyclone Classic, Cascade, Milair, Hydro-Dry, VTX, Ventex and Peter Storm MVT. I've used several of these and found that whilst none of them breathe as well as the laminates they are an improvement over non-breathable coatings and the best ones work very well indeed. Improvements are going on all the time and it may well be that soon a coating will equal a laminate in terms of performance.

Laminates are the most effective (and most expensive) breathable fabrics and there are far fewer of them than the coatings, with just two generally available, Gore-tex and Sympatex. One of the few others is the British-made microporous Porelle, available in a 48 per cent polyester, 27 per cent polyurethane, 25 per cent nylon three-layer laminate called Aquatex and available in garments from Blacks.

Gore-tex, which started the breathable waterproof revolution, is a microporous membrane made from the wonderfully named polytetrafluroethylene whilst *Sympatex* is a hydrophilic one made of rather mundane polyester. Both membranes are laminated to a wide range of fabrics, mostly different sorts of nylon though in some cases polyester or polycotton. The thicker these fabrics are, the more durable the garment is, but the lower the breathability. In three-layer laminates the membrane is stuck between two layers of nylon to produce a hard-wearing but stiffish material. The glue dots used to stick the layers together also cut down on breathability. More breathable but perhaps less durable are two-layer laminates, where the membrane is stuck only to an outer layer and the inner lining hangs free, and drop liners where the membrane is left loose between an inner and outer layer or else is just stuck to a very light inner layer. This design minimises the number of seams, which is a bonus point.

Which works best? It depends on the membrane and the materials used for the inner and outer layer, so there is no easy answer. My experience, based on extensive use of several garments, is that in three-layer laminates Gore-tex performs slightly better than Sympatex, but that both membranes breathe better in two-layer or drop-liner form than any three-layer laminate. The one I've found to work best of all is the two-layer type where the laminate is the inner layer. In these forms there's little to choose between Gore-tex and Sympatex. There are still times of course when you can expect condensation to appear in either of them.

When it comes to durability however Sympatex has the edge. I've twice worn out Gore-tex three-layer garments on walks lasting several months and three times had jackets made of the fabric fail on me in heavy rain so that I ended up soaked. I've given Sympatex two-layer and drop-liner garments more use than Gore-tex ones which have failed, and have not yet had one leak so that is what I now choose, especially for long treks. There are far more makers of Gore-tex garments however, so there is more choice of styles (Berghaus, The North Face, Phoenix, Marmot and Sprayway all make top-quality Gore-tex garments as do Craghoppers, Karrimor, Ultimate, VauDe and Jack Wolfskin in Sympatex). Remember too that compared with other breathable fabrics both work very well.

One problem with all these fabrics is that after a time—it's impossible to say exactly how long—the water repellency of the outer or face fabric, which causes rain to bead up and run down the garment, wears off and the material starts to absorb moisture. When this happens you will notice damp patches appearing on the outer of the garment. As well as adding to the weight and taking time to dry this also impairs its breathability, so when it happens it's worth coating the jacket with one of the special treatments described below. Being very aware of this problem fabric manufacturers are working hard to create water-repellent coatings that are more durable. Certainly they now last a lot longer than they did in the late 1970s when they usually failed after no more than a week or so.

Breathable Waterproofs without Membranes or Coatings
A totally new way of making a garment waterproof and breathable was launched whilst I was writing this book. Paramo clothing, created by Nick Brown of Nikwax, is not coated and does not contain a membrane, yet it is claimed to be as waterproof as the best laminates and far more breathable. So new is it at the time of writing that only a Rain/Track Suit designed for runners rather than walkers is available. Thanks to Nick Brown I have been able to try this out and at least come to some tentative conclusions. Paramo clothing is made from Pertex, a tightly woven nylon that is water- repellent and windproof and Parameta, a knitted, raised (i.e. with a slight pile on one side) polyester-based fabric that has the capacity ('the extraordinary capacity', say Paramo) to pump liquid water in one direction only, from inside the garment outwards. Both layers are breathable and are industrially treated with Nikwax TX.10 Waterproofing Compound. The principle behind the clothing is that the combination of the water-deflection of the Pertex outer with the pumping action of the Parameta inner makes the garment waterproof whilst the Parameta also expels condensed perspiration as well as moisture vapour to the outside, something no laminate will do. Because garments can be retreated with TX.10 at home the proofing is renewable, something else you can't do with laminates or coatings. And because they are treated with TX.10 the zips and seams are waterproof without being taped or covered by flaps.

All this sounds too good to be true. But my first trials with the Paramo jacket, a simple design with zip front, attached hood and two zipped hem pockets that weighs 500g/17oz, suggest that it works. The first thing I noticed is that the garment is far more breathable than any MVP waterproof, as breathable in fact as a non-waterproof windproof layer. After taking a long steep climb at as fast a speed as I was capable of on a day of bitter cold and wind in the Scottish Highlands I arrived breathless at the top to find the inside bone dry but the Pertex outer steaming with evaporating sweat. It's performed in exactly the same way on short walks and runs in heavy rain showers and kept me dry as well, though I haven't yet tried it in a long downpour, which is the real test.

Walkers' garments from Paramo, and perhaps other companies, that work on this principle should have appeared before this book is published. Watch out for them in the shops and for reviews in the outdoor magazines.

Non-Breathable Waterproofs: These are made from nylon coated with polyurethane or neoprene. The first is cheap but eventually cracks and peels off. The second is more expensive (though still cheap when compared with the top breathables) but very hard-wearing. Both will see you soaked in sweat after a hard day's walking in wet weather. The only way to remove that moisture is to ventilate the garment, hardly practical if it's pouring down, though a way to limit the dampening effect is to wear a windproof layer under the waterproof one and trap some of the moisture between the two layers, something I always did before breathable fabrics were available.

Whilst moving you will still feel warm even if your undergarments are wet with sweat, as heat is kept in along with the moisture, so it's better to wear a non-breathable waterproof shell than a breathable non-waterproof one—rain being much colder than perspiration. When you stop though you'll cool down rapidly unless you put on extra clothes.

Non-breathable garments are really only worth considering if you wear a windproof top most of the time and a waterproof only in continuous heavy rain. Designs are much the same as for breathable garments, with weights running from 200g/7oz for an ultralight polyurethane-proofed top to 900g/2lb for a tough, long-lasting neoprene-coated one.

Design: The material is not enough on its own to ensure that a garment will perform well. The design is nearly as important. Of prime importance is that clothing be waterproof by construction. With regard to condensation the more opportunities there are for ventilation, the less problems there will be, so all closures and fastenings should be adjustable. The two basic choices are between zipped front-opening and over-the-head garments. Having tried both this is one instance where I would always go for the full opening jacket simply because over-the-head ones can be difficult to put on in a strong wind. The only exception is with the ultralight waterproofs I carry when I don't expect to need rainwear at all but take something 'just in case'.

Here I use a pullover design because these are lighter than front-opening ones and in this case weight is the prime requirement. No design is fully waterproof though. Wind-driven heavy rain will find its way into any garment somewhere given time. The best will keep out most precipitation most of the time and that's all you can hope for.

Length is really a matter of personal choice. I like hip-length garments as these allow the legs greater freedom of movement, but many people prefer longer ones, even knee-length, arguing that these cut down the number of times you need to wear overtrousers.

Seams are the most crucial features for ensuring maximum waterproofness. If these are not proofed in some way they will leak. In breathable fabric garments and the more expensive non-breathables, the seams are usually tape-sealed, the most effective way of making them watertight. In cheaper garments they may be coated with a special sealant instead. If you happen to have a garment with uncoated seams you'd better acquire a tube of sealant, available from any outdoor shop, and apply it yourself. You can also do this too when the original sealant cracks and comes off—as it always does. Taped seams can peel off too, though this is very rare.

The front zip is the other major source of leakage. This must be covered with a single or, preferably, a double waterproof flap closed with either studs or velcro. Even so, after facing into driving rain for any length of time you may find a damp patch inside the zip where water has found its way in, often at the top of the collar. A high collar helps prevent this. It's important too that the covering flap comes all the way to the top of the zip. Most zips are two-way ones, opening from the bottom as well as the top. These are slightly more awkward to use than single ones (you have to slot the parts together at the bottom, which can be difficult with numb fingers), and have no advantages that I can see except perhaps to allow ease of movement in very long garments.

Hoods are clearly potential leak points. Good ones fit very closely round the face when the drawcords are tightened without leaving a gap under the chin. Detachable or foldaway hoods that wrap around a high collar generally provide better protection than fixed hoods, though they are more awkward to use. I find the slight inconvenience worthwhile however. A wired or otherwise stiffened peak can be useful to keep off hail or driving rain and people who wear glasses tell me that such a peak is essential if they are to see properly in wet weather. The best hoods move with your head so that you can look to the side without finding yourself staring at the inner lining, as is the case with all too many designs. Clearly the best way to check this is to try the hood on but a quick assessment can be made by looking at the hood seams. One single seam running back to front over the hood generally means it won't move with you. If there are two seams rather than one, or a single seam that runs around or across the hood from one side to the other, the hood is more likely to provide good visibility. There's no denying though that the hoods that give the best protection in bad weather are also the ones that limit vision the most. However I'd rather have the protection than the visibility, especially on those days where the rain drives down for hours and swirling mists hide the view. In winter weather I sometimes wear a pile-lined Gore-tex cap with a large peak instead of a hood in light showers and under one in storms and blizzards when it gives better protection than any hood on its own. It's too warm outside the snow season however, though I suppose an unlined cap might work as well. Whether you wear such a cap or not your jacket hood must be big enough for you to wear warm headwear underneath, whether a full balaclava or a lightweight knitted hat.

Sleeves need to be cut full under the arms to allow for free movement and to stop them riding up when you lift your arms. Again, trying a garment on is the best way to find out how well the sleeves are cut. Some of the more sophisticated jackets now feature 'articulated' sleeves—ones with a built-in curve at the elbow. How much of an advantage this may be I don't know but I can't say I've ever missed it. Underarm zips are found on some, principally American-made, garments. Reports suggest that they allow for better ventilation but also tend to leak in heavy rain, which is perhaps why they haven't found favour with manufacturers in the wet British Isles (though see Buffalo clothing below for a similar design that works). The cuffs on sleeves need to be adjustable as they are an important ventilation point. I like simple external velcro-closed ones rather than the neater,

but more awkward, internal storm cuffs, and I abhor non-adjustable elasticated ones as I find my arms overheat and run with sweat very easily in them.

Pockets are undoubtedly useful but making them waterproof is difficult, not to say downright impossible, so I prefer a minimum number. In fact just one mapsize chest pocket is adequate for me. Hem pockets are usually inaccessible under a fastened pack hipbelt and even if they're not, I don't like carrying anything in them as they then flap against the legs which I find irritating. However, as shell jackets, particularly the more expensive ones, are often used as general-purpose garments as well as in the outdoors, people want plenty of pockets and most jackets provide them. Pocket openings should always be covered by flaps whether they are zipped or not, and the seams should be taped or sealed on the inside. The most water-resistant hem ones hang inside the jacket, attached only at the top. The best compromise between waterproofness and accessibility for chest pockets is for them to have a vertical zipped entrance placed under the front flap but outside the front zip. Pockets inside the jacket keep out the rain but you have to open the jacket front and let it in to use them. Those on the outside of the jacket that have angled flaps and zips are the best for access but the first to leak in heavy rain. An advantage of pullover-type garments is that they usually have a single large 'kangaroo' pouch on the chest which is the easiest sort to use and very water-resistant.

Pockets don't need to be made from the same material as the rest of the garment. A lightweight unproofed nylon is adequate (avoid cotton as it absorbs moisture). The best though is a mesh pocket as found on Patagonia shell garments because you can ventilate by opening the pocket, and it adds the minimum of weight. This is particularly effective on a garment with two outside chest pockets with angled openings like the Patagonia Storm Jacket, as with both pockets open but still protected by their flaps, you can ventilate the whole chest and armpit area.

Mesh is also the best material for the inner lining on garments that have one, as two-layer laminates and many microporous coated ones do, again because of its light weight and because it helps moisture reach the breathable layer as quickly as possible. If it's made from a wicking fabric, as many now are, all the better. Woven linings, even nylon ones, I've found become wet with condensation, however breathable the outer layer. Makers who use mesh linings include Patagonia, Marmot, Phoenix and Berghaus.

Drawcords are needed at the collar for tightening the hood and are often found at the waist, though the hipbelt prevents snow and rain entering via the hem and seals in warmth—too effectively all too often. Self-locking toggles are a boon on drawcords. Trying to untangle an iced-up tiny knot with frozen fingers in order to lower your hood is not easy or fun.

Finally a note on the trend for shell garments with extra sets of zips for attaching warmwear. I hate it. It adds weight for no practical purpose and puts the cost of garments up. I say this on the basis of brief usage only, but I feel it strongly. As far as I can see it's done purely so that the combined garment can be worn as a warm town coat. Personally I don't find the effort of donning two garments so great that I can't manage it.

Weights: Shell garments range in weight from 175 to 900g/6–32 oz-plus. Those at the lower end are too light except for trips when you don't expect to need a waterproof but carry one just in case, or else when you regularly use an 'almost-waterproof' windproof top, as they won't last long if worn very often. Those above about 750g/26oz are just too heavy. Garments in the 450–700-g/16-25-oz range are where most waterproofs with reasonable durability are to be found and also where there is the biggest choice.

My Selection: Having had the opportunity of trying out most of the materials available, including at least one of each type of breathable fabric, my choice for places and times when rain is likely, as it is on most of my trips, is a Sympatex jacket, the Craghoppers Cloudbreaker. This has a polycotton outer with a separate Sympatex lining plus a wired, foldaway hood, two external chest pockets, two hem pockets, waist drawcord and double, velcro-closed, flap. The weight is a rather heavy 700g/25oz but the material works well in heavy rain and wind-driven sleet and the design is excellent, especially that of the hood, one of the best at combining maximum visibility with maximum protection I've come across. The only disadvantage is that the pockets aren't waterproof. The drop-liner construction means the Cloudbreaker breathes better than three-layer garments or ones with the laminate glued to the outer layer. The reason, I think, is that the Sympatex stays warmer as it is protected by the polycotton from the cold outside air and moisture is therefore less likely to condense on it. After much wear the polycotton outer does start to absorb water and requires reproofing. I used a Cloudbreaker on both the Canadian Rockies and Yukon walks, and was well pleased with its performance, comfort and durability.

When rain is unlikely or will occur only in short bursts (the Sierra Nevada of California in summer, the Norwegian mountains in winter, a heatwave anywhere), I carry a Patagonia Featherweight Shell Pullover weighing just 175g/6oz. This is a short ripstop nylon top coated with Patagonia's H2NO Light proofing. It has an attached hood and a large, mesh-lined front pocket. It is neither very breathable nor very waterproof, but it keeps out drizzle and showers—a little more if worn over a windproof top. Since I coated the seams with sealant as Patagonia suggested, it is more waterproof than it was when new.

These choices may well change in the near future however as developments continue apace in the field of waterproof fabrics. Whilst I was writing this section makers Akzo announced a new Sympatex membrane that is a third lighter than the original one (10 microns instead of 15 for those who understand these things), making it more breathable but still as waterproof and durable. Another new development is that Craghoppers are to produce a new two-layer garment, to be called the Galebreaker, with the same Sympatex inner as the Cloudbreaker but with a Tactel microfibre outer which should be less absorbent, faster-drying and perhaps lighter than polycotton whilst still being as breathable and comfortable. Robert Saunders, more noted for their tents, have launched a set of microfibre clothing claimed to be waterproof though not coated or containing a membrane. Coatings themselves, especially hydrophilic ones, are being improved with regard to durability and breathability all the time and new names are constantly appearing on the market. Paramo and Buffalo clothing offer other ways of staying dry that I'm still evaluating. The best advice I can offer is to watch the advertisements and reviews in the magazines and check out the manufacturers' catalogues before you buy a new waterproof.

Overtrousers: Waterproof overtrousers are available in the same range of materials as the jackets. Weights run from 140 to 700g/5–25oz depending on the fabric. I find most overtrousers uncomfortable and restrictive so I wear them as little as possible, far less often than my waterproof jacket. Therefore I usually only carry a lightweight pair, often the 140-g/5-oz Patagonia Featherweight Shell Pants which have an adjustable waist, lower leg zips and zipped slits for access to trouser pockets.

In continuous rain I've found the best way to keep my legs warm and dry is to wear thermal long-johns under my overtrousers. I only wear a pair of long trousers in between in bitterly cold weather and strong winds. However, most legwear (see below) will keep you warm when wet and dries quickly so I often don't bother wearing overtrousers at all. Many people don't even carry them. The Paramo trousers look as though they might be suitable as general legwear as they are breathable and comfortable, yet still function as waterproofs when it's raining. They weigh 260g/9oz, have an elasticated waist, lower zips and a small zipped pocket inside the waistband.

Features to look for in overtrousers are adjustable waists, and zips in the lower leg that are long enough to allow you to pull them on without taking your boots off. If these have gussets behind them more water will be kept out. However, I find the zips catch in such gussets so I prefer not to have them. For winter use when you are wearing crampons or skis, trousers with full-length two-way zips are useful. This type can also be ventilated more easily by unzipping the sides from the waist down to the knee when necessary. Salopette types that cover the chest are designed for mountaineering and alpine skiing. Some people like them for ski touring but I find them too hot. They are also heavier and bulkier than trousers.

Windproofs: The advent of breathable waterproof fabrics was hailed as a weight-saving boon, as only one garment needed to be carried for both wind and rain. Whilst this is true I find that even the best materials are far less breathable than non-waterproof windproof ones and that waterproof jackets are never as comfortable as lightweight windproof tops. Paramo clothing looks as though it might prove to be the exception to this, but at present I usually carry a windproof top as well as a waterproof one, unless weight is a real problem.

There are two approaches to this combination. One is to carry a double-layer water-repellent windproof jacket plus an ultralight waterproof. The other, which is more common, is to carry a single-layer lightweight windproof top and a standard-weight waterproof. For most trips I adopt the second approach but for ski tours in countries such as Norway, where heavy rain is unlikely but cold winds almost guaranteed, I use the first.

Double-layer jackets come in similar designs to waterproof ones and weigh in the 500–1400-g/17–49-oz range which is why you wouldn't want to carry a full-weight waterproof as well. The lightest are made from various polyester, cotton and nylon mixes which dry quickly and are very comfortable, but not very water-resistant. The best is probably 50/50 polyester cotton as used in the Rohan Pampas Jacket (750g/26oz) and many more. I've used this garment on many trips and it works well. However if you want more waterproofness then the fabric to go for is Ventile, a tightly woven 100 per cent cotton material that blocks out most rain. For day use Ventile is very nearly waterproof. I've walked in one for nine hours in continuous heavy rain and stayed dry. The problem is that Ventile is heavy (jackets run from 900 to 1400g/2–3lb) and that in rain it soaks up so much moisture that it can double in weight. It then takes a very long time to dry unless there is something like a tumble-dryer available. If you can't dry it overnight then the next day it will leak as the whole garment will be saturated. For backpacking use this means Ventile garments need protecting from the rain by a waterproof layer which makes for a heavy load. I only use my Ventile jacket (a Survival Aids Arctic Ranger, weighing 1090g/38oz) for hut-to-hut ski tours and day walks because of this.

Single-layer windproof tops, often called windshirts, make much more sense as they can double both as a mid-layer shirt to keep a cool breeze off the inner layer and also as a shell to keep stronger, colder winds off your warmwear. They aren't as water-repellent as double garments though, so a fully waterproof top needs to be carried as well. The most water-resistant are probably Ventile ones, such as the Survival Aids Windstoppa (525g/18oz). This is described as keeping out 'all but the heaviest shower'. My brief usage of one suggests that this is so.

For years I used a Rohan Moving On II, a 300-g/10½-oz polycotton pullover top with a zipped chest pocket, large lower hand-warmer pocket, short neck zip, stud-fastened cuffs and adjustable hem but no hood. It functions very well, though its water resistance is marginal. However the latest nylon and polyester microfibre fabrics are lighter, more water-repellent, faster-drying and more durable than polycotton whilst being just as windproof and just as comfortable. Beware though of those that are coated, as these are often both less breathable and less waterproof than actual waterproof breathable fabrics, a rather negative achievement. The number of manufacturers making single-layer and even double-layer microfibre garments is increasing all the time. Fabric names to look out for include Pertex, Climaguard, Supplex, Versatech, Technique, Finesse, Microft and ICI Tactel. If worn over a pile jacket, single-layer garments made from these fabrics will keep out a surprising amount of rain. At the same time they are more breathable than any fully waterproof fabric. The top I now use most often is a short over-the-head Buffalo Running Smock made from Pertex nylon. It weighs just 200g/7oz and features a hood, large velcro-closed front pocket, neck zip and side zips that run from the armpits to the hem. The last are for ventilation and ease of use. Its packed size is minimal and I rarely leave it behind.

A COUPLE OF HERESIES

1: The Buffalo Double P System
The layer system is the accepted way of dealing with the wide variety of weather conditions found in the wilderness. It usually works and works well, but it does require constant adjustment and there are times, usually when the weather is cold and wet, when finding the right combination of layers can be difficult if not impossible. In stormy weather the whole system depends on the shell layer. If that stops functioning you will soon be cold and wet regardless of what is worn underneath. Such failures do occur. I know people who have gone back to non-breathable waterproofs after a soaking in a breathable one saying they'd rather be wet but warm with sweat than cold and wet from the rain. I myself have had microporous breathable jackets cease working on three separate occasions, which is why I now prefer hydrophilic

breathables, especially Sympatex, as these have so far proved more dependable.

There is an alternative to wearing several layers though, and that is to wear just a single garment. For extreme conditions, argues designer Hamish Hamilton, that is the answer. Just one layer of his Buffalo Double P clothing is claimed to replace wicking underwear, warmwear and shell. Made from Pertex and pile (hence 'Double P'), Buffalo clothing is designed to function best in the foulest conditions such as heavy wind-driven rain in near-freezing temperatures, but also to be comfortable in more equable conditions. The Buffalo system consists of just three garments: trousers/salopettes, shirt and jacket. There are variations in design according to the usage envisaged (four types of shirt for instance), but the main difference is between the Standard Range which uses Pertex 5 as the outer layer and the Professional Range which uses the harder-wearing and more wind- and waterproof Pertex 6.

The premise behind Buffalo clothing is that it is more important to remove sweat than to keep out rain in order to stay comfortable, especially as the latter is ultimately impossible since all shell garments leak at cuffs or neck eventually or else cause undergarments to become sodden with sweat. Buffalo clothing is designed to be totally condensation-free, warm, windproof and 'highly rainproof', the last meaning that a single Buffalo layer will keep out rain falling at a rate of up to 1cm/½in per hour, which is most rain outside of a cloudburst. The polyester pile provides the warmth and wicks away perspiration whilst the Pertex shell keeps out the wind and allows moisture from within to spread over its surface and quickly evaporate. The two fabrics in combination keep out most rain whilst two layers of Buffalo clothing should deflect the heaviest downpour. If the clothing does become saturated (from falling in a river for example), it dries quickly and keeps the wearer warm. Other advantages of the system are a lighter pack (no spare clothing other than socks is needed) and fewer stops because less clothing adjustment is needed.

These are quite incredible, not to say wild-sounding, claims. Can they be substantiated? In my experience—and much to my astonishment—the answer is yes. Others, including experienced arctic explorers and members of several mountain rescue teams used to the worst of Britain's winter weather, have come to the same conclusion. For extremes of wet cold Buffalo clothing is now well proven.

The garment I have used most is the Standard Range Mountain Shirt. This over-the-head top has a short neck zip, side zips running from armpit to hem for ventilation, a velcro-attached hood, velcro-adjusted cuffs, lower hand-warmer pockets and a chest pocket. The weight is 620g/22oz (this is for the P5 shirt without a hood—the P6 one weighs 640g/22½oz and the hood 70g/2½oz). It is designed to be worn next to the skin and without a shell garment on top. Indeed if you wear other garments, says Hamish Hamilton, you will overheat and then chill when you stop and your sweat cools.

I first used the shirt on a two-day mountain orienteering event in the Galloway hills of southwestern Scotland. The weather was some of the worst I've ever been out in, with lashing rain, winds that knocked you off your feet and bitter cold. After an hour or so of fighting uphill wearing a synthetic thermal inner layer, a thin wool shirt and a microporous breathable jacket I was soaked to the skin and starting to shiver. I stripped off all my layers, donned the Buffalo shirt and, because I hadn't a hood for the shirt, my shell garment, and continued. I stayed warm for the next eight hours of battering by the storm, though when I reached the overnight camp I found the Pertex outer of the shirt soaked. Once I removed the shell jacket it dried very quickly and I stayed warm. At no time did the pile next to my skin feel damp. The next day in cold, windy but dry weather I wore the shirt on its own and found that by using the side and neck zips I could prevent overheating and stay comfortable. I only met one person who said he'd stayed dry during the first day of the event. He too had been wearing a Buffalo shirt, this time with a hood.

Further use has convinced me that the shirt is effectively waterproof and also very breathable. Any sweat that has occurred, such as on my back and under my pack shoulder straps, has disappeared rapidly when I've stopped; the pile has wicked it away at an amazing rate. When wearing the shirt whilst skiing in temperatures well below freezing, I've experienced no icing up either. However I've found the salopettes too warm even in the coldest weather. I sweat profusely in them and although they dry quickly when I stop, I don't like the hot clammy feeling they produce when I'm moving. In winter the Mountain Trousers (450g/16oz), which I haven't tried, might prove more suitable, though I suspect they would also be too hot in above-freezing temperatures. The Mountain Jacket (990g/35oz) is designed for wearing over the shirt at stops and in really cold conditions. I haven't used one but have found that a down top (lighter and less bulky) works well, as I've found I only need an extra layer when the temperature is below freezing and it therefore isn't raining. But I can imagine situations with days of continuous rain at around freezing point when the jacket could well be useful.

For places with guaranteed wet cold, stormy weather (such as many arctic and sub-arctic regions, especially Iceland, the Scottish Highlands in winter and other northerly destinations swept by wet ocean winds) the shirt is probably the best garment available. I would happily rely just on it and the trousers and jacket as long as the forecast was bad enough, though I haven't yet tried this full system out. In mixed weather I usually carry other garments as well as the Mountain Shirt, because of my concern about overheating. I'm aware though that I haven't yet really used Buffalo clothing enough to fit it into my overall system. On trips where weather may vary from severe storms to hot and sunny I want to try out the shirt along with a thermal tee-shirt and an ultralight waterproof to see if that will cover all conditions—as I expect it will. The possibilities of the Buffalo system go beyond just clothing to wear during the day too. In conjunction with Pertex/pile sleeping bags the clothing can be used for bivouacking and camping.

2: Vapour Barrier

The second heresy, which has been around much longer than the single-layer one, challenges the idea of breathability. Our skin is always slightly moist, however dry it may feel. If it really dries out then it cracks and chaps, and open sores appear. To keep a layer of warm moist air around the skin we constantly produce liquid—either sweat or, when we aren't exercising hard, 'insensible perspiration'. The aim of breathable clothing is to remove this moisture from the skin as quickly as possible and transport it to the outside air where it can evaporate. In doing so heat loss inevitably occurs. There is also, as we have seen, the problem of maintaining breathability in severe weather conditions.

The vapour-barrier theory says that instead of trying to remove this moisture from the skin we should try to keep it there so that its production and attendant evaporative heat loss will cease, enabling us to stay warm and our clothing to stay dry, as it won't have to deal with large amounts of liquid. To achieve this one wears a non-breathable waterproof layer either next to or close to the skin, with insulating layers over it. Because heat is trapped inside, less clothing need be carried. Because of the way they work, vapour barriers are most efficient in dry cold, that is in temperatures below freezing, as when the humidity of the air is high, heat loss by evaporation falls anyway. A further advantage of vapour barrier clothing is that by preventing moisture loss it helps stave off dehydration, a potentially serious problem in dry cold conditions.

When I first read about vapour barriers my immediate thought was that surely wearing one would result in being soaked in sweat. However as several reputable outdoor writers said vapour barriers worked, I decided to give it a try rather than reject the idea out of hand.

Apparently if you have a hairy body waterproof fabrics feel comfortable worn next to the skin. However I'm mostly hairless and I find vapour barriers feel instantly clammy unless I wear something under them. The ideal material is a thin non-absorbent synthetic such as polypro. Initially I used a set of old polyurethane-coated lightweight waterproofs as a vapour-barrier suit. A few outings with these showed that whilst I did overheat rapidly in them when walking and I started to sweat even when the temperature was several degrees below freezing, as warmwear for sitting round camp they were superb. Indeed I was as warm wearing my vapour-barrier top under a pile jacket as I was when wearing a down jacket over it. And when used for sleeping, the vapour barrier added several degrees of warmth to my sleeping bag, but being low in bulk and having a slippery surface didn't make me feel restricted or uncomfortable.

I was impressed enough with these first experiments to change my waterproof suit for a lighter and more comfortable purpose-made vapour-barrier one. The Patagonia VBL

(Vapour Barrier Liner) Shirt and Pants are made from a soft-coated ripstop nylon and weigh just 110 and 80g/4 and 3oz respectively. The shirt has a zip front and velcro-closed cuffs, the trousers a drawcord waist and velcro-closures at the ankles. They perform very well, yet after a first winter of delighted use I find I rarely wear them any more. This is partly because all attempts at wearing them to walk in have resulted very quickly in overheating (though I've never been out in them in temperatures below −10 °C/14 °F and rarely in those temperatures, which probably means I've not tried them in cold enough conditions). However, it is also because, despite the fact that I know they will keep me warm, I somehow don't have any real confidence in them. A down jacket looks warm, and carrying one is psychologically reassuring. Two thin pieces of nylon just don't have the same effect. Nowadays I tend to carry the VBL suit as an emergency back-up for sleeping in in winter, in case temperatures are worse than expected, but I very rarely use it.

Vapour barriers can also be worn on the feet and hands in the form of plastic bags or thin plastic or rubber socks and gloves. Again I've tried both and have found they work, but again most times I usually don't bother. If your feet do become very cold and wet however, an emergency vapour barrier worn over a dry thin sock with a thicker sock over the lot does help them warm up. I used this combination near the end of the Canadian Rockies walk when I had to ford a half-frozen river seven times in a matter of hours and then walk on over frozen ground in boots that were splitting and socks with holes in. Dry inner socks and plastic bags made a huge difference to my feet.

LEGWEAR

What is worn on the legs is not as important as what is worn on the upper body, but it still matters with regard to both protection from the weather and comfort. In particular legwear needs to be either loose-fitting or stretchy so that it doesn't interfere with movement when walking. Long trousers are also needed to keep you warm in camp and also perhaps in your sleeping bag if it's very cold.

Shorts

Shorts are my favourite legwear and I wear them whenever possible. Nothing else provides the same freedom of movement and comfort. If the upper body is kept warm shorts can be worn in surprisingly cold conditions and I carry them on all except winter trips, though strong winds, insects and rain often mean that they stay in the pack. Any shorts will do, as long as they have roomy legs that don't bind on the thighs. Many people wear cut-down jeans, a good way to use up worn-out clothing. Running shorts are the cheapest and lightest types available (my 100 per cent polyester Nike ones weigh just 60g/2oz), though they are very flimsy and don't stand up well to contact with granite boulders, rough logs and other normal wilderness seats. I carry them on trips when I doubt whether I'll wear shorts but want a pair in case the weather is kinder than expected.

When I know I'll wear shorts I prefer more substantial ones, preferably with pockets for use when travelling and in towns. For years I used Rohan ones (50/50 polyester/cotton, 220grams/8oz), which have six pockets, four of them zipped, and a double seat. They are very hardwearing—I have pairs which survived both my Pacific Crest Trail and Continental Divide walks. They are expensive though and in the latest models I've found the cut in the legs a little tight for real freedom of movement, leading me to suspect that style rather than function is now playing a part in their design. Also, unlike most running shorts, Rohan and the similar shorts now available from many other companies don't feature a built-in brief so underpants have to be worn as well. This makes them bulky and uncomfortable to wear under trousers, a feeling added to by the pocket and fly zips. It's only a minor point but I do find it convenient to be able to pull on trousers over my shorts without having to remove the latter when the weather changes and having a built-in brief does save the snippet of weight of a pair of underpants.

It was at the start of the Canadian Rockies walk that I finally found the nearest to ideal shorts I've yet come across. I'd brought a pair of polycotton ones with me that I hadn't had a chance to try out until the first day's walk, which consisted of a stroll along Upper Waterton Lake with just a daysack. This was enough to show me that the shorts were too tight in the leg, so I spent a few hours browsing and trying on shorts in the outdoor shops of Waterton townsite on the edge of Waterton Lakes

National Park. In one of them I bought a pair of Patagonia Baggies Shorts (52 per cent cotton/48 per cent nylon, with a polyester inner brief, drawcord-adjusted elasticated waist, two front pockets, one rear pocket, weight 140g/5 oz). I wore them for most of the next three and a half months and they proved very comfortable and highly durable. The wide-cut legs made them easy to walk in whilst the material dried very quickly when wet. Following the Rockies walk I've worn them for short trips in the British hills and two two-week treks in the Pyrenees, after the last of which I threw them out as they'd torn along the side seams. Around four months of wear is, I think, quite reasonable for such a lightweight garment. Other companies offer similar shorts to the Baggies but I stuck with Patagonia and bought another pair for my Yukon walk.

Trousers
Sadly the climate does not always allow for the wearing of shorts on their own. Indeed in some summers in the British hills I've hardly worn them at all. I always carry trousers anyway for wear around camp or if the weather changes or biting insects make wearing shorts a game for the dedicated masochist only. Around camp and in cold weather long-johns can be worn under shorts. This is something I often intend doing but rarely do as it means removing my shorts before donning the long-johns. It's much easier to pull trousers on over shorts when extra warmth is needed (and also simpler to take off trousers rather than long-johns when you warm up).

Trousers fall into two categories: those that will be worn mostly in mild conditions but which may have to cope with cold stormy weather and those designed only for the latter. Whether trousers are full-length or breeches-length—called knickers in America—(coming just below the knee) is a matter of personal choice. I used to wear the latter all the time but for the last ten years or so I've preferred full-length trousers for no particular reason I can think of except perhaps that I feel less conspicuous entering a strange town alone and on foot wearing trousers rather than breeches. The same applies to travel by aircraft or train. The only exception is for snow and particularly ski trips, when I wear gaiters all the time. Then I prefer breeches as I find long trousers tucked into gaiters uncomfortable.

Jeans and corduroy trousers are popular with many people, despite the fact that they are cold when wet and take an age to dry—potentially dangerous attributes in severe conditions, though they can be minimised by the wearing of overtrousers. Other objections to jeans-type trousers are that they are heavy, too tight and not very durable. I find them so uncomfortable I no longer own a pair, even for everyday wear.

For three-season use I favour lightweight trousers of the type made popular in Britain by Rohan with their Bags but now found in many if not most outdoor-clothing ranges. Generally these trousers weigh between 250 and 375g/9–13oz, are made from cotton mixed with polyester or nylon in a 50/50, 65/35 or similar ratio, have double knees and double seats, and have a multitude of pockets, many of them zipped. The material is hardwearing, windproof, quick-drying and comfortable. As well as the Rohan Bags (50/50 polycotton, 285g/10oz), which I used on the Pacific Crest Trail and the Continental Divide, I can vouch for trousers from Craghoppers (whose 50/50 polycotton Trail Pants I used on the Canadian Rockies and Yukon walks—the weight is 285g/10oz); Troll (Tramps, 66/34 cotton/nylon, 255g/9oz); and Survival Aids (50/50 polycotton, 240g/8½oz). There are many more which are probably just as good. The main thing to check is the fit, especially round the legs, as now that many people are using such trousers for everyday wear (as I do and have done for a decade) many styles, including Rohan Bags, seem to be shrinking in order, I suspect, to look more fashionable. That indeed is one reason why I've changed from Rohan Bags to other makes. Another reason is that many of the newer designs such as those from Troll have elasticated waists rather than conventional ones with belt loops, which I prefer as I don't like wearing a belt under a pack hip-belt and anyway stretch waistbands can do just that when you pig out in a restaurant after a long period on dried food! I'm not too bothered about the exact arrangement of pockets though at least one stud-closed or zipped one is useful for money and wallet when travelling to and from the wilderness. Thigh pockets, if large enough, can be useful for carrying maps.

I wear lightweight trousers in any conditions where I find shorts a little too cool, usually donning them on top of the latter. If the weather becomes really cold or on frosty evenings or mornings around camp I wear thermal long-johns under them (currently Craghoppers Sportant Fresh ones, 100g/3½oz). Worn over long-johns and under overtrousers lightweight trousers will cope with most weather outside of winter whilst you are on the move, the combination of three layers being more versatile than one thick pair of trousers.

Slightly heavier, but considerably warmer and more waterproof, than cotton-mix trousers are Ventile cotton ones such as Survival Aids Mountain Trousers (450g/16oz). My only severe weather usage of these, during four days of sleet, snow and high winds in April in the Scottish Highlands, suggests they might well obviate the need for overtrousers and prove adequate for most conditions short of the severest winter ones.

I also like the look of the trousers that are starting to appear in the same synthetic microfibres as windshirts, such as Climaguard, Technique, Tactel and Finesse. These should be harder-wearing, more water-repellent and faster-drying than cotton-mix ones whilst being as comfortable and light in weight. Troll have some nice designs in Tactel nylon in their Omni range, as long as you don't mind the bright stripes and patches—which I must admit put me off wearing them (though reasonably plain blue ones are available). Berghaus's Technique Pants come in tracksuit-type design with elasticated waist and ankles plus two side pockets and a zipped rear pocket into which they fold. They weigh just 200g/7oz. I have a pair on test and the material is as comfortable next to the skin as polycotton and the cut is roomy. I've not used them much at the time of writing but enough to feel that they or similar trousers will soon replace my polycotton ones.

A popular alternative to lightweight trousers is tracksuit-type bottoms which have the advantages of being relatively inexpensive and very durable. These are usually a little warmer, though less windproof, than the thinner poly-cotton trousers. Their stretchiness makes them very good for rock scrambling or skiing, activities where non-stretch designs can bind at the knee. I've tried two models, both in 100 per cent polyester (avoid cotton-mix sweats, these hold moisture and take a long time to dry). Winter-gear Trax are conventional tracksuit bottoms in design with only one tiny internal pocket, foot stirrups and piping down the outer seam. They weigh 275g/10oz. Heavier (420g/15oz) but more practical are Troll's Rock Bottoms which have two standard front pockets as well as an internal one, double material on the seat and upper legs and elasticated ankles. Both garments I find comfortable but I miss the windproof qualities of polycotton and also find that when it's calm I overheat more easily, as I do if I wear long-johns underneath in bitter winds. So whilst I will continue to wear them for scrambling and skiing in mild conditions I'm going back to more conventional legwear for straightforward walking.

As I find two layers on the legs less comfortable and more restricting than one, I wear thick trousers when I know conditions will be cold enough. For twelve years my winter walking trousers have been Rohan Super Striders (63 per cent nylon, 34 per cent viscose, 3 per cent elastane). My pair weigh 660g/23oz, though 800g/28oz is the current catalogue figure. These thick, warm, stretchy, non-absorbent, windproof breeches are ideal for snow and wet-cold conditions. I rarely wear overtrousers over them as they're warm when wet and fairly quick-drying. I only take them on walks when I know I'll wear them every day, however, as the weight and packed bulk precludes carrying them in the pack. As I find them too warm in temperatures much above 5 °C/42 °F, this restricts them to winter use. Craghoppers make a similar pair (the Ra Breeches) as do Field & Trek, but otherwise such garments are rare. For warmer weather, I have a pair of Rohan Outsiders (500g/17oz), thin, stretchy synthetic breeches which are useful for scrambling and walking in areas like the Cuillin Hills on the Isle of Skye, as polycotton materials abrade easily on rough rock and don't give enough freedom of movement for awkward manoeuvres. They (along with many other excellent Rohan garments) are no longer available but Craghoppers do a similar pair, the Ra Lites, which probably perform as well.

In the Super Striders material I also have a a pair of Rohan Super Salopettes (weight a horrific 860g/30oz), which I use for skiing as I like the protection from snow the high back and chest gives me when I fall over! Again these are winter-only garments and again Craghoppers and Field & Trek (and also Calange) make similar models—better ones in fact, as Rohan now only make full-length leg ones with zip-off gaiters which look clumsy and bulky to my eye and which weigh 1475g/52oz.

There are walks, particularly long ones spanning different seasons, when warm trousers are needed for use in camp, perhaps even for sleeping in, but are not needed for walking every day, if at all. Weight becomes important here so the stretch breeches described above are out. Ventile trousers might do (see above) but the obvious material is pile as it is warm, light (typical weights run from 270 to 625g/9½–22oz), non-absorbent and quick-drying. However, it is bulky and not very windproof, and this told against it for me, at least until the thin fleeces came along. I've owned a pair of Helly-Hansen nylon pile Polar Trousers (500g/17oz) for many years but rarely use them, as in even a gentle breeze I have to wear overtrousers on top which immediately makes them too hot. On the Canadian Rockies walk I took a pair of Mountain Equipment Ultrafleece Trousers and was delighted with them. They are very light (270g/9½oz), low in bulk, comfortable to wear, instantly warm, quick-drying and reasonably windproof. During the last part of the walk, which took place in September and October, I wore them in camp as evening and morning temperatures were always below freezing, and as I was in bear country I couldn't cook and eat in the tent. During the last ten days I wore them for walking as well, finding that they stood up to the wind quite well and were not too hot when blizzards forced me to wear overtrousers on top. My pair have two open front pockets and an elasticated waist, but current models have zipped pockets. My only reservation about them is that the material doesn't stretch, which is why I don't wear them for skiing, but the cut is generous enough for this not to matter when walking.

Alternatives to the Ultrafleece trousers might include the Buffalo Pertex-covered pile trousers which I haven't used, but which are bulkier and heavier (though still only 450g/16oz and you wouldn't have to carry overtrousers as well), and probably warmer. Lined polycotton and synthetic trousers are a possibility too and have the advantage of being fully windproof. Rohan and Craghoppers both make polycotton trousers lined with microfibres (Insuflex-lined Winter Bags and Isodry lined Thermo-Trails at 625 and 540g/22 and 19oz respectively), both of which I've tried and found too hot for walking in all but the severest sub-zero weather. They're nice for wearing in camp, however. Better (that is covering a wider temperature range) were the Rohan Warm Bags (520g/18oz), lined with the thermal polyester Dryline, but again these are no longer available. I still wear mine occasionally on winter walks and I have friends who sorely lament their passing. Patagonia's Capilene Pants with Shell (448g/16oz, the shell is nylon) could well be an adequate substitute, however, as could Abris's Jura Plus polycotton trousers with brushed polyester lining. There seem to be few other warm trousers around other than pile ones, so the choice is limited. Wool or wool-mixture ones used to be common. Indeed my first winter walking trousers were made of Derby Tweed. Although warm, they were heavy and itchy and soaked up rain. When wet they would rub my inner thighs raw and take days to dry out. After my first weekend in Super Striders I never wore them again. Perhaps it's not surprising that wool trousers are now hard to find.

For really severe weather, down-filled trousers are available. I've never been out in conditions anywhere near cold enough to warrant even considering these, but in case you do it's worth knowing they exist. Unsurprisingly there isn't a wide choice. RAB make down salopettes (900g/2lb), as do Mountain Equipment, who also make down trousers, both available with Gore-tex shells. The North Face catalogue offers Lhotse Side Zipped Down Pants (750g/26oz) and the Marmot one Down Pants (540g/19oz) and 8000 Metre Pants (935g/33oz). The last have as much goose down in them as the lightest down sleeping bags! I expect there's more available if you look. I suppose you could even use a pair along with a down jacket instead of a sleeping bag. The only person I know who ever owned a pair, Chris Ainsworth (who was given them secondhand) was unable to see a use for them so he had them remade as a down jacket. Vapour-barrier trousers worn over long-johns and under fleece or pile and shell trousers would probably prove as warm as down ones. Whenever I've worn VB trousers, usually just under polycotton trousers, for walking I've almost instantly overheated though I have found them useful for campwear and for sleeping in, and would certainly consider them for any trip where weight was a real problem or the likelihood of needing warm trousers was remote but

enough of a possibility to make me want to carry something.

HATS

Although the percentages quoted differ (anything from 20 to 75 per cent) it's generally agreed that a large amount of heat is lost from the head if it is unprotected. In order for the brain to function efficiently the blood supply to the head is constant, regardless of conditions. The capillaries that lie just below the skin do not close down to conserve heat as they do on other extremities like the hands and feet. Hence it is essential to protect your head in order to stay warm. 'If you want warm feet, put on a hat' may be something of a cliché but it is nevertheless true. It's also true that if you start to feel hot the first item of clothing you should remove is your hat.

Traditionally walkers and mountaineers have worn thick woolly balaclava helmets, rolled up to form hats in milder weather, pulled down in storms. I wore one when I began backpacking but found it too hot much of the time and also unbearably itchy on my forehead, so it's many years since I last possessed a woollen balaclava. Pile and fleece ones are available now which don't itch but which aren't windproof and, when worn under a hood, are rather too warm, at least for me.

Instead of one thick balaclava I carry a number of thinner hats, adopting the layer principle for my headwear. The base layer and the one I carry all year round is a simple knitted hat (bob hat, watch cap and, in Canada, tuque are other names). Every outdoor shop offers a selection of these in synthetic fabrics, usually acrylic, or wool, and in various colours and patterns, and I now own several in differing thicknesses, the lightest weighing 50g/2oz, the heaviest 80g/3oz. I prefer the synthetic ones over wool as I find they dry more quickly when wet and keep their shape better, though both types eventually stretch and need a hot wash to shrink them back to size. Having said that, I've just bought, though not yet worn, an REI Ragg wool hat with polypropylene lining (80g/3oz) that I suspect just might become my favourite warm hat. Pile and fleece ones can be found too but like the balaclavas I doubt whether they are very windproof.

Most of the time a knitted hat is all I need to keep my head warm. In winter and cold weather and on long trips, when I like to have a spare hat in case I lose one (as I did on the Canadian Rockies walk when I foolishly tucked it into my pack hipbelt rather than a pocket when I removed it whilst bushwhacking, only to discover it had been plucked away by the vegetation when I stopped to camp), I also carry a headover or neck gaiter. This is a tube of material that can be pulled over the head to form a thick collar or scarf and also worn as a balaclava and even rolled up to make a hat. I have both a Best wool one and a Survival Aids polypro one (130 and 70g/4½ and 2½oz respectively), though I find I use the latter most of the time as it's not as warm as the former in which I tend to overheat. Worn in conjunction with a knitted hat it provides the same protection as a full-weight balaclava whilst not feeling as bulky or restrictive. Headovers are also available in silk which is probably excellent and pile which would I think be too warm for me. Thin balaclavas made from polypro, chlorofibre, Capilene or silk are popular with some people but I prefer headovers as they can be worn as hat, balaclava and neck-warmer rather than as just the first two. I know people though who wear a thin balaclava instead of a knitted hat and carry a headover as well.

As I don't like hoods on my warmwear, whether pile or down, I usually carry a third hat in winter for wearing at stops and in camp. This is a Lowe pile-lined, peaked Gore-tex cap with ear flaps. The weight is 100g/3½oz. It's very warm and weather-resistant making it ideal for below-freezing temperatures, especially if it's windy. I've hardly ever worn it whilst on the move but I was glad of it during a ski ascent of the Hardangerjokullen ice cap in Norway, when I wore it under my Sympatex jacket hood and over a polypro headover in a bitter and strong wind, and was still barely warm enough. There are many caps of similar design available, of which Outdoor Research's Hat For All Seasons looks good as the pile lining is removable from the Gore-tex shell so both can be worn separately. A waterproof outer isn't necessary though; a much cheaper and just as functional option is Helly-Hansen's nylon-covered pile Helly Hat. Down versions exist too, one of which I bought many years ago. It's too hot however and with the ear flaps down it cuts out all sound, so I never use it.

As well as keeping you warm, hats can keep you cool and many people wear brimmed hats of cotton, felt, wool or other fabrics as protection against the sun. I've tried doing so but found that I feel hotter under such hats than without them, perhaps because I have a thick head of hair. If it thins as I grow older I might well discover the advantages of shading my head from the sun. Instead I prefer simply to use a cotton bandanna as a sweatband and to seek shade when I stop if it's searingly hot. If soaked in cold water a bandanna headband keeps you very cool as the moisture evaporates. A friend of mine resorts to the old handkerchief knotted at the corners idea if he feels his head growing too warm. However sun hats are needed by many people and there is a large choice. Light colours would seem appropriate as these should reflect the heat and be cooler than dark ones but I can't speak from experience. Even when crossing the Mohave Desert and the deserts of New Mexico in baking temperatures I didn't wear a sun hat.

The above was written before I went to the Yukon where I found a hat was essential, not just to keep off the sun, which in July was painfully hot (hotter than I remember it being in a the desert), but also to keep leaves and twigs out of my hair when bushwhacking and to hold a head net in place when the bugs were bad. It was for this last reason that I decided to take a hat but I left for Canada without one, having failed to find a model that felt comfortable for even a few seconds in a shop. Then in Whitehorse I discovered the Canadian-made Tilley Hat. This is a cotton duck hat with a wide brim and a fairly high crown somewhat reminiscent of an Australian bush hat. The instructions (it comes with a detailed leaflet!) say the fit should be loose, the double cords for the chin and the back of the head are used to hold it in place in windy weather. This I find is the key to comfort. With space in the crown and no tight sweaty line across my forehead I discovered I actually liked wearing the Tilley Hat, so much so that I wore it when I didn't really need to, finding that it warded off light showers and was far less restrictive than a jacket hood and that sprayed with insect repellent it kept bugs off my face without the use of the head net. The weight is 125g/4½oz and the hat comes with a lifetime guarantee. Certainly mine, although very battered-looking, is in good condition after a summer's hard usage. The colour of my Tilley

Hat is 'natural' (i.e. off-white) but brown ones are available for those who want something darker. Having looked at and tried on many hats over the years, I'm glad to have found the Tilley, which I think is vastly superior to anything else available.

GLOVES & MITTS

Cold hands are not only painful and unpleasant but they make doing even the simplest task such as opening the pack or unwrapping a granola bar very difficult. As with hats I adopt the layer system for gloves and mitts, finding several layers more adaptable than one thick one. Except at the height of summer I always carry at least one pair of gloves. So-called liner or inner gloves of a synthetic wicking material such as polypro or Capilene are ideal. They are thin enough to wear whilst doing things like pitching the tent or taking photographs, yet they keep the hands surprisingly warm and at around 28g/1oz a pair are hardly noticeable when in the pack. They don't last long if worn regularly, though, and I go through at least one pair every winter, finally abandoning them when the holes become too big. Wool and silk versions are available, which may be more durable though probably not as quick-drying, which is one of the reasons I prefer synthetics.

In really cold weather liner gloves aren't warm enough so I wear a pair of wool mitts over them. Mitts are warmer than gloves as the fingers are kept together and don't have to be warmed separately. As the only purpose of this layer is to keep the hands warm it seems to make sense to wear mitts. I bought my wool mitts in Iceland and they are very warm even when wet, and quite wind-resistant. They weigh 120g/4oz. Now that I've treated them with TX.10, they don't absorb much moisture and dry fairly quickly. The Dachstein mitts found in most outdoor shops are effectively the same. Pile and fleece mitts are available too but unless they are covered they aren't windproof. I've tried Gore-tex shelled ones but find them too bulky and inflexible and often too warm. I may buy some nylon covered ones though, such as Helly-Hansen's Polar Mittens, which are much lighter and softer, as alternatives to the wool ones for my next long walk.

In really bitter stormy weather when my hands aren't warm enough in the wool mitts I also wear a pair of Gore-tex overmitts. Mine are Lowe ones with a rough grip material on the inner side for holding on to ice axes and ski poles and two velcro-closed straps for tightening them over sleeves. These straps are designed to be done up with mitts on so when you've put on one mitt you don't find it impossible to put on the other, as you do with mitts that have elasticated closures. The Lowe overmitts weigh 150g/5¼oz. They work well but I find that three layers feels very bulky and restrictive, which is why I am considering buying the Polar Mittens in the hope that they'll replace the two outer layers. The fact that they're not waterproof doesn't matter as they should be warm when wet and quick- drying. My interest in them has been stirred by a couple of ski tours I've done in Norway with Chris Ainsworth on which he wore cheap unbranded nylon covered pile mitts which kept his hands very warm. They were at least as effective and far simpler to use than the three-layer systems the rest of us wore. (Note: in fact for the Yukon walk, I bought some Field & Trek Polarmitts (80g/3oz) which I only wore in the blizzards of the last few days, though then they were essential. They were warm even when wet, and I could well use them as my standard mitts for all but the most severe weather.)

I've made up my own set of gloves and mitts from separate sources but many companies now offer mitt systems consisting of inner gloves, pile or fleece mitts and breathable overmitts (usually Gore-tex, though there are some Cyclone ones around and I expect Sympatex will appear soon). If you need to buy mitts and gloves together these could be worth looking at. One point in their favour is that the component parts are designed to fit on top of each other.

Because of the bulk and lack of feel when wearing three layers, I've tried insulated alpine ski gloves for ski touring. I have a pair of Gates Thinsulate-lined Gore-tex ones (175g/6oz), which are warm and allow good dexterity. However I'm on my third pair, having taken two back to the shop because they split at the base of the fingers. I doubt whether this third pair will prove any better, as I've seen other similar gloves tear in the same way. By the end of a six-week ski tour in the Canadian Rockies a companion's brand new pair of pile-lined gloves were split along several seams, whereas my three-layer system was completely intact. The number of seams and curves in padded gloves is so great that making them durable seems highly difficult. Simple mitt designs, on the other hand, have little to go wrong with them.

Losing a mitt or a glove in bad weather can have serious consequences. I once dropped a wool mitt I'd tucked under my arm whilst getting something out of my pack. Before I could grab it, it was whisked away by the wind to disappear into the grey, snow-filled sky. Luckily I was about to descend into the warmth of the valley which was only a short distance away. Even so my hand, clad in just a liner glove, was very cold by the time I reached shelter. Since then I've adopted two precautions. One is to attach wrist loops (often called 'idiot loops') to my mitts so that they stay attached when I take them off. I use thin elastic shock cord for this. Many mitts now come with attachments for wrist loops, while some, like my Lowe overmitts, come with loops as well. On my Icelandic wool mitts I simply pushed the shock cord through the wool about 2cm/$\frac{3}{4}$in from the cuff. The other precaution I take, unless weight is a serious problem, is to carry a spare pair of mitts or gloves. I do this particularly on ski tours where it's inadvisable to travel with your hands in your pockets.

If all else fails, spare socks can be worn on your hands. I used this ploy at the end of the Canadian Rockies walk during a bitterly cold blizzard when my hands weren't warm enough in liner gloves and wool mitts. With thick socks added my hands went from achingly cold to comfortably warm, not to say hot. Unfortunately if your feet are cold the reverse procedure is not possible!

BANDANNAS
Barely an article of clothing, though this seems the best place to discuss it, the bandanna is an essential piece of equipment. This 28-g/1-oz square of cotton acts as headband, brow wiper, handkerchief, pot-holder, dishcloth, flannel, towel and neck shader (when tucked under another bandanna worn as a headband or a sun hat). I usually carry two, keeping one threaded through one of the loops on my pack shoulder straps so I can use it to wipe sweat off my face whenever necessary. I rinse my bandannas out frequently, tying them on to the back of the pack to dry. Before I first went backpacking in the USA I used large handkerchiefs rather than bandannas, as I'd never found the real thing in

Britain. But isn't a bandanna just a large handkerchief anyway? Yes, except that it's a very large handkerchief, larger than any I've found in Britain. So whenever I visit North America I return with a fresh supply of bandannas. However, I have seen some on sale in the Pyrenees recently so perhaps they'll be available in British outdoor shops before too long.

CARRYING CLOTHES
Nylon stuffsacs are the ideal containers for most clothing, especially compressible down- and synthetic-insulated items. Weights run from 28 to 110g/1–4oz depending on size and thickness of material—thin ones are fine for use inside the pack. I usually carry all my spare clothing in a stuffsac in the lower compartment of my pack with my down jacket, if carried, in its own stuffsac inside the larger one for extra protection. Dirty clothing usually languishes in a plastic bag at the very bottom of the pack. Waterproofs and clothing I may need during the day (windshirt, warm top, etc.) moves around according to how much space I have, sometimes living at the very top of the pack, at others at the front of the lower compartment. They are always accessible though. I don't pack these garments in stuffsacs but use them to fill out empty spaces in the pack. Head- and handwear lives in a pack pocket, usually the top one, or in the bumbag if I expect to need it during the day.

TREATMENT AND CARE
At home I simply follow the washing instructions that should be sewn into every garment. These need to be noted carefully, as many fabrics that are tough in the field can easily be damaged by washing them at the wrong temperature, by spinning or by using the wrong washing powder or a fabric conditioner. I've shrunk enough synthetic underwear over the years to ensure that I now read labels fully. Fabrics like polypro and other synthetics and pile and fleece work best if they're kept as clean as possible. However, certain others can be damaged by too much washing. This is especially so with down, which is reckoned to lose a little of its loft and therefore its warmth every time it's washed, and to some extent with wool, which loses natural oils. I sponge dirty marks off the shells of down garments but have never washed one, and would only do so if it reaches the stage where the down has formed hard balls

and no longer keeps me warm. I don't like washing waterproof garments either, as I suspect that doing so shortens their life too. Again, bad stains can be sponged off if you're bothered.

Special down and breathable waterproof soaps are available and Nikwax make a shampoo called Loft for wool, down, polyester and waterproof materials, which leaves the water-repellent qualities intact. They recommend it for their Paramo clothing and also for Gore-tex. I've used it and it seems to work. I avoid harsh detergents anyway, using Ecover washing powder, which doesn't strip away water-repellent treatments and natural oils or harm the environment.

Most outdoor clothes can be stored flat in drawers, but down- and synthetic-filled garments should be kept on hangers so that the fills can loft (i.e. expand). Prolonged compression can damage them. It's worth checking zips and fastenings before garments are put away. It's irritating to say the least to discover as you're hastily packing for a trip that a zip needs replacing or a button sewing back on.

On a walk, garment care is minimal and in cold and wet weather non-existent. On trips of a week or less I never wash anything; on longer ones I rinse out underwear, socks and, if they are very grubby, other items every week or so if it's sunny enough for them to dry quickly. This shouldn't be done in a stream or lake of course, but in a cooking pot using water from your large camp water container. I don't use soap for this—removing sweat and debris is the aim, not producing stain-free garments. A length of cord strung between two bushes makes a washing line or garments can be hung on the back of the pack whilst walking. On walks lasting more than a few weeks town stops usually occur, if only to pick up supplies, and where there are towns there are launderettes. I generally wash everything whenever I find a launderette, keeping just my waterproof overtrousers to wear. For that reason I don't like carrying fabrics like silk that require special care. I want everything to go in a 40 °/105 °F or 50 °C/125 °F wash together and then be able to stand up to tumble-drying on a high heat afterwards.

Clothing performance, especially with regard to water-repellency, falls off with use. There are various products available that can restore this to some degree and even some that improve it. Nikwax have been the leader in this field in recent years with their Texnik and TX.10 products. The first is a spray (pump-action not aerosol—Nikwax point out that even CFC-free aerosols contain dangerous, usually inflammable, substances) for non-breathable coated nylons. I haven't used it so I can't say how effective it is. I do know people who've used it to coat maps however, and they have been very pleased with the results.

TX.10 is a 'total immersion waterproofing' which is to say you soak the garments in it, either in a bucket or by putting them through a washing machine cycle using TX.10 instead of powder. It's suitable for wool, polyester and down. TX.10-proofed garments are said to absorb less moisture and dry faster without losing any breathability, and I've certainly found this to be so with my wool mitts which have been TX.10 treated, and to a lesser extent (because I think it was fairly water-resistant anyway) with my Ultrafleece sweater. I also treated a very old well-worn double polycotton jacket that had never been very water-resistant, and found that it kept out heavy rain for an hour or so rather than the few minutes it had before. I intend eventually to proof my wool socks and other polycotton clothing, as I'm convinced enough that TX.10 improves performance to feel it's worth doing. It shouldn't be used on all garments though, so you should check the maker's instructions. Hamish Hamilton for example recommends that no treatment of any sort is applied to his Buffalo clothing, as he says it increases the likelihood of condensation occurring.

Other similar sprays and treatments are available, particularly from Grangersol who have their own total-immersion waterproofing called Super-Pel plus well-established sprays such as Fabsil and Nylopruf, and one called Superproof for restoring the water-repellency of the outside of breathable fabrics. Edelrid do a range of soaps for washing down and synthetic insulations, whilst the makers of Ventile make a special reproofing fluid for that fabric. Many garment-makers offer their own treatments too. REI also have their own compounds for washing breathable waterproof fabrics (Revive II), down and synthetic insulations (Loft II), and polypro and silk (Refresh). I must say though that I use none of these. Only TX.10 seems to offer enough improvement to make me bother doing anything other than wash my clothing.

Shelter:
Camping in the Wilderness

Silence. A ragged edge of pine trees, black against a starry sky. Beyond, the white slash of a snowslope on the distant mountainside. A cocooned figure stirs, stretches. A head emerges from the warm depths, looks round in wonderment then slumps back to sleep. Hours pass. The stars move. An animal cry slices through the quiet, lonely and wild. A faint line of red light appears in the east as the sky lightens and a faint breeze ripples the grasses. The figure moves again, sits up, still huddled in the sleeping bag, then pulls on a shirt. A hand reaches out and the faint crack of a match being struck rings round the clearing. A light flares up then a sudden roar breaks the stillness. A pan is placed on to the blue ring of the stove's flame. The figure draws back into its shelter, waiting for the first hot drink and watching the dawn as the stars fade slowly away and the strengthening sun turns the black shadows into rocks and, farther away, cliffs, every detail sharp and bright in the warm light. The trees turn green again as warm golden shafts of sunlight slide through on to the silent figure. Another day in the wilderness has begun.

Nights like that and others when the wind rattles the tent and the rain pounds down are what distinguishes backpacking from day walking and from touring from hut to hut, hostel to hostel or hotel to hotel. Only by staying out in the forests and mountains, the deserts and moorlands, is it possible really to experience nature, to live in the wilderness instead of escaping back to the confining, restricting comfortable barriers we have constructed to keep out the earth. On all my walks I seek those precious moments when I feel part of the world around me, when I merge with the trees and hills. Such times come most often and last longest when I spend several days and nights living in the wilderness.

The modern backpacker uses nylon tents and high-tech sleeping systems to stay warm and dry but anyone who thinks these act as barriers against the wilderness has never lain in a tiny, flimsy tent listening to the wind roaring down the valley and waiting for the next gust to shake the fabric, wondering if this time it will be torn apart leaving the user face to face with the storm.

Shelter is needed to protect the backpacker against cold, wind and rain and also insects and in some places the sun. What shelter is needed depends on the type of terrain, the time of year and how spartan you are prepared to be. Some people like to sleep in a tent every night whatever the weather, others regard them as for the worst conditions only. Robert Peary, the first man to reach the North Pole, never used a tent or a sleeping bag but slept out in his furs curled up beside his sledge. Most mortals however require a little more shelter than that! In order of the protection they provide, the forms of shelter are bivouac bags, tarps, tents and huts and bothies, with snowholes as a winter option.

BIVOUAC BAGS

Sleeping out under the stars is the ideal way of spending a night in the wilderness. With no barrier between you and the natural world you have come to be part of, you can experience directly the sights and sounds of the night. The last things you see before you fall asleep are the stars and the dark edges of trees and hills. Then at dawn you wake to the rising sun and can lie watching the return of colour and the waking of the world. Often these are the most magical times of the day, lost to those sealed in a tent.

All too often of course the weather is not so kind, and even if it is fine when you fall asleep, it can be the cold feel of raindrops on your face at four in the morning instead of the first rays of the sun that wakes you. The simplest way of dealing with such changes of weather is with a bivouac or bivi bag. Basically this is a simple waterproof envelope into which you slip your sleeping bag when the weather turns wet or windy.

In case of emergencies the heavy-duty plastic bivi bags available from most outdoor shops and weighing 300–400g/10–14oz are better than nothing, but they are open at the head end and, being non-breathable, retain condensation which soaks back into your sleeping bag. Many years ago I used a down-filled sleeping bag in one of these on a wet night in a conifer forest and had one of the most uncomfortable nights out I've ever spent. I can still clearly remember waking frequently to find my sleeping bag becoming soggier and soggier from both condensation and the rain that seeped in at the open end. Dawn was very welcome and I've never used such a bivi bag since, though I often carry one on day walks just in case of an unplanned night out. Lightweight versions for emergency use only exist. I have a Survival Aids one weighing just 100g/3½oz that comes in a sealed foil pouch. It's made from such thin polythene that I doubt whether it would last more than one night at most, so I only take it on trips when I don't expect to need to bivouac but when, if the unexpected happened, such a bag would be better than nothing. I note from the label that it can also be used 'to make an equipment bag, flotation aid, desert still or dewtrap' and that the label itself can be peeled off the pouch and used as a waterproof patch. Also available are thin, lightweight metallised 'space blankets' which I particularly do not recommend

as they tear easily and are hard to wrap round yourself in windy weather. They may be fine for wrapping round the shoulders of runners at the end of road marathons, but they are useless for protecting shivering walkers benighted in a mountain storm.

My night out in the plastic bivi bag occurred before the advent of Gore-tex and other breathable fabrics, and caused me to give up bivouacking except in perfect weather, and even then only with a tent to hand. Now however there is a large selection of breathable bivi bags available and these work well. Most of them are made from Gore-tex, though Sympatex ones are starting to appear. The cheapest have polyurethane-proofed undersides, not necessarily a disadvantage if you place your sleeping mat inside the bag. All have hoods of some sort, closed either with a zip or drawcord, and the bigger ones will also hold some of your gear. Weights depend mostly on how simple or complex the entrance is and run from 450 to 790g/16–28oz. Ones with vertical, diagonal or curved zips or even arm openings like the REI Cyclops Bivy Sack (790g/28oz) are only worth considering if you intend bivouacking regularly. Straight-across zips or draw-cord closed entrances are adequate for occasional use. Any shelter that has a pole or poles I regard as a tent, including the very smallest ones, which often appear in catalogues as 'hooped bivis'.

The practical as opposed to aesthetic advantages of bivouacking are a light pack and the ability to sleep in many places where a tent couldn't be pitched, such as in the lee of a boulder, on a mountain top or under the shelter of a spreading tree. However, although a good bivi bag will keep out rain and wind there are still problems when you don't want to be cocooned in it, particularly when cooking. Even if the weather is good, biting insects can make bivouacking a nightmare—although some bags do come with insect netting. Indeed one, the Survival Aids Gore-tex Cobra (780g/28oz), comes with a wide netting mouth the top of which can be suspended from a branch so that you can lie inside without fabric touching your face. Overall though, unless the night will be calm and dry (how cold doesn't matter) and insect-free, I prefer to sleep in a tent and be able to cook, eat, read, write and contemplate the world outside in comfort. This doesn't mean I never carry or use a bivi bag though, as there are situations, even when tent camping, when one can come in useful.

The bag I've used most is a Survival Aids Gore-tex Bivi Bag with a simple horizontal zipped entrance covered by a flap. It weighs 540g/19oz and once kept me dry in a down sleeping bag during several hours of heavy rain—after I'd realised that to prevent leakage through the zip it should be below rather than above me. That was several years ago. I now rarely carry it on summer trips, simply transferring to the tent if the weather changes when I'm sleeping out. In winter I sometimes use it inside my tent to keep off condensation drips and for extra warmth—I've found a bivi bag adds several degrees to the range of a sleeping bag. I used one for these reasons on the Pacific Crest Trail walk on the colder and wetter nights, and the system worked well, allowing me to carry a light sleeping bag that wasn't too hot on warmer nights. I've also used it when snowholing to keep off drips from the roof and in damp bothies. Now eight years old, the bag isn't as waterproof as it once was, and I wouldn't like to rely on it again on a wet night. I haven't replaced it though, but instead use the Sympatex/pu bivi bag section of my Bivvybug Niche tent, even though it has only a drawcord-closed top and no hood, as this is adequate for the usage I put a bivi bag to. The weight is 560g/20oz. On the rare occasions when I intend to sleep out without at least having a tent nearby in case of bad weather, I now prefer to use a Buffalo Pertex/pile sleeping bag rather than a bivi bag, because of its greater efficiency.

TARPS

Constructing your own shelter from sheets of plastic or nylon (tarps) and cord is something hardly any backpacker does these days. Lightweight tents are far more appealing providing, as they do, much greater protection against wind, rain and insects and being usable in places where there is no attachment for a tarp within sight. This is to be welcomed as, properly used, tents also have less impact on the land. In particular they are too valuable to be left behind, unlike plastic sheeting, torn bits of which can all too often be found littering the wilderness—especially since the growth in 'survivalism', which has led to a return to shelter building with no matching commitment to no-trace techniques. Since even when they are carried out

plastic sheets are still a waste problem, my own view is they should not be used at all.

Tarps do still have a use though in those parts of the world where problems with bears mean that you shouldn't eat or store food in your tent. On both the Canadian Rockies and Yukon walks I carried a 360 x 360cm/12 x 12ft sheet of proofed ripstop nylon with grommets for attaching guylines along each side, to use as a kitchen shelter in wet and windy weather. I used it enough for it to be worth its 450g/16oz. In bad weather I erected it as soon as I stopped so that I could shelter under it whilst I donned extra clothes and unpacked the rest of my gear. On the many occasions that I made camp in cold, wet, windy weather, the protection it provided whilst I cooked and ate was essential. I usually pitched it as lean-to, slung between two trees on a length of cord, but on occasion I made more complex structures, using fallen trees and branches as makeshift poles. On sites where there were picnic tables I found I could string the tarp over a table and have a sheltered sitting and eating area.

Whilst catalogues and shops are packed with tents, lightweight tarps are now hard to find. Mine was specially made up for me. Anyone with a sewing machine could make one in no time by buying a sheet of nylon, hemming it and adding a few grommets for guylines and pegs. The only ones I've seen on offer recently that look worth considering are the Survival Aids Basha, a 432 x 324cm/14 x 10½ft sheet of proofed nylon with eight border loops and one central one that weighs 600g/21oz, and the Outdoor Products range of coated nylon ones, the smallest of which weighs 625g/22oz and measures 215 x 275cm/7 x 9ft. Otherwise most of those available seem to be reinforced polyethylene ones. As the lightest of these weighs 675g/24oz yet measures only 180 x 240cm/6 x 8ft—barely adequate for solo use—I wouldn't recommend one for any but the shortest trip. The one advantage they have is that they are very cheap.

GROUNDSHEETS

When sleeping out, with or without a bivi bag or tarp, a groundsheet is useful, especially if the ground is wet, both to protect the sleeping bag and to spread out items that need to be kept clean and dry. I also carry a groundsheet when I'm using basic mountain huts or bothies, as the floors in these are often wet and muddy, and when I sleep in a snowhole. I used to use one under the floor of my tent in order to prolong the life of the latter, but I no longer do so, as the materials used for tent floors are much more durable than they used to be.

Most of the groundsheets offered in outdoor shops and catalogues are designed for car camping and are far too heavy for carrying in a pack. Polythene sheets are much lighter but they don't last long, also a disadvantage of the orange plastic survival bags many people use as groundsheets. Such materials cannot be pegged to the ground either, which is necessary if it's windy. Proofed nylon can be used but is relatively expensive and heavier weights are needed than for tarps if it is to last long. I've not seen nylon groundsheets in stores or catalogues so you'd probably have to buy a sheet of it and make your own.

The best ready-made groundsheets I've come across are the laminated aluminised polyethylene, polyester and fibre-glass sheets that are available from time to time in various thicknesses and weights. They are identifiable by being blue or red on one side and silver on the other. Don't confuse them with the similar-looking but thin and useless 'space blankets' that are often stacked with them in shops. The latter won't last one night as a groundsheet without tearing. The blue one I currently have measures 128 x 200cm/4 x 6½ft, weighs 500g/17oz and is grommeted at each corner and sold under the name Sportsman's Blanket. Lighter ones (340g/12oz) sold as All Weather Blankets are available but I've found them less durable. Both types are far superior to plastic sheeting however. I've found that they tend to crack and then leak at the fold points (they come ready-folded) long before they are punctured or torn by use. When I replace the one I have, which is near the end of its life, I intend rolling the new one rather than folding it to see if it lasts longer. You can use one of these blankets as a tarp in an emergency, though they are a bit small for this. One occasion when mine proved useful in this capacity was during a prolonged thunderstorm in Yellowstone National Park in the Rockies, when I wasn't carrying a full-sized tarp but didn't want to cook in my tent, because of bears, or to sit outside in the cold storm. So I slung my Sportsman's Blanket, carried as a groundsheet for when I slept out under the stars, between two trees as a lean-to and used my pack as a seat under it while I cooked and ate and watched the lightning flashes light up the forest and the rain bouncing off the sodden earth. I've used one of these blankets as a sunshade too, silver side out, when resting in shadeless desert.

TENTS

For most backpackers most of the time, shelter means a tent. A tent provides more protection from the weather than a bivi bag. What a tent gives is space: the space to sit up, cook and eat in comfort, read, make notes, sort out gear, play cards and watch the world outside. In a tent you can relax at the end of a hard day, whatever the weather.

Selecting the right tent isn't easy though, as they come in all shapes and sizes and there is a multitude of models. It's made harder because few shops have the space to display many tents, and there are therefore limited opportunities for seeing a variety of models pitched and being able to crawl in and out of them and assess how well each one suits your needs. There are public tent displays in various places in many countries (the biggest is held in Holland in September), but most people cannot get to these. Good advice in a shop, and a study of the catalogues and magazines, is therefore very useful. However, this can lead to confusion unless you know what you are looking for, so before a choice is made some questions need to be answered. When and where will it be used? How many must it sleep? How critical is weight? The answers should help you narrow the field to just a few models, after which price and personal choice (How do you feel about the colour? Is the shape attractive?) come into play. Hopefully the discussion below of how tents work and what features and designs to look for will help.

A tent's main purpose is to protect the occupants from wind, rain and snow. To do this it must be wind- and waterproof. For wilderness use it must also be light and low in bulk when packed, whilst having the strength and durability to cope with severe weather. To achieve this the material a tent is made from is very important.

The Condensation Problem

Tents have the same problem as shell clothing which is to repel rain whilst letting condensation out. Although they don't have to cope with

Wintergear Sapphire/Blizzard elongated geodesic dome.

vast outpourings of sweat, they do have to deal with the moisture constantly given off by the human body, which over the period of a night amounts to a lot of liquid and to which may be added that from the drying out of wet clothes and the steam from cooking. As with clothing, there is no perfect solution. In tents the problem is usually minimised by having two layers or skins, a breathable non-waterproof inner and a sealed waterproof outer or flysheet. The theory is that moisture passes through the inner fabric and is then carried away by the flow of air circulating between the two layers. If condensation does occur it will be on the flysheet and it will run down the latter on to the ground, any drips being repelled by the inner. To some extent this works. However, moist air is only carried away if there is a breeze and if it can escape. As warm air rises the ideal way to do this is to have a vent high up on the flysheet so that a chimney effect is created whereby cool dry air is sucked in under the bottom edge of the flysheet and damp air is pushed out at the top. Few tents have vents though, as it's hard to make these waterproof. But many have two-way door zips, and I always leave at least the top few inches of these open unless rain starts coming in through the gap. If it's a choice between protection and condensation I close up the tent, and let the flysheet become soaked. To prevent this moisture reaching the inner tent, it's important that the gap between it and the flysheet is big enough so that a wind cannot push the two together.

Condensation is worst in calm, humid conditions when, even if all the doors are left open, you can wake to find streams of water running down the flysheet. Nothing can prevent this

except sleeping under the open sky. I once woke on a misty night to find drips falling on me from the tarp, open on three sides, under which I was sleeping. Where insects are a problem, as in Scotland during the summer, I've sometimes felt as though my tent was turning into a sauna as I've cooked inside the vestibule with all the doors shut tightly, producing clouds of steam that promptly condensed on the flysheet. Being warm and damp is preferable to be eaten alive, however!

A more serious problem occurs in below-freezing temperatures, as then the inner tent can become so cold that moisture condenses on it and then drips back on to the sleeper below. If this happens it's better if it becomes even colder so that such moisture freezes—something I have had happen. Again ventilation provides a partial cure, weather permitting.

Double-walled Tent Fabrics

Most two-skin tents are made of nylon or polyester and these are undoubtedly the best fabric, having all the properties outlined above. Cotton, the traditional tent material, has too low a tear strength at the weights needed to make really lightweight tents. The few all-cotton models that are available are in traditional styles and start at around 5kg/11lb in weight, which is fine for base camps or where you have porters, but not for the backpacker. Very fine cotton is sometimes used for the inner for tents with nylon flysheets and some people prefer it, saying it helps reduce condensation and feels pleasant. Even the lightest cotton inners are heavier than nylon ones though, and they absorb condensation, which makes them even heavier, especially as they then take a long time to dry. Also if you brush against a wet cotton inner you will get damp and perhaps cause a drip.

Unproofed nylon inners, in contrast, absorb no moisture, dry quickly and are very light. Ones designed for warm-weather use have mesh panels for ventilation whilst keeping out insects. On any tent that may be used where insects are a problem, a mesh as well as a solid door panel is useful, as it performs the same function. Flysheets may be polyurethane or elastomer silicone-coated. Both keep out the rain. Weights for both inner and outer nylons are in the 30–60-g-per-square-metre / 1–2-oz-per-square-yard range, the lighter ones needing slightly more care than the heavier, though all are quite tough. Flysheet seams may leak unless sealed, which can be done with a tube of adhesive sealant—available under various names from most outdoor shops. Many tents now come with fully taped seams whilst some that don't, such as those from The North Face, come with sealant.

Breathable Fabric Tents

Breathable fabrics are used to combat condensation in tents as in clothing and there are many Gore-Tex models available. They have the advantage of being easy to pitch, as there is only one layer, but there are limitations to their performance. In order to maximise the breathability of the material, they are usually small tunnels or domes—in larger tents breathable fabrics don't seem to work at all. I used a Gore-tex tent (a Wintergear Eyrie cross-over pole dome, no longer available) on the Pacific Crest Trail, a walk that lasted five and a half months, so I have a good idea of how they work. In the snowbound High Sierras where the temperature fell to around −10 °C/14 °F every night and the humidity was very low, I had no problems with condensation whereas my companions in two-skin tents found their flysheets frozen solid each morning. However in wet weather, which I had on many nights in the Washington Cascades in September, I found condensation a real problem with moisture running down the taped seams of the tent and forming pools on the groundsheet. On many rainy mornings I had to pack the tent wet and then pitch it still sodden in the evening, by which time the moisture had spread all over the groundsheet. I kept my down sleeping bag dry by sleeping in a Gore-tex bivi bag inside the tent. Although in theory Gore-tex works on the variation in pressure between the inside and the outside of the material I found that it made no difference to the levels of condensation, whether I closed the tent doors or not; the condensation related solely to the outside humidity level.

I have not rejected Gore-tex tents, however, but still use one on short trips when the forecast is good, or on longer ones in areas where prolonged wet weather and high humidity are unlikely. Six months before writing this I went on a two-week walk in the eastern Pyrénées. I took my Gore-tex Phoenix Phreerunner tent and never once had a drop of condensation inside. However I wouldn't use a Gore-tex tent on a serious winter trip after what happened on a ski crossing of the vast Columbia Icefield in the Canadian Rockies. We had two similarly sized tunnel tents, one a two-skin model, the other Gore-tex. Instead of four days our crossing took eight because of blizzards, and we spent several days trapped in the tents. The two of us in the two-skin tent stayed warm and comfortable, if bored. The condensation that formed on the flysheet and in patches on the inner at night mostly dried out during the day. Conditions meant that communication between the two tent groups was minimal, so I was shocked to discover, when we finally descended from the icefield and made camp in the shelter of the forest, that the pair in the Gore-tex tent had had a rough time and that their down sleeping bags were wet with condensation and barely providing any insulation. Their tent, they said, had been sodden inside and constantly dripping on them since the first night.

Groundsheets

Tent groundsheets are made from nylon, and they vary from 60–100g/2–3½oz per square yard pu-coated ones—the lightest but least durable—to PVC ones at 230g per square metre/8oz per square yard for really long life but a heavy pack weight. Medium-weight Neoprene ones at 115g per square metre/4oz per square yard are perhaps the best compromise between weight and toughness. Not so long ago pu groundsheets had a reputation for leaking after only short usage and most people, myself included, put another groundsheet underneath to prolong its life, but this also increased the weight of the tent. The latest pu groundsheets are tough enough not to need such care. The 60-g/2-oz one on the tent I used on the Canadian Rockies walk was still waterproof after 80 nights' use without any protection being used under it.

Poles

These are either rigid or flexible, depending on the design of the tent. The first are always made from aluminium alloy, the second usually so, though some are made from fibre-glass. There are claims that hollow fibre-glass poles are stronger as well as lighter than alloy ones. This may be so, but I've never used a tent with such poles. I have used flexible alloy ones extensively though and found them excellent. Flexible poles may be pre-bent (i.e. they are curved when new). If they are not pre-bent, they often develop a curve with use. This is not something to worry about—just don't try and straighten them as they may break. Poles with the sections linked by elastic shockcord are the easiest to use, especially in tents where they are threaded through sleeves. Sprung metal is used in a few rigid-pole models instead of shock-cord. Unlinked poles can be a nightmare in sleeved pole tents as the sections tend to come apart inside the sleeves. I would avoid poles made from solid fibre-glass for this reason. With shock-cord-linked poles it's almost impossible to lose sections (though I managed it once after the shockcord had snapped, and I had to use a tent that dipped a little on one side for a few weeks until new poles arrived). You also don't have to fiddle around putting the right pieces together every time you pitch the tent. Nesting poles have sections which can be packed inside each other. Some rigid poles come in this form. The only advantage is in lower bulk for packing, which is not enough in my view to counteract the lack of shock-cord, especially as it can sometimes be difficult to remove the inner sections.

Most flexible and some rigid poles are attached to the tent, either the inner or the outer, by threading them through nylon or mesh sleeves and then fixing the end in a grommet or tape loop. A few makers use clips or even shockcord to hang the tent from the poles, which is said to be faster to use than sleeves. Never having tried them I can't comment. I am quite happy with sleeved poles.

Poles are very strong when the tent is pitched but vulnerable to breakage when lying on the ground. This is especially so with long, thin flexible ones. Take care not to tread on them! Take

care too not to use them to hold on to when entering and leaving the tent. I had a flexible pole break once when my companion put all his weight on it when leaving the tent. As this was during a gale in a remote area of Norway in winter I had to hurriedly scramble out of my sleeping bag, throw on some clothes and repair it, which I did by slipping a short alloy sleeve over the break and binding it in place with tape. Such sleeves come with most flexible pole tents and I always carry one, though that's the only time I've used it.

Pegs

Although much is made in advertisements and catalogues of free-standing designs that require no pegging, in reality every tent needs holding down in wind. How many pegging points are needed is another matter. Fifteen to twenty pegs is a reasonable number. Some tents require less. Long heavy steel pegs aren't necessary. I usually use 18-cm/7-in round alloy pegs (10g/$\frac{1}{3}$oz each), which hold in most soils, though I always carry a few 15-cm/6-in alloy V-angle pegs for softer ground (15g/$\frac{1}{2}$oz each). As pegs are easily mislaid I take two or three more than the number needed to pitch the tent. Mind you, I've returned on many occasions with more pegs than I started with, having found ones other people have lost. I carry pegs in a small nylon stuffsac, as supplied with most tents, in a pack pocket so that I can easily find them when I pitch the tent.

Guylines

Depending on the design, tents need anything from two to a dozen and more guylines to keep them taut in a wind. More than ten I think is too many for a tent that will be taken down and repitched every day. Most tents come supplied with a full set of guys, but some only have the main ones plus attachment points for others. I find it pays to attach these extra guys as they're usually needed in a storm. I'd rather have plenty of guylines and leave them tied back when it's calm than not have enough. To avoid confusion and to help when sorting out tangles, different-coloured guylines are useful, especially when several are attached to the tent at the same point. If the guylines are tied back in loops when packing your tent they are less likely to tangle, and I always try to do this—though in cold stormy weather I often forget, being more

The North Face Tadpole semi-geodesic.

interested in packing quickly and moving on. Undoing knots with numb fingers the next night I then curse myself for not taking more care when packing. Metal locking sliders come with most guylines. If they don't you can buy them separately. There are a number of knots that will grip when under tension but slide when it's released. It could be worth knowing these in case you need extra guylines and have no sliders—or even to use instead of sliders. I usually forget them but find that if I need one that I can eventually come up with something that works! As nylon stretches when wet, guy-lines should be pegged out tightly and the sliders or knots locked. If it's very wet and windy I generally go out and tighten them again before going to sleep.

Size and Weight

These two are directly related. Tents come in a wide range of sizes from tiny bivi tents that are barely big enough for one person, to monsters that will sleep four Himalayan mountaineers and hold all their gear. In terms of floor area, the most important factor is clearly that there should be room to lie down and stretch out without pushing against the walls or either end. I normally camp solo but I find that the smallest tents aren't big enough for me as I like to have enough space to lay out items I want to hand on either side of my sleeping bag. I usually leave my pack outside so I'm not bothered about having space for that as well. How much space a tent for two should have depends on how cramped they're prepared to be and how friendly they are. Be warned that many tents described in catalogues as sleeping two assume very close friendships! Ones described as for 1–2 people really only sleep two in an emergency. Better are the two-person ones, though even some of these are more suited to solo use. Few tent-makers give the floor areas of their tents, which is a pity. One that does is The North Face. However all give length and width so a comparison between sizes can be made.

The height of the inner is important too. If you spend any time in your tent—and unless you only camp in heatwaves and dry sunny climates (in which case why are you carrying a tent anyway?) you will—room to sit up and move round in is welcome. I find tents that don't allow me to sit up straight so confining

that I don't use them despite their low weights. The key factor here is the distance between the floor and the top of your head when you're sitting cross-legged. If you know that then you can work out from catalogues which tents will be roomy and which will give you a crick in the neck. For me that distance is 90cm/35in, so I always look for a tent with an inner height of at least that. If two of you want to sit up then that height should run the length of the inner.

As well as the size of the inner you need to consider the vestibule, if any. If you expect to cook and store gear in it regularly, as most backpackers in Britain's wet and windy climate do, then it needs to be roomy enough for you to do so and still have room to enter and leave. It should be high enough for a stove to be used under it without any danger of the fabric catching light too. Tents for two often have double vestibules and although they are heavier, this does make sitting out a storm much easier. For areas where you usually live outside and only use the tent for sleeping in such as the Pyrénées and the California High Sierra in summer the size of the vestibule isn't so crucial whilst in bear country where you never cook, eat or store food in the tent you don't really need one at all.

Because I like a view from my tent whenever possible, I also like vestibules with zipped doors that can be rolled out of the way. It's not quite the same as bivouacking but lying with my head by the door looking at the stars and the trees and the heather is far better than spending a fine evening or night encased in a nylon cocoon. Some tents only offer slits to look out of. I prefer those where the whole front or side of the tent can be opened up.

Making big, roomy tents is no problem. Making big, roomy, *lightweight* tents is, even with modern materials. I was surprised to find, on checking some data for a magazine article on tents I was writing, that at the time I was using tents that were 20–25 per cent heavier than the ones I'd carried a decade earlier. I had, I realised, been seduced by complex designs and masses of room. In that article I wrote that I would no longer carry a tent that weighed more than 2kg/4½lb for solo use, and I've stuck to that ever since, the only exceptions being when I've tested heavier tents for magazine reviews. Keeping the weight down when you share a tent is easier. I've used a 2½-kilo/5½-lb tent for snow camping with two and not felt cramped, and there are plenty in the $2\frac{1}{2}$-$3\frac{1}{2}$- kg/$5\frac{1}{2}$-$7\frac{3}{4}$-lb range that provide ample room. Note that whilst some tent-makers include stuffsacs, poles and pegs in the weights they quote for their tents in their literature, some don't.

Stability

Once you've struggled in the dark to cram gear into a pack under a thrashing sheet of nylon after the wind has snapped one of your tent poles the stability of your tentage becomes a matter of great concern. At least it has been for me since I found myself in that situation, especially as I was alone, it was pouring with rain and I had to make a long descent in the dark to the valley where the only shelter I could find in the middle of the night was in a public toilet. The incident occurred in the English Lake District in August. If it had been somewhere far more remote in winter I could have been in serious difficulties.

Over the years I've actually had three tents collapse on me, twice because of the wind and once because of a very heavy wet snowfall, and on two occasions I've camped with others whose tents have been blown down. I've also slept peacefully in a well-designed tent during a gale that blew down less-stable models nearby and shook others so hard that the occupants had little sleep. Even if your tent stays up, you'll be too exhausted to enjoy the next day, if it thrashes so wildly that you spend the night expecting it to collapse at any minute.

How concerned you need to be about the ability of your tent to withstand high winds and heavy snowfall depends on where and when you use your tent. For three-season, low-level, sheltered site camping it's not a major concern. For high-level, exposed sites it is for winter mountain camping stability should be a prime factor in your choice of tent. A host of factors determine how stable a tent is, including its shape, the materials it's made of, the number of poles and how they are arranged, and the number and position of guylines. The last item is particularly important in preventing a tent from shaking violently in high winds. For stability I look for a tent with no large areas of unsupported material, sleeved poles and plenty of guylines. When pitched a stable tent will feel fairly rigid when you push against the poles. Makers describe tents as three- or four-season

models and this can be used as a guideline. However, high winds can occur in summer and the best three-season tents are as stable as four-season ones. What they lack is often extra space, snow-shedding ability and large vestibules rather than stability.

Remember though that stability is relative. Gales that strip roofs off buildings and blow down trees can easily shred the strongest four-season mountain tent. In strong winds your experience and ability to select a sheltered site can be as important as the type of tent you have. In storms, when pitching the tent seems impossible, it's better to go on, even after dark, in search of a more sheltered spot. If I can tell that the night will be rough or think that the weather is worsening, I often change my plans in order to reach a sheltered site by nightfall. If you really have to camp in storm-force winds, seek out whatever windbreaks you can, such as piles of stones or banks of vegetation, and consider sleeping out in a bivi bag, if you are carrying one, or even wrapped up in your tent. It may be uncomfortable, but it is better than having your tent destroyed in the middle of the night and then having to bivouac.

Inner or Outer First—The Great Pitching Debate

Traditionally tents were pitched inner first with the flysheet thrown over as an extra when it rained. However, to cope with the wet and windy British weather some tent-makers began designing models that pitched flysheet first so that the inner could be erected under cover and kept dry. The disadvantages of this method are that the inner cannot be used on its own, as you might want to do on dry nights when insects are a problem, and that unless the way the inner connects with the flysheet is very well designed it may sag and will certainly flap in windy weather. Inners that pitch first are held taut by the poles and don't flap much. The best of them can be pitched so quickly that even in heavy rain they don't become very wet.

Tent-makers argue vehemently about this, but having used tents of both types for long periods of time, I've come to the conclusion that it doesn't matter which way the tent pitches, unless you want to use the inner alone. Overall design and quality of manufacture are far more important factors than whether the inner pitches first or not. So when I'm considering tents I am

The North Face Westwind three-pole tunnel.

not too concerned which bit of it pitches first, though I do check that I can put up an inner-first tent very quickly and that the inner on a flysheet-first model can be hung tautly.

Design

Since the advent of the first dome tents in the early 1970s tent designers have created a bewildering array of shapes, some of them quite bizarre. Overall though these developments have led to a superb range of tents: lighter, roomier, tougher and more durable than ever before.

Traditional: Before the forests of waving flexible poles appeared, all designs were variations on the standard ridge tent, a solid structure still popular with many backpackers. The general shape is rectangular but to save weight the lightest ones often taper in width and height to a short pole at the rear. The simplest but least stable and most awkward to use are those with upright poles at either end. A-poles make for a far more stable tent and also leave entrances clear. The classic design for high mountain camping has them at either end. Some models, known as transverse designs, open along each side with upright poles in the middle of each door. These provide much more room than any other traditional design but have the least stability because of the large areas of unsupported flysheet. Tents with two uprights at the front and one at the rear—a design that gives more headroom than A-pole models—have just about disappeared, apart from those made by a few tiny specialist companies like Wilson Tents.

Many manufacturers have dropped all rigid-pole tents, but quality models are still available from Vango, Phoenix, Saunders, Fjallraven,

Ultimate, Field & Trek and a few others.

Domes: Good though the best traditional tents are I think that flexible-pole models are vastly superior and I haven't used a rigid-pole tent for nearly a decade, except for one model I had to test. Flexible pole tents, with their steep sides and curved roofs, give far more usable space for the weight than rigid-pole models. It's easier to live in half a sphere than a triangle.

Dome tents are the biggest of the different flexible pole designs and can be defined as those where the poles cross each other at some point. They are the roomiest tents available and have the advantage of being self-supporting, so that they can be pitched and then moved to the ideal position—if there's no wind. One does hear stories of tents taking off like giant balloons never to be seen again. There are two types: geodesic and cross-over pole domes. Geodesic domes are highly complex structures in which four or more long poles cross each other at several points to form roomy, stable tents that, whilst on the heavy side (4kg/9lb upwards), have developed a good reputation for mountaineering and polar expedition use. Overall, however, they're too heavy for most backpacking trips. Simpler in design are cross-over pole domes where two or three poles cross at the apex to give a spacious tent that is lighter than a geodesic, though not as stable. Weights start at $2\frac{1}{2}$kg/$5\frac{1}{2}$lb. Both geodesics and cross-over pole domes are popular so the choice is large. Makers include The North Face, Jansport, Gregory, Walrus, Moss, Phoenix, Wild Country, Ultimate, Kelty, Jack Wolfskin, Fjallraven, VauDe, Eureka, Wintergear and REI.

Neither geodesic nor cross-over pole dome designs can be scaled down to make solo tents. However this category contains the most stable and roomy two-person tents available. My favourite winter camping tent when I'm not going solo is the four-pole elongated geodesic Wintergear Sapphire which weighs $3\frac{1}{2}$kg/$7\frac{3}{4}$lb and has recently been revived after a hiatus in production under the new name of Blizzard. It has large vestibules at each end and enough room for two to sleep, live and cook under cover. Being rectangular there is more usable floor space in this design than in the usual hexagonal geodesic shape. Headroom is excellent. I've had four sitting in it playing cards during a storm! It's pitched inner first, has sleeved poles and goes up on fourteen pegs very quickly indeed. The inherent shape is so stable that only two side guys are needed. I've used it in storms and blizzards everywhere from the Halingskarvet mountains in Norway to the Pyrénées and the Isle of Skye and never felt insecure in it. When other tents are shaking like jellies the Sapphire just sways slightly from side to side. I've also lived in it for 36 hours at a stretch without feeling cramped or falling out with my tent partner. The Sapphire was the first tent of this stretched geodesic type, though others have now appeared under various brand names, including Phoenix, Wild Country, REI and Eureka, which probably perform as well.

Lighter are three-pole semi-geodesics, cross-over pole domes with a third pole added at the front. In some models—the better ones in my experience—the back of the tent is tapered to the ground to give a very stable wedge shape. I used the Wild Country Voyager (mine was 2.7kg/6lb, though current models are 2.9kg/6½lb) on the Continental Divide walk and found it roomy, durable and good in gales and even heavy snowfalls, when the flattish roofs of these designs can be a problem. It's described as a two-person, three-season tent. Whilst I enjoyed the space I wouldn't carry that weight of tent on a long solo walk again. Similar tents are available from The North Face, Eureka and Ultimate and there are undoubtedly more I haven't seen.

Although there are several tents in the 2.9–3.3-kg/6½–7¼-lb range, there are few semi-geodesics really light enough for solo use, and those that there are tend to achieve low weights by using lighter materials. The 1.95-kg/4¼-lb North Face Tadpole for example has only mesh side walls and doors on the inner. It's ideal for warm-weather use (it has a three-season rating) but, as I've found, cold breezes can blow under the flysheet and through the mesh so it's not for the cold.

Tunnels: In tunnel tents the poles form hoops that are parallel to each other. The tiniest tents come into this category, single-skin bivi tents, some with just one pole, that weigh between 1 and 1½kg/2¼–3¼lb. These are so low and narrow however that I feel claustrophobic just looking at one, and I've never tried one out. The simplest models that can be called real tents have two hoops and weigh upwards of 2kg/4½lb. Ones with the poles far apart, leaving large areas of material between them to

catch the wind, are not very stable. However tents with poles which are close together so that there is less material between them, with the shape tensioned by pegging out each end, are much more wind-resistant. Vango's Hurricane tents (four models from 2.3 to 4.5kg/5–10lb) have a zipped-in inner so that the whole unit goes up together but can be split for drying, and are very roomy and very stable. I've used two double-hoop tents, the 3.7-kg/8¼-lb Hurricane Beta and a similar, though smaller, 2½-kg/5½-lb tent from the German company Jack Wolf-skin called the Pocket Hotel. Both have stood up well to strong winds and have plenty of space for two. I've also examined though not used the Norwegian Hilleberg range of tunnels tents and am very impressed with both the design and the quality of manufacture. For solo use the 2kg/4½lb Nallo 2 looks superb with masses of room and a large bellend.

However, I prefer three-pole tunnel tents, particularly those where the poles are different sizes, with the biggest in the middle. My reasons for liking this design are based on several years' usage of The North Face Westwind. At just 2.4kg/5¼lb (though current versions are listed as 2.74kg/6lb) it's just light enough to carry for solo use on short trips, though in line with my recent resolution on weight I no longer do so. It's also very stable, having resisted gales in places as far apart as Iceland, the Cairngorm mountains in Scotland and the Columbia Icefield in the Canadian Rockies. The high centre pole makes for a great deal of living space. Two of us found it adequate for the several days we spent trapped by a blizzard on the Columbia Icefield. My only complaint is that the single-zip door in the flysheet means that it's impossible to open the door in fine weather and sit or lie in the tent watching the world outside. However, the current model has two zipped doors and looks to be much better in this respect. Like all The North Face tents, the Westwind pitches inner first. Phoenix make two flysheet-first three-pole tunnels, the 3-kg/6½-lb Phalcon and the 3.6-kg/8-lb Phunnel, that look as good as the Westwind though I've used neither of them, and there are other similar tents around.

Like domes, tunnel tents are very popular and most tent-makers have at least one in their range. As well as the companies already mentioned names to look for include Walrus, Kelty,

Wild Country, Ultimate, Survival Aids and Sierra Designs.

Single-hoop Tents: The problem with solo tents is that weight and size are related. Whilst a smaller floor area is acceptable in a solo tent, lower headroom isn't, at least not for me. Yet slimmed down versions of the designs described above result in tents you can barely sit up in (the Hilleberg Nallo 2 being the only exception). The answer is to be found in single-hoop models, a style that really only works for solo tents, though some will sleep two. As the name suggests this design features one long single flexible pole. Transverse models, where the pole runs across the width of the tent, as in the Robert Saunders Spacepacker and Spacepacker Plus (1.75 and 2.18kg/4 and 5lb respectively), have huge vestibules either side but little headroom at either end of the inner, something I dislike. Better headroom and inner living space is provided by models where the pole runs the length of the tent, though these have only one vestibule.

Single-hoop tents can be remarkably stable for their weight if the guying system is good, and my favourite solo tents lie in this group. They are Phoenix's Gore-tex Phreerunner and double-skin Phreeranger (both 1.8kg/4lb). These feature short ridge poles for added inner headroom and nine guylines for stability. I use both, but overall I prefer the Phreeranger for long trips, unless I know conditions will be mostly dry, because of the double-skin construction. There is ample space inside for storing gear, for sitting—the high point is 97cm/38in—and for lying down, as you sleep along the line of the poles. I used Phreerangers on the Canadian Rockies and Yukon walks and found the performance excellent, even in the worst rain and snow storms. The triangular guying system is essential in these conditions, though in calm weather I don't bother pegging the six side guys out. The back three are always needed as they help give the tent its shape. With all the guys 15 pegs are needed, the inner requiring no pegs as it attaches to the flysheet by shockcord, hooks and rings at ground level. The tent can be erected in a few minutes. The single vestibules on these tents are big enough for me, though extra care should be taken when using a stove or even a candle under them, but for those who find them on the small side Phoenix offer larger EB (Extended Bell) versions which add 250g/8oz to the Phreerunner and 150g/5oz to the Phreeranger.

There are hardly any other single-hoop tents available. One of the few is Jack Wolfskin's Starlight, so called because the inner, which pitches first, is made of insect netting. This, plus the lack of a vestibule, means that although it only weighs 1.95kg/4½lb it has plenty of room for two. These same factors also mean it is only a fair-weather or summer model.

I nearly put the Bivvybug Niche in the next section but decided it fits more suitably here, even though it is very much a hybrid, being a bivi bag with a single-hoop canopy over the head end. This allows the user to sit up and cook under cover in a unit that weighs just 1.025kg/2¼lb. More than that, it combines the freedom of sleeping out under the stars with the protection of a tent. If the night starts out fine you can lie in the bivi bag with the canopy flat behind you knowing that if the weather changes you can erect it in seconds without leaving your sleeping bag. The Niche bivi bag comes in either Cyclone or Sympatex with a pu nylon groundsheet, and the canopy in elastomer-coated ripstop nylon. Zips and velcro fasten the bivi bag to the canopy. The latter is large enough to provide storage and cooking space either side of the sleeper. It's an ingenious design, the only hooped bivi that works in my view. I've found it roomy enough to spend several evenings sealed inside during heavy rain without feeling at all restricted. Just six pegs see it up though I've added four more and a couple of extra guylines (it comes with just two). In terms of space for weight nothing compares with it and you can use the bivi bag separately. My only concern is to do with insects, which I can imagine

The Bivvybug Niche single hoop/bivi.

creeping in under the edge of the canopy, though David Platten of Bivvybug says burning a mosquito coil inside will keep them out. An optional midge screen is available for the main door. Except in places which are full of bugs, I find I'm using the Niche more and more, and I'm delighted at the lack of weight and bulk. Although it is starting to appear in a few shops; the Niche is mainly available by mail-order, at least in Britain. If you're interested write to Bivvybug, Boscarhyn, Syra Close, St. Kew Highway, Bodmin, Cornwall, PL30 3ED, Great Britain.

Hybrids: Flexible poles can be used in an amazing number of configurations and some strange tent shapes have resulted, many from Moss. These usually cannot be classified in any category, as they take design features from many of the groups above, hence my description of them as hybrids. For example the Saunders Satellite tents (two models, the Standard, 1.7kg/3½lb and the Plus, 2kg/4½lb) are a mixture of ridge and tunnel designs. They have an upright pole at the rear, a large hoop at the door for good headroom and then another upright in the vestibule, which is thus very large. A total contrast is Phoenix's Phreebooter which is a single hoop tent with a smaller hoop added at the front and a curving ridge pole linking the two. The result is a very roomy yet lightweight (2.4kg/5¼lb) two person tent. What will appear next is anyone's guess.

Pitches and Pitching—Minimum Impact Camping

One of the pleasures of backpacking is camping in a different place every night. This can also be one of the horrors if you are still stumbling round in the rain looking for a site long after dark. In areas such as the national parks of the USA and Canada where there are prepared backcountry sites that must be used, finding a pitch isn't a problem. And in other popular areas, especially along long-distance paths, you will find plenty of well-used sites. If you take time to look at such places and work out why they have been used so regularly you'll soon learn what to look for when selecting a site. There are both practical and aesthetic criteria involved. For a good night's rest as flat a site as possible is essential and it must be on ground that is fairly firm and dry. Often a slight slope has to be accepted. When that's so I find that,

like most people, I have to sleep with my head uphill, otherwise I develop a bad headache and cannot sleep. Sometimes the slope can be so gentle as to be hardly noticeable until you lie down and try to sleep. When that's the case I just turn round in the tent and sleep the other way, something I've done groggily on many occasions. If its very windy a sheltered spot makes for a more secure and less noisy camp, but if insects are a problem a site with a breeze is to be welcomed and I often head uphill to camp when I am in mosquito or midge country. Water is a necessity at a site unless you carry it to what you know from the map or previous visits will be a waterless pitch, as I sometimes do.

From the aesthetic point of view the ideal site has a wonderful view, preferably from the tent door, and interesting surroundings to explore. The practical aspects come first however. Beautiful scenery doesn't look so good in the cold half-light of dawn if you've spent the night trying to get comfortable on lumpy sloping ground or wondering when the wind will tear the tent down.

When I'm in unknown country where there are no 'official' sites I generally work out over breakfast each morning where I want to be that evening and select from the map a probable area for a site. More times than not when I arrive in the area I find a reasonable spot quite quickly. If an obvious one doesn't present itself within minutes however I take off the pack and explore the area. If this doesn't produce a spot I'm happy with I shoulder the pack and move on. At times, especially when hours of daylight are short, this can mean continuing into the night. I did this several times towards the end of the Canadian Rockies walk as the late autumn days shortened. One day I picked a small lake on a watershed for a camp only to find when I reached it, half an hour or so before dark, that the area round it was a quagmire, beyond which were steep slopes. Circling the lake I saw that there was nowhere to camp, so I continued on down into the forest, my headlamp picking out the trail ahead. For some time I descended a steep hillside where it would have been a waste of time to even look for a site. Eventually the trail, which was not marked on my map, reached the valley bottom, crossed the creek and started to climb the other side. There was no flat ground. As there was water however, the first since the lake, I stopped and searched for a site. I found one between two fir trees. There was barely enough room for the tent but there was just enough flat ground for me to sleep comfortably. In the morning it looked as makeshift a site as you could imagine, the sort of place where no one would dream of camping in daylight, but it had served its purpose.

At times like that, when my selected site turns out to be unusable and I have to continue, tired and hungry, into the night I remind myself that my experience has shown that a site will always turn up but that it may require a little imagination to make the most of what seems unsuitable terrain. Perfect pitches are wonderful, yet many of those I remember most are the ones, like that in the northern Rockies, that were snatched almost out of thin air.

Minimum-impact camping is a necessity if we are to have pristine wild lands to visit in the future. The list of prohibitions below may not seem to accord with the freedom of backpacking but I'd rather follow them and be able, in most areas, to choose where I camp than to have my sites selected for me as in North American national parks.

'Wild' sites used for just one night should be left spotless, which means no trenching round tents, no cutting of turf and no preparation of the tent site. Previously unused sites should always, but always, be left with no sign anyone has been there. This means camping on bare ground or forest duff, or else on vegetation such as grass that will be least damaged by your stay—which shouldn't last longer than one night. If it does, move your tent or tents each day if the site is one that seems easily damaged. Paths from tent to water are easily created by groups, though solo campers can make them too. If you use a water container big enough to hold all the water for your camp, trips to the waterside can be minimised. Use a different route each time as well. Fires should only be lit if you can do so without leaving any sign of them when you depart. Rocks moved to hold down tent pegs—very rarely necessary though often done—should be replaced in the streams or boulder fields they were taken from. Too many rings of stones mark regularly used wild sites all over the world. I've spent hours removing such rocks from sites everywhere from the Scottish Highlands to the Rocky Mountains. The less sign that anyone has used a site, the less chance anyone will use it again so when you leave make sure you obliterate all evidence you've been there, roughing up any flattened vegetation as a last chore.

Of course you will often camp on sites that have been used before. If a site doesn't appear to have been used very often I feel it is better if possible to pass it by or even to stop and disguise as far as possible the signs of its use. A well-used site should be re-used however, and the temptation to create a new one avoided. Using such sites limits the impact in an area to one place. Just because the site has a worn look to it of course, you shouldn't add to the damage. This can be minimised by using bare patches for the tent and already existing fire-places if there are any. Tidying up the place may encourage others to camp there rather than make new sites. And as with every site, leave nothing and alter nothing.

One problem that is rare but does occur is that of flooding. What should one do about it, given as I've said that trenching round tents is out? I've only been swamped three times. On the first occasion I was able to move the tent to a higher, drier site nearby but on the second there was nowhere else to go and a lengthy thunderstorm was sending streams of rain running under the groundsheet. This had my companion and me running round barelegged, draped in rain jackets, digging shallow diversion ditches with our ice axes. I wasn't happy doing this, even though it was because the site was so well used that the hard-packed soil wouldn't soak up the water, but I also wasn't happy at the thought of the tent being flooded. After the storm we tried as well as we could to replace the earth and minimise the signs of our trenching. On the third, much more recent occasion, again when camping on a well-used, hard-packed pitch, I woke to find the groundsheet floating on a pool of water. A short shallow trench dug with my toilet trowel allowed this to drain off and this time there was little damage to try to repair. My view now is that whilst trenching should never be done on a pristine site or before it is absolutely necessary, if there really is no other choice a minimum amount of digging is justifiable if soil is replaced afterwards and the site is well used.

Compared with finding a site, setting up camp is easy. I don't have a set routine, it all depends on the time and the weather. In cold or wet weather, when I'm very tired or if darkness is imminent, I pitch the tent immediately and chuck in the gear I'll need overnight. I then fill my water bottles, crawl into the tent, change into warm or dry clothes if necessary, set up the stove and sort out my gear in comfort whilst the water boils for a hot drink. By the time it has boiled, I'm comfortably in my sleeping bag. The whole operation from starting to pitch the tent to taking the first sip can be done in ten minutes, though I usually like to do it in a more leisurely 15 or 20. The key is knowing your tent so well that you can pitch it when you're too tired to think. For greatest weather resistance and strength tents should be pitched very taut and guylines tightened until, in Phoenix's words, 'you can play a tune on them'. This will also minimise flapping and noise. When there's plenty of daylight and it's warm and sunny I may just sit and relax for half an hour before I do anything.

In some places and at certain times setting up camp is not so easy. If the terrain is rocky and pegs won't go in you may have to attach loops to the pegging points and tie them and the guylines to rocks to hold the tent down. I've only ever done this a couple of times, but when I have it's been essential and one of the many reasons I always carry a length of cord. Deep snow is even more of a problem, as tent pegs are just about useless. However if there's total snow cover you'll be carrying items such as ice axes, crampons, skis and ski poles, all of which can be used to support the tent, again through extra guylines tied to the pegging points if necessary. In soft snow it's wise to stamp out a hard tent platform first—most easily done whilst wearing skis or snowshoes. A snow shovel is also useful for this, especially when it comes to the final levelling of the site. If you have to use pegs bury them lengthways and pack the snow down on top. Once the temperature falls below zero they'll freeze in place. Come morning and you'll probably need an ice axe to dig them out. Sticks could be used instead of pegs. Another alternative, which I've never tried, is to fill stuffsacs with snow, attach guylines to them and bury them. There are also special wide pegs available for snow camping, which again I've never used—I'd rather improvise, as they look rather heavy and bulky.

Whether on rock, snow or nice firm soil, the actual pitching of a tent is easy. You just follow the instructions that come with it. A practice run

The Phoenix Phreeranger single hoop.

in the garden or on open ground near your home is always advisable with a new tent, both to familiarise yourself with how it goes up and to check that all the bits are there. Wind is the one thing that can complicate tent-pitching. There are so many different ways of putting up tents that detailed advice is impossible but in general I've found it wise in windy weather to peg out the end of the inner or outer, whichever pitches first, that will face into the wind and then thread or clip the poles into position before raising the tent off the ground. In a strong wind it may be necessary to lie on the tent whilst you do this. Speed is important here as tents are very vulnerable to damage when thrashing around in the wind. Once the basic shape of the tent is established the rest of the pegging can be done in a more relaxed manner. If the site allows, rectangular or tapered tents should be pitched with the tail or end into the wind as then they will shed it more easily. Keeping the door in the lee of the wind is a good idea for cooking too. Rain is not as much of a problem as wind, though with inner-first tents you'll want to be quick.

When striking camp I usually pack the tent last so that it can air and any condensation can dry out. In rain I pack everything under cover, including the inner if it's a flysheet-first model. In very heavy rain you can collapse an inner-first tent, leaving the flysheet pegged out, withdraw the poles and then stuff the inner into its bag from under the flysheet so that it stays dry. Shock-cord-linked poles should always be *pushed* out of their sleeves. If you pull them they're likely to come apart. In very cold conditions the pole sections may freeze together. Don't try to force them apart, as they may break. Instead grit your teeth and rub the joints with your hands until the ice melts. In bitter cold I do this with liner gloves on to prevent the metal sticking to my skin. If poles freeze like this, the chances are that any condensation will have frozen to the flysheet. At times this may be coated with ice on the inside and frost on the outside. All you can do then is shake as much of it off before you pack it, unless the day is sunny and you have time to wait for it to thaw and then evaporate.

Care

During a walk tents look after themselves. I try to dry off any condensation before packing the tent, but if the morning isn't sunny this may not always be possible. Spreading tents over bushes or dry ground or hanging them over a length of cord or branch is a good way to do this. Dirt can be wiped off pegs if there's much of it. Most tents come with two stuffsacs for poles and pegs but only one for the flysheet and inner. I always add a stuffsac, both because two small units are easier to pack and to keep dry inner tents separate from wet flysheets. The easiest way to pack tents is, appropriately enough, to stuff them into their stuffsacs. This is also best for the tents. If they are carefully folded, cracks in the proofing may eventually occur along the creases. In the pack the tent always goes near the top so that it's accessible for pitching the next night. I slide the poles down one of the corners of the pack between the sides and back. Unlike some people, I don't strap them on the outside of the pack, as I fear they might be damaged there or even fall off and be lost. Pegs live in a pocket, as I've found that if they are kept in the main pack they tend to work their way down to the bottom.

At home I always hang the tent up to dry before storing it in its stuffsacs. Although nylon will not rot, mildew can form if a tent is stored wet and will leave both a stain and an unpleasant musty smell. Particular care should be taken with Gore-tex tents, as they can appear dry even when damp, as moisture can be hidden in the material. Poles too should be dried before being stored to prevent corrosion. They should also be wiped down if you've been camping anywhere near the sea, as salt corrodes them very fast.

MOUNTAIN SHELTERS

In many wilderness areas there are unlocked shelters available for use by walkers. These usually provide shelter from the elements but no more, so that the user still needs a sleeping bag, mat, stove and warm clothing. Some countries, like Scotland where they are known as bothies, have chains of them and some long-distance routes like the Appalachian Trail can be walked using shelters almost every night. In some areas, especially in North American wildernesses, such shelters may be open on one side. The most luxurious I've found are in Scandinavia where the purpose-built pinewood huts contain wood-burning stoves with supplies of logs, bunk beds, cooking utensils and food supplies. There is a charge for these huts, payment being made via a box on the wall—an honour system that works. Mostly though mountain shelters are very basic. In general I prefer the freedom and solitude of a tent or bivouac, but in bad weather such shelters can be a blessing and I always like to know where they are in case I need them.

SNOW CAVES

In deep snow an alternative to pitching a tent is to dig a shelter. Snow is a good insulator and cuts out all wind. Inside a snow cave it is always calm and quiet even when a blizzard is raging outside. To dig a proper one takes time—several hours at least—so you need to stop early if you're planning on doing so. Ice axes, cooking pans and toilet trowels can all be used to dig with but a proper snow shovel speeds up the process greatly. Whatever you use, digging snow is hot work so strip off your warmwear or it will become soaked with sweat. To start with a bank of snow at least 2 metres/6ft deep is needed. Into this you dig a narrow horizontal trench. Once this is well into the snowbank the area around it can be dug out at around waist level to form sleeping platforms. These are raised so that cold air will sink into the trench. The roof should be curved and as smooth as possible to minimise drips. How big you make the cave depends on how many it must shelter, how much time you have and how much snow there is. The entrance should slope upwards out of the cave and be kept small to prevent snow and wind blowing in, but there should always be an air inlet to prevent carbon monoxide build-up when you are cooking.

If you need to dig a snow shelter because of a storm and there is little time any sort of structure will do. Mountaineers have survived high in the Himalayas in body-size snow coffins for several days and nights when necessary. A simple trench can be roofed with tilted snow blocks or with skis, over which are spread flysheets or tarps, the edges held down with snow. The aim is simply to get out of the wind.

Be careful where you put things, especially small items, in a snow shelter (and when digging it)—even more so than when camping on snow—as it's easy for them to become buried.

SLEEPING BAGS

Whether you sleep out under the stars or the weather forces you under a tarp or into a tent or bivi bag you need to be able to keep warm at night which means for most people using a sleeping bag. You hear stories of people who just pile on extra clothes at night, but I've never met anyone who does this by choice (an enforced bivouac when you aren't carrying a sleeping bag is another matter), and it sounds both uncomfortable and inefficient.

The sleeping bag serves the same purpose as warm clothing, which is to trap warm air and prevent the body cooling down. The details of how the body loses heat are described in the clothing section so I won't go into them again here, but like clothing the sleeping bag must allow invisible perspiration to pass through it (unless a vapour barrier is used). If you're intending to sleep out in it without shelter, your bag should also be wind-resistant and have a quick drying shell.

Fill

Choosing a sleeping bag is much easier than choosing a tent, as there are far fewer designs. The biggest decision to be made regards the type of insulation or fill. The ideal material would be lightweight but very warm, low in packed bulk, durable, non-absorbent, quick-drying, warm when wet and very comfortable. Unfortunately this ideal doesn't exist so choices have to be made as to which of those properties are most important—which in part depends on when and where you camp and what shelter you use. There are two types of fill, synthetic and waterfowl down. Pile-insulated bags are also available but these are so different to the others that they'll be dealt with separately.

Synthetics: When I started backpacking, synthetic-filled sleeping bags were far too heavy and bulky to consider carrying in a pack. However, since Du Pont launched Fibrefill II in the mid-1970s a whole host of good synthetic fills, all varieties of polyester, have appeared on the market and there is now a wide selection of reasonably lightweight bags to choose from. There are two basic types: chopped fibres and continuous filaments. The idea of both is to produce fine webs of material that will trap air when uncompressed and keep the sleeper warm, but which will pack down to a small size for carrying. Chopped fibres are short sections of fill, often with a hole or holes running along their length. Continuous filaments are endless strands of fibre. Which is best is a matter of debate. My view is that the quality of manufacture of the bag as a whole is more important than which fill it contains. In continuous fills there are only Polarguard and Hi-Loft Hollowfibre, but there are many versions of chopped fibres including Quallofil (with four holes in it), Hollofil (one hole), Isodry, Microsoft, Hollowfibre, Fibrefill and others including ones exclusive to a particular bag maker like Gold-Eck Loft Technology (a hollowfibre). Those which are capitalised are brand names, a guarantee of quality at a higher price. Unbranded ones are cheaper but don't have the backing of a company name.

The advantages of synthetic fills are cost, ease of care and resistance to moisture. The last is the feature which is used to sell the bags, often under the slogan 'warm when wet'. Unfortunately this isn't true. Nothing is warm when wet. What matters is how fast something dries. As synthetic fills are virtually non-absorbent they won't soak up vast amounts of water and so will dry fairly quickly. Also, as the fill doesn't collapse when it is saturated, much of its warm-air-trapping thickness is retained. This means that a wet bag will start to feel warm in a comparatively short space of time, certainly compared with a down-filled one (see below), as long as it is protected from rain and wind. You can't sleep outside in a storm in a synthetic-fill bag and stay warm however, something you can do with a pile one. Using a synthetic-filled bag is not a reason for neglecting to keep it as dry as possible.

The disadvantages of synthetic fills are a short life, less comfort compared with down or pile and more bulk and greater weight for the same warmth when compared with down. Though synthetics are cheaper than down to buy, in the long run down costs less. Mountain Equipment, who make both down and synthetic bags, estimate that with average use a down bag will last twelve years but a synthetic one only four.

Down: This is the accepted fill for the lightest, warmest sleeping bags and the best when weight and bulk are critical factors, as nothing comes anywhere near down for compactness and low weight combined with good insulation. It is also very durable and comfortable to use. The fluffy undercoating of ducks and geese, down consists of clusters of incredibly thin filaments which trap air and thus provide insulation. No synthetic microfibre comes anywhere near down for weight, lightness, thinness or air-trapping ability. Unlike feathers, down clusters have no stalks. There are disadvantages though. Down must be kept dry, as it loses virtually all its insulation when wet and soaks up so much moisture that it takes a very long time to dry. Indeed drying a down bag out in bad weather is just about impossible—only a hot sun or a tumble-drier will do the job. Keeping a down bag dry means packing it in a waterproof bag and always using shelter when it rains. Down bags should also be aired whenever possible to remove any moisture picked up from humid air or your body during the night. This doesn't mean that looking after a down bag need be difficult or a chore. I've used down bags on almost all my long walks and never yet had one get more than a little damp.

When I began backpacking however, I used a feather- and down-filled bag, bought in a sale as a 'second', and I twice slept in this when it was wet. One occasion was when I was sleeping on an absorbent open-cell foam mat in a single-skin proofed nylon tent in heavy rain. The condensation was horrendous and as it ran down the walls it was greedily soaked up by the foam and then transferred to my bag. By morning I was lying fully clothed under the bag and feeling very cold. Once it was light I packed up and went home. Luckily it was September and my camp was at sea level. The second occasion was when I bivouacked out in a forest in the rain using a plastic bivi bag as mentioned previously, when again the sleeping bag became damp through condensation and leakage, though not as sodden as previously. These unpleasant experiences didn't put me off using natural-fill bags though, just single-skin proofed nylon tents, open-cell foam pads and plastic bivi

bags! I'd probably have stayed dry on the first occasion if I'd had a proper sleeping mat and on the second if I'd had a breathable fabric bivi bag.

There are several different grades of down and two different types. Pure down is usually at least 85 per cent down, the remainder being small feathers, which are impossible to separate from the down. Down and feather fills are usually at least 50 per cent down (many are 70 per cent or 80 per cent) but feather and down ones are less than 50 per cent. The last, along with all feather fills, have just about vanished as synthetic fills are as durable and give the same warmth for the same weight, as well as being easier to care for. One way to tell how pure a down fill is, is to feel it to see how 'stalky' it is, as the presence of stalks means the presence of feathers. Whatever the mixture, down may come from either geese or ducks. Goose down is generally regarded as warmer, weight for weight, than duck down. It is also more expensive. The more space a given amount of down will fill, the higher its quality, as the thickness or loft determines the warmth. Measuring the volume an ounce of down will fill gives a scale for this, the resulting figure being called the fill-power. However, many manufacturers don't give the fillpower for their down so it's hard to make comparisons. Three that do are RAB (550 and 700+ fillpower for their duck and goose downs), The North Face (550+ and 625+ for their two grades of goose down) and Marmot (650+ goose down). Overall it's probably safe to assume that most pure downs will have fill-powers of between 500 and 650 cubic inches per ounce (I have never seen metric figures quoted for this).

Shell Materials

Whether down or synthetic, the fill must be contained inside other materials. Nylon is the best as it is lightweight, hard-wearing, wind- and water-resistant, non-absorbent and quick-drying. The latest softest nylons are comfortable against the skin and so are suitable for the inner as well as the outer shell. Because nylons in the past felt cold and clammy, many people prefer cotton or polycotton inners and these are still available. They are however heavier, more absorbent, slower to dry and less easy to keep clean. After several months of continuous use a polycotton inner feels sticky and quite unpleasant—I speak from experience! A nylon one however, as long as it's aired occasionally, stays fairly fresh, as it doesn't absorb sweat or dirt.

Pertex nylon makes a particularly good shell material as it has all the properties of other nylons plus a very pleasant feel. It also spreads moisture out rapidly over its surface, which speeds up evaporation. The polyester microfibre Versatech, used on The North Face's top-of-the-line bags, is meant to be even more moisture-repellent. A breathable waterproof outer shell like Gore-tex provides the best water-resistance and a few bags are offered with this as an option. It adds to the weight and cost though, and unless all seams are sealed it will still leak. Drying out damp Gore-tex-covered bags can be difficult too. I prefer a separate Gore-tex bivi bag as a waterproof cover for a sleeping bag. On the Columbia Icefield crossing in the Canadian Rockies (see Tents), I used a Gore-tex bivi bag and a down bag whilst the others used Gore-tex-covered down bags. The atmosphere in the tents when we were pinned down for days by a storm was so humid that I slept in the bivi bag every night. By dawn the outside of it was damp but my sleeping bag was dry and I was able to pack the latter away but leave the former out to dry. My tent companion had to turn his bag inside out to air it and had much greater problems keeping it dry.

A few bags come with special inners designed to increase the warmth, usually by reflecting back body heat. Kelty's Solarsilk inner fabric is one example—a silver material claimed to be completely breathable and to lower a bag's temperature rating by 5 °C/9 °F without adding extra weight.

Shape and Size

As a sleeping bag keeps you warm by trapping your body heat, the closer it fits the more efficient it is. A bag with lots of room in it means a bag with lots of dead air space to heat up. To counter this most sleeping bags are tapered from head to foot. Most also have hoods, as the head is a prime source of heat loss if uncovered. The result is known as the mummy bag, presumably from a resemblance to an ancient Egyptian corpse. It's the standard shape for high-performance lightweight sleeping bags. In the late 1970s Mountain Equipment discovered the limit to how close-fitting a bag can be when they launched bags that they called 'tulip-shaped', which were very body-hugging indeed—too much so in fact for the public didn't buy them. The company had to enlarge their bags again and put a regretful note in their next catalogue to the effect that the new bigger models were not as efficient as the tulip-shaped ones, but seemed to be what people wanted.

The size of your sleeping bag is important too. One that is too big either in width or length means more air space to be heated and more weight to be carried. Too small a bag will be uncomfortable however, and not very warm where you push hard against the shell and flatten the fill. Bags come in different lengths and widths and many companies offer two sizes in each model, so finding a reasonable fit isn't too difficult, though very tall people will find their choice limited (bags from Scandinavian makers such as Fjallraven and Ajungilak and Northern Feather seem the biggest) and short people may find they end up with a bag a little too long. It's worth actually climbing inside a bag on the floor of the shop and seeing how it fits before buying, even if you do feel a little conspicuous doing so.

Construction

How the fill is held in a sleeping bag has a great bearing on its efficiency. In order to prevent the fill, whether synthetic or down, migrating, it is contained in channels which give sleeping bags their familar look. Generally these run right round the bag.

To create these channels the inner and outer of a bag have to be stitched together. The simplest and lightest way of doing this is with straight-through stitching. However, the oval channels thus created are not the best shape for allowing the fill to expand fully or to keep it spread throughout the channel. The main problem with this construction though is that heat escapes through the stitch lines. Even so this is an adequate construction for bags that will only be used in above-freezing temperatures, and it is found in most of the lightest synthetic bags and a few down ones.

To cut out this heat loss the inner and outer can be connected by short walls of material to make rectangular boxes, hence the name box-wall construction. If the walls are angled it is called slant-wall construction. Virtually all down bags intended for cold-weather use have these internal walls. This system can't be used for synthetic fills though, as these are fixed in layers.

Instead two methods are used: double-layer and shingle. In the first, two or even three sewn-through layers are used, with the stitch-lines offset to cut out the cold spots, a rather heavy though quite efficient method. The shingle construction where slanted layers of overlapping fibre are sewn to both the inner and the outer, is reckoned to be lighter and to allow the fill to loft more easily.

Whatever the internal construction, a bag's channels are usually split in two by lengthways side baffles to prevent all the fill ending up on the top or bottom. Some bags, usually light-weight down ones, dispense with these side baffles on the grounds that it might be useful at times to be able to shift the fill to the top or bottom of the bag to give more or less warmth. Personally I would distrust such a construction, fearing that the down would move whether I wanted it to or not. In contrast RAB's top goose down bags are divided lengthways into quarters with four rather than two full-length baffles in order to prevent down shift, while to prevent the fill from moving away from the important chest area, Mountain Equipment bags have short vertical channels in the upper section of the top of the bag. RAB bags also have channels of different widths with the narrowest ones over the chest, again to keep the down there. Some synthetic bags, such as Gold-Eck's lighter ones and the Kelty Soft Touch series, have the side baffles set at ground level so that two-thirds of the fill is in the double-layer upper section and just a third in the single-layer base.

The problem with this and other bags which have more fill in the top than the bottom is that not all sleepers keep their bags the right way up, and that includes me. I often wake to find the hood above me, having turned the bag completely over during the night. For that reason I prefer to have the fill equally distributed.

To prevent compression of the fill, many bags have the outer shell cut larger than the inner, which is known as differential cut. Whether this is necessary or not is a matter of debate amongst bag makers. I've used bags with and without it and can't see that it makes much difference.

Building a bag that fits the body closely without being restrictive has been a problem makers have been trying to solve for years. Mountain Equipment's tulip bags showed the limits people would tolerate. At the end of the 1980s a new approach was developed by Moun-tain Equipment themselves and by Kelty, namely elasticated inners that give a body-hugging fit but which move with the sleeper, who therefore doesn't feel constricted. In the autumn of 1989 Mountain Equipment introduced down bags with elasticated inner seams. They say that this construction increases warmth by reducing heat loss through convection by cutting out dead air space and also, because the elastication increases the box size, by allowing the down to loft more easily. This efficiency should mean lighter bags for the same warmth. Do they work? I think so. I used the 960-g/2lb 2-oz Lightline, which has a 450-g/16-oz fill, on the Yukon walk and found it very warm. Even when the temperature dropped to −6 °C/22 °F I didn't need to wear any clothes in it. I haven't made a direct comparison with an equivalent non-elasticated bag but I wouldn't expect quite such warmth from such an amount of fill. The elastication I found noticeable at first because I'm not used to being in contact with a bag at every point, but as it's non-restrictive and moves when you do I soon became used to it and decided that it is more comfortable than standard constructions, mainly, I think, because of the complete absence of cold spots. This elasticated construction is found in all the bags in Mountain Equipment's top-of-the-range Classic series, as well as the ultralight Dewline bag.

At about the same time as Mountain Equipment developed their elasticated construction in Britain, Kelty developed their similar Soft Touch Concept in the USA. This, which I've not seen but only read about, involves a stretch tricot that 'forces the liner to hug your body yet does not restrict movement while sleeping'. As the bags are Quallofil ones it means that body-hugging bags are now available with both synthetic and natural fills. Using a different method there are also pile bags in which the inner space can be reduced as described below.

Design Features
Hoods: A good hood should fit closely round the head and have a drawcord for adjustment, whose self-locking toggles can be easily reached and slackened when the bag is done up tight. Most hoods fit well, few are easy to adjust from inside. Bags for use in below-freezing temperatures should have large hoods in which you can bury all bar the nose or, in my case, the back

of the head as I like to keep my face warm and I don't find being enveloped in nylon and down claustrophobic, at least not when it's skin freezingly cold. Bags for warmer conditions sometimes have smaller hoods or even no hood at all to save weight. In above-freezing temperatures I rarely do up the hood. Indeed I often fold it out of the way under the bag.

Shoulder Baffles: A filled, drawcord-adjusted collar or neck baffle to prevent draughts is a feature of many bags, especially those designed for cold weather. I'd not used one until recently but having done so I think they are a good idea as it means you can close the bag up round your shoulders whilst leaving the hood open.

Feet: To keep your feet warm a sleeping bag should have a shaped or boxed foot section. If the two halves of the bag are simply sewn together at the foot your feet will push against the fill, compress it and then feel cold. A boxed foot is one where an extra circular section is added. On some designs this is itself divided into channels, while on others it is just a single unit. On cold-weather bags a boxed foot may contain an offset double layer of fill or, in down bags, have internal box walls.

Zips: It's hard now to find a sleeping bag without a side zip, except for the very lightest down ones. For years I distrusted zips on sleeping bags, seeing them as adding weight and letting heat out, and also as a potential source of disaster if they failed. However, I've now used models with zips and have come to a grudging acceptance of them, though I can still see no real advantages. I know in theory that you can unzip them when you're too warm and let cool air in and that they make getting in and out of the bag easier. Being used to non-zip models though, I automatically pull bags on and off without using the zip even if there is one, and ventilate by undoing the hood and sliding my shoulders out. Couples can zip two bags together to make one big one if they so wish. Those I've spoken to tell me they rarely if ever do this.

But, as I say, most bags have zips and most of the zips are full-length ones. To prevent heat loss zips must have filled baffles running down the inside. Unfortunately such baffles are ideally placed for the zip to get caught in them so a stiffened anti-snag strip is also necessary. In my experience these are far from perfect, but they do lessen the number of times the zip catches.

If a zip is two-way you can stick your feet out to cool off if you overheat, whilst keeping the rest of you warm. I suppose in fact you could even waddle round outside wearing your bag as a somewhat restrictive but very warm coat, though I can't imagine when you would want to do so.

Warmth and Weight

Rating sleeping bags for warmth is very difficult, though some attempt must be made to do so. Most companies give their bags either season ratings or temperature ranges. The latter is the most useful, as the problem with the former is that it doesn't tell you the area or the altitude at which the seasons apply. Usually five seasons are listed, the fifth meaning extreme cold. Moreover, bags warm enough for deep winter use will be too hot in most summers, yet these are usually listed as four-season models. Generally the ratings for seasons seem to be: one-season down to 5 °C/9 °F, two-season down to 0 °C/32 °F, three-season down to –5 °C/23 °F, four-season down to –15 °C/5 °F and five-season below –15 °C/5 °F. Where temperatures are quoted they may be given as the lowest at which the bag should keep you warm or the temperature band in which a bag should be comfortable. Perhaps more useful are the figures, such as those given by Gold-Eck, which give you a temperature range plus an extreme rating or when using a bivi bag as well. Thus their Husky 1000 is recommended for temperatures between 20° and –8 °C/68° and 18 °F but has an extreme rating of –17 °C/2 °F. A bag's warmth is dependent on its thickness or loft as well as its shape and construction method and a useful thickness scale is given by Fjallraven for this, assuming the use of a 10mm+ thick mat and the absence of wind:

Min.temp:	+5 °C	–10 °C	–20 °C	–30 °C	–40 °C	–50 °C
Loft:	4 cm	6 cm	7cm	8cm	9cm	11cm

This is for the loft over the body, not the total thickness of the bag. Where makers give loft figures you need to check whether it is for the whole bag or just the top half—the second is the more important figure. For example the loft quoted for the Gold-Eck bag referred to above is 12cm/4¾in. This is for the whole bag though, which is why the rating is only for –8 °C/18 °F. The slightly lower figure than Fjallraven's is probably due to the Husky 1000 having a double top but a single-layer base.

There is one big problem with all this: the human body. Everybody's metabolism is different. Some people are warm sleepers, some cold. Those who, like me, come in the first category have a great advantage, being able to use lightweight bags at lower temperatures than they're rated for. Those who feel the cold can shiver a summer night away in a bag made for the polar ice cap. I have a friend who sleeps buried in a four-season mummy bag at the same time as I'm comfortable half-out of a summer model. Other factors influence how warmly you'll sleep too. Food is fuel is heat, so however tired I am at the end of a long day I always eat before going to sleep if it's cold as I've found that if I don't I wake in the early hours of the morning feeling chilly. (If it's warm and I don't eat I wake because I'm hungry!) Although the obvious thing to do if you wake feeling cold in the night is to put on some clothes, a carbohydrate snack can also help warm you up. Tiredness itself can also keep you shivering long after you expect to be warm. The weather matters of course, and in more ways than just temperature. High humidity means a damp bag (though it may feel perfectly dry) and less loft plus conductive heat loss. This can mean that you feel colder when the temperature's around freezing and the humidity is high than you do when it's several degrees below freezing but dry. Wind reduces a bag's efficiency, as does sleeping under an open sky with no barrier to prevent heat loss by radiation. It would take a long time to heat up the universe! So if you bivi out regularly you'll need a warmer bag than if you always use a tent. Using a sleeping mat of some sort makes a huge difference too, especially if the ground is wet or frozen, and I always carry one. All this means that the temperature rating of a bag should only be taken as a guide. The type of backpacking you do and the type of sleeper you are are also needs to be taken into account.

High loft requires more fill, which means more weight, so it's not a good policy to buy a very warm bag to ensure comfort on the coldest nights. This is where down-filled bags have a great advantage as they are much lighter than synthetics across all temperature ranges, running from 500g/1lb 3½oz for ones suitable down to 5 °C/41 °F to 2400g/5¼lb for −15 °C/5 °F and below models. Synthetics go from a reasonable 990g/2lb 3oz to a hefty 2950g/6½lb. Just on the basis of weight alone I would choose a down bag.

Models and Choices

The number of sleeping bags available runs into the hundreds, though the number of designs is far fewer. However it's fairly easy to reduce the choice to a handful of models that fit your specific criteria. For myself I always look for the lightest, least bulky bag—which means one with a down fill—which meets my needs. These are to keep me warm whilst sleeping unclothed in a tent in the average temperatures expected for the time of year and the area. If the temperatures are cooler than average and I feel chilly, then I wear clothes. As I backpack year round, for the last decade I've used two bags, one for when temperatures will mostly be well above freezing and one for when they'll be mostly below. For the first, for years I used the Mountain Equipment Lightline with 450g/16oz of down fill and a total weight of 900g/2lb because it was the lightest quality bag available. I found I could use the Lightline down to −5 °C/23 °F without needing to don clothes, but that above 10 °C/50 °F it was a little too warm. In the late 1980s several lighter bags appeared and I changed to a RAB Micro 300 with 300g/10½oz of goose down fill and a total weight of just 625g/1lb 6oz. Construction is stitch-through, the hood is small and there is no zip, but this simple bag keeps me warm down to 5 °C/41 °F without need of clothes and cuts the weight and bulk of my load. I used it on the first half of the Canadian Rockies walk and it kept me warm throughout, though I needed to wear thermal underwear on the few nights the temperature dropped below zero. Mountain Equipment make a similar bag, the Dewline, also with 300g/10½oz of fill but even lighter at 550g/1lb 3-oz. It has box-wall construction and elasticated inner seams which together could make it usable to below freezing without clothes.

So far my use of the new elasticated Mountain Equipment Lightline Bag (450-g/16-oz fill, total weight 960g/2lb 2oz) suggests that this will be adequate down to −10 °C/14 °F and maybe even −15 °C/5 °F. The Lightline also has slant-wall construction, shoulder baffle, full-length zip and V-baffles over the chest. At 205cm/80in in length and with a 70-cm/27½-in maximum width, it's the right size for me and is my current choice for walks where I expect temperatures below 5 °C/41 °F.

There are fewer makers of down sleeping bags than synthetic ones and owing to the cost of the fill, virtually all are of high quality—it's not worth trying to cut costs. As well as RAB and Mountain Equipment models, I have used bags from The North Face and Field & Trek and found them very good. I took the F&T Golden Oriole Expedition with 565-g/20-oz goose down fill and 1190-g/2lb 10-oz total weight on the second half of the Canadian Rockies walk and slept warm in it unclothed in temperatures of −10 °C/14 °F whilst the North Face Superlight with 680g/24oz of goose down and a total weight of 1350g/3lb kept me warm in similar temperatures on the Columbia Icefield. Other down bags come from Marmot, Feathered Friends, Slumberjack, Karrimor, Vango, Fjallraven, REI, VauDe, Caravan, Cotswold and more.

I can't say I use synthetic bags except when I'm sent one for test and review purposes, but I'm aware that they are the ones most people buy. Overall I find down softer and more comfortable, as it drapes round the body better as well as being lighter and lower in bulk. If I'm bivouacking or snow-holing and want a bag that'll keep me warm when wet then I use a pile one (see below). However, synthetic fills are improving all the time and ones that rival down warmth for weight may be with us soon. In the meantime I view cold-weather synthetic bags as simply too heavy to consider. For above-freezing temperatures though there are a number of good bags available. I took a Karrimor Mountain Tiger with a single-layer Isodry-KS fill and a weight of 990g/2lb 3oz on a two-week summer walk in the Pyrénées. The bag was warm enough for me to sleep unclothed in it down to 5 °C/41 °F, but on the few nights it dropped to freezing I needed thermal underwear. This makes it equivalent to the 625-g/1lb 6-oz Micro in performance at a third more weight—not that 990g/2lb 3oz is an unreasonable amount to carry.

Both Kelty and Gold-Eck have bags with very good warmth/weight ratios, at least on paper. They achieve this by the use of thin reflective layers called Solarsilk by Kelty and Thermoflect by Gold-Eck and also in the Keltys by the use of an elasticated construction. The fills are Quallofil and Loft Technology respectively. The lightest Solarsilk Soft Touch bag weighs 1250g/2lb 12oz and is rated to −7 °C, again roughly a third more than an equivalent down bag such as the 960-g/2lb 2-oz Lightline. Gold-Eck's Husky 1000 weighs 1300g/2lbs 13oz. It's rated to −8°C/18 °F although as I haven't yet used it below freezing I don't know if it'll live up to this. Because of its large size I rather suspect that for me it won't, though for someone of a much bigger build it might.

Making other comparisons from catalogue data does seem to confirm that even the best synthetic bags weigh at least a third more than down ones with the same warmth rating. In cold-weather bags it seems to be well over a third. However you do the sums though one thing is clear: for the same warmth synthetic bags weigh significantly more than down ones. I've also found that whilst down bags often have conservative warmth ratings, synthetic ones often have very optimistic ones! For those, the majority it seems, who do want a synthetic bag, other quality models come from Mountain Equipment, The North Face, Sierra Designs, Slumberjack, Ajungilak, Field & Trek, Vango, Snug Pak, Cotswold, Fjallraven, REI, Caribou, Jack Wolfskin, VauDe and undoubtedly far more.

Pile Sleeping Bags

After a flurry of interest in the late 1970s in Britain, sleeping bag makers lost interest in pile bags. In other countries the interest never seems to have been there in the first place. Yet pile bags have much to offer, being reasonably inexpensive, incredibly hardwearing, very comfortable and—their special virtue—the exception to the rule that nothing is warm when wet. Pile bags achieve this amazing feat by the speed with which they both wick moisture away and dry when wet. Pile on its own isn't wind- or water-resistant though so with one exception those few makers who offer pile sleeping bags make them up as liners to increase the warmth of conventional bags. The exception is Hamish Hamilton whose company Buffalo specialises in pile sleeping bags and clothing covered with tightly woven Pertex nylon. The latter makes the bags windproof and very water-repellent, so much so that you can sleep warm in one whilst it's raining. I've slept out on a snow-covered hilltop in November in a Buffalo bag and been warm and comfortable yet woken to find a strong cold wind blowing and the foot of the bag lying in a pool of water. For bivouacking in wet, cold and windy weather Buffalo pile bags are ideal.

The range consists of three models: the Lightweight Outer, the Superbag and the 4S Outer/Inner combination, plus a Pertex inner called the Thermaliner. All the bags are tapered in shape, with full-length central zips and close-fitting hoods (drawcord-closed cowl-type hoods won't work on a pile bag). As a body-hugging fit is essential for maximum warmth the bags come in two sizes, medium and large. The one I've used most is the 4S (it stands for four-season) combination which consists of two separate bags that fit inside each other, the outer being Pertex-covered, the inner just pile. Together the bags weigh 2720g/6lb (medium size), which separates into 1475g/3lb 4oz for the outer, 1245g/2lb 12oz for the inner. Used in combination they have kept me warm sleeping unclothed at −6 °C/21 °F, and with Buffalo clothing would clearly go much lower. If weight and bulk are crucial, a lighter down inner is available called the Sundowner, with either a 400 or a 600-g/14 or 21-oz fill. Any lightweight down bag could be used instead, of course. On its own I've used the outer down to 7 °C/45 °F with thermal underwear. Again the addition of Buffalo clothing would add much warmth.

However it's the other two bags, introduced during the writing of this book, that I think offer most as they are lighter and much less bulky than the 4S. At the time of writing I have just received one of each of them for test but I have not had time to test them fully yet. The Lightweight Outer weighs just 830g/1lb 13oz (medium size) and packs down very small. It's rated for summer use only, though it has been used with Buffalo clothing in very cold conditions on ice caps in Iceland. The Superbag weighs 1800g/4lb, has a baffled double front zip and three internal shockcord adjusters to reduce dead air space. Arm zips are also fitted so that you can sit up in the bag and cook and eat without losing any protection. Buffalo rate it three/four-season on its own but again recommend wearing the clothing inside in extreme conditions and also the Thermaliner which adds another 240g/8½oz to the weight. The packed bulk is reasonable especially if you use the compression stuffsac that comes with the bag, though this adds 100g/3½oz to the weight. I've spent one night in it so far, bivouacking out on a closed-cell mat in windy weather with light wet snow falling and a temperature hovering around freezing. I used the Thermaliner, which can be fastened inside with toggles and loops to prevent it twisting, and wore the Buffalo Mountain Shirt and Trousers plus pile socks. I was very warm and although the outer shell became quite wet with melted snow none soaked through. My only complaint is that I felt claustrophobic with the short zip, which closes the hood tightly over the face, done up.

These bags might seem heavy compared with down bags but you don't need a tent or even a bivi bag (Buffalo recommend carrying a standard 340-g/12-oz plastic bivi bag for use in heavy rain but many users don't bother and stay comfortable). If I am carrying a tent then I take a down bag but if bivouacking, snow-holing or sleeping in damp, leaky mountain huts or bothies I use a Buffalo bag. Other suggestions for using the bags from Hamish Hamilton are to slide your sleeping mat into the bag when it's raining so that you don't get cold from compressed wet pile under pressure points and not to wear absorbent clothing (cotton, wool or down) in a pile bag, as this will become wet.

The Buffalo concept is so different from any others that I would suggest that any reader interested in it contact the company at Meersbrook Works, 19 Valley Road, Sheffield, S8 9FT, Great Britain for more information.

No one else makes anything similar, though Survival Aids sell a version of the 4S with added arm zips, made for them by Buffalo, called the Allweather Sleeping Bag. Otherwise pile liners from companies such as Mountain Equipment and Field & Trek are all that is available.

Carrying

Many people, especially those who use external-frame packs, like to strap their sleeping bags under the packbag. It seems to me though that, however good your stuffsac, this leaves your sleeping bag vulnerable to rain, dirt and damage. As it's not an item I'm likely to need during the day I pack my bag at the bottom of the pack. If it's a down-filled one I first stuff it into an oversize stuffsac then roll it into a proofed nylon sac liner. The reason for the oversize stuffsac is to enable the bag to mould to the curve of the pack around the lower back and hips and fill the corners. A rounded stuffsac packed to bursting, as provided with most bags to show how small they go, is very hard to fit in a pack without leaving lots of unfilled space. This is especially so with compression stuffsacs, so when I carry a pile bag I simply shove it by the handful into the bottom of the pack, saving myself a little weight in the process. Even if the pack leaks I find the pile absorbs very little moisture and what it does take up dries quickly and doesn't affect the performance.

Care

In the field all sleeping bags benefit from being aired whenever possible to allow any moisture to evaporate. This is especially important with down bags as these can absorb a surprising weight of moisture overnight. It's also a good idea with down bags to remove them from their stuffsacs well before use so that the fill can expand, and to give them a shake before climbing in to help ensure even distribution of the fill. Neither of these actions make the slightest difference to synthetic or pile bags.

Small cuts or holes in the fabric should be patched with sticky-backed ripstop nylon from the repair kit to prevent any fill escaping. This is usually adequate, though it could be reinforced with a sewn patch on your return home, with the stitch lines coated with seamseal to make them downproof.

At home the most important thing to do with down and synthetic bags is not to store them compressed, as in time this means the fill won't expand fully and the bag won't keep you as warm. Synthetic bags suffer most from this; prolonged compression leads to a completely flattened fill. Instead bags should be stored so that the fill can loft, which means either flat (mine live on top of a wardrobe), hung up or in a very large bag. If the last it should be a non-proofed bag so that moisture can escape. Cotton or polycotton are ideal. Some makers such as The North Face and Mountain Equipment provide storage bags with each sleeping bag. Pile bags can be stored in their stuffsacs without any harm coming to them.

This is all that needs to be done until the bag needs cleaning. With pile bags this is no problem as they can be machine washed in exactly the same way as pile clothing, and of course they dry very quickly. In fact it's advisable to wash them whenever the pile starts to flatten out to maintain the warmth. On long trips this could even be done by hand in the field. Synthetic bags can also be machine washed but shouldn't be dry-cleaned.

Cleaning down bags is a very different matter and one fraught with danger. First, every time you clean down it loses a little of its insulating properties, so it should only be done when the fill is so dirty that it no longer keeps you as warm as it should anyway. If it's just the shell that is dirty it can be freshened by airing and wiping off spots with something like Stergene. Eventually though, every bag needs to be thoroughly cleaned. The problem then is that down absorbs vast amounts of water and the bag becomes very heavy. If it is lifted when wet, the baffles may tear under the weight of the wet down, so most instructions say bags should be hand-washed in a bath or large tub. It must then be dried quickly in a large tumble drier to prevent the down forming clumps. Finally special soaps are needed, as standard washing powders strip the natural oils from down and thus shorten its life. The whole procedure sounds so tedious and time-consuming that I must admit I have never tried it. I have always sent down bags away to be washed or dry-cleaned by experts. As well as relieving me of the task, I also think this makes it more likely that my bag will survive the process. A few manufacturers such as Fjallraven say down bags can be machine washed but I wouldn't be prepared to risk damaging an expensive bag by doing this. Many experts think that improper cleaning ruins more down bags than anything else, including prolonged use.

If you decide to have someone else clean your bag where do you go? To find local cleaners, if there are any, contact the shop you bought the bag from or the manufacturers for their recommendations. Only some dry-cleaners can handle down-filled items and it's very important that the bag be well aired afterwards as the fumes from the chemicals they use are poisonous. Some dry-cleaning agents also ruin down so you need to be sure the company you use know what they're doing. I prefer to have the bag washed rather than dry-cleaned as I think this is safer, though it is harder to find someone who offers this service. In Britain one specialist company which does and which will do so by post is W.E. Franklin (see Appendix Three for address) who also offer a dry-cleaning service and who clean bags for RAB Down Equipment. Their prices are very reasonable, around a twentieth of the cost of a new bag.

Reconstruction

There may come a time when the shell of your down-filled bag is so filthy it makes your skin crawl and no cleaning company will touch it. This happened to me with the Field & Trek Golden Oriole bag I used on the Continental Divide walk. This had a polycotton inner (current models are Pertex, a much better fabric), which after 157 nights' use was in an appalling condition. Dry-cleaners I approached (I didn't know of W.E. Franklin then) wouldn't handle it, saying the polycotton was rotten and would disintegrate during the cleaning process. As the expensive goose down fill still lofted quite well and kept me warm I was loath simply to throw the bag away, so I had it remade. This included washing the down and cost less than half the price of a new bag. The resulting product is not only a better fit, as I could specify the length, but weighs 900g/2lb rather than 1250g/2lb 12oz, as the new shell is a Pertex one. I've been using this remade bag for four years and it's proved well worth the money.

To find a company that will remake bags ask at your local outdoor shop and also check the small ads in the outdoor press. I know of two companies that offer this service in Britain. Duvet Designs (see Appendix Three for address) make jackets as well as sleeping bags, using the down from unwanted or worn-out articles. Their sleeping bags are of slant-wall construction with nylon shells (cotton is optional for the inner), hood and shaped foot, and come with a stuffsac. Extra down can be added if you want a warmer bag. Mountaineering Designs (See Appendix Three) offer a similar service but only for sleeping bags. Their mummy bags have nylon/cotton shells and slant-wall construction. Again extra down can be added if required, though they point out that a cheaper way to make a warmer bag is to use the fill from two old sleeping bags. With both companies the cost is less than half that of a new bag.

Liners

The obvious way to improve the warmth of a sleeping bag is to wear clothes in it. However you could use a liner instead. If you always use one it does help keep your bag clean. But then again so do clothes if you wear them to sleep in every night. It makes more sense to me to carry clothing rather than a liner, as you can wear it in and out of the sleeping bag. Also many liners twist around you during the night and cause frustrating tangles. Personally I find I sleep best and feel most comfortable if I sleep naked in a bag without a liner so that's what I generally do, only donning clothes if I feel cold.

Liners are available in cotton, polypropylene, silk, Pertex and coated nylon. The first I'd discount entirely because of its weight, absorbency and slow drying time. The second makes more sense, a typical liner weighing 450g/16oz, though that's more than a set of polypro underwear weighs. Silk at 125g/4½-oz really is light and also low in bulk and I do have a North Cape silk liner that I've used on occasion. It's what I'd recommend if you really want a liner. The Buffalo Pertex Thermaliner is rather more versatile, as it can be used as a cover as well as a liner. Its weight is 250g/9oz which includes a zip and a hood, unlike other liners. I use it as intended, with Buffalo pile sleeping bags, whose performance it does improve, but I haven't bothered otherwise. Tangling isn't a problem as the liner and bag can be attached to each other by way of toggles and loops.

Coated nylon is a different matter as it forms a vapour barrier that keeps moisture in and stops evaporative heat loss. In dry cold, especially when the temperature is well below freezing, a vapour-barrier liner (VBL) can add a surprising amount of warmth. However again I prefer to wear VB clothing because of the versatility and I've never in fact used a VB liner—there are only a few available, one of which comes from the North Face. (See Clothing chapter for how VBs work.)

MATS AND PILLOWS

Insulation in the form of a sleeping mat is needed under all types of sleeping bag to prevent ground chill from striking upwards where the fill is compressed under your body weight. In summer weather some hardy souls manage without a mat just using clothing under their bags but most people, myself included, use a mat year round.

There are two sorts of sleeping mats in general use, air beds and covered open-cell foam having just about vanished as far as backpackers are concerned. The choice is between closed-cell foam mats and self-inflating open-cell foam-filled mats. The first are lightweight, reasonably cheap and hardwearing, but very bulky to carry.

Although they are an efficient form of insulation they don't add much in the way of softness and so can be quite uncomfortable when used on bumpy or stony ground. These mats may be made from either pressure-blown or chemically blown foam. The first are warmer, more durable and resist compression better than the second but as the two look identical you have to rely on the makers to tell you which is which and they don't always do so. The synthetics they're made from don't really matter though Evazote (EVA), Ensolite and polyurethane are common ones. Mats come in different lengths, widths and thicknesses. I find three-quarter-length (about 145cm/57in) ones adequate as I use clothes as a pillow and under my feet if necessary. This saves a little weight and bulk. There are many makes, a popular one in Britain at least being Karrimor's Karrimat which comes in four types, using both sorts of foam, and a variety of sizes. A three-quarter-length four-season pressure-blown Karrimat weighs just 250g/9oz. I've found the most comfortable closed cell mat to be Cascade Designs' EVA Ridgerest which has a deep ridged pattern that adds softness and traps air for greater warmth. Although the bulk is more than flat-surfaced mats the weight is low, just 255g/9oz for a full-length (182-cm/72-in) Ridgerest. Because of their bulk closed-cell mats are normally carried on the outside of the pack wherever there are convenient straps.

Cascade Designs are better known though for the first and best self-inflating mat, the Therm-A-Rest. I've used one now for nearly a decade. The pu-proofed nylon shell of these mats is bonded to an open-cell polyurethane foam core that expands when the valve at one corner is opened. A few puffs of breath helps speed up this process. Once the mat has reached the required thickness the valve can be closed to prevent the air escaping. The comfort and warmth the Therm-A-Rest provides is astonishing. I've slept on stones and not noticed and been comfortable on snow when others were using two closed-cell foam mats. Every time I've loaned one to dubious friends they've gone out and bought one at the earliest possible opportunity. During the writing of this book I used a closed-cell foam mat for the first time in years to see how it compared. I found I had to take much greater care in selecting where I slept and that even on the softest ground it was far less comfortable than the Therm-A-Rest.

There are two weights of Therm-A-Rest—Standard and Ultra-Lite—and two lengths—three-quarters (119½cm/47in) and full (183cm/72in). Standard ones expand to a thickness of 3.8cm/1½in and weigh 680/1lb 8oz and 1020g/2lb 4oz for the two lengths. Ultra-Lites expand to 2.54cm/1in and weigh 480/1lb 1oz and 795 grams/1lb 12oz. Unsurprisingly my choice is for the three-quarter-length Ultra-Lite. One of these lasted through both the Continental Divide and Canadian Rockies walks plus all the trips in between before finally puncturing round the valve where a repair proved impossible. I estimate that I'd have gone through at least four closed-cell foam mats in that time, which puts the initial high price of the Therm-A-Rest into perspective. Before the Ultra-Lites were available I used a three-quarter-length Standard model which I took on the Pacific Crest Trail.

Although heavier than a closed-cell foam mat a Therm-A-Rest is much less bulky and can be folded and packed down the back of the pack where it is protected from damage. Care is needed in use too and I don't throw my Therm-A-Rest down on the bare ground and sit on it without checking for sharp objects that might puncture it. If I'm not using a tent I always carry a groundsheet to put the Therm-A-Rest on. In case the mat does spring a leak a repair kit containing patches, glue and a spare valve is available. It weighs very little and I always carry it.

Various copies of the Therm-A-Rest have appeared on the market but all those I've seen are heavier and bulkier and don't look as well made or durable. I'd recommend sticking with the original.

For a pillow I simply use a pile or down top, sometimes packed in a stuffsac. I've tried using my boots as some people do, but have found them very uncomfortable. For those who prefer more comfort than folded clothing there are a number of lightweight pillows available. Inflatable nylon- or PVC-covered ones can be found in many outdoor shops. They weigh around 155g/5½oz and take up very little room. Caribou offer the Quallofil-insulated Pack-It Pillow with a cotton/nylon/polyester shell and a weight of just 115g/4oz plus a pocket into which clothes can be stuffed for more firmness.

Snow holes can be surprisingly comfortable: Denise Thorn reading out a storm in the Cairngorms of Scotland.

PREPARING FOR BED AND COPING WITH THE NIGHT

There can be no right way to prepare for bed, but for those who are interested, this is what I do. Once a campsite has been selected and my shelter, if any, erected I lay out my Therm-A-Rest and open the valve. If the ground is cold and I want to sit on the mat I generally blow it up rather than wait for it to expand. Then I pull out my sleeping bag and lay it out on the mat. Depending on the temperature I may lie on or in the bag whilst I cook, eat, read, make notes, study the map, watch the stars and the trees, daydream or otherwise while away the evening until I start to feel sleepy. Then I usually strip off my clothes, arrange a pillow, lie down and adjust the sleeping bag until I feel warm enough.

Most nights don't need coping with because I sleep right through. The roar of the wind wakes me on occasion. If I can't go back to sleep when it does, I read and may even start up the stove and have a hot drink or some soup, anything rather than lie wide awake wondering if the tent will hold. On the rare occasions when the tent has collapsed, I've abandoned camp in the dark. Usually though I simply don't have quite enough sleep and I am glad to see the first grey distorted edges of daylight through the flysheet. What do you do though when you wake feeling chilly long before dawn? First, if you haven't done up the hood of the sleeping bag or have the zip partly open, adjusting those may well be enough. Nights grow colder as the hours go by, so you may need to adjust the sleeping bag to stay warm quite often. I'm so used to doing so that I barely wake at all but just fumble with the drawcords and sink back to sleep. The next stage if you're still cold is to don some clothes and have a snack. If wearing all your clothes doesn't make you warm then you've seriously underestimated the capabilities of your sleeping bag and clothing or else the temperatures are extremely cold for the area and time of year. All you can do then is shiver through until dawn with the aid of hot food and drink, then get out and not make the same mistake again.

111

The Wilderness Kitchen

FOOD AND DRINK

One of the joys of backpacking is taking the first sip of a hot drink at the end of a long hard day. Often it's the anticipation of that moment that keeps me going for the last hour or so. The tent is up, your boots are off and you can lie back and start to unwind. You may eat and drink whilst lying in the tent with a gale raging outside or sitting outside, back against a tree or boulder, admiring the view. Either way this period of relaxation and renewal is a crucial part of living in the wilderness, one of the aspects of backpacking that differentiates it from day walking.

Your choice of food plays a large part in how much you enjoy life in the wilds in terms both of the nutrition provided and of the pleasure you gain from eating it. The possibilities and permutations are endless so your diet can be constantly varied. Wilderness dining has two extremes: gourmet eaters and survival eaters. The first like to make camp at lunchtime so that they have several hours to set up their field ovens, bake cakes and bread and cook their multi-course dinners. Only a few kilometres are walked each day and a campsite may be used for several nights. Survival eaters on the other hand breakfast on a handful of dry cereal and a swig of water and are up and walking within minutes of waking. Dozens of kilometres are pounded every day, and lunch is a series of cold snacks eaten on the move. Dinner consists of a freeze-dried meal 'cooked' by pouring hot water into the packet or, for the real die-hard, just more cold snacks.

Most people of course fall somewhere between these two extremes. I should warn those who tend towards the gourmet approach that I lean heavily towards the survival one, so this is not a book in which you'll learn how to bake bread or make soufflés. If you're interested in doing so I'd suggest having a look at Rick Greenspan and Hal Kahn's appropriately titled *Backpacking: A Hedonist's Guide* (Moon Publications), which is also good for fish dishes for those handy with a rod. A book of recipes for those gourmets who also favour wholefoods and a less indolent form of backpacking is Vikki Kinmont and Claudia Axcell's *Simple Foods for the Pack* (Sierra Club Books). Be warned though. The foods may be simple, but the cooking and particularly the preparation, much of which can be done at home, often isn't, at least to my mind. Even so there are meals in here that even I might be tempted to make (though as I've had a copy of the book eleven years and not done so yet it seems unlikely!). Most of the meals are vegetarian, though some include fish. Meat-eaters interested in similar menus might like to look at Margaret Cross and Jean Fiske's *Backpacker's Cookbook* (Ten Speed Press). Other useful-looking cookbooks are June Fleming's *The Well Fed Backpacker* (Random House) and Gretchen McHugh's *The Hungry Hiker's Book of Good Cooking* (Knopf).

Many of the facts and figures quoted below

have been taken from David Briggs and Mark Wahlqvist's *Food Facts* (Penguin), a fascinating volume which I recommend to anyone interested in pursuing the subject further.

Hot or cold?

Hot food provides no more energy than cold food and cooking food can destroy some vitamins, though certain starches like potatoes, beans and lentils need to be cooked to make them more digestible and, in the case of the last two, to destroy substances that make utilising their protein difficult. One way to cut the weight of your pack significantly would be to eat only cold food and dispense with the need for stove, fuel and cookware. I've often thought of doing so. When it comes to the point though I always take food that needs cooking, on the grounds that on short trips the extra weight is so slight as not to matter and on long trips the psychological boost of hot food is essential, especially if the weather turns cold and wet. I find daydreaming about the steaming soup and hot dinner I am going to have as I trudge through the last remaining hour of a bleak windswept day excellent for lifting my spirits. If cold food was all I had to look forward to I don't think it would have the same effect. And if anyone becomes really cold and wet, shivering and on the verge of hypothermia perhaps, hot food and drink is a great, perhaps essential, help. Certainly in winter when snow may have to be melted to obtain water and a hot meal can send waves of welcome warmth coursing through your cold, stiff body I wouldn't recommend trying to survive without a stove and hot sustenance.

Composition

Food consists of a number of components, each of which is needed by the body. The main ones are fats, proteins and carbohydrates. All three provide energy but also serve other functions.

Fats release their energy slowly and can be stored in the body to be used when required. Because fats are digested gradually they are not a good food for providing quick energy. This, combined with the fact that your body cannot easily digest food and undertake strenuous exercise at the same time means eating much in the way of fat before the evening isn't a good idea. Eating fats as part of your evening meal however enables them to release their energy during the night and help keep you warm. Sources of fat include dairy products, margarine, eggs, nuts and meat. Much is made by nutritionists of the difference between saturated and polyunsaturated fats, the current wisdom being that you should cut down on foods high in the first (butter, animal fat margarine, cheese, whole milk, lard, chocolate) and replace it with those high in the second (polyunsaturated vegetable margarines, low fat spreads, vegetable oil). This is in addition to cutting down the total amount of fat in the diet anyway as it can clog up arteries and lead to heart disease as well as cause obesity. Some fat is needed by the body, but nothing like the amount most people in developed countries eat.

Protein is needed to renew muscles and body tissue. During digestion proteins break down into the amino acids they're made from. The body then rebuilds these into muscle and tissue protein. Complete proteins contain a full complement of amino acids and are found in meat, eggs and dairy produce. Incomplete proteins lack one or more amino acids and are found in grains and pulses. However by combining foods from these categories complete proteins are created. Thus a stew with beans and barley in it provides all the amino acids. As the body either burns as fuel or stores as fat protein that isn't immediately used for muscle regeneration, protein should be eaten in small amounts at every meal.

Carbohydrates are turned directly and quickly into energy by the body and so are the foods most needed by the backpacker. There are two types of carbohydrate: simple and complex. The first are basically sugars (sucrose, dextrose, fructose, glucose and honey), the second starches (grains, vegetables, pulses). Generally it's the latter you should try to eat most of as they provide energy over a longer period of time than the former, and also give fibre, vitamins and minerals. Fibre in particular is essential to the diet if you aren't to become constipated — a potential problem for the backpacker living on dehydrated food for a long period. Sugars will give you a quick boost when you're really tired, but it won't last.

What proportion of your diet should consist of each of these components is a matter of debate amongst nutritionists, the current advice is to eat less fat and protein and more carbohydrates.

This is a conclusion that most backpackers, especially those who undertake long walks, will have come to anyway, I suspect, as it's carbohydrates that speed you along the trail and which you crave when food runs low. I estimate my backpacking menu is probably 60-70 per cent carbohydrate, the rest split equally between fats and proteins.

Vitamins and minerals are also components of foods but not ones you really need worry about on trips of less than a month in duration. Even if your diet is deficient in them for short periods of time it shouldn't do you any harm. On long trips however the lack of fresh food could mean you need to add a vitamin and mineral supplement to your diet. Advice is mixed on this — as are my views. I took a daily multivitamin with minerals supplement on both the Pacific Crest Trail and Canadian Rockies walks but not on the Continental Divide one, whilst on the Yukon trek I took a gram of vitamin C a day. The supplements appear not to have made much difference as I was ill on none of these except for the Yukon walk when I suffered a bad cold for a few days. I may still take a vitamin supplement on future long walks though. At the very least it does no harm and it just may ensure that no deficiency occurs.

Calories and Weight

Calories are well known as a measure of the energy value of food. In fact there are two different calories, both units of quantity of heat. The Large or kilocalorie is the one used for food and represents the amount of heat needed to raise 1kg of water 1°C. Correctly this should be called the Calorie with a capital C or the kilocalorie (kcal) though it's often called just the calorie on food packets. Sometimes kilojoules are used instead of kilocalories. There are 4.2 kilojoules to the kilocalorie.

How many kilocalories a person needs per day depends upon their metabolism, weight, age and sex as well as how active they are. Metabolism is the processing of food by the body into living matter. This is an extremely complex and not fully understood process but what is known is that after protein has been used for tissue-building and carbohydrates and fats for fuel (energy) any surplus is stored as fat. This means that if you eat more kilocalories than you use you will put on weight, and if you eat less, you will lose it. Putting on weight is not usually a problem for the backpacker, but losing it may be. What is important is the weight of food you need to carry in order to have enough energy.

Everyone's metabolic rate differs, though in general the fitter and more active you are the faster you will burn up food whether you are working or at rest. Figures are available for the kilocalories needed for 'everyday life' for people of different sizes. For someone of my height (173cm/5ft 8in) and weight (70-73kg/154-161lbs) it's around 2500 kcals a day. Of that 1785 kcals makes up the basal metabolism, which is the energy required simply to keep the body functioning. This is based on 1100 kcals per 45kg of bodyweight. Any extra energy output uses up more calories so it's clear that my backpacking menu must provide more than 2500 kcals a day.

How many are needed can be worked out roughly from figures that are also available for the kilocalories needed for different activities. I hadn't worked this out before writing this book —my food planning for walks was done on the rather hit-and-miss basis of hoping that by carrying the same weight of food on each walk I'd have about the same number of kilocalories. However I've made some calculations here as I was curious to see how closely my field-based figures compared with scientifically calculated ones and I feel that such an exercise could perhaps be useful to others in planning their food supplies.

These figures are adapted from *Food Facts*.

Activity	Kilocalories per hour	
	58-kg/128-lb woman	70-kg/154-lb man
1: Sleeping, resting, fasting	30–60	60–90
2: Sitting, reading, desk work	60–90	90–120
3: Sitting typing, playing piano, operating controls	90–150	120–180
4: Light bench work, serving in shop, gardening, slow walking	120–210	180–240
5: Social sports, cycling, tennis, cricket, light factory work, light farm work	180–300	240–360
6: Heavy physical labour, carrying, stacking, cutting wood, jogging, competitive sports	240–420	360–510
7: Very hard physical labour, intense physical activity, heavy lifting, very vigorous sporting activity	600+	720+

If we include walking with a pack at the upper end of category 5 and the lower end of category 6 then men need 360kcals per hour and women 240. If you walk for about seven hours a day, not including stops, as I do, that works out at 2100kcals for a woman and 2520 for a man (5 and 6 per minute respectively). Splitting up the rest of the day into nine hours' sleeping and resting (category 1), which requires 270–540kcals (women) and 540–810 (men), and 8 hours of category 4 (spent setting up camp, cooking, packing, 'slow walking' around the site) which requires 960–1680kcals (women) and 1440–1920 (men) we end up with totals of 3330–4320kcals (women) and 4500–5250 (men). These figures are very rough of course but they seem on the high side. You could argue, however, that much backpacking comes into category 6/7 and requires more not less energy than given here.

I say that the figures seem rather high because my actual experience is that I only need around 4000kcals a day on trips of no more than a few weeks. The reason for the discrepancy is probably that the figures are for the so-called 'average' woman or man and none of us fits them exactly. Even so, such exercises are at least interesting and possibly useful to those who would like to be precise about how much energy they use and where it comes from.

On longer walks my appetite goes up dramatically after the first couple of weeks and I now plan for more food from that time onwards. I guess, though I haven't worked it out exactly, that on long treks I average at least 5000kcals a day. On treks in bitter weather even more may be needed because of the cold and even more again on ski tours as skiing uses up energy at a far greater rate than walking.

Many foods these days have the calorie content listed on the packaging, which is useful in making comparisons and compiling menus. I always check labels to see if the kilocalories are listed when scanning the supermarket shelves for new foods. Unlike most people who are looking for calorific information I'm searching for high-calorie not low-calories foods. As such information is not always available on food labels here's a list of the kilocalories per 100grams/3½oz dry weight of a selection of foods useful for backpacking, plus the percentages of fat, protein and carbohydrate they contain:

Food	Kcals per 100g/3½oz	% fat	% protein	% carbohydrate
Dairy produce, fats and oils				
Margarine	720	81.0	0.6	0.4
Low-fat spread	366	36.8	6.0	3.0
Vegetable oil	900	100.0	-	-
Instant dried skimmed milk	355	1.3	36.0	53.0
Cheddar cheese	398	32.2	25.0	2.1
Edam cheese	305	23.0	24.0	-
Parmesan cheese	410	30.0	35.0	-
Eggs, dried	592	41.2	47.0	4.1
Low-fat cheese spread	175	9.0	20.0	4.0
Dried fruit				
Apples	275	-	1.0	78.0
Apricots	261	-	5.0	66.5
Dates	275	-	2.2	72.9
Figs	275	-	4.3	69.1
Peaches	261	-	3.1	68.3
Raisins	289	-	2.5	77.4
Vegetables				
Potato, dehydrated	352	-	8.3	80.4
Tomato flakes	342	-	10.8	76.7
Baked beans	123	2.6	6.1	19.0
Nuts				
Almonds	600	57.7	18.6	19.5
Brazil nuts	652	66.9	14.3	10.9
Coconut, desiccated	605	62.0	6.0	6.0
Peanut butter	589	49.4	27.8	17.2
Peanuts, roasted	582	49.8	26.0	18.8

Food	Kcals per 100g/3½oz	% fat	% protein	% carbohydrate
Grain products				
Porridge oats	375	7.0	11.0	62.4
Muesli, sweetened[1]	348	6.3	10.4	66.6
Pasta, white	370	-	12.5	75.2
Pasta wholewheat	323	0.5	12.5	67.2
Rice, brown	359	-	7.5	77.4
Rice, white	363	-	6.7	80.4
Flour, plain	360	2.0	11.0	75.0
Flour, wholemeal	345	3.0	12.0	72.0
Baked products				
Granola bar[2]	382	13.4	4.9	64.4
Crispbread, rye	345	1.2	13.0	76.3
Oatcakes	369	15.7	10.1	65.6
Bread, white	271	-	8.7	50.5
Bread, wholemeal	243	-	10.5	47.7
Biscuit, chocolate	525	28.0	6.0	67.0
Fig roll	356	5.6	3.9	75.4
Cake, fruit	355	13.0	5.0	58.0
Meat and Fish				
Beef, dried	204	6.3	34.3	-
Beef, corned, canned	264	18.0	23.5	-
Salami	490	45.0	19.0	2.0
Salmon, canned	151	7.1	20.8	-
Sardines, drained	165	11.1	24.0	-
Tuna, drained	165	8.2	28.8	-
Sugars and sweets				
Honey	303	-	0.3	82.3
Sugar, brown	373	-	-	96.4
Sugar, white	384	-	-	99.5
Chocolate, milk	518	32.3	7.7	56.9
Custard, instant	378	10.2	2.9	72.6
Drinks				
Cocoa mix	391	10.6	9.4	73.9
Coffee	2	-	0.2	-
Tea	1	-	0.1	-
Complete meals:				
Pasta & Sauce[3]	384	4.7	13.1	77.1
Vegetable Goulash & Potato Mix[4]	375	11.9	15.9	54.4
Vegetable Cottage Pie[5]	391	3.0	16.3	66.5
Thick Pea Soup[6]	333	5.3	17.0	58.0
Bean Stew Mix[7]	349	2.9	17.5	67.3
Fruit & Nut Bar[8]	420	28.0	17.0	56.0

These figures are taken from a variety of sources including *Agricultural Handbook No.8: Composition of Foods* (US Department of Agriculture) as reproduced in *Mountaineering: The Freedom of the Hills*, 4th Edition, *Food Facts* by David Briggs and Mark Wahlqvist and manufacturers' specifications.

Notes

1: *Taken from Gateway's Fruit & Nut Muesli*
2: *Jump Tropical Fruit Cereal Bar*
3: *Crosse & Blackwell's Romana Pasta Choice*
4: *Bilsons Easy Cuisine*
5 & 6: *Hera Complete Meals & Soups*
7: *Be-Well Easy Beans*
8: *Bear Valley Fruit-'n-Nut Pemmican.*

If you use calories purely as criteria for choosing foods, what these figures suggest is that you should live solely on margarine, vegetable oil, dried eggs, nuts and chocolate in order to carry the least weight! I doubt whether you'd feel very well or find walking very easy, however, as all these are very high in fats. In fact fats have 9kcals per gram, whilst proteins and carbohydrates have just 4. By using the above list, it is possible to work out the approximate calorific content of most foods by seeing what group they fit into and what the average is of that group. The diet of complex carbohydrates (dried skimmed milk, dried fruit, dried vegetables, pasta, rice, oatcakes, muesli and granola bars), plus a little fat (cheese, margarine) that I eat and recommend gives a measure of around 400kcals per 100g/3½oz. So to have 4000kcals a day you have to carry 1kg/2.2lb of food per day, which, as it happens, is about what I do carry. This diet should also provide enough in the way of protein. Only if your diet is based on sugars do I think you run the risk of not having enough protein.

It's worth checking the calorie content of any food you intend carrying as there are significant variations between makes and high-calorie carbohydrate foods mean less weight than low-calorie ones. After compiling the table above I'm glad I don't carry tinned fish, as many do, as the weight per calorie (including the can which you have to carry) is very high. However I really should give up my coffee in favour of cocoa! On short trips, weekends say, in warm weather weight isn't a major concern, and I often take loaves of bread, fresh fruit, tinned food and anything else I fancy that I find in the larder. But in cold weather when you have a much bigger and heavier basic load and particularly on long treks when a week or more's food has to be carried weight matters a great deal. Unfortunately it's on short trips that you can get away with taking less food, as you'll be back home in a few days and on long trips that you must carry enough food to meet all your needs. I've read of people who can manage on around 450–700g/16–24oz of food per day without, apparently, subsisting on margarine and nuts. I can't, at least not for more than a few days. I need that 4000kcals to keep me going, a little more on ski and cold-weather treks, so it has to be 1000g/35oz a day. Powdered drinks, condiments and other odds and ends are included in this total, and it roughly divides into 150g/5oz for breakfast, 400g/14oz for dinner and 400g/14oz for during the day. The main evening meal usually weighs around 200g/7oz, the other 200g being made up of soup, margarine, herbs and spices, milk powder, coffee and sugar. These figures give approximately 600, 1600 and 1600kcals for the three meals.

Carrying 1kg/2.2lb a day means 7kg/15lb a week, 14kg/30lb a fortnight. Two week's worth is the most I now ever consider carrying and

I only do that if there's really no other choice. On the Pacific Crest Trail I carried 20kg/44lbs of food on the 23-day crossing of the snow-bound High Sierra which made for a 45-kg/100-lb load as I also had snowshoes, ice axe, crampons and cold-weather clothing. I couldn't actually lift the pack off the ground but had to put it on whilst sitting down then slowly and carefully stand up. The weight was ridiculous and it was only my lack of awareness of what such a load would feel like that made me try to carry it. And I still ran short of food, probably because of the extra energy I needed to carry such a weight. Never again! Two weeks food is the most it is reasonable to carry.

Knowing what weight of food you need per day helps minimise the chance of finishing a long hike with food left in your pack. To do so is particularly galling at the end of a two-week trek that began with a very heavy load. I know that if the total weight of my food comes to much more than 1kg/2.2lb a day I've packed too much, so I jettison some.

To keep the weight down to 1kg/2.2lb a day on long walks and in cold conditions I increase the amount of fat somewhat, usually by adding more margarine and cheese to evening meals. In extreme cold fats also help to keep you warm as they gradually release energy. Polar explorers often consume appallingly large amounts of fat every day, as it's the only way they can consume the 7000–8000 calories they need. Eating that amount in carbohydrates would mean huge loads and never-ending meals.

Bulk
This is something that doesn't matter on one- or two-night jaunts but can be a problem on longer trips. Fresh, canned and retort (where cooked food is vacuum wrapped in foil) goods as well as being heavy are also bulky, so dried foods are the backpacker's staple for long-haul treks. By removing the moisture from foods the calorie content is kept but the weight and bulk are drastically reduced. The simplest method of drying food is under a hot sun. Because this doesn't remove as much moisture as other methods it's not used for many foods, though some fruits, such as bananas, may be sun-dried. Air-drying, where the food is spun in a drum or passed on trays through tunnels through which hot air is blown, produces what are generally described as dehydrated foods. As this

damages the cell structure, reconstituted dehydrated foods don't taste much like the original—hence the common dislike of them. In spray-drying, the food is sprayed at high speed into a high hot-air-filled cylinder. This is used to dry milk, cheese and coffee. The most complex and expensive means of sucking the water from foods is freeze-drying, whereby food is frozen very quickly (flash-frozen) so that the moisture in it turns to ice, the crystals of which aren't large enough to damage the cell structure. The food is next placed in a vacuum at a low temperature in which the ice turns directly into vapour without passing through a liquid state (a process called sublimation), again leaving the cells undamaged. Freeze-dried food is costly compared with dehydrated food because of this complicated process, but it does taste better. It often doesn't need cooking before it can be eaten—just the addition of boiling water—because the food can be cooked before being freeze-dried.

Cooking Times and Methods

The time food takes to cook affects the amount of stove fuel you have to carry and also how long you have to wait for a meal at the end of the day. If you generally wander only a few kilometres each day or travel in country where fires are acceptable, cooking times may not be significant. When you're crouched exhausted and hungry over a tiny stove at the end of a long day with a storm raging all around, knowing your energy-restoring dinner will be ready in five rather than 30 minutes can be very important. Also, as you go higher and the air pressure drops so does the boiling time of water, which means that cooking times go up, as those listed on food packets are for sea level. The ratio is approximately double the cooking time for every 5°C/9°F drop in the boiling point of water. This temperature drop occurs for every extra 1500metres/5000ft of altitude. So at 1500 metres/5000ft the cooking time is twice what it would be at sea level, at 3000 metres/ 10,000ft nearly four times as long, at 4500 metres/15,000ft seven times and at 6000 metres/20,000ft an appalling thirteen times. In Britain of course these figures don't mean much, but in other areas such as the Pyrenees, the Alps, the mountains of Western North America and in particular the Himalayas, they need to be taken into account.

These figures are important as most food suitable for backpacking requires cooking in boiling water. Many people like to fry foods, especially for breakfast. However, cleaning the greasy pan can be very difficult and oil or cooking fat has to be carried, so I rarely fry food. You can bake and roast if you have a fire for cooking, but I've never done so. (I did warn you I'm not a gourmet outdoor cook!) Anglers often carry foil to wrap trout in before placing them in the embers of a fire—the one type of roasting I can see makes sense.

There are many foods, from cup-a-soups to eat-from-the-packet freeze-dried meals that don't require cooking at all, just boiling water and a quick stir. Their taste is usually far inferior to meals that require a little simmering, but I generally carry a few for those times at the end of long hard days when I want hot food quickly and I'm not too fussy about the taste. I also take them when bivouacking, as I may then need to produce a meal in a gale. In that case I want to spend the least possible time cooking. Mostly though I use meals that need 5–10 minutes' simmering, as these for me are the best balance between tasty and fast food.

Cooking times can be helped along by presoaking some foods in cold water. This works with dried vegetables, dried meat, soya products and pulses, but not with pasta or rice. Some people put food to soak in a tightly capped bottle during the day so that it's ready for cooking when they reach camp, but I've never done this. My logical reason is that I don't want to carry the extra weight of the water but I suspect that the real reason is that I can't be bothered.

Fuel—though not time—can be saved with most foods that need simmering by bringing the water to the boil, adding the food and then turning off the heat. As long as a well-fitting lid is used the food will then at least partially if not completely cook in the hot water. I often do this when I make camp with plenty of time to spare, re-heating the food when I'm ready to eat.

What's Available

There are so many foods suitable for backpacking these days that attempting to list them all would require a book to itself. Here though are some suggestions biased heavily towards my own diet. Suitable foods can be found in supermarkets and grocers, wholefood stores and outdoor shops. All the foods you need can in fact be bought in supermarkets and their prices are the lowest. However you're likely to end up with quite a few processed foods full of additives, which may affect your decision. Care is also needed in checking cooking times. One packet of soup may take five minutes to cook whilst the almost identical one next to it on the shelf takes twenty-five. Wholefood stores supply unadulterated foods and a wider variety of cereals, dried fruits and grain bars than supermarkets, though the number of supermarkets selling wholefoods is increasing rapidly. Outdoor shops are where you'll find the foods specially made for backpackers and mountaineers. Lightweight, low in bulk, often freeze-dried but expensive, these are fine if you have the money and don't mind the taste. I've tried a wide variety of them and have found those from North America to be generally very good and worth buying, but those from Britain awful-tasting and to be avoided.

The best I've found come from the Californian company Alpineaire whose foods I ate on the Continental Divide walk. Even after five and a half months I hadn't grown tired of the food, so after trying vastly inferior British meals on the Canadian Rockies walk I returned to Alpineaire for the Yukon walk. Alpineaire foods are additive-free, use wholemeal pasta and brown rice and include both freeze-dried and dehydrated items. The range includes breakfast dishes and evening meals plus soups and light meals for those who cook lunch. They are available by mail order—see Appendix Three.

Offering a wide choice of specialist outdoor foods by mail order, including Alpineaire ones, are Trail Foods (see Appendix Three). They supplied me for my Pacific Crest Trail walk which is how I discovered Alpineaire. Other brands available from them are Mountain House, Richmoor and Backpacker's Pantry. There are other mail-order food suppliers in North America; the small ads in *Backpacker* magazine are the best place to look for them.

The Basic Breakfast: The only hot sustenance I normally have first thing, when I'm still bleary-eyed and trying to come to terms with being awake, is a mug or two of coffee with sugar and dried milk (combined weight at most 10g/0.3oz). To eat I have 110g/4oz of muesli or granola with dried milk (10–20g/0.3–0.6oz) and a few spoonfuls of sugar (about 15–20g/0.5–0.6oz) unless the brand already contains the latter. I

have no preference for any particular make— there are many good ones. Every supermarket and wholefood store offers several varieties. If it's cold enough for the water in the pan to have frozen overnight I tip the cereal on top of the ice, then heat the lot on the stove to make a sort of muesli porridge.

For those who prefer hot food every morning proper porridge is of course a possibility and there are various dried omelette and pancake mixes available from outdoor food suppliers, though I can't say I've tried any. You can of course eat anything at any time of the day. I have one trail companion who eats instant noodles for breakfast—not a food I could face at the start of the day! An experienced hiker I travelled part of the Pacific Crest Trail with ate trail mix for breakfast. I've tried it but find it too dry. Another I met on the same walk ate instant freeze-dried meals three times a day for the whole six-month walk, something else I couldn't contemplate.

The Lengthy Lunch: Walking with a pack requires a constant flow of energy, not sudden large inputs interspersed with periods of fasting, so I eat several times during the day. Often the first mouthfuls of 'lunch' are eaten soon after breakfast and before I start walking. Some people like to stop and make hot drinks during the day or even cook soup or light meals. I don't, as I rarely stop for more than ten or 20 minutes at a time and I am happy to snack on cold foods and drink cold water. Also, the days when I'd most like something hot are those when the weather's so cold or wet that stopping for more than a couple of minutes is a bad idea. In such conditions I'd rather keep moving and make camp earlier. On days when long halts are pleasant I don't feel the need for hot food.

A staple snack food is that mixture of dried fruit, nuts and seeds known as trail mix or gorp, as well as a host of other names. At its most basic it consists of just peanuts and raisins, but more sophisticated and tasty mixes can include bits of dried fruit (my favourites are papaya, pineapple and dates), a range of nuts, desiccated coconut, chocolate or carob chips, sunflower and sesame seeds, handfuls of crunchy roasted cereal (granola) and anything else you fancy. I prefer trail mix to be on the sweet side, others prefer a more savoury taste but there are so many possibilities that it can be different for every trip. I find I can easily eat 75-100g/2½-3½oz a day. I generally add any dried fruit I buy to the trail mix. The exception is sun-dried bananas which come in 250g/8oz blocks; these are too large so I eat them as an alternative to the mix.

I used to eat several chocolate and other candy bars every day but following the recommendation to cut down on fat and sugar and increase complex carbohydrates, I no longer do so. Instead I munch on cereal or granola bars, usually three or four a day. Two examples from the many such bars now available that I happen to have in my supply store at the time of writing are the 40-g/1½-oz 197-kcal carob-topped Castaway bar containing oats, carob coating (raw sugar, hydrolysed vegetable oil, skimmed milk powder, whey powder, carob flour, emulsifier—soya lecithin), raw sugar, vegetable oil, honey, wholemeal flour, coconut, hazelnuts, sesame seeds, soya lecithin, almonds and sea salt and the 21-g/¾-oz Jump tropical fruit bar containing mixed fruit pieces (dried apricot, dried papaya, dried banana), crisped rice, glucose syrup, rolled oats, vegetable oil, sugar, malto dextrin, glycerine, honey, sugar syrup, natural flavourings, citric acid, corn starch, vanilla and salt.

I also often carry a more substantial cereal bar, usually some form of sweetened oat biscuit or flapjack; those made by Suma are a particular favourite. However the best lunch foods I've discovered are the California-made Bear Valley Meal Pack and Pemmican bars which I took on the Continental Divide and Yukon walks. There are four varieties: Fruit 'n' Nut, Carob, Coconut Almond and Sesame Lemon. They are filling, packed with kilocalories (420, 470, 415 & 435 respectively), tasty and surprisingly light at just over 100g/3½oz per bar. They also contain all eight essential amino acids and so are a good source of protein. I ate at least one every day of the five-and-a-half-month Divide walk and two or more a day in the Yukon and never grew tired of them. The ingredients of each bar are much the same with the Fruit 'n' Nut bar, the basis of the range, containing malted corn and barley, non-fat milk, honey, wheat germ, raisins, walnuts, soy flour, soy oil, wheat bran, pecans and grape juice. As far as I'm aware they haven't yet crossed the Atlantic, which is a shame. If I ever do a trip where I eat only cold food these bars will make up the main part of my diet.

All the above foods are to a greater or lesser degree sweet-tasting. Having some savoury foods as a contrast is a good idea and I usually carry some form of bread substitute such as biscuits, crispbread or crackers plus a cheese or vegetable spread. Oatcakes are my favourite biscuit; my daily ration of six weighs 75g/2½oz and contains 275kcals. I like spreads that come in squeeze tubes as these are easy to use and don't create a mess (unless they burst). Spreads in tubs and foil I find ooze round the edges and smear themselves on your clothes and the sides of the plastic bags they have to be kept in. Primula make a good range of cheese spreads weighing 150g/5oz per tube. As one tube lasts me four days that works out at 37½g/1.3oz a day. My current favourite is Dairy Spread with cheese, garlic and herbs (contents: blended low fat cheeses, reconstituted skimmed milk/whey powder, emulsifying salt, garlic powder, parsley, preservative), which has 262kcals per tube, but there are many others. I'm not too bothered at the low energy content as I regard it as more of a flavouring than an essential food item. Meat eaters often carry paté or salami to go with biscuits whilst those with a really sweet tooth can take jam or honey, both of which are available in plastic squeeze bottles or tubs.

The Dehydrated Dinner: A one-pot dehydrated or freeze-dried meal forms the basis of my evening repast. It's possible to concoct such meals at home from basic ingredients but I prefer to use complete meals which I then doctor to suit my taste buds. There's a wide variety of these on the market at a wide variety of prices. As I have said, my favourites come from Alpineaire, available only in North America. Although this has not always been the case, all Alpineaire dishes require only the addition of boiling water and a 7–10-minute wait before you can eat them. A typical meatless example (they do beef, turkey, seafood and chicken dishes too) is Mountain Chilli (contents: cooked freeze-dried pinto beans, soy protein, tomato powder, cornmeal, freeze-dried corn, spices, bell peppers, onions and salt), which has a net weight of 200g/7oz and which makes two servings. Well, maybe, if you're not hungry, haven't been walking all day and have lots of other food to eat. I have no problem eating the whole 850g/30oz and 680 Kcals in one go. In fact when searching shop shelves for evening meals I look for dry weights of around 200g/7oz and ignore the number of servings, as I know that's what I need. If the amount is well below 200g/7oz I only carry it if I'm planning on adding extra food.

In Europe, where Alpineaire meals are sadly unobtainable, I find that I mostly live on pasta dishes. One staple dish is that perennial hikers' favourite on both sides of the Atlantic, macaroni cheese. Kraft Cheesy Pasta is the commonest brand (contents: pasta, cheese, dried skimmed milk, dried whey, salt, emulsifying salts, lactic acid, colour). It cooks in six minutes and comes in 190g/6¾oz packs, just right for a single meal though the pack says 'serves 2–3'. The makers advise adding milk and margarine to the dish. I add extra cheese as well. Slightly more sophisticated are the Crosse & Blackwell Pasta Choice dishes, though these do require supplementing as the dry weight is only around 100g/3½oz. A typical example is the Romana (contents: pasta tagliatelle, mushrooms, tomatoes, green peppers, maltodextrin, white wine powder, skimmed milk powder, hydrolysed protein, hydrogenated vegetable fat, paprika, starch, salt, yoghurt powder, flavour-enhancer (sodium glutamate), wheatflour, emulsifiers, onion extract, sugar, spices and garlic extract). This takes five minutes to cook and provides 670kcals with the addition of the butter and milk the makers advise. I substitute margarine for butter and add plenty of cheese as well.

There are various meals available in Britain that sound as though they should be equivalent to Alpineaire ones but for some reason unknown to me they don't taste anything like as good and need heavy seasoning to make them palatable. Haldane Foods make many of these, under the Hera label for wholefood shops and Raven for outdoor ones. They come in 200-g/7-oz packs and a variety of flavours, mostly soya-based. Each pack contains two 100-g/3½-oz sachets and I've found the best way to use them is to cook a sachet (simmering times 5–10 minutes) along with an equal weight of rice or pasta plus some herbs and spices. To my palate the most tasty of these meals is the Vegetable Cottage Pie which contains instant potato. Be-Well Easy Beans, also made by Haldane, I find tastier than the Hera ones but the packs are smaller at around 156g/5½oz. Varieties include Bean Stew, Lentil Curry and Haricot Bean Goulash. I must admit though that whilst these meals should be healthier than the more adulterated supermarket pasta ones described above it's the latter that

I much prefer and use most often.

Found in both North America and Europe, are oriental noodles with flavour sachets, usually sold under the name Ramen, that cook in about four minutes. Westbrae Ramens, using wholemeal flour for the noodles and without added chemicals, are my favourites. These are found in wholefood shops. There are half a dozen versions all weighing 88g/3oz and making 255g/9oz of cooked food, so extra ingredients are needed to make a full meal; packet soups, cheese and margarine being what I use. Supermarkets sell white flour versions such as Super Noodles which I sometimes use.

Whatever meals you choose a selection of herbs and spices will enable you to change and improve their taste when required. I carry garlic powder (fresh cloves on short trips), curry or chilli powder, black pepper and mixed herbs but not salt, which I don't like. Margarine, cheese and milk powder add kilocalories as well as taste and bulk to meals. I also sometimes use packet soups to add flavour to a boring meal. Conversely soups can be used as the base for a meal with pasta, rice, cheese, dried milk and other ingredients tipped in to increase the food value. I often mix foods like this on the last few evenings of a long trip, using up whatever I have left. If I am buying pasta or rice to add to soup I look for the quick-cook varieties.

I usually carry packet soups anyway and eat a bowl before having my main meal, unless I'm very hungry. The ones that require simmering for five or ten minutes taste best (I like Knorr brand), but instant soups have been improved a great deal since they were first introduced and require less time and fuel to prepare. The biggest problem with them is the serving size, a meagre 200g/7oz when rehydrated that provides only 118kcals. I solve this problem by eating two sachets at a time, the dry weight of which is 55g/2oz. Again, adding margarine and cheese will increase the energy content. The tastiest soups I've found come, again, from Alpineaire and these provide far more energy than most others. In fact with a little cheese and margarine added they will do as a main meal. There are several varieties, weighing between 94g/2½oz and 125g/4½oz and providing 194–318kcals per packet. They require no cooking—7–10 minutes' soaking in boiling water is all that's required.

Staple foods I almost always carry are margarine, dried milk and cheese. With the first I find I use around 50g/1¾oz an evening so a 250-g/9-oz tub lasts me five days. In the USA Parkay liquid margarine is available in a squeeze bottle at a weight of 450g/16oz. This is much easier and less messy to use than a tub and far less likely to crack or spill. I wish such a product was available in Europe. Tubes of margarine appear occasionally but are generally impossible to find, and also the only one I've tried tasted awful. I also calculate the weight of cheese needed for a trip on the basis of around 50g/1¾oz a day (twice as much if it is a main part of the meal). On long trips I plan on using up any cheese in the first few days out and so eat the lowest-calorie meals I'm carrying then. Instant dried skimmed milk adds taste and calories to any dish as well as being needed for breakfast cereals and tea or coffee. There are numerous makes; Marvel is a common one. Again North America provides the best brand, Milkman Instant Milk, which tastes more like fresh milk than any of the others. I prefer those that contain nothing but milk powder rather than those that contain an array of chemicals. The latter are usually found, ironically but I suspect deliberately, in plastic imitation miniature milk bottles. A standard 198-g/7-oz pack of instant milk will make 2 litres/3½pt and lasts me at least four or five days.

Coffee and sugar make up the final part of my evening sustenance. Three or four mugs an evening means carrying 22g/¾oz sugar and 6g/0.2oz of coffee per day. Despite being English I don't drink tea, but those who do seem to find a large supply of teabags essential—though I've noticed that an amazing number of mugs can be wrung from just one bag when supplies run low. Cocoa and drinking chocolate are other alternatives. Although they supply plenty of kilocalories, unlike coffee or tea, and are available in convenient sachets I rarely carry them.

Variations: The above is what I take on most walks that last more than a few days. There are variations of course. On two- or three-day trips I may carry bread rather than biscuits. Indeed I sometimes make up a packet of sandwiches for each day's lunch. Retort foods are feasible then too, being lighter and tastier than canned goods, though heavier and bulkier than dried ones.

Cold weather and winter treks in northern latitudes (in which I include the British hills) bring about the biggest change in my diet. Short daylight hours mean more time spent in camp and less on the move, whilst increased cold means a need for more kilocalories. These factors lead me to take slightly less day food but more for the evening. In particular I usually add some sort of sweet as a third course. Instant custard with dried fruit added is a favourite. An 87-g/3-oz packet (contents: sugar, cornflour, hydrogenated vegetable oil, skimmed milk powder, maltodextrin, whey powder, starch, lactose, caseinates, salt, flavourings and colours) provides 378kcals even before you add any dried fruit.

Emergency Supplies

For many years I carried at the bottom of my pack a compressed block of silver-foil-wrapped emergency rations known as Turblokken, on the assumption that it would keep me going if I ran out of food. I eventually ate it when I did indeed run short of food during a five-week walk in the Scottish Highlands. I could have reached a resupply point in a day but that would have meant not climbing some of the mountains that lay on my route so I decided to try and live on the Turblokken. My journal records that it was 'fairly tasteless but kept me going'. I never replaced it however and have since relied on carrying just a little extra food, such as a 250g/8oz block of dried bananas in case of emergency, plus supplies for one day more than I expect the trip to last in case bad weather slows me down or keeps me in camp. If you can catch fish or know which insects and plants are edible you can of course try to 'live off the land' (see Wild Foods).

I've only once run out of food in a really remote area—one where I couldn't walk out to a supply point in a day or two. My situation was not made any easier by the fact that I was also somewhat unclear as to my exact whereabouts. This was on the Canadian Rockies walk and I had to ration my food severely for several days, emerging from the forest extremely hungry but without having run out of energy. I learnt that, if you have to, you can get by on remarkably little food, at least for a short time. I would go to great lengths to avoid such a situation recurring however. Once is more than enough.

Packaging

Plastic bags of all sizes are essential for carrying food. I bag everything that needs repacking, including coffee, sugar, dried milk, trail mix, muesli and meals such as macaroni cheese that come in cardboard cartons. If I need them I tear off cooking instructions and put these in the bag with the food. The only items I keep in their cardboard containers are oatcakes and other bread substitutes as these are very vulnerable to breakage. I also keep margarine tubs and cheese in plastic bags in case of leakage. Packets of soup, granola bars and complete meals which come in light foil containers don't need repacking but can be bagged together so that it's easy to see what you have left of any foodstuff. This also means that if a foil pack tears or bursts the contents are kept in one place. The best bags I've found to be Ziploc—yet another item only available in North America. I buy large quantities whenever I'm over there as I've found European versions tear more easily and have less secure closures. Less easy to use but found in every supermarket are freezer bags with wire twist tie closures. I also keep and reuse the bags that supermarket bread and vegetables come in. Most plastic bags are quite tough but I always double-bag heavy, messy items such as sugar and I always carry a few spare bags in case one splits.

Outdoor shops are full of plastic containers for food but I've not found many that are actually much use. One of my main objections to them is that as they are emptied they still take up the same space in the pack, whereas plastic bags compress to almost nothing. Polyethylene squeeze tubes, in which you can put the required amount of semi-liquid foodstuffs such as jam or margarine seem like a good idea but I find that they break very easily, leaving an unholy mess in the food bag, so I no longer use them. Hard plastic egg boxes are available for those who carry fresh eggs. I haven't done so for years but when I did I used to pack them inside my cooking pots and I don't recollect ever having any breakages. The only plastic containers I regularly use are empty plastic film canisters in which, after washing them out, I carry herbs and spices. Flip-top lids with shake holes are available to fit these canisters and I have a pair (weight with canisters: 21g/0.75oz) for the ones that hold black pepper and curry powder. They work well.

To keep my food together in the pack I use large heavy duty plastic bags, transparent ones so that I can easily see where things are. These I close at the top with an elastic band. On long treks and especially in bear country where food has to be hung from a tree branch at night, I use nylon stuffsacs, which are less convenient but far tougher and more durable. When I'm carrying more than a week's food at a time I use two of these which makes it easier to find items. I put day food, which tends to be the bulkiest of my rations, in one bag and camp food in the other. Two bags are also easier to pack than one large one.

Resupply

On trips of up to a week, resupplying isn't a problem. Unless your route passes through a place where you can buy food you simply carry all you need. On longer treks though, especially ones that run to a month or more, you have to plan how you will resupply. Often, especially in Europe, it's easy to come down to a town or village at least once a week to do so. If you're prepared to accept whatever may be available and live at times on a peculiar diet, you can rely on the local shops providing for your needs. I've done so and it can be quite interesting! Most small shops can provide packet soups, biscuits, bread, cheese, candy and chocolate bars, coffee and tea but dried meals and even breakfast cereals can be hard to find. This can mean carrying more weight and bulk than you'd like in order to have enough kilocalories.

What I prefer to do, and have done on all my long walks in North America as well as several in Scotland, is send supplies to myself to be collected along the way. In this way I know what is in each supply box and can plan accurately and also include other items such as maps and camera film in the same boxes. The obvious places to send supplies to are post offices. They should be addressed to yourself 'Poste Restante' in Europe and 'General Delivery' in North America. They should also be marked 'hold for walker' and have a date on saying when you intend to collect it. I also write to post offices to tell them what I'm doing. In future I will also ring them after mailing my supplies to check that they've arrived as during the Canadian Rockies walk one box went astray, causing me a week's delay. Some mail-order food suppliers such as Trail Foods and Alpineaire (see 'What's Available' above) will ship food to post offices along your route, a service I used on both the Pacific Crest Trail and Continental Divide walks. If there are no post offices where I need to resupply then I approach a park or forest service ranger or warden office or else the nearest youth hostel, lodge or motel to ask if they will hold supplies for me. I've never yet been refused though some of the latter places have made a small charge (I always offer payment when I write).

You can cache food in advance if you have the time or else have someone who can do it for you. I've never done this but if someone had cached food for me I would want to be absolutely certain I could locate where they had put it. Obviously cached food has to be in an animal-proof container and hidden where only you can find it.

The alternative to caching food is to have it dropped by helicopter or brought in by bush plane. I considered such methods for the remote northern section of the Canadian Rockies walk but rejected it, mainly on the grounds of the high cost but also because I wasn't happy about bringing noisy machines into the wilderness unless it was absolutely necessary. Instead I tried to carry all my food for this 500km/300mile section. I took 17 days' food but spent 23 in the wilderness. I was lucky in that it was hunting season and there were a number of remote outfitters' camps in use, whose occupants fed me as I passed through. Without them I wouldn't have completed the walk. Of course I could and should have contacted them in advance and asked if they'd take supplies in for me, which is what I would do on a similar venture.

Food Storage In Camp

On most trips I like to keep my food in the tent, which means it's easily accessible and protected from small animals and birds. If you leave the tent door open bolder creatures, both domestic and wild, may venture in however. Camped on a quiet farm site in North Wales many years ago I was woken abruptly in the middle of the night by something furry brushing against my face. Startled, I sat up with a jolt, just glimpsing a dark shape sliding under the flysheet. A quick scan round with my headlamp revealed the nature of the culprit as it lit up the muddy paw prints of the farm cat crossing the groundsheet to my food bag, out of which the animal had pulled and then gnawed a lump of cheese. As I was lying near the food bag I guess that

the cat had relaxed as it ate the cheese and brushed against my face.

I try never to leave food outside on the ground, even if it's in the pack, as this is a sure way to feed the local wildlife. Sharp teeth will quickly make holes in the toughest materials. Even food left in the tent vestibule may be pinched. I once led treks for an Outward Bound school in Scotland that used to finish on the Isle of Skye at a coastal campsite where we could reprovision with fresh food. On every trek, despite warnings, students would leave their supplies, usually bread and bacon, just inside their flysheet doors only to have the local seagulls and sometimes even the local sheep steal them.

Bear bagging

If I'm camped near trees I often hang my food bag from a low branch to protect it from animals. Where bears may raid campsites in search of food, as in many areas in North America, food bags need to be hung high above the ground and well away from the trunk of the tree. The general advice is that they should be at least 4 metres/13ft above the ground, 2 metres/6ft below any branch and 3 metres/10ft away from the trunk. There are various ways of doing this, all requiring 15 metres/50ft or more of nylon line. The simplest method is to tie a rock to the end of the line, throw it over a branch a minimum of 6 metres/20ft above the ground at a point over 3 metres/10ft from the trunk, haul up the food until the bottom of the bag is a good 4 metres/13ft or more high then tie off the line round the trunk of the tree. This only works however in areas where there are big enough trees with long and strong enough branches, which usually means when you are deep down in the forest.

Around the timberline the trees are usually smaller and with shorter, down-curving, snow-shedding branches. Here it is usually necessary to suspend food bags between two trees about 7 metres/23ft apart, which involves throwing one end of the weighted line over a branch, tying it off and then repeating the process with the other end over a branch of the second tree. Make sure you keep the line between the two trees within reach as the food bag is tied to this before being hauled up until it is halfway between the trees and 4 metres/13ft off the ground. If you're on your own this method can be very difficult to put into operation. All I can say is persevere. I've spent the best part of an hour hanging my food in this way, expending a lot of energy on curses as branches broke and rocks whirled off into space or spun round branches leaving a tangle of line to unwind. But whenever I've felt like giving up I've thought about losing my food to a bear and gone on until my food is secure. I only use this method, however, if I can't find a suitable single branch within reasonable distance of my camp.

In a very few areas the bears have worked out that breaking a line rewards them with a bag of food. In these places, such as Yosemite National Park in California, neither of the above methods work and a counter-balance system is required. This is difficult to set up as it involves throwing the line over a branch that is at least 6 metres/20ft high, tying a food bag to the end of the line and hauling it right up to the branch, then tying a second food bag (or bag of rocks if you haven't enough food) to the other end of the line, pushing any spare line into the bag, and finally throwing or heaving the second bag into the air so that both bags end up 4 metres/13ft or more above the ground and 3m/10ft from the tree trunk. If a loop of line is left at the top of one of the bags this can be hooked with a stick or your staff to pull the bags down the next morning.

All the above methods make setting up camp more complicated and there is a tendency not to bother at the end of a long, hard day or in bad weather. Certainly when I make camp after dark I often make do with my food suspended somewhere I wouldn't be happy with in daylight. I always do hang it though, as not doing so can have consequences far beyond just losing my food. A bear that finds food at a campsite may start raiding it regularly and become such a danger that it has to be destroyed.

Generally in bear country it's wise to camp near trees and I've nearly always done so. If you end up far from any timber the advice is to store food well away from your tent in airtight plastic bags, which is what I did in the northern Yukon, where there are few trees big enough to hang food in. It is possible to buy 'bear proof' plastic cylinders though these are quite bulky. They could be worthwhile for habitual above-timberline bear-country campers though. In certain areas, such as the Slims River Valley of Kluane National Park in the Yukon where grizzly bears are very common, they are now com-

pulsory and can be hired from park offices.

Finally it should be noted that in this context 'food' includes items such as toothpaste, soap, insect repellent, sunscreen, food-stained clothing, dish clothes and dirty pots and pans. All these smell attractive to bears.

'Wild' Foods

I'm often asked why I don't 'live off the land' during long wilderness treks. The phrase conjures up the carefree image of a walker ambling along munching on nuts and fruits plucked from the trailside bushes and whisking tasty trout from every stream. In fact finding enough to eat unless you hunt animals with snare and gun or spend a long time fishing is very difficult and does not fit in with walking far each day. I also think that as our wild lands are limited and fragile we should take no more from them than we absolutely must, which means going into them with all the food we need. If every wilderness traveller relied on plants for food, popular areas would soon be stripped bare.

Fishing is perhaps an exception to this, mountain tarns and streams often seeming prolific in trout, and the stocks are unaffected by regular fishing. I wouldn't like to rely on fishing for food, but I can see that keen anglers might well want to carry light fishing outfits (and licences) in areas known for their fish and supplement their diets with some fresh food. Rick Greenspan and Hal Kahn's *Backpacking: A Hedonist's Guide* (Moon Publications) contains useful information for the would-be backcountry angler if you want to know more on this subject.

As some plants, especially some fungi, are poisonous, you should know exactly what you're eating if you do decide you'd like the occasional fresh item with your dehydrated dinner, so carrying a field guide and being able to identify plants is important.

WATER

Note: Whilst as elsewhere I have below given both metric and imperial figures for measurements I have not done so for volume because the British and American imperial systems are different. Three different figures seems just too much! Instead I have just used metric figures. For those who need to translate—a litre is near enough a quart in both the USA and the UK.

Whilst you can manage without food for a surprisingly long time, this is not the case with water. Dehydration can kill in a matter of days and long before you are in real danger you'll cease to enjoy what you're doing as your mind becomes dulled and your perceptions numbed. On any walk, knowing where water sources are and what the condition of the water is likely to be is very important. In many places water is not a problem, unless there's too much of it, but in others, especially desert or semi-desert areas, the location of the few water sources can determine your route. One of the first things I want to know about a region I'm visiting for the first time is what the position is regarding water supplies.

How much water you need per day varies from person to person. It also depends on the prevailing weather conditions, the amount of energy used and the type of food carried. I can walk all day without a drink in cool, damp conditions, though I don't recommend this. But on a very hot day in an area where there is no shade I may drink a litre an hour. Estimating needs for overnight camps is easier; with the dried foods I eat I need at least two litres, preferably more—and that is just for cooking and drinking, not for washing either myself or my pans.

When there's plenty of water such calculations are academic, but when you have to carry water they become important as water weighs a kilogram a litre. In desert areas of the southwestern USA I've carried up to 8kg/17½lb of water, a massive amount when added to the weight of your pack. Luckily it's rare to have to carry anything like that, at least for a whole day. 'Dry' camps (ie ones away from water sources, often high up on mountain ridges or even summits) may require the carrying of 3 or 4 litres of water (remember you need enough to get you to the next source as well as for use in camp), but this can often be picked up well into the day and only carried for a few hours.

Snow covered country is odd, for although everything is shrouded in solid water effectively it is a desert. You can become dehydrated as quickly travelling across snow as across sand; the dry air sucks moisture out of your body. The thirstiest I've ever felt has been when skiing all day in hot sunshine with no shade and not enough liquid. Eating snow cools the mouth but provides little real relief. The answer, easily given but not so easily carried out, is to melt enough snow in camp (see below) to keep you well supplied during the day.

Ideally, whether you are in a desert or a rain forest, you should never allow yourself to become even slightly dehydrated. The best way to avoid this is to drink regularly whether you feel thirsty or not. In practice there will be times when dehydration creeps up on you and only when your mouth starts to feel sticky and your tongue swollen do you realise how thirsty you are. Warning signs of incipient dehydration are a reduction in urine output and a change in the colour of urine. The paler it is the better. If it is dark, you need to drink a fair amount of water quickly.

Sources

Streams, rivers, lakes and ponds are the obvious sources of water, their locations easily identified from the map. In areas dotted with these features little water need be carried and you needn't worry about running out. Care is needed though to check contour lines and see exactly where the water is. Often the high ridges that make for superb walking can be far above any water, and in such places it's better to carry full bottles than make long descents and reascents when you need a drink. Watch out too for dotted rather than solid blue lines on the map, as these usually mean seasonal water sources. The rushing stream in June, heavy with snowmelt, may have vanished completely by late September.

If large water sources are really scarce then it may be necessary to hunt out tiny trickles and small seeps. To find these look for areas of richer coloured, denser vegetation and for depressions and gullies in which water may gather or run. Overall though it's best to rely on maps and guidebooks for information on the whereabouts of water. In desert areas successful water location is crucial. My experience is limited to crossings of the Mohave Desert and the semi-deserts of southern California on the Pacific Crest Trail, and the deserts of New Mexico on the Continental Divide. Each time I linked guaranteed water sources that were never more than 40km/25miles apart. Even so I often carried four litres of water at a time. For those intending more serious desert ventures and who want to know about caching water, desert stills and similar solutions, I recommend a look at Colin Fletcher's *The Complete Walker III* (Knopf) which goes into this in great detail. Most 'survival' books also cover desert travel but, unlike Colin Fletcher's book, are not written specifically for the backpacker.

Treatment

The real problem with water is not in finding it but in deciding whether what you find is safe to drink. Some water clearly needs purifying before it can be drunk but all too often there is no clear indication of either purity or con-tamination. Even the most sparkling, crystal-clear mountain stream may not be safe to drink.

The dangers come from a wide variety of micro-organisms which cause diarrhoea and dysentery—sometimes mild, sometimes severe. Giardia, which causes a virulent stomach dis-order curable only by specific antibiotics, is the one that has received most attention, at least in North America, but there are plenty of other nasties about.

So how do you judge and what do you do? Personally I've always drunk water untreated, as long as it looks clear and I'm above any habi-tations or livestock herds, but I'm aware that I risk picking up giardia. I've only once though had a serious bout of diarrhoea after a wilder-ness trip and the cause, although undiagnosed, wasn't giardia. It's certainly wise to find out about water in any new area you visit but also to be aware that travelling far from home can in itself lead initially to an upset stomach. If you're really worried about stomach disorders then treat all water regardless but note that this too has dangers. In the Montana Rockies during my Continental Divide walk I regularly met members of a large party doing the same trek. Most of them were very worried about giardia and filtered or boiled all water before drinking it. Whilst restocking and resting in the town of Butte after several weeks of very hot weather I met one of this party walking down the street looking rather pale and very thin. I was sur-prised to see him as when we'd last met he'd been intent on taking a more roundabout route than me. When I spoke to him I discovered that he'd staggered out of the mountains feeling weak and sick. He didn't have giardia—he was suffer-ing from severe dehydration through not drink-ing enough. He wouldn't drink unfiltered water and he hadn't time to filter anything like the amount he should have been drinking.

There are three ways of purifying water: boil-ing, treatment with chemicals and filtration.

Visibly dirty water can be filtered through a bandanna as can glacier melt water full of sedi-ment but this on its own doesn't remove the most dangerous organisms so it should still be treated. The surest way to kill off dangerous organisms is by boiling but this is impractical except for water which is drunk in camp because of the amount of fuel it uses up and the time it takes. Iodine and chlorine tablets are lightweight and simple to use but neither is fully effective, though iodine is rated better than chlorine. Both make the water taste foul so if you use either of them I'd suggest carrying fruit-flavoured crystals or powder to add to it to make it drinkable. Potable Aqua, which comes in $100g/3\frac{1}{2}oz$ bottles, is a common brand of iodine tablets. I used chlorine on the Pacific Crest Trail and Potable Aqua on the Continental Divide, on both of which at times I drank from really filthy stock ponds. I never became ill so presumably both worked. Tablets don't last long so you can't store them in your first aid kit and bring them out to use three years later, expect-ing them to work. Iodine crystals, which are reckoned to be more effective than tablets, are available from chemists and drug stores but care is needed in their use; iodine is poisonous if too much is ingested. The Polar Pure Iodine Crys-tal Kit $(100g/3\frac{1}{2}oz)$, available from REI, con-tains crystals, thermometer and instructions and is perhaps safer to use than crystals alone.

Filtration is probably the best method to use in areas where all water has to be treated. There are a number of devices on the market, mostly easy to use but heavy to carry. I have no direct experience of any of them but the 350g/12oz First Need Water Purifier is one of the lightest and its replaceable charcoal-based filter is said to screen out pesticides and many chemicals, which boiling won't do, as well as micro-organisms larger than 0.4 microns. It purifies a litre of water in 90 seconds. The established name is the Katadyn Pocket Water Filter which has a silver-quartz-impregnated ceramic filter which screens out organisms larger than 0.2 microns. Unfortunately though it weighs 650g/23oz.

Flavourings

Personally I find clear cold mountain stream water the most refreshing drink there is, which is one of the main reasons I'm reluctant to treat water unless it is absolutely necessary. Whilst filtered water simply loses a little of its zest and sparkle and tastes a little flat, chemically treated water tastes so awful that you just have to add something to it. Powdered fruit-flavoured drink mixes are the obvious solution. However the ones that used to be common in British supermarkets under the names Appeel and Rise 'n Shine vanished off the shelves in the late 1980s. As I hardly ever treat water in the British hills and rarely anywhere in Europe and I don't use such mixes otherwise, this is only a minor inconvenience. Those who like to flavour all water will have to adopt one of the alternatives mentioned below. In North America every store still seems to carry such mixes with Kool-Aid by far and away the commonest brand. Three versions are available, those to which sugar must be added, those containing sugar already and those containing artificial sweeteners. I've found the sugared ones the most useful. If you're carrying the stuff you might as well have a few extra kilocalories along with it.

Healthier alternatives to sugar and chemical concoctions are electrolytic salt and vitamin C mixes. Redoxon tablets, which are found in chemists and drug stores, and come in lightweight metal tubes, combine fruit flavours with high doses of vitamin C, but are quite expensive. Sports shops sell various types of fruit-flavoured high-energy or electrolytic salt replacement drinks. The electrolytes concerned are potassium and sodium chloride and they are depleted through heavy sweating. Whilst drinks containing them may be necessary for runners I don't find they are needed for walking—though they could be in desert regions. Such drinks have almost replaced salt tablets, though the latter are still available. There is much debate as to their usefulness. I carried salt tablets across the Mohave Desert but never used them—but then I don't seem to have a great need for salt as I don't normally add any at all to my food. I find the answer to heavy sweating and walking in hot weather is to drink little and often.

Carrying: Bottles, Bags and Flasks

Even on trips in well-watered country some form of water container is needed. These are available in aluminium and plastic and in a wide variety of shapes, sizes and makes. Aluminium has the advantage of keeping liquids cool in summer but unless it's lacquered inside it will contaminate water with drink mixes added. Plastic bottles warm up quickly but the contents don't taint. When little water needs to be carried, half-litre bottles are adequate but for general use I prefer litre ones, and I carry at least two in desert areas.

The standard aluminium bottles, and the ones I use, are the Swiss-made round red- or blue-lacquered Sigg Drinks Bottles (the uncoated silver ones are for stove fuel), which come in 0.6- and 1-litre sizes at weights of 110g/4oz and 140g/5oz. Sigg bottles are very tough and have screw tops with rubber seals that don't leak—at least none of mine ever have. However they also have narrow openings which can be awkward to fill from seeps and trickles. I generally use mine on trips where hot weather is expected and I don't want lukewarm water. Other aluminium drinks bottles include those from Markhill whose rounded bottles are ceramic-coated to prevent tainting and come in 0.4-, 0.75- and 1-litre sizes, and Laken, whose flat-sided bottles come in 0.75-, 1.0- and 1.25-litre sizes and have clip-on lids permanently attached to the bottle. Markhill offer clip-on and screw-top lids.

Laken and Markhill also make high-density, high-strength polythene bottles. Lakens are flat-sided, have attached screw tops and come in 0.5-, 1.0- and 1.5-litre sizes. Markhills are round and come in 0.75- and 1-litre sizes. They look durable and well made though I've never tried either. For years I've used Nalgene heavy-duty food-grade plastic bottles which are round in shape, have wide mouths for easy filling, screw tops and come in 0.5- and 1-litre sizes. I generally use the larger one, which weighs 100g/3½oz, lighter than many other bottles, yet very hardwearing. Nalgene bottles don't leak, unlike some of the cheaper unbranded bottles available, which must be kept upright in the pack. They are available with tops either attached to plastic rings round the bottles' neck or unattached. I've always used the second but having now twice let the lid slip through my fingers into a rushing stream and been very lucky to find it again, on both occasions after an hour or so's search amongst the boulders, I think that when I need a new bottle I'll change to the first. Whatever drinks bottle I carry it always lives in an outside pack pocket where I can get at it easily.

On most trips I only carry one rigid water

bottle, so I need something else for camp use. Of course in arid areas where you need several full bottles during the day, nothing extra is needed for overnight. Some people who only carry a single bottle make do with this plus their cooking pots in camp. Apart from the hassle of constantly having to go and fetch water whatever the weather, this practice is environmentally unsound as it means you're more likely to camp on sensitive stream and lake margins to be as near to water as possible. Moreover, the constant wanderings back and forth fetching water create paths and scars. Collecting all the water needed for camp at one go is both convenient and has less impact on the area, so I carry containers big enough to do so.

As several rigid bottles are heavy and bulky, I carry a light collapsible one that holds $7\frac{1}{2}$ litres/1 gallon, yet weighs only 100g/$3\frac{1}{2}$oz. This is the Field & Trek Water Bag which consists of a double flexible plastic inner bladder and a tough nylon outer with leakproof spigot and two webbing handles. All the parts are replaceable, whilst ripstop tape can be used for emergency repairs during a trip. They are quite durable but can be damaged, especially by fire and ice. Hot sparks from the first can melt holes in the fabric whilst if the contents freeze, slivers of ice can pierce it when the bag is folded up.

In North America similar bags appear under a variety of brand names but in Europe I've seen no others, though there are a number of alternatives, all inferior in my view. The clear plastic water carriers that roll up on to a wooden bar I find too fragile, as I do collapsible plastic jugs. Both crack and spring tiny holes very quickly. However Ortlieb and Liquipak bags, which come in a variety of sizes from 1 litre upwards, seem to have a good reputation. Ortlieb bags are made from coated nylon/PVC material with welded seams and come with an amazing five-year guarantee. Liquipak ones have plastic inners and nylon outers into which they fold. To my eye neither looks as functional as the simple yet effective Water Bag, and they cost considerably more.

Four litres of water usually sees to all my needs in camp, so I find the Water Bag is more than big enough. Filling it in fast running water is easy, especially if you can place it under a small cascade. However in slow-moving or still water I find it best to fill it from my rigid bottle. Other uses of the Water Bag are as a portable

shower (hang it from a tree and stand underneath) and, so I'm told, as a water pillow. What it isn't good for though is carrying water! I've carried it full a number of times, usually strapped to the back of the pack, and I've found the water in it sloshes about, altering the balance of the load in an unnerving way. For distances that take less than an hour to walk I actually prefer to carry it in one hand by its strap. If a lot of water is going to have to be carried far though, rigid bottles are the ones to choose.

In really cold weather thermos-type flasks can be useful and to my surprise I find I now often carry one in winter. It serves two functions. In camp I often fill it with hot water last thing at night so that in the morning I have warm water that soon comes to the boil, speeding up my departure on short winter days. If it is filled before leaving camp it provides hot drinks (usually coffee, but sometimes hot fruit juice or soup) during the day. This is welcome when it's really cold and when the water in your ordinary bottle has frozen, as it avoids the need for a long stop while the stove is put into action. The catalogues and shops are full of unbreakable stainless steel and reinforced plastic flasks and I keep meaning to buy one. But each time I pick one up and feel the weight I put it back on the shelf and reflect that I've only ever broken a couple of ordinary much lighter flasks. My current one is an actual Thermos (although used generically this is a brand name), which holds half a litre and weighs 400g/14oz. To protect it I carry it at the top of the main compartment well away from the sides and wrapped in a spare item of clothing. Because it has its own plastic mug I don't carry a separate one when I take the flask. An alternative to flasks could be the insulating covers that are available for Sigg and other water bottles but I have no experience of these.

THE CAMP FIRE

Minimising the Impact: to Light or Not to Light

Sitting round a camp fire staring into the flames on a cold evening is for many people the ideal way to end a day in the wilderness. Even in areas such as the British hills, where the lack of trees makes having a fire difficult, people like to light them, especially if they're using bothies. However, in too many areas too many badly

A folding grill is useful when cooking over a fire.

situated and constructed fires have left scars that will take decades and more to heal, and too many trees have been stripped of their lower branches and even hacked down to provide fuel. Even collecting fallen wood can damage the environment if not enough is left to replenish the soil with nutrients and provide shelter for birds and animals and food for insects and fungi.

The alternative is to use a stove for cooking and clothing and shelter for warmth. Doing so eliminates the need to light fires but also takes some of the pleasure out of backpacking. Most experts seem to agree however that it's not necessary to stop lighting fires completely, and I for one am grateful for this. An essential element in wilderness living would be lost if camp fires could never be lit. What is necessary is to treat fires as a luxury rather than to depend on them for warmth and cooking and to ensure that they have the minimum impact on the environment. Landowners and managers may ban fires in certain areas for periods of time, perhaps just weeks in a drought when the fire risk is high but decades if a damaged area is being left to recover. In North American national parks fire permits may be needed and you may be required to carry a stove. Such regulations can seem restrictive but they are necessary to prevent the further degradation of popular areas. Fires, whether officially permitted or not, are inappropriate in some areas

anyway. In particular fires shouldn't be lit at and above the timberline as the growth rate of trees and woody plants there is very slow and the soil is so poor that all the nutrients from dead wood are required to replenish it.

In other areas though fires can be lit even on pristine sites without significant harm to the environment, as long as you know what you're doing. The ideal places for fires are below high-water mark on the coast and below the spring flood level along rivers, as any traces will be washed away and there is usually plenty of wood to burn. Fires on beaches and river banks can be lit on shingle and sand too so that scars aren't left.

Using mineral surfaces in other areas when possible minimises the impact there as well. Alternatives are flat rocks and bare earth or sparse vegetation. Rich meadowland should never be scarred by having fires lit in it. If a rock is used as the base then mineral soil should be heaped on to it to a depth of 8cm/3in or more to prevent blackening by the fire. On the ground a shallow pit should be dug so that the fire is lit on mineral soil not vegetation or forest duff. Material that is removed should be piled to one side so that it can be replaced when you leave. I use my toilet trowel for such excavations, which take only minutes when a suitable spot is found.

What should not be done on a pristine site

is to build a ring of rocks around a fire. This serves no purpose, yet it is the first task undertaken by many people when constructing a fireplace. Presumably the idea is to contain the fire and prevent it spreading. The best way to do this though is to make sure the area around the fire is cleared of flammable materials. A site 60–80cm/24–32in across is big enough. You should also make sure that there are no low branches or tree roots above or below the fire and that you pitch your tent well away, preferably upwind so that sparks can't harm it. Other gear, especially if it's nylon, needs to be kept away from fires too.

To ensure that no sign is left of your fire no partially burnt wood should be left behind and ashes should be scattered widely before the pit is refilled with the soil or duff removed when it was dug. Spreading duff and loose vegetation over the site helps conceal it. The remains of fires lit on rocks should be scattered too and the soil used as a base returned to its source.

On well-used sites there are often many rock-ringed fire-places, and you should use one of these rather than make a new fire-place, even a minimum-impact one. If there's time I like to dismantle the least-used fire rings and scatter any ashes and charcoal in the hope that they won't be used again. In some designated backcountry sites in North American national parks metal fire-boxes are provided. Obviously where this is done they should be used. Cut wood may also be supplied on such sites to prevent the forest around being damaged.

Where wood has to be collected this should be done with care too. First and foremost no wood should be removed from living trees, and that includes dead wood. Snags are needed by wildlife and can also add to the attractions of a place. Nothing is worse than a campsite surrounded by trees stripped of their lower branches and the ground bare of any fallen wood. In areas of high use it's best to go farther afield to find wood rather than take even more from the overused land on the edges of the site. Shorelines and river banks are good places to scavenge for wood. You should also only collect what you will use and only small sticks that you can break by hand, as these are easily burned to ash. Axes and saws are not required.

Lighting and Tending the Fire

There is a certain mystique to firelighting, and pages of text are devoted to it in survival and woodcraft books, with many different types of fires described. Basically though, the secret of fire lighting is simple: start small with dry tinder. Paper is good for the latter, but I wouldn't carry it just for this purpose. I lighten my load by burning pages from the books I read as tinder. Food wrappings can be used as well. If you have no paper then the finest of twigs, tiny pine cones, dry leaves and moss and any other dry plant material can be used. If it's wet, look for kindling under logs and at the base of large trees where it's usually dry. Good kindling can be created by half-slicing small slivers off a dry twig to make a feather-stick.

Once you have a small pile of kindling, build up small dry twigs around it in a pyramid, making sure that there is plenty of air space. A flame can then be applied to the kindling. When the twigs start to catch, slightly larger pieces of wood can be added. Don't overdo it though—it's easy to smother a new fire. It doesn't matter at this stage what shape you want for your fire. That can be set up once the fire is burning well. I have no preference for any shape and let the fall of the wood determine what I end up with. If I'm cooking over the fire I usually try to arrange an area of hot coals at one end to balance my pans on as it's coals rather than flames that provide heat. Small metal grills with short legs make cooking over a fire easy and I carried a Coughlan's Fire Grill (310g/11oz) in the Yukon where I cooked over fires often, so it was worth the weight.

Fires shouldn't be left unattended and the ashes should be cold before you leave the next day. If you're not scattering them to the four winds because they're in a well-used fire-ring and you've had a morning fire it's a good idea to douse them in water to make sure they're out. Don't throw foil or silver-lined food wrappings into a fire as they won't burn up properly unless you're prepared to fish them out and carry them with you when you leave. This applies to hut and bothy fires as well. I've spent many hours cleaning out fire-places in such shelters that have become blocked by foil.

STOVES

Carrying a stove removes the necessity for lighting a fire, with all the environmental impact that entails—a good reason in itself to do so. A stove also ensures that you can have hot food and drink whenever you want or need it. I always carry one, as do most backpackers from Britain. In many home areas, especially the unforested open hill country most suited to wild camping, lighting a fire isn't really an option.

The practical advantage of a stove over a fire is that you can have hot food and drink quickly and whenever you want it. A stove cuts you off from the world around you less than a fire too, especially after dark. Where a fire blacks out all your surroundings a stove doesn't, allowing you to observe the stars, the silhouettes of the peaks high above, the reflection of moonlight in the nearby lake, the quick flit of a bat or the slow purposeful glide of an owl. And when you turn the stove off you can hear the night too, hear the silence or the wind, the scuttlings of small animals, the splash of fish. A fire cuts out all of this. At the end of a long day when you end up setting up camp, perhaps in the dark, feeling very tired, setting up a stove is easy. Gathering fuel and lighting a fire takes far longer and much more energy. And in stormy weather a stove enables you to lie in your sleeping bag inside your tent and still be able to cook hot meals. There's nothing like waking up to the sound of wind and rain on the flysheet and being able to reach out an arm, light the stove on which a pan of water was set ready the night before and in a few minutes have a hot drink ready to set you up to face the weather outside.

Compared with other items of equipment there isn't a great deal of choice amongst stoves. The difference between those that there are is marked however. In some situations a stove that malfunctions is no more than a nuisance. In others it can be a serious problem, particularly if you're relying on it for cooking dried food or if you need it to melt snow for water and lighting a fire is not an option. Some stoves work well in the cold and in windy conditions, others don't. To have to wait a long time for a stove to produce hot water when you're cold, wet and tired can at the very least be dispiriting, and if anyone is on the verge of hypothermia it could be dangerous.

I was tempted at this point to produce a table comparing the weights, rate of fuel consumption and boiling times of various stoves of the sort found in catalogues, magazines and other backpacking books but I resisted because such charts can be misleading. There are many factors which affect a stove's performance in the field as opposed to in a controlled environment; moreover individual stoves of the same model can perform very differently. One obvious error perpetuated by these charts is that alcohol stoves like the Trangia take longer to boil water than others. This may be so in still air and if the time taken to set up and light the stove isn't taken into account. However, in real as opposed to artificial situations, such stoves can be faster than any other. Indeed they work best in the sort of stormy weather in which it's difficult to light many other stoves, never mind bring water to the boil. Weights aren't really comparable either as some models include windshields and pansets in the total, and the amount of fuel you have to carry for a given period affects the weight actually carried as well—more so on long trips than the weight of the stove.

To generalise, a half-decent stove should bring half a litre of water to the boil within five minutes of being lit as long as the burner is adequately shielded from the wind. And no stove should weigh more than 600–700g/21–25oz unless pans and windshield are included.

Fuels

The availability of fuel in the areas you visit may well determine which stove you end up with, especially on a long trek where you need to buy more fuel every week or so, or in places which you have to reach by flying, as airlines don't allow the transportation of flammable materials. The choice is between solid fuel, liquid fuel in the form of burning alcohol, kerosene/paraffin or white gas and cartridges containing butane or butane/propane. In different areas of the world different fuels have found most favour, which is worth knowing if you like to range widely in your explorations, as I do. In North America white gas dominates, in Scandinavia alcohol, in the Alps and Pyrenees butane and in Africa and Asia kerosene. This doesn't mean that you won't find other fuels in those places, just that you're more likely, especially in out of the way places, to find those that local people use.

How much fuel you need per day depends not only on the type of stove you have but also on the weather (how cold is the water? how windy is it?) and the type of cooking you do. If you cook three meals a day and use foods with long cooking times you'll use more fuel than someone like me who cooks just one meal

Stoves and accessories, clockwise from top left Trangia alcohol stove, Peak 1 Multi-fuel stove, can of Coleman fuel, 1-litre Sigg fuel bottle with pourer spout, 0.6-litre Sigg fuel bottle, 0.6-litre MSR fuel bottle, Epigas Alpine stove and Epigas 250 butane/propane cartridge, Edelrid Scorpion cartridge stove, Optimus 123 white gas stove. Centre MSR Whisperlite Internationale white gas/kerosene stove.

a day, only boiling water for a hot drink at breakfast and not using the stove at all during the day. The figures given below show how long fuels last me for my cooking needs. If yours are different you'll need to adapt them. Also, they can be more or less doubled if snow has to be melted for fuel, as it takes the same amount of energy to produce a given amount of water from snow as it does to bring the same amount of water to the boil. The figures also assume the use of a full windshield with all stoves, whether supplied or not.

Models and Choices

A stove needs to fulfil a number of criteria. It must be capable of bringing water to the boil under the most horrendous conditions you are likely to encounter, it must be small and light enough to carry and it must be as simple as possible to operate. Stability is important too, particularly with stoves that will be used with large pans.

Solid Fuel: I don't find solid fuel tablets and jellied alcohol, which are available under vari-

ous names, efficient enough to be worth considering, though I did meet a hiker on the Pacific Crest Trail who boiled water three times a day for his instant eat-from-the-bag freeze-dried meals in a metal cup balanced on two stones or small earth walls over a large solid fuel tablet. This is not a way I would choose to operate, but it did help keep his pack weight down. If your cooking needs are minimal or you usually use a fire, solid fuel could be worth considering. Names to look out for include Cari-cook and Esbit (tablets) and Firestar (alcohol) and there are tiny metal stoves, just fuel holders really, available too under the same names.

Alcohol Stoves: Although available in most countries under various names usually involving the words alcohol or spirit (methylated spirits in Britain, *alcool à brûler* in France, denatured alcohol, rubbing alcohol or marine stove fuel in the USA and Canada, T or Rod spirit in Scandinavia), the fuel for alcohol stoves can be hard to find and very expensive. Chemists, drug stores and hardware stores as well as outdoor shops are places to look for it. In Scotland, and perhaps other places, it may be necessary to sign the poisons register when buying meths, as it's generally known in Britain, and you may only be able to buy half a litre at a time. It's the only fuel not derived from petroleum and the only one burnt unpressurised as a liquid, which makes it a safe fuel. It's clean too, evaporating quickly if spilled. For these reasons it's a good fuel for any trips where you'll regularly be cooking in the vestibule of the tent. It's not a hot fuel however, producing only half as much heat as the same weight of gasoline or kerosene, and I find that a litre lasts me little more than a week. This makes it heavy to carry on long trips compared with other fuels.

Alcohol is most popular in Scandinavia and the Swedish-made Trangia stormcookers are probably the safest and simplest stoves available, and also the ones that work best in strong winds. They come as complete units including burner, windshield/pan support, pans, lid and potgrab, which fit together to form a compact unit for carrying. The burner consists of a short hollow-walled open cylinder with jets around the top into which you pour fuel—50ml/2fl oz will fill it. To light it you simply touch a match to the alcohol. The burner rests inside a rigid aluminium windshield which contains fold-out supports onto which the pans are placed. With a lid over the top you have a virtually sealed unit, so heat loss is minimal. There are small holes in one side of the windshield base which can be turned into the wind to create a draught and a stronger flame. Alcohol stoves are the only ones I know that boil water more quickly when it's windy. The flame can be controlled somewhat by dropping a simmer ring over the jets so that only the surface of the reservoir is burning and then partially covering this with a flat metal disc, which you knock into place with a spoon or knife until you achieve the required degree of heat. It's a crude system and awkward to operate. Basically Trangias are not designed for cooking meals that need long simmering.

The unit can be set up very quickly and has little that can go wrong; the only maintenance needed is to prick the jets occasionally. Trangias are silent in operation and you can often hear water coming to the boil. They are safe too, though you need to be careful when using one in daylight as the flame will then be invisible. The biggest danger is in inadvertently trying to refill a still burning stove from a fuel bottle,

as this could cause the bottle to ignite. For this reason, if the stove goes out during use I refill it by pouring fuel into the burner lid and then into the burner. If the lid caught fire I would simply drop it into the burner well, perhaps suffering singed fingers. As a full burner only lasts for half an hour at the most (depending on the wind and use of the simmer ring), refilling while the stove is in use is often necessary. Trangias don't flare however, so they are the safest stove for use under a tent flysheet. They are also very stable. One thing they do that many people don't like is blacken the outside of pans. I can't see why this is a problem. In theory blackened pans should absorb heat faster than shiny silver ones so I make no attempt to clean the exterior of Trangia pans.

When packing up the stove I pour any unused fuel back into the fuel bottle after it's cooled, as if it is carried in the burner it always seems to leak. I also pack the burner in a plastic bag and carry it separately from the pans so that it doesn't dirty their insides and leave a lingering smell of meths.

There are two sizes of Trangia, each available with two aluminium pans and a lid and with and without a kettle. For solo use the Trangia 27 is ideal; including pans of 1- and 1.1-litre capacity and a lid and potgrab, the weight is 795g/1lb 12oz (without the pans and potgrab the unit weighs 425g/15oz). Substituting the 0.6-litre kettle for one of the pans brings the weight up to 830g/1lb 13oz. The larger 25 and 25K (i.e. with kettle) models have 1.5- and 1.75-litre pans and a 1-litre kettle and weights of 1.02kg/2lb 4oz and 1.22kg/2lb 11oz, which is too heavy for one but fine for two or three. There are also versions with teflon-coated pans but these are heavier and you have to carry wooden or plastic implements to protect the non-stick coating, so I feel the standard ones are more practical. Also heavier are the stainless steel pans now available for the Trangia 25 but not the 27.

I've had a Trangia 27 since the early 1970s. At one time it was my regular stove for all treks and it's been all over Scotland, to Norway in summer and winter, to Iceland and on a Land's End–John O'Groats walk. Although dented, it still works perfectly. There is so little to go wrong that it's just about indestructible. Indeed I have heard of a Trangia which was run over by a truck simply being beaten back into shape then returned to use. I still take my Trangia on short winter trips and when bivouacking, as it's the one stove I know that will work regardless of the conditions. I've even used it when I had to put a rock on top of it to prevent it from being blown away. I don't take it on long trips any more, though, because of the weight, both of the unit itself and the fuel.

The Swiss company Sigg make an almost identical stove called the Traveller (1150g/2½lb) but otherwise the only alternative to the Trangia is the rather more complex Optimus 81 Trapper, also made in Sweden, which comes in a large size only that weighs 970kg/2lb 2oz. It comes complete with two pans of 1.9- and 2-litre capacity plus lid and looks similar to a Trangia except that the burner is a felt-lined open-ended tube that acts as a wick when soaked in fuel, the capacity being 0.25 litres. A lever projecting from the lower edge of the windscreen operates a plate which covers the base of this tube. By means of this plate the amount of air entering the burner and thus the heat output can be controlled. To refill the stove a plastic tube with a closed base is slid into the burner and fuel poured in from a plastic measure that comes with the stove. When it's full the felt is saturated with fuel but there is no liquid alcohol to spill even if the stove is turned upside down. I've even seen a lit one rolled along the floor as a demonstration of how safe it is. I don't recommend trying this! When lit the stove burns as well as the Trangia whilst the flame is far more controllable. Although it's slightly more complex to use it's much better than the Trangia at simmering. The Trapper doesn't blacken pans either.

For solo use the Trapper is too big and heavy but it's just right for two people. Two experienced backpacking friends of mine, Chris and Janet Ainsworth, use a Trapper on winter trips and praise it highly. I concur with their view after seeing how fast their Trapper boiled over a litre of water from snow on a ski tour in the Norwegian mountains. An overnight storm had worsened at dawn and we'd packed up and fled from our exposed campsite without bothering with breakfast. As soon as we found a boulder big enough for the four of us to cower behind out of the full force of the wind we stopped for some much-needed sustenance and a hot drink. The Trapper was set up and lit and produced boiling water almost before we'd got the mugs ready. Few stoves could have matched it for speed, and many would have been very difficult to use in such circumstances.

White-Gas and Multi-fuel Stoves: White gas is probably the most efficient stove fuel, being easy to light and burning very hot. In the form of automobile fuel it's available everywhere and as far as stove use is concerned it's very cheap. However stove fuel lines and jets clog up quickly if they are run on it and need very frequent cleaning, and many makers state firmly that automobile fuel shouldn't be used in their stoves, so calling them petrol stoves as they are known in Britain is rather misleading. Instead of automobile fuel they should be run on specially refined stove fuel, sold under various names, the most common being Coleman Fuel, or as a second choice on unbranded white gas, which is sold in hardware stores. In North America both of these are readily available and fairly cheap but in Europe they're not so easily found and are far more expensive. Whatever form it comes in, this is a volatile fuel, igniting easily if spilled, and so great care should be taken with it. I always use stoves that run on it in North America because it's the only fuel you can guarantee being able to buy just about anywhere. Because it burns so hot I find a litre lasts me at least ten days.

Unlike alcohol stoves white gas models burn vaporised not liquid fuel, which means that the fuel has to be pressurised. Once stoves are alight the heat from the flames keeps the fuel line hot so that fuel in it expands and turns to gas. Multi-fuel stoves—included here because they are basically white-gas models that can be adapted to run on other fuels—enhance this by having a loop of fuel line pass through the flame to ensure vaporisation. This is particularly useful when they are used for burning kerosene. In the simplest stoves the fuel is transmitted from the tank to the burner via a wick that leads it into the fuel line. These stoves have to be pre-heated or primed before they can be lit to ensure that the fuel vaporises before passing through the jet. Stoves with pumps are easier to light.

Because they burn pressurised fuel all the stoves in this category can flare badly during lighting and great care is needed if they are to be used in a tent vestibule. Overall I can't recommend them for regular tent cooking. Except for the MSR models all white gas stoves have built-in fuel tanks. They operate best when these are half to four-fifths full and they should never be totally filled as the fuel can't then expand and you won't be able to pressurise the stove fully. I find it best to top up fuel tanks last thing before packing away the stove in the morning. That way I'm unlikely to run out whilst cooking the evening meal. If this does happen you must wait for the stove to cool down before you can refill it.

There are two types of burner found on these stoves; roarer and ported. In the first, the same as that found in paraffin stoves, a stream of vaporised fuel is pushed out of the jet, ignites and hits a burner plate which spreads it out into a ring of flame. The biggest disadvantage of roarer burners is the noise. In ported burners the flames come out of a ring of jets, just like a kitchen gas cooker. These are much quieter than roarer burners. As far as I can tell neither type is more efficient than the other, though ported ones are easier to control and thus better for simmering.

The choice in these stoves is larger than with alcohol or paraffin ones though virtually all come from three makers: Optimus, MSR and Coleman. The first is Swedish, the others hail from the USA.

The Optimus 123R Climber, previously known as the Svea 123 and still often referred to as such, has been around for decades and until the MSR and Coleman models took the market by storm in the 1980s it was one of the most popular white-gas stoves, especially for the solo backpacker, because of its lightness, compactness and ease of use. It was in fact the lightest white gas stove at 510g/1lb 2oz until the MSR models appeared. Owing to its reputation and low weight I used it on the Pacific Crest Trail and because it performed faultlessly on that long trek I used one again on the Continental Divide. As well as white gas, it can be run on unleaded petrol.

In design the 123 looks like a brass can with perforations. This is made up of a simple roarer burner unit screwed into a 0.13-litre/$\frac{1}{4}$-pint capacity brass fuel tank and a circular windshield/pan support unit that fits round the burner. A small aluminium cup fits over the top to protect the burner when it is in the pack. Entry to the tank is by a screw-on cap which has a built-in safety valve designed to release pressure in the event of the tank overheating. If this happens the jet of fuel that spurts out will almost certainly become a jet of flame, so it's wise always to use the stove with the tank cap pointing away from you and away from anything flammable like your tent. The 123's burner is operated by a key that fits on to an arm jutting out from the burner. The key can be inserted through the windshield but placed inside it when packed.

To light the 123 it's necessary to heat the tank slightly to make the fuel expand and some of it vaporise, as there is no pump. The simplest way I've found to do this is to fill the shallow recess at the foot of the burner tube with about a teaspoon of petrol from the fuel bottle and light it. By the time the last of the flames are dying away the tank should be sufficiently warm so that as you turn the key and open the jet the burner catches. If you miss this point a quickly applied match will usually light the stove. The flame should be blue. If it's yellow the stove hasn't been pressurised enough and is burning semi-liquid fuel. It needs to be turned off and reprimed, though with less fuel. Once lit the key can be used to control the flame but the range is rather limited. The key also controls a built-in jet cleaner which is operated by turning the key beyond the 'on' position. This should be done infrequently to avoid widening the jet hole. In use the 123 is quite powerful but it does require a separate windshield in a strong wind; the one with it is not adequate. Because the tank is below the burner the stove mustn't be fully surrounded by a windshield in case the tank overheats. Stability is adequate with small pans but care is needed if large ones are used, owing to the tall narrow shape.

Optimus also make two other white-gas stoves, though I have little experience of them. The newest one is the Eagle 1000 which seems to be an attempt to update the 123. The burner is the same key-operated one but it is set atop a larger 0.2 litre tank which will burn, say Optimus, for 65 minutes as opposed to 50 for the 123. A tapered windshield, rather more solid than the 123's, fits over this leaving gaps for access to the fuel tank and key arm. As this windshield doesn't protect the flame I doubt whether it will be of much use. A small pan support sits on top of it. Unfortunately this doesn't clip on in any way but remains detached, which doesn't seem very stable to me. Even worse, it's only 10cm/4in in diameter and any pans much wider than this, as most well-designed ones are, wobble alarmingly. Optimus have obviously realised this as the 1000 is also available with a tall, narrow 1.2-litre pan into which the stove unit fits for carrying. With this pan the whole unit is 25cm/9in high but only 12cm/5in wide, and when the pan is full it balances very badly. Overall, without having used it in earnest, I can't say I'm very impressed with this stove, which seems inferior in design to the 123. The stove unit weighs 425g/15oz, the pan adds another 115g/4oz.

The 8R Hunter has been around for years and also has the same key-operated burner as the 123, but it is fitted into a metal box with the 0.13 litre tank alongside it. Its weight is 625g/1lb 6oz. Stability is better than the 123 because of the lower profile, but keeping the tank pressurised is apparently more difficult because it isn't directly below the burner.

Optimus also make a triple-fuel stove, the 111 Hiker, which looks like the 8R but which has a built-in pump and is much larger and heavier at 1530g/3lb 6oz. The fuels are white gas, kerosene and alcohol. Like its predecessors, the 111 and 111B which burnt gasoline and kerosene respectively, the 111T is ideal for large groups and expeditions, being very stable even with the largest pans.

The Coleman Peak 1 Feather 442 and Peak 1 Multi-Fuel stoves are high-tech looking constructions seemingly bristling with levers and knobs. Both have ported burners set atop 0.28 litre fuel tanks and built-in pumps so don't need priming except in very cold weather. The original Peak 1 weighed 795g/1lb 12oz and a complicated procedure was needed to light it. My only experience with it was not a success as during a week of cold stormy Cairngorm winter weather Chris Ainsworth, whose stove it was, and I had great difficulty getting it to light, finally resorting to pouring fuel over the tank and burner, throwing in a match and standing back, a dangerous procedure that I definitely don't recommend. We also found it needed a separate windshield which added to the weight. The stove has now been relegated to summer base-camp use and Chris uses a Trapper alcohol stove for winter trips. However the latest version, the Feather 442, weighs a little less at 645g/1lb 7oz and is reputedly easier to light, one control lever having been dispensed with. It will also run on unleaded petrol.

The newer Peak 1 Multi-Fuel stove seems a much better performer however, and is significantly lighter at 525g/1lb 2½oz though still quite bulky. Lighting the stove involves pressurising the tank by 25–50 strokes of the pump, lighting the burner, then pumping 15–30 more strokes. This is simpler and takes less time than priming a stove and makes flaring less likely. For some reason the Multi-Fuel Peak 1 seems to light better in the cold than the old white gas one. I've lit the stove in a strong breeze first time in temperatures around freezing point. A separate windshield is still required for good efficiency and quick cooking times however, even though the pentagon-shaped windshield round the burner means it won't blow out in a wind. A neat tapered plastic ring round the base means the short legs can be adjusted to keep the stove level on uneven ground. I haven't used the stove enough yet to come to a definite decision about it but it looks a good contender for winter use, especially for groups of two and more.

The multi-fuel claim is a bit of an overstatement though, as this is basically a unit that runs on stove fuel or white gas but which can be converted to use paraffin. Dual-fuel would be a more accurate description. The instructions say clearly 'never use regular or premium leaded automotive fuel'. To enable it to use paraffin the burner and generator must be changed, a complex task requiring the use of a small spanner that I would not like to carry out in the field. Also the burner/generator and spanner add an extra 75g/2½oz to the weight if carried.

The MSR X-GK II is probably the most powerful lightweight stove available and it really deserves the name multi-fuel as it will run on white gas, leaded and unleaded petrol, aviation fuel, paraffin, diesel and more, though you may have to clean it regularly with anything other than stove fuel. It consists of a roarer burner with a long fuel tube that fits into a pump which in turn plugs into a fuel bottle, obviating the need for a tank and enabling the burner to be fully shielded from wind without danger of its overheating. To this end a folding foil windscreen and reflector are provided with the X-GK, which also has a built-in sparker for ignition. For melting snow the X-GK is unsurpassed but for more general use it is, if anything, a little too powerful, especially as regulating the flame is difficult. For group cooking or when you don't know what fuel you might have to use it seems a good choice. The latest version weighs just

400g/14½oz including the windshield, astonishing for the power provided. To this of course has to be added the weight of a fuel bottle (see below), the lightest of which weighs 115g/4oz. It is also maintainable in the field and a maintenance kit weighing 56g/2oz is available.

MSR's other pressure stoves, the WhisperLite and WhisperLite Internationale, are in essence the same, the only difference being that the first will only burn stove fuel/ white gas whilst the second will also burn kerosene. Both are small collapsible spidery looking stoves with quiet ported burners—hence the name WhisperLite—which, like the X-GK, save weight by having pumps that plug into fuel bottles so that tanks aren't needed. At 340g/12oz each these are lighter than any other pressure stoves except the X-GK by a considerable margin. That weight includes the pump and also the folding aluminium foil windscreen and reflector supplied with each stove. To light these stoves you pressurise the fuel by pumping, release a little into a cup below the burner by opening the valve which is situated on top of the pump, light this to prime the stove, then as the flame dies down reopen the valve. The whole process takes only a few seconds. Flame control is limited so simmering over these stoves is difficult, but they are as powerful as much heavier models and ideal for solo use. If you want to use kerosene in the Internationale all that's needed is to change the tiny jet unit—which takes seconds—for the one marked K supplied with the stove. The windscreen means they work efficiently in stormy weather, especially if you fold them so that no space is left between them and your pans. Again both stoves are maintainable in the field. The maintenance kits weigh 42g/1½oz. As well as spare parts these include a jet pricker. I carried an Internationale on the Canadian Rockies and Yukon walks, and it has proved very reliable, performing as well now as when it was new. The only attention it needed was to the leather pump washer which dried out (I regreased it with margarine and it worked perfectly), though I did have it fully serviced by the British distributor between the walks. Currently the Internationale has replaced the Optimus 123 as my first choice for long walks as it's easier to start up, lighter, smaller, more stable and performs better in wind whilst being just as efficient and reliable.

Kerosene Stoves: Kerosene (or paraffin) is the traditional stove fuel. It's easily obtained, reasonably cheap and burns hot. Like gasoline it's known under various names, some of them very similar, so it pays to check carefully when abroad that what you buy is what you think you're buying. In France for example it's called *petrole*, in Germany and Scandinavia *petroleum*. *Essence* and *benzine* always mean gasoline.

Kerosene won't ignite easily so if it is spilled it is relatively safe—certainly far safer than white gas. However this means that lighting the stove requires a separate priming fuel such as meths, solid fuel tablets or kerosene-soaked paper. It tends to flare during lighting and so should always be started up outside. I find it a messy fuel and hard to work with and so I only use it as a last resort in a multi-fuel stove; I also find it stains badly and takes a long time to evaporate, leaving a strong smell. Some people swear by it though. When I said I disliked it in a magazine article I received an irate letter from a reader saying that it was clear that I was in the pay of non-kerosene stove-makers, had never used a kerosene stove and didn't know what I was talking about. Others who feel as strongly will no doubt continue to use kerosene. I, and I suspect many others, won't.

Optimus's 96 Mini Camper and 00L Camper stoves are the classic kerosene stoves, having been around for decades. Essentially they are the same stove in different sizes, the 96 having a 0.28-litre capacity tank, the 00L a 0.56-litre one. Both stoves require assembling before use then pumping and priming with another fuel before they can be lit, which is a time-consuming process. Flaring is likely during lighting, so this shouldn't be done under a tent flysheet. Once lit the flame can only be controlled by opening a valve and releasing some of the pressure—a crude method. They are noisy in use as they have roarer burners. They're also relatively heavy to carry at 595g/1lb 5oz for the 96 and 1.13kg/2lb 7oz for the 00L. Although the flame is very powerful and both stoves have small windshields to protect the burners, their efficiency can be increased in breezy conditions by using a separate full windshield. My experience with these stoves is limited to use of the 00L when I led treks for an Outward Bound school in Scotland, as these were the stoves used by the centre. Some of them dated back 40 years, which shows how durable they are, but I have to say that after one trip with them I reverted to using my own Butane cartridge stove in preference.

Optimus make one other, much more modern, portable kerosene stove, the 85 Loke Expedition, which looks like the Trapper alcohol model as it comes complete with two pans, lid and windshield. Although it weighs 1430g/3lb 2oz it would not need an additional windshield and looks a highly efficient unit for group use. Its existence also begs the question why small white-gas stoves haven't been developed in this style.

Butane and Butane/Propane Cartridge Stoves: Light, clean, simple to use; cartridge stoves are the choice of the majority of backpackers, especially those who don't undertake marathon treks or head deep into the winter wilderness. The fuel is liquid petroleum gas, kept under pressure in a sealed cartridge. The most popular version is pure butane which is available worldwide and relatively cheap. However, owing to the low pressure in the cartridges—necessary because their walls are thin to keep the weight down—butane won't vaporise properly in temperatures much below 5°C/41°F, making it a fuel for summer use only. Also, as the cartridge empties and the pressure drops so the burning rate falls until a point is reached when the heat produced won't bring water to the boil. Cartridges can be warmed with the hands or stored inside clothing or sleeping bags to keep them warm, but I find this a lot of trouble. Reports of Himalayan mountaineers successfully using butane cartridge stoves in bitterly cold temperatures would seem to contradict the fuel's bad cold weather reputation, but there is a reason for this. The thinner air of high altitudes means reduced air pressure outside the canister, which in turn means less obstruction to the gas leaving the cartridge. This is useful for backpackers who camp high as well as for mountaineers. At 3000 metres/9800ft butane stoves will work down to −10°C/14°F. At lower altitudes the answer is to use butane/propane-mix cartridges, which work well in below-freezing temperatures, as propane vaporises at a much lower temperature than butane. However it is such a volatile substance that if used on its own it requires very thick-walled and heavy containers. Lightweight canister mixtures are usually 85/15 butane/propane. I find a standard 200–250g/7–9fl oz cartridge lasts three or four days.

In the USA a purer butane called iso-butane can be bought as an alternative to butane/propane but reports suggest this isn't as efficient in the cold. REI, for one, recommend that iso-butane cartridges should be kept above −2°C/28°F. The availability of butane cartridges in general is good in Europe, where the blue 200-g/7fl oz Camping Gaz ones can be found just about everywhere, but not so good in North America, where distribution is very patchy. The more useful resealable cartridges are not so easy to find, though Epigas ones are now quite common in Britain, and they and others are starting to appear in many places in Europe and North America.

All cartridge stoves have ported burners and are quiet in use. The heat output is easily adjusted, making them excellent for simmering, but the flame must be protected from wind. Most stoves come with small windshields fitted round the burner. If you always cook in a tent vestibule these may be protection enough but for outside cooking I've found them inadequate and a separate windshield is needed. There are two types of cartridge: those in which the cartridge valve is self-sealing and can be removed for carrying at any time, and those in which the cartridge must be left on the stove until empty.

The latter are typified by the Camping Gaz Bleuet C206, probably the most popular lightweight stove in the world. It consists of a burner/pan support unit that clamps on to a 200g/7fl oz butane cartridge, a spike at the end of the fuel column piercing the cartridge. The result is a tall structure that isn't very stable especially with large pans. An optional stabilising base helps with this. The weight is 280g/10oz. Although the pan supports fold away for packing, because the cartridge can't be removed, it's an inconvenient shape to carry. Once a three-season model at best, the introduction of butane/propane cartridges that fit the Bleuet means that it can be used year round. It's not the most powerful stove though, and overall not one of my favourites. But it is durable. I know of models over 15 years old that are still in regular use.

There are two smaller Camping Gaz models designed specifically for those to whom weight is crucial. The Globetrotter comes complete with two 0.56-litre nesting pans plus handle, though no lid, and uses the small 90-g/3fl oz GT butane/propane cartridges. With the pans it weighs just 450g/16oz. Like the Bleuet it consists of a burner/pan support unit that clamps on to the cartridge. I've never used a Globetrotter, and I suspect that I would find the pans too small, but at least one experienced backpacker I know, Graham Huntington, praises his. In contrast to the Globetrotter, the Rando '360 takes the tiny resealable 55-g/2-fl oz tubular Rando butane cartridges which screw into the side of the stove to give a stable unit. The Rando also comes with nesting pans of 0.8- and 0.3-litre capacity and a pot grab. It has folda-way combined leg and pan supports and can be packed inside the pan-set along with two cartridges. The weight is 227g/8oz. The burning time of the cartridges is no more than an hour, so for most people, a cartridge a day is needed. When I tried out a Rando stove I was quite impressed, especially with the windshield, the only one on a cartridge stove that worked in a strong gusty wind. I also found it worked satisfactorily on snow covered ground in temperatures around 5°C/41°F. I don't like the pans though, which are tall and narrow—an inefficient shape for quick heating and one in which it is easy to burn food. My biggest doubts about both the Globetrotter and the Rando '360 are to do with cartridge availability, as each can only be used with a specific non-standard cartridge. I've seen these in so few places that I would suggest that anyone using one of these stoves carry all the cartridges for a trip with them.

The most suitable stoves for backpacking, in my opinion, are those which will fit a variety of both sizes and makes of self-sealing cartridges. There are over 25 makes of cartridge worldwide, with the same size thread and valve. A very useful list of what brands are available where is published by Epigas, the originators of self-sealing threaded cartridges. Try writing to them at Wear Mill, King Street West, Stockport, Cheshire, SK3 0AJ, Great Britain for a copy. Cartridges may contain butane or butane/propane and come in sizes ranging from 100 to 500g/3½ to 17½fl oz and in a number of shapes. Low-profile ones like Epigas's 250g/9oz butane/propane one are the most stable. Tall, thin cartridges should be used with stabilising bases. There are also adaptor units available for turning Camping Gaz 206 cartridges into self-sealing ones for use with these stoves.

There are two ways in which stoves attach to self-sealing cartridges. The most basic models simply screw into the top of the cartridge. More complex but far more efficient are those which have a flexible tube running from the burner to the cartridge. These are to be preferred, because the burner can be safely encircled with a windshield, something you shouldn't do with the screw-in burners because of the possibility of the cartridge overheating and exploding. I use an MSR foil windscreen with tube connected stoves, as it weighs only 50g/1½oz and is available as a 'spare'. Screw-in models require a heavier folding windshield, which must be taller than the MSR one because of the height of the stove plus cartridge. They also need a plastic stabilising base weighing around 75g/2½oz with all cartridges except the 250-g/9-fl oz low-profile ones to minimise the chance of being knocked or falling over, always a stronger possibility than with tube-connected stoves. These factors make the total weight carried higher with screw-in stoves than with tube connected ones.

The lightest tube connected stove is the Scorpion which weighs just 235g/8oz. It has a typical wide and low three-legged profile and breaks down flat for carrying. Assembly takes only a few seconds. Care must be taken to keep the cartridge upright, as if it topples over the sudden rush of fuel into the burner causes it to flare and then become blocked with partially burnt fuel. It won't then work again until the jet is cleaned. The Scorpion is fine for solo use but not really powerful enough for two or more. However there is a larger version, the Scorpion 2, which I haven't used but which is reputedly very powerful. It weighs 375g/13oz.

The German-made tube-connected Markhill Ministove has four fold-out legs, adjustable pan supports and a very flexible metal spring-coated fuel line, plus a fairly efficient looking windshield. Its weight is a reasonable 310g/11oz. This stove looks to be one of the few small gas stoves that is stable with large pans, because of its extra wide profile. Two versions in which the burner is integrated with a windshield are also available; the Stormy with 1.3- and 0.9-litre pots, chain assembly (to enable mountaineers to hang the stove during bivouacs on narrow ledges), plus a stove/windshield unit, weighs 720g/1lb 9oz; and the Stormy Camp with 1.8- and 1.5-litre pans weighs 1.08kg/2lb 6oz.

Cartridge stoves, other than the Bleuet, have never really taken off in North America because of the scarcity of cartridges, but this is changing with the introduction of such a stove by one of the big names in white-gas stoves, MSR. Their Rapidfire looks like a Whisperlite and comes with the same foil windscreen and reflector. The total weight is 355g/12½oz. I've not used this stove but given MSR's reputation I would expect it to work well.

The tube-connected stove I've used most and like best is the Epigas Alpine (the current version is the Mark 3). Weighing 345g/12oz, the Alpine looks much like the Scorpion but close examination suggests that it's better made. A number of features make it a very safe stove. One is that, like Epigas's other stoves, but unlike most others, there is no gas escape when the cartridge is attached. It also has an anti-flare liquid feed burner system so that if the cartridge is knocked over or even inverted it won't flare. I've tested this and it works. The stove folds flat without being taken apart and has pan supports that can be locked into either of two positions to hold small and large pans. I've used the Alpine extensively and found it very durable and the burner very powerful. Using the Alpine I find a 250g/9fl oz butane/propane cartridge lasts me four days, less if snow has to be melted. It's my first choice for trips of two weeks or less in all but the worst conditions.

Epigas also make screw-in stoves including the minute Micro, which at 145g/5oz is the lightest stove I know. Its burner is claimed to be as powerful as that of the Alpine and it has fold-in pan supports to make it really compact when packed. It's designed for use with Epigas's ultralight 100-g/3½-oz butane/propane cartridge, but will also work with larger ones. I've not tried this stove but it looks a gem, ideal for short trips. A more standard-sized screw-in stove I have used is the Epigas Backpacking Stove which weighs 200g/7oz and folds flat. It works well but I prefer the Alpine, despite the extra weight, because I can use the MSR windshield with it. A similar stove, though it doesn't fold flat, is the Trekker, made by Primus—a name well known to older backpackers as for decades it was the leading name in kerosene stoves. It weighs 220g/7¾oz and has a very powerful burner. It's also available under the name Super Trekker with an aluminium cook-set consisting of a 2-litre pan, a kettle and a frying pan lid; the total weight is 770g/1lb 11oz. Markhill also make a screw-in burner called the High Power Stove which weighs 195g/7oz. This will take large pans but would, I suspect, be unstable with small cartridges if used with them.

Before leaving cartridge stoves I must mention the one big disadvantage: the disposability of the cartridges. Too many lie glinting in the sunlight at the bottom of once-pristine mountain lakes or jut half-buried out of piles of rocks in wildernesses the world over. What to do about this I don't know. Perhaps mountain shops and cartridge makers could offer a deposit system with a refund for the return of 'empties'. Ultimately though, the answer must lie with those who use the stoves.

The Dungburners

There is one type of stove I haven't yet mentioned—those that burn natural materials that can be found around a campsite such as twigs, pine cones, bark, charcoal and dried dung. The last item has given these stoves the generic name of 'dungburners'.

At least three very similar models exist. They all work by using a tiny battery operated electric blower to fan the flames of a small fire lit in the well of the stove. The stoves consist of a base on which is mounted the blower, above which is a circular stainless steel combustion chamber with air channels inside an aluminium shell. One C-size battery is said to power the fan for at least eight hours. One version, available in the USA, is called the Zip Stove or Super Sierra. This weighs 425g/15oz. Accessories include a 1-litre aluminium pot and lid, a grill and a lightweight fire starter called Zip Fire that comes in small blocks and is claimed to light even when soaked. European versions include the Turbo Cooker, which comes complete with a 1-litre aluminium pan, stainless steel frying pan/lid and pot grab, total weight 800g/1lb 12oz, and perhaps the most interesting of the three models, the Markhill Wilderness Stove. This weighs 500g/17½oz and has a fan that can be powered by an optional solar cell plate instead of a battery. The latter weighs 165g/6oz. A Trangia-type alcohol burner can be used in the stove as well.

Such stoves may seem no more than an interesting curiosity, but reports suggest that they work well and that the weight saved in fuel is worthwhile, so they could be worth considering for trips in wooded country. I've never used one but I'm thinking of doing so.

Safety and Maintenance

All stoves are dangerous and need care in use. The most important safety point is never to take a stove for granted. Always check that any attachments to fuel tanks or cartridges are secure and that tank caps and fuel bottle tops are tight and controls turned off before lighting a stove. The detailed instructions that come with all stoves should be studied carefully and practised, especially with kerosene and gasoline models, before heading off into the wilds. When you're cold, wet and tired and it's half-dark and you desperately need a hot meal, it's important that you can safely operate your stove virtually automatically.

A stove should be refilled with care after checking that there are no naked lights such as burning candles, other lit stoves or camp fires anywhere nearby. This applies whether you are changing a cartridge or pouring fuel into a white-gas stove tank. If you are in a tent or hut it's best to go outside to refuel to ensure that there is no spillage inside.

Overheating of cartridges or fuel tanks is another potential hazard, completely overcome by tube-connected gasoline or cartridge stoves and impossible with meths ones. When the burner is directly above or alongside the fuel tank care should be taken to allow enough air flow round the tank or cartridge. I've already mentioned that windshields shouldn't fully surround such stoves. Stones shouldn't be used to stabilise them either, and if large pans are used that overhang the burner, you need to check periodically that too much heat isn't being reflected off these on to the fuel supply.

In operation, stoves are most dangerous during the lighting sequence, when they can flare badly. For this reason you should never have your head over a stove when you light it. It might flare more than you expect. Nor should a stove be lit close to any flammable material, particularly your tent. Lighting a stove with open air above it whenever possible is the best way to avoid trouble, even if this means sticking it out into the rain to do so and then bringing it back into the tent vestibule when it's burning properly. If you do light a stove in the vestibule, the door should be open so that it can be pushed out quickly if anything goes wrong. If you have to do this, be careful where the stove goes if there are other tents around. I was once walking across a crowded campsite on a cold, blustery winter day when I saw a bright yellow flash inside a nearby tent. A second later a blazing gasoline stove came hurtling through the tent flysheet, leaving behind a neat hole, to land near my feet. If there'd been another tent close by the results could have been disastrous.

A real threat if a stove is used inside a closed tent is carbon monoxide poisoning which can be fatal. All stoves give off this odourless, colourless gas and consume oxygen. In an enclosed space they can use up all the oxygen, replacing it with carbon monoxide. Ventilation is always required when a stove is in use. In a tent vestibule air can usually enter under the edge of the flysheet, but this may not be the case if you are pitched in snow, or when valances are in use. In those cases having a two-way outer door zip is useful, as the top few centimetres can be left open to ensure a good air flow.

I don't like using stoves in the inner tent under any circumstances, partly because of the possibility of carbon monoxide build-up but mainly because of the danger of fire. However, in tents without vestibules, it may be necessary in severe weather.

The nearest I have ever come to a serious stove accident was when cooking in the vestibule of a tent pitched on snow. A severe blizzard had trapped us on the same site for four nights during the last of which the wind had battered the tents so much that we'd hardly slept at all. To keep out blown snow I lit the white-gas stove in the vestibule with the door zipped shut. The burner caught but the flame was sluggish. 'Pump it some more,' suggested my companion. Without thinking I did so. There was a sudden bright surge of flame, then the whole unit was ablaze as liquid fuel shot out of the jet. Two suddenly energised bodies dived for the door zip and yanked it open. I threw the stove out and plunged my singed hands into the cooling snow. My eyebrows and face were also slightly burnt, I discovered later. In retrospect we were very lucky. That moment's carelessness could have left us, at best, without our tent and gear, and at the worst badly burnt or even dead. I guess lack of air was the cause. Whatever it was, I should have opened the door and tried to revive the stove outside. As it was the flysheet zip had partially melted and wouldn't close so in future storms we had to cook in the inner tent, which we did with great care with the stove standing on a pan lid to prevent the groundsheet melting.

On two other occasions I've been present when a stove has caught fire, once outside and once in a mountain hut when the owner had to hurriedly eject it through the door. Each time a white-gas stove was involved and my view now is that, as most of the makers state, these are best used outdoors and not in tents or huts. The safest stoves are meths ones, followed by cartridge models and one of these is what I use for regular tent cooking.

Most stoves need little maintenance. Except for those with built-in self-cleaning needles the jets of any stove may need cleaning with the thin wire stove-prickers (weighing a fraction of a gram) that come with most stoves. I always carry one, and on long trips two. I only use them when the stove's performance seems to be falling off however, as too much usage can widen the jet and lessen the burn rate. Rubber seals on tank caps and cartridge attachment points should be checked periodically and replaced if worn. Again I carry spares on long trips. In the case of tank caps, this usually means carrying a complete cap. On the Pacific Crest Trail I was glad I did so as the original one on my Optimus 123 started to leak after four months' constant use.

Fuel Containers and Tank-filling Devices

Liquid fuels don't usually come in containers suitable for carrying in the pack, either because they're too large or too fragile or they leak once opened. There are many plastic and metal fuel bottles available. Plastic ones are fine for alcohol and some are said to be suitable for white gas and kerosene, but I'd rather trust metal bottles to hold such volatile fuels. It's important that any fuel bottle is robust and has a well-sealed, leakproof cap. Almost standard, and the ones I've used for years for all fuels, are the cylindrical Sigg bottles, available in three sizes: 0.3 litres (70g/2½oz), 0.6 litres (115g/4oz) and 1 litre (142g/5oz). These extremely tough silver aluminium bottles have leakproof screw caps with rubber gaskets and can be used as fuel tanks for MSR white-gas stoves. MSR don't recommend them as such because they make their own similar bottles in near-enough the same three sizes and weights. With the Internationale I carry just a 0.6-litre MSR bottle on trips of a week or less, adding a 0.6-litre Sigg bottle for trips where more than a week's fuel

has to be carried at one time or where snow must be melted, and a 1-litre Sigg bottle on really long treks. With the Trangia a full 0.6-litre bottle sees me through three or four days, a 1-litre one through a week. Markhill also make fuel bottles in 0.4-, 0.75- and 1-litre sizes which can be used as fuel tanks with MSR stoves. I've not used these but they look as good as the others.

Filling small fuel tanks directly from standard fuel bottles is almost impossible without spilling, as there is no way of controlling the flow. However there are various ingenious devices available for overcoming this. I have a Sigg pouring cap and spout bought many years ago for filling my Optimus 123 tank. This is a standard cap with a small plastic spout inserted in one side and a tiny hole drilled in the other. By placing a finger over the hole the flow down the spout can be controlled. Such a cap has the disadvantage that you have to remove the normal cap, screw in the pouring one, fill the stove then change the caps again. To avoid losing either cap I keep them linked with a piece of shockcord. A better device looks to be the one marketed in similar versions by REI as the Super Pour Spout and Olicamp as the Ulti-Mate Pour Spout/Cap because it replaces the standard top of a fuel bottle completely. By turning the spout one way it opens and can be used for pouring, by turning the other it seals again. How easy it is for such a cap to be opened inadvertently I don't know but I'd want to check before I used one. A different, very secure-looking cap with an automatic valve closure comes with the Markill-Matic Safety Fuel Bottle, available in 0.4-, 0.75- and 1-litre sizes. Again I have no experience of this. For filling fuel bottles themselves from larger containers I use a small plastic funnel bought in a hardware store. This has a built-in filter and weighs only a fraction of a gram. I usually carry it on long treks when I may have to refill with white-gas that isn't as clean as the Coleman Fuel I normally use. For example on the Yukon walk I found that the Goldex Camper Fuel that was often all I could buy quickly blocked the jet of my stove unless it was filtered.

Windshields and Other Accessories

As I've said, windshields are needed with all stoves if they are to function efficiently. All MSR stoves come with foil windscreens whilst solid

MSR XPD Heat Exchanger fitted to MSR Alpine pan and Whisperlite Internationale stove.

alloy ones are part of the structure of Trangia, Sigg and Trapper alcohol stoves, the Loke kerosene stove, the Markhill Stormy and Stormy Camp cartridge models and all the natural fuel burners. No other stoves come with adequate windshields as components. For low-profile, tube/attached cartridge stoves the MSR foil windshield is ideal and adds only 50g/1¾oz to the weight. For taller stoves with fuel tanks and cartridges that mustn't be fully shielded from air flow, larger, heavier windshields are necessary. They can be made by stiffening sheets of foil-backed nylon or canvas with wire rods (knitting needles are apparently good for this) that project below the material and can be used to anchor it in the ground. When I used the Optimus 123

regularly my windshield was a folding Coghlan's one made up of five sheets of aluminium with tent-peg-like anchor rods at either end. It is very efficient and durable and also works well with screw-in cartridge stoves but adds 225g/8oz of weight. This gives the 123 a total weight of 735g/1lb 9oz as against the Internationale's 340g/12oz, reason in itself for my preference for the latter. A similar windshield is the eight-section Olicamp Folding Aluminium one, which weighs 270g/9½oz. Whatever windshield you use, it should extend well above the burner if it is to be effective.

To make starting the 123, 8R and 1000 stoves simpler, especially in cold weather, Optimus offer a Mini Pump that replaces the fuel cap. I've never used one because it can't be fitted to the 123 when the windscreen/pot support is in place, and I've never fancied trying to fit that with the stove alight. Reports suggest that great care is required with these pumps as there is a danger of overpressurising the tank and perhaps blowing the safety valve.

Also available to help with priming are various pastes—almost essential if you use kerosene stoves. Optimus Burning Paste in 50-g/1¾-oz tubes is one example. Alternatives are broken up solid fuel tablets, tiny amounts of meths and as a last resort kerosene-soaked paper.

An innovation new at the time of writing is the MSR XPD Cook Set with Heat Exchanger. This consists of two stainless steel pans of 1½-

and 2-litre capacities with frying pan/lid and pot grab plus a corrugated aluminium collar for the stove that is meant to reduce boiling time by directing more heat up the sides of the pan. This heat exchanger, claim MSR, increases the stove's efficiency by 25 per cent. As the weight of the exchanger is just 198g/7oz it could save weight overall on long trips. On short ones the advantage would be mainly in faster boiling times. The pan-set weighs 740g/1lb 10oz, too heavy for solo use but fine for duos. I would save weight by leaving the larger pan behind and substituting a stainless steel mug. The heat exchanger folds up to fit inside the pans for carrying. Although designed for MSR stoves, the exchanger can be used with other brands. It won't work with pans less than 16cm/6in in diameter though, which cuts out many small solo units.

Stove Lighters and Fire Starters

Matches are essential for lighting fires and starting stoves and I usually carry several boxes of strike-anywhere ones, each sealed in a small plastic bag. One lives in my food bag, one in the stove bag and one in the plastic bag with the toilet paper. On long trips I may carry a fourth as well, also kept in a food bag. The combined weight is only a few grams. I keep them in the original box, but waterproof metal or plastic matchsafes are available that weigh around 30g (1oz) or so, which I suppose I should use for the extra protection they give. Book matches I don't like, as the striker wears out quickly and half the matches never seem to work.

The likelihood of several boxes kept in different places in the pack all becoming soaked is remote but it could happen if, for example, you fell in a river, so carrying some form of emergency back-up fire starter is a good idea. In my repair and oddments bag I always keep a box of waterproof, windproof Lifeboat Matches, available from Survival Aids and other companies. Each waterproof plastic canister contains 25 large matches, has strikers top and bottom and weighs 20g/¾oz. They really do work but beware of the hot embers left after one has gone out. Less efficient alternatives are the water-resistant matches available under the Greenlite and Coughlans labels. These are standard-sized matches, come 40–50 to a box and are cheaper than the quite expensive Lifeboat ones, making

them a viable alternative to ordinary matches for those worried about dampness.

An alternative to matches are cigarette lighters, and I often carry a cheap 20g/¾oz disposable butane one instead of one of the boxes of matches. The advantages of a lighter are that the spark alone will ignite white gas and butane, though not kerosene or alcohol—at least not easily—and that if it gets wet it's easily dried, whilst a sodden box of matches is useless. Refillable lighters like the classic gasoline Zippo (58g/2oz) would be an alternative.

I've not tried the more esoteric fire lighters like flint and magnesium (38g/1.3oz), which works by chippings scraped from a magnesium block being ignited by sparks caused by drawing a knife across a flint, and the Permanent Match (15g/½oz), which has a brass 'match' that lights a gasoline-soaked wick when struck. Carrying one might be an idea on long remote wooded country trips. Other methods of fire lighting using natural materials, though much touted in survival manuals, strike me as being singularly unworkable in the conditions when you might need a fire most, that is, when it's cold and wet. For ultimate protection in really bad weather I would rather rely on my tent, sleeping bag and clothes than a fire.

UTENSILS

Many people seem to carry an inordinately large amount of kitchen gear. One advantage of minimal cooking is that it requires minimal tools. My basic kit consists of a 1-litre stainless steel pot with lid, a 0.6-litre stainless steel cup, a small knife and two spoons, total weight 450g/16oz. This serves my needs both on weekends and on long summer trips.

Pans

Many stoves now come with pan sets of varying degrees of quality and usefulness. The only one I really like is the Trangia 27 aluminium cook set which consists of a 1-litre pan, a 1.1-litre pan and a frying pan/lid weighing in total 325g/11½oz and an optional 0.6-litre kettle weighing 110g/4oz. With other stoves I used to use the smaller and lighter Field & Trek Lightline Billies, also made of aluminium. There are four sizes of pan ranging from 0.7- to 1.7-litres plus lids to fit. For solo use the 1-litre one is ideal. Complete with lid it weighs 110g/4oz.

There are plenty of other aluminium cook

Kitchen utensils: clockwise from left, MSR Alpine stainless steel pans; Field & Trek Lightline billy and lid; Trangia kettle, pan, frypan/lid and potgrab; stainless steel mug; plastic mug; Lifeboat Matches; lighter; Lexan plastic spoons.

sets available but not many of the same simple design as the Trangia and Lightline pans, which don't have handles and which are wide and fairly shallow with rounded bases. Attached handles or bails I find a nuisance in aluminium cookware as they are prone to overheat. Tall, narrow pans, such as come with some stoves, heat up slowly, or at least the food at the top does. This may still be lukewarm when the food at the bottom is burning.

Owing in part to concern about the possible long-term effects of ingesting aluminium, even the minuscule amounts from cooking pans, several stainless steel cook sets have appeared on the market. Apart from the health factor stainless steel is easy to clean, non-corroding, scratch-proof, tough and long-lasting and it doesn't taint food. It is far superior to aluminium. I found this out on the Canadian Rockies walk when I carried an aluminium pan and a steel cup. At the end of the three-and-a-half-month walk the pan was pitted and corroded inside whilst the cup looked as good as new. The problem with stainless steel though is the weight. Some of the best come from Evernew, but their smallest set, consisting of 1-litre

and $\frac{3}{4}$-litre pans plus frying pan/lid and plastic cup, weighs 595g/21oz, which compares badly with the 198g/7oz of the equivalent-sized aluminium Field & Trek Lightline Solo Set. Admittedly the Evernew pans have fold-out handles but this can hardly account for the weight difference. Another example is MSR's Alpine Cook Set, the same as the one that comes with the Heat Exchanger, with $1\frac{1}{2}$- and 2-litre pans plus lid and pot lifter, which weighs 735g/26oz. This would be a fine set for two people. The lightest stainless steel pans I've found are those from Olicamp. I have a 1-litre copper-bottomed pan taken from a larger set that, with its lid, weighs 212g/7$\frac{1}{2}$oz, only 100g/3$\frac{1}{2}$oz more than the Lightline. This is now my standard pan for solo trips, despite the fold-out handles which, unlike those on aluminium pans, I find stay cool except when cooking over a wood fire. Other stainless steel cooksets are available from Markhill and Coleman.

Complete pan and windshield sets designed for specific stoves are available from companies like Markhill (for Camping Gaz Bleuet, Optimus 123 and Coleman stoves) and Sigg. An example is the Sigg Tourist Stainless Steel Cook

Kit that fits the Coleman Feather 442 and the Camping Gaz Bleuet. It has 1.2- and 1.6-litre pans, frying pan/lid, windscreen and pot lifter, and a weight of 735g/26oz, fairly low for steel utensils. The use of these sets obviates the need for additional windshields.

Lids are important as water will boil far faster if one is used. Many are designed to double as frying pans as well but people who use the latter tell me these don't work very well and recommend carrying a separate frying pan, preferably with a non-stick coating. At weights of 340g/12oz and upwards you have to be pretty dedicated to fried food to bother with one.

Pot lifters

Far superior to fixed handles are simple two-piece pot lifters that clamp firmly on to the edge of a pan when the handles are pressed together. I've used my 25-g/1-oz Trangia one on almost every trip for nearly 20 years. Not all are as of high a quality though; some thin aluminium ones soon distort and twist out of shape. To make close-fitting lids easy to lift off pans I put them on upside down with the rims pointing upwards. Lids that leave a large gap, like Trangia ones, can be put on the right way up and the pot lifter inverted to grip them. Some people use bandannas or thick items of clothing as insulating cloths for lifting pans but I have worries about hot liquid soaking through or my hand slipping, and prefer a lifter. Now that I usually use the Olicamp pot with its fold-out handles and a lid with a plastic knob I only carry a pot lifter when I intend to cook over an open fire, as then the pan handles can become very hot.

Plates or Bowls

I usually eat out of the pan and so don't bother with plates or bowls. However twosomes and bigger groups can't easily do this. Outdoor shops are full of shallow plastic utensils that look suitable but aren't as they spill easily and don't hold much. It is better to use a deep plastic mixing bowl of the type found in the kitchen sections of department stores. These are cheap and weigh only a few dozen grams. A handle can be made by melting a hole near the rim and threading a piece of thick cord through it into which the fingers can be entwined. This idea comes courtesy of Todd Seniff who produced such a bowl on the Canadian Rockies ski tour.

I was impressed, as the standard camping store plastic plate I'd brought had proved next to useless. Some people eat out of their mugs but if you do that you can't have a drink at the same time.

Mugs

These are essential and may be made of plastic or metal. The first are light and cheap but not very durable (in constant use I find the best last no more than a few months before dirt-collecting uncleanable cracks and splits develop causing me to retire them mostly on hygiene grounds). They also hold tastes and so should only be used for one type of liquid. If you have tomato soup in the evening, however well the mug is washed the morning coffee will have a faint soupy taste to it. A typical 0.42-litre one weighs 20g/$\frac{3}{4}$oz. Lexan ones could be better as this material is claimed not to retain tastes and to be unbreakable. The REI 0.3-litre Lexan Cup weighs 85g/3oz.

The alternative to plastic is metal, but this must be stainless steel. To drink out of aluminium or enamel mugs you need asbestos lips. This means that the ones that come with Optimus 123 and MSR X-GK stoves and double as burner covers are actually fairly useless except for cold drinks. I tend to leave them at home. Stainless steel however is ideal for mugs as the lip remains cool, it doesn't taint, it doesn't scratch and it's long-lasting. I have a 0.6-litre one bought several years ago from REI. It's called the Cascade Cup, weighs 110g/4oz and has a clip-off handle that folds away under the cup. Having a wide base, it can be used as a small pan and I frequently use it as such, heating water for drinks in it. Unfortunately I haven't seen it or anything like it in any catalogues recently. I rather wish I'd bought two.

The Cascade Cup is clearly a large version of the Sierra Cup, a 0.3-litre wide-topped shallow cup very popular in North America. I've tried one of these and frankly find it hopeless. Drinks cool far too fast because of the shape, it topples over very easily and, worst of all, it's simply not big enough. There are conventional stainless steel mugs available; the one I have weighs 110g/4oz and holds 0.6 litres. It can just about be used as a pan on stoves with pot supports close together like the Optimus 123 and the Epigas Alpine, but it's not really the right shape for this. I take it on trips with others when

I'm sharing a cook set and won't be using my mug as a pot. If keeping drinks hot for long periods is important then double stainless steel mugs which are claimed to do just that are available in 0.3- and 0.4-litre sizes. They're heavy though—the smaller one weighing 198g/7oz.

Eating implements

Lexan plastic works well for cutlery, but despite claims to the contrary, it does in time discolour and it can be broken. A soup spoon and teaspoon together weigh 10g/0.35oz. Other plastic spoons will break under the weight of a baked bean and aren't worth bothering with. Metal cutlery weighs a little more but lasts longer and I expect when my current Lexan spoons break I'll go back to raiding the cutlery drawer. Special clip-together camping sets seem unnecessarily fussy and anyway nearly always include a fork which is useless for the type of food I eat in the wilderness. A knife is useful in the wilderness kitchen, if only for opening food packets, but also has so many other functions I've included it under General Accessories in the next chapter.

Washing Up

One advantage of stainless steel is that it cleans much more easily than aluminium, especially worn pitted aluminium. Generally a wipe-round with a damp cloth is enough. For hygienic reasons it's advisable to clean pans and utensils thoroughly though, which I do with boiling water. I don't carry any detergent or washing-up liquid. It's unnecessary and a pollutant, even if biodegradable. Nor do I wash dishes directly in a stream or tip waste food into one. Dirty washing up water should always be poured on to a bare patch of ground or into thick vegetation. To make dish washing easier it's advisable to pour cold water into a pan once it's empty to stop food residues cementing themselves to the inside. Some foods are worse than others for this—porridge is particularly bad. Hard-to-clean pans can be scoured with gravel or even snow to remove debris. (You can also do this if you've forgotten your dish cloth.)

I often wash up without leaving the tent by boiling water in the dirty pot, scrubbing it out with the scourer backed sponge I carry (weight—a fraction of a gram), pouring the water away at arm's length, then rinsing it out with cold water.

Carriage

I generally pack my stove, pans and utensils together in a small stuffsac. What I don't do is pack the stove inside the pans as I find that this tends to dirty the latter, although being able to do so is touted as an advantage of many small stoves. Fuel bottles are normally carried in outside pockets just in case of leakage (though on the Yukon walk they resided in the bottom of the main pack compartment for three months with no problems) whilst cartridges usually end up in the bottom of the top compartment of the pack where they are out of the way. The stove and pans end up here too as I rarely use them during the day. If you cook at lunchtime you will obviously need to pack them somewhere more accessible.

SITING AND OPERATING THE KITCHEN

I like to site my kitchen next to my sleeping bag, which means either in the tent vestibule or next to the groundsheet if I'm sleeping out. That way I can have breakfast in bed—a good way to face a cold or wet morning and nice at any time. The stove needs to be placed on bare earth or short sparse vegetation if the heat from it is not to cause damage. If the plant growth is long and luxurious I try to find a flat rock to place the stove on, to avoid singeing the vegetation. The rock must of course be returned to where it came from when you have finished. Once the stove is set up I sort out the food I need for the evening before I light it. Then when all the kitchen items are arranged near the stove and I know where everything is, I start cooking.

This pattern requires modification in two very different circumstances. The first is in country where bears are a potential menace. Here it is advisable to site the kitchen at least 100 metres down-wind of where you sleep as the smell of food might attract a bear during the night. I look for a sheltered spot with a good view and, because I won't have my mat and sleeping bag to lie on and in, a log or tree stump to sit on and perhaps another to use as a crude table (in bear country you are nearly always camped in woods). Utensils, as long as they're clean, I leave in place overnight. Dirty ones should be hung with the food.

The other modification is required when camping on snow. Often the cold means that eating from the sleeping bag is essential. The problem is to prevent the stove melting down through the snow. Some form of insulation is needed for this and I often use a small square of closed cell foam, cut from the corner of an old mat, which now has deep grooves in it where it has partially melted from the hot metal of stove bases and legs. For some time I've meant to glue a covering of silver foil over it to prevent this happening. If you don't have a piece of foam to use, other items can be pressed into service. In the snowbound High Sierras on my Pacific Crest Trail walk I balanced my Optimus 123 on the thick natural history guide to the area I was carrying—the book surviving remarkably well! At other times I've used the blade of a metal snow shovel. An alternative to cooking from the sleeping bag in deep snow, which is especially useful when there are two or more of you, is to dig out a kitchen. Any type of construction is possible but I've found the best to be a simple bench shape with a back of snow and a trench for the feet. The seat and back can be lined with insulating mats for warmth and the stove set up on the edge so that you can sit and cook.

Unless I've stopped very late in the day, evening meals are leisurely affairs. I start with a hot drink, follow that with soup, then generally have a break from the stove while I read, write, study the map, daydream or watch the wind stirring the grasses, the clouds building and dissolving, ants removing specks of dropped food and whatever else is going on around me. A faint feeling of hunger usually stirs me to action within an hour of finishing my soup and I cook my main meal in the same unwashed pan (I reason that traces of soup will add extra flavour). As I eat the meal my mug is back on the stove boiling water for an after-dinner hot drink. Before going to sleep I may have another if I'm feeling really thirsty, with perhaps a granola bar to stave off middle-of-the-night hunger pangs. The stove and utensils are then left in place so that I can make breakfast with as little effort as possible. If there's any chance of an overnight frost I place a pan of water on the stove. That way if it freezes all I have to do is light the stove to melt it. Thawing out a frozen plastic water container is difficult, though turning it upside down means you will be able to use any water that hasn't frozen. When it looks like being very cold I bring a bottle inside the tent and wrap it in stuffsacs and spare clothing to try to prevent it freezing. People do apparently take bottles into their sleeping bags with them but I fear a leak too much to do this. If you have a thermos-type flask, this can be filled with hot water last thing at night, ready for the morning.

Breakfast only requires boiling water for coffee and preparing a bowl of cereal. It may take ten minutes or two hours depending on the weather, how far I have or want to travel that day and how I'm feeling. Usually I start packing up to move on whilst finishing the second cup of coffee, and I'm generally starting walking an hour or so after waking up.

149

The Rest of the Load

To make any walk both safe and enjoyable a whole host of small items are needed. Some of these are essential on every walk, some are never actually necessary although carrying them may well enhance your stay in the wilderness. I am always surprised at just how many odds and ends I end up with in the pack yet when I examine what I carry none of it is superfluous to my needs. Everything of course relates to some activity, and knowing how to use the items is, as always, important so I will describe the techniques as well as the gear.

LIGHT

In the far north at midsummer it's light 24 hours a day, and no artificial light source need be carried. In the same places (Alaska, Northern Canada, Greenland, Iceland, Lapland) there is no daylight at midwinter. Then no one goes backpacking. Most treks take place in areas further south however, where some form of light is needed summer and winter. How much you need depends on where you are and when. The further north you are the less light you'll need in summer, the more in winter. In Northern Scotland for example mid-June sees 20 hours of daylight, mid-December barely seven.

Two sorts of light are needed; one for use whilst walking and one for use in camp. The walking light will do for camp; but not vice versa.

Head Lamps and Torches

These are the lights needed for walking and setting up camp when it's dark, something you may never intend doing, but which will probably occur at some point in your walking career. It's wise therefore to be prepared. Not so long ago flashlights or torches, as they are called in the USA and the UK respectively, had a reputation for being unreliable, always going wrong just when you needed them most. My field notes from the 1970s and early 1980s confirm this. I went through a considerable number of different torches, constantly trying new ones in the hope that they would prove better than ones that had failed. Even in 1985 I had two fail on me during the Continental Divide walk, finishing that trek with a large and heavy store-bought handtorch. The 1980s however saw a wave of new tough and longlasting torches and headlamps on the market. One reason for the unreliability of older designs lay in the on-off switches which soon developed loose connections. Many current models don't have switches. To turn them on you simply twist the lamp housing. Others, usually the larger ones, have recessed switches that aren't easily damaged or switched on by accident.

Hand-held lights are cheaper and lighter than headlamps and there is a much greater choice. Two names dominate the ones suitable for backpacking: Tekna and Maglite. Each produce a range of units. A typical Tekna product is the Camper 2AA which has a waterproof tough ABS plastic body, adjustable focus and an interesting battery-life indicator—red indicating less than 25 per cent power remaining, yellow 25-50 per cent and green more than 50 per cent. It will run for five or six hours on two alkaline AA batteries at 20°C and weighs 85g/3oz including the batteries. The Mini-Maglite AA takes the same batteries and runs for the same length of time but weighs 115g/4oz because of the aluminium body. It also has a beam that adjusts from wide to spot. There are many larger sizes, the biggest being far heavier than any walker would want to carry. Many other makes exist, and every outdoor shop offers a selection. Other reputable names include Durabeam and PeliLite.

I don't use any of these though, as many years ago I stopped using hand held lights, finding a headlamp far more useful as it enabled me to have both hands free for various tasks, especially pitching the tent and cooking. I'd previously done these tasks whilst gagging on a torch held in the mouth, stopping every few minutes to recover. I find walking with a headlamp easier than with a hand-held light too. They were first developed for alpine mountaineering to make pre-dawn starts easier, and many of the best ones come from mountaineering equipment manufacturers. Early models had poor reputations as they involved trailing wires to pocket-held battery packs which were always catching on things and being ripped out. Then the first ones to put the battery case on the headband located it at the front behind the lamp itself which made the unit uncomfortable to wear for very long. A few of these are still around.

Since the early 1980s I've used a Petzl Zoom Head Lamp, a French product now widely recognised as the best around. I've certainly found it very comfortable and reliable. The battery pack fits on the back of the head and there is a strap running over the top of the head as well as the usual adjustable headband. The actual lamp unit pivots up and down to make directing the beam easy. The lamp is switched on by twisting its housing and goes from spot to flood. Two spare bulbs can be stored behind the lamp unit. The weight without batteries is 150g/5oz. The standard battery is a flat Duracell MN 1203 alkaline 4.5V one (weight also 150g/5oz) which is virtually unobtainable in North America— which is why I didn't take my Petzl on the Continental Divide walk. I regretted that decision, as I found out too late that there is an adaptor available that takes three AA cells and weighs, with batteries, 70g/2½oz and which I used on the Canadian Rockies walk. Petzl say that at 20°C the 4.5-v battery provides light for 17 hours, the three AA ones for 8. I've used a Petzl with 4.5-v battery for all-night winter walks without the light fading and find that one will last for several weeks of normal use. This is with the standard 3.8-V/0.2-A bulb which gives a 30-metre/ 100-foot beam. If the more powerful and long-lasting 4-V/0.5-A halogen bulb which gives a 100-metre/325-ft beam is used the flat battery lasts six and a half hours, the three AA ones two and three-quarter hours, again at 20°C. I've always found the standard bulbs adequate, preferring the longer battery life.

At a weight of 300g/10oz (with 4.5V battery), the Zoom Headlamp is a little heavy to carry for northern summers, when a light isn't needed very often or for very long. Petzl have thought of this however and the answer is their Micro headlamp which takes just two AA batteries, the total weight being 150 g/5oz. Again this has a pivoting lamp. The battery unit is mounted on the forehead but is so light that it doesn't feel uncomfortable. The beam reaches 10 metres/33ft and the battery life is five hours. The bulb is a 2.5-V/0.2-A one and a spare can again be carried behind the lamp unit.

Battery life declines in the cold but for less than extreme temperatures these standard head lamps are adequate. If you're going where it's really cold there is a version of the Zoom Lamp called the Arctic which features a battery pouch that you hang round your neck and keep next to your body so that it stays warm. This only takes the halogen bulb but with the 4.5-V battery is reckoned to last six and a half hours at -40°C, twice as long as the Zoom version.

There are other headlamps around but none I've seen look as well made or as comfortable as the Petzls. Having found a light that is reliable I'm sticking with it. I carry my headlamp in a small stuffsac along with a spare battery in a pack pocket so that I can find it quickly when I need to. Lights used to switch themselves on so easily in the pack, owing to their protruding switches, that it was essential to reverse the batteries for carrying to prevent them being drained. This isn't necessary with the Petzls and, I expect, with most other modern lights. In camp I always keep the light to one side of the head of my sleeping bag when it's not in use so that I can reach for it in the night if necessary and find it without too much trouble.

Whatever torch or headlamp you use it's wise to carry spare batteries and bulb on all trips. I always use the widely available alkaline batteries, but alternatives are rechargeable nickel-cadmium and long-life lithium ones. You can't recharge the former during a long trek, though. The latter, although expensive, could be worth considering for cold weather use, when they are meant to last considerably longer than alkaline ones. Lithium batteries also maintain a steadier beam throughout their lives rather than going into a slow decline like alkaline ones. Some reports however suggest that lithium batteries aren't as reliable as they need to be for backpacking. Ordinary carbon-zinc batteries whether standard or heavy-duty are too short-lived to be worth bothering with unless they're all you can find in a tiny store miles from anywhere.

Candles

Batteries are heavy, expensive and polluting even when carried out, so I try to minimise their use. Also a general, diffuse light is more useful in camp than a single beam. All I carry for this purpose are candles, usually the short stubby long-life ones that weigh up to 198g/7oz when new but which burn for 10–30 hours depending on their size. I use these mainly because they will stand up on their own. I place candles on the ground or a flat rock in the tent vestibule,

or, if I am sleeping out, near the head of my sleeping bag, always checking to make sure that if one falls or is knocked over it won't land on anything inflammable. I never bring a candle into the inner tent or stand it on a groundsheet. On cold, dark winter nights I am always amazed at how much warmth and friendliness a single candle flame can give off inside a closed tent, especially if the stove windshield is placed behind it as a reflector (and of course to keep off breezes). Used like this I think a lit candle is fairly safe as long as you don't leave it unattended. Take care though to blow it out before you refill or light a stove or change cartridges, and make sure the flysheet above the candle isn't too close. I've melted tiny holes in two flysheet doors through not paying enough attention to this.

Candle lanterns which protect the flame from wind and which can be hung up are available, but having tried a couple of rather complex and fragile models many years ago I've not bothered with them. Current models look far better than the ones I remember using however, so I may get round to seeing what they're like one day soon. The most common glass and aluminium design with wire handle, made by a number of firms and offered in several catalogues, regulates the flame as the candle burns down for constant light, weighs 180g/6oz and lasts 8–9 hours

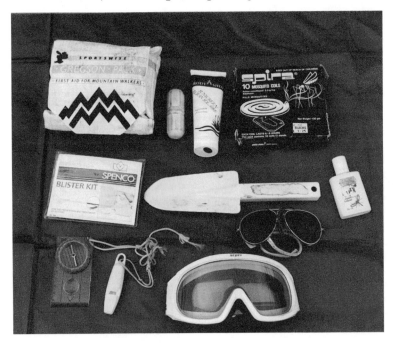

Accessories – clockwise from top left Gregson First Aid Pack, Coghlan's snake bite kit, sunscreen, mosquito coils, insect repellent, toilet trowel, glacier glasses, snow goggles, whistle and compass, blister kit.

with one candle. The glass slides into the metal base for carrying. Replacement candles come in packs of three that weigh 140g/5oz.

Candles also make good fire starters and can apparently be eaten in an emergency. Some are available with built-in insect repellent for summer nights in mosquito and midge country. I doubt whether the latter are very edible!

White-Gas, Kerosene and Cartridge Lanterns

As with candle lanterns, a few experiences with fragile and heavy butane lanterns many years ago made me lose interest in these items. Although there are now some much tougher, lighter models available I'm still not convinced that they're really worth bothering with, at least by solo backpackers. Apart from anything else the hiss they emit would probably drive me crazy. But for those who are interested here are a few details.

All these lanterns have glass globes that surround and disperse the light from a glowing lace-like mantle which in turn surrounds a jet. Both the globe and the mantle are highly breakable. If the lantern is to be carried in a pack they must be protected in some way. Looking through the catalogues, the one that catches my eye as probably the most useful is the Epigas Micro Lantern which weighs only 200g/7oz and has protective lightweight steel bars around the globe. The output is a bright 75–80 watts. It runs off a resealable cartridge, the ideal one being the Epigas 100-gram/3½-oz butane/propane one. No other lantern touches it for weight. Camping Gaz's Lumogaz, one of the few others that run off cartridges, weighs 540g/19oz. White-gas and kerosene lanterns are even heavier, the classic Coleman Peak 1 is a typical example at 850gs/30oz.

Lightsticks

Seemingly no more than a curiosity (at least for backpacking) lightsticks are thin plastic tubes that are bent to break an internal glass capsule and allow two non-toxic (we are assured) chemicals to mix and produce light, 'greenish' light according to one stockist. This gives 'three hours' reading light, nine hours' marker light, 30 minutes' work light and five minutes' distress-marker ultra-high intensity light'. The weight is 28g/1oz. I've never carried one.

HEALTH & BODY CARE

First Aid

You should be able to repair yourself in the event of injury or accident, at least enough to survive until help arrives or you stagger to the nearest road or habitation, especially if you travel alone. Taking a Red Cross, St John's Ambulance Brigade or similar first-aid course is a good idea. Alternatively, many outdoor schools offer courses specifically about wilderness first aid. There are many books on the subject too; recommended ones include *Medicine for Mountaineering*, edited by James A. Wilkerson (The Mountaineers) and *Medical Handbook for Mountaineers* by Peter Steele (Constable). Be warned though, a close study of either of these may well convince you that wilderness travel is so dangerous that you're lucky to have survived so far and you'd better not go back again! The antidote to this is a glance through the statistics of accidents in the home and on the road. Driving to the wilderness is far more hazardous than anything you do when you get there.

As well as a little knowledge a few basic medical items are needed. Outdoor shops are full of pre-packaged first-aid kits, few of which are actually worth buying. You can usually put a better one together more cheaply by browsing the shelves of your local chemist. This is what I always did until the Sportswise Gregson Pack appeared on the British market. This excellent first-aid kit consists of a fluorescent yellow, reinforced PVC, soft waterproof case that opens up to reveal a number of waterproof compartments containing first-aid items for specific injuries plus fold-out instructions directly relating to the contents, the idea being to help someone who's inexperienced or panicking. It also contains notes on mouth-to-mouth ventilation, the recovery position, hypothermia and shock. It's a comprehensive kit—not light at 450g/1lb, but surprisingly compact. I now carry the First Aid for Mountain Walkers Gregson Pack (there is also one for canoeists) on every trip. It lives in a side pocket for quick access and has proved very durable, only looking a little battered after the 124-day Canadian Rockies walk. The medical-grade contents, compiled in conjunction with first-aid organisations and mountain rescue teams, consist of:

Plastic emergency whistle	for summoning help–six long blasts, pause, repeat

Rescue call-out card and pencil	to send with someone going for help
15 x 10-cm sterile ambulance dressing	major bleeding
2 sterile lint dressings	severe bleeding
17-cm elastic net	to hold dressing on head wound
25-cm fabric plaster	minor cuts and blisters
5 antiseptic wipes	minor cuts and blisters
triangular bandage	arm fracture/shoulder dislocation
4 safety pins	
7. 5 x 5-cm crepe bandage	ankle sprain/arm fracture
10 x 10-cm sterile non adherent burns dressing	burns
10 x 500-milligram paracetamol tablets	pain
1 pair blunt/sharp nurse's scissors	

The only modifications I make to the Gregson Pack are to carry more material for blisters and, on long trips, more pain-killers. On major walks in remote country I also carry a course of prescription antibiotics in case of illness or infection. If you need any personal medication, that will have to be added to the kit as well of course.

There are other pre-packaged kits, that may be worth a look, including several from REI, but none has the mix of instructions and items that characterise the Gregson Pack. Groups will want to carry larger and more comprehensive kits, perhaps containing items like inflatable splints. If you make up your own kit the ideal container for it is a plastic food box as it prevents the contents from being crushed.

Tooth Care

Those who, like me, have teeth which are more metal than enamel and which require regular treatment may well want to carry an emergency temporary repair kit with them as well as having a check-up immediately before a long trip. Tooth care kits containing mirror, multi-purpose tools, spatula, mixing tray, dental cement, catalyst and instructions, and weighing 30g/1oz are available from Survival Aids amongst others.

Wash Kit

There are two schools of thought regarding washing on backpacking treks. One says 'little or never', the other, in the words of Hugh Westacott in *The Walker's Handbook*, says that 'before retiring for the night, and whatever the weather, the backpacker should strip off and thoroughly sponge the body from head to foot'.

The very thought has me shuddering, which tells you which approach I adopt. It's surprising how long you can go without washing. I managed 23 days in the High Sierras during my Pacific Crest Trail walk. When every drop of water you use has to be produced laboriously by melting snow over the stove, washing suddenly becomes of little importance. A minimum of cleanliness is needed for reasons of hygiene if nothing else though, and I usually manage to rinse my face and hands most days, however cold. More thorough washing I save for when I get home or, on long trips, the shower in a motel or campground at a resupply stop. In hot weather I wash more often, if only to stay cool. Water bags make good showers when hung from a tree. If left in the sun for a few hours beforehand the water is surprisingly warm. Overall though, being grubby from natural dirt seems to do no harm.

Soap is something I never carry. Even the biodegradable versions shouldn't be allowed to enter wilderness waters. If you can't manage without soap use a phosphate-free one, try to use as little as possible and dispose of the water you wash in well away from any lake or stream. Deodorants, cleansers and other cosmetics have no place in the wilderness either and should be left at home.

I don't carry a flannel or towel either. Both are heavy and slow to dry. A bandanna does for the former, an article of clothing for the latter, pile jackets are particularly good and I use one after a shower at a campground.

All my wash kit consists of is a toothbrush, a small tube of toothpaste and a comb. The first two live in a tiny stuffsac and weigh all of 20g/¾oz. Like soap, toothpaste should be deposited a long way from water. The comb lives in my 'office' (see below), and is carried so that I can make an attempt at looking respectable on reaching a town. Men with beards don't need to think about shaving gear. Although I normally shave, I don't in the wilderness even though the resulting scraggy attempt at a beard looks pretty awful. Men who do want to shave may be interested in the tiny battery shavers available for travellers, such as Braun's Minishaver (130gs/4½oz) which runs on two AA batteries.

Fending off Insects

In areas where biting insects such as mosquitos or midges regularly swarm in summer, some form of repellent is essential if you are to remain sane. You can cover up with tightly woven clothing that is light in colour (dark colours apparently attracting insects), and even wear a headnet (cotton mesh, 30g/1oz, to be worn over a brimmed hat) but you'll still need repellent. The most effective substance is diethyl-methyltoluamide (DEET for short), the active ingredient in most insect repellents. Well-known brands include Muskol, Cutters, Jungle Juice, Repel and Apica. Liquid repellent is the most useful, 30 ml/1 fl. oz weighing 30g/1oz. DEET will repel most biting insects including ticks. Insects home in on carbon dioxide, which is given off by the skin. DEET works by interfering with their senses, so as they approach the skin the signals given out tell them the source of CO_2 is moving away from them. I keep insect repellent either in my bumbag or a pack pocket so it's easily accessible. It should be kept well away from plastics such as pocket-knife handles and cameras as it dissolves these, turning them sticky and pliable.

Unfortunately DEET has recently been found to be harmful to the skin after sustained use and it shouldn't be used by children at all or by adults for long periods. One hundred per cent DEET repellents are not a good idea for regular use. More dilute versions of DEET with only 25-50 per cent active constituent are one alternative. Non-Deet ones include Spectrum Repellent, a mix of cinnamon, clove, eucalyptus, lemon, thyme and sandalwood in a coconut and vegetable oil base which sounds most fragrant, and oil of citronella, a traditional insect repellent that's making a reappearance in the light of the news about DEET. How effective these are I don't know but I intend to find out. In the meantime I've been using a Scottish product called Bug Off, which is only 12 per cent DEET. A 60ml/2fl oz bottle weighs 60g/2oz. I took Bug Off on my Yukon walk and found it successfully repelled mosquitoes and black flies, whilst on the Isle of Skye I found it kept midges, the worst insects I've ever encountered, from biting me. It's now my first choice in repellents. Less likely suggestions for keeping off insects are to take massive doses of vitamin B or to eat lots of garlic. However I know one person who crushes garlic and smears the juice on his skin which, he says, keeps Scottish midges at bay. What effect it has on anyone else I leave to your imagination!

In an enclosed space such as a tent vestibule, and perhaps under a tarp if it's calm, burning a mosquito coil will keep insects at bay. Candles containing insect repellent are available too but these are much heavier than coils and anyway it's during long light summer evenings that insects are a nuisance. Ten coils, each lasting eight to ten hours, with holder weigh 130grams/4½oz. The active ingredient is something called alletherin. In Scotland, where midges are a major hazard in summer, I use these regularly. My normal practice when midges are about is to pitch the tent as fast as possible, fill my water bag, climb in the tent, zip the door shut, light a mosquito coil and stay there until dawn. As midges will enter by the thousand under a flysheet if no coil is burning I set a coil up last thing at night, then sleep with the insect-netting inner door shut. By dawn this is often black with hungry midges and the vestibule is swarming with them. I unzip a corner of the netting, reach a hand out, strike a match and light the coil. Then I retreat and close the netting again. Within five minutes most of the midges will be dead, the inner door can be fully opened and I can breakfast in peace. I keep the coil burning though until I leave the tent. The tent often becomes hot and stuffy and stinks of burnt coil when I do this, but it's better than being bitten or having to eat breakfast whilst running round in circles as I've seen people doing. Even if you dose yourself with repellent the midges will still make your skin and scalp itch maddeningly by crawling all over any exposed flesh and in your hair, even though they won't bite.

Ticks are usually no more than an irritant but they can carry fatal diseases, so checking for them in areas where they are endemic (local knowledge is useful here) and at times when they appear (usually late spring/early summer) is a sensible precaution. Ticks crawling on the body can be detached and crushed. Ones embedded in the skin can be removed by touching them with gasoline- or kerosene-soaked cotton or paper so that they withdraw their mouthpieces and then picking them off carefully with tweezers. Twisting or burning them is not advised as the mouthparts will remain in the wound. The wound should be cleaned thoroughly. Ticks attach themselves by being brushed off the ends of grasses and leaves, where they wait for victims to pass by, so care should be taken in thick undergrowth. Wearing long clothing helps and repellent can be dabbed on cuffs and ankles. At night body searches can locate ticks that may not yet be attached. It helps if there are two of you for this. REI offer a Tick Kit consisting of a 6x magnifier, curved tweezers, antiseptic swabs and instructions, weighing 56g/2oz.

Bee and wasp stings can be very painful. There are various remedies. Sting Eze is a liquid anti-histamine available in a 50-ml/2-fl oz bottle which is said to be effective, whilst REI offer a Sting-X-Tractor Kit containing a suction venom extractor. I've no idea if it works. People who have an adverse reaction to such stings should carry their own medication.

Sunscreen
Protecting your skin against the sun is a necessity—burnt shoulders are agony under the weight of a pack and a peeling nose can be very painful. And in the long run there is the risk of skin cancer. To minimise the chances of burning, sunscreens should be used on exposed skin whenever you are in sunlight, even if you think sunburn is unlikely. There are a host of sunscreens on the market, all with a sun protection factor (SPF) number. The best are creamy rather than greasy and don't wash off in sweat—at least not quickly. The higher the SPF, the more protection is given. SPFs of 15 and above give virtually total protection and are recommended for high altitudes where ultraviolet light, the part of the spectrum that burns, is stronger (it apparently increases by four per cent in intensity for every 300 metres/1000ft of altitude). I burn quite quickly and need screens with SPFs of 10-12 applied several times a day. A 100-ml/3½fl-oz tube lasts me around a week in consistently sunny weather. Snow reflects sunlight, so all skin including under your chin and around your nostrils needs covering with sunscreen when crossing bright snowfields especially at altitudes above 2000 metres/6500ft. Brimmed and peaked hats help shade the face and cut the need for sunscreen.

If you do burn there are various soothing creams and lotions that help reduce the suffering, but it's best to avoid this happening in the first place. I don't carry any sunburn treatment.

Lipsalve
Lips can suffer from windburn as well as sunburn and crack badly in very cold conditions, so a tiny tube of lipsalve is a good addition to the load. Every chemist or drug store sells them and they weigh only a few grams yet can save days of pain.

Sunglasses
Most of the time I don't wear sunglasses, preferring to accustom my eyes to bright sunlight. Only during snow travel do I regularly wear sunglasses as then they are essential to prevent snow blindness even when the sun is not shining brightly. I learnt this the painful way on a day of thin mist in the Norwegian mountains. Because visibility was so poor and wearing sunglasses made it worse I didn't wear them but skied all day straining to see ahead. My eyes became sore and itchy, and by evening I was seeing double and my eyes were very painful except when closed. Luckily it was the last day of my trip, otherwise I would have had to rest for at least a couple of days to allow my eyes to recover. I was lucky too that I did not suffer complete snow blindness. What I think happened was that although no sunlight was visible the mist was very fine and a lot of sunlight was being filtered through it.

The main requirement of sunglasses is that they cut out ultraviolet light which most specialist ones do but many cheap high street shop ones don't. In Britain there are no standards for sunglasses, but in the USA there are three classifications: cosmetic, general purpose and special purpose. The second two are the ones worth buying. For general use look for grey or brown lenses as these render colours accurately. Glass ones are scratch-resistant, polycarbonate are lighter in weight. Names of quality glasses include Bolle, Vuarnet, Ray-Ban and Oakley. For snow use the glacier types with side shields are a good idea, and at high altitude essential. The problem is that they are prone to fogging with condensation. I have a pair, weighing 28g/1oz (56g/2oz with hard case), but I haven't used them since I acquired a pair of Oakley Eyeshades with a large wraparound lens that protects against light from the side almost as well as side shields and which rarely fogs. They weigh 42g/1.5oz and come with snap-off, snap-on ear pieces which minimise the chance of breakage and grey scratch-resistant lenses that cut out 100 per cent ultraviolet light. They are promoted as cycling glasses but I find them ideal for ski touring.

People who wear prescription glasses can buy overglasses that fit over the top as well as clip-on dark lenses. I don't wear glasses but to me the former seem the more practical.

Keeping glasses on, especially when skiing, can be a problem. The answer is to have a loop that goes round your head or neck. Glacier glasses often come provided with these, and for those that don't have them there are various add-on ones available that slip over earpieces. Names include Croakies, Chums and I-Ties and they weigh around 15g/½oz. I use Croakies with my Oakley glasses and they work well.

In really severe blizzard conditions, goggles rather than glasses may be needed and on ski tours I carry a pair of good quality Scott alpine ski ones (100g/3½oz). They have an amber double lens which improves visibility, so you can see more clearly in haze. They're what I should have worn when I nearly suffered snow blindness in Norway. There are foam mesh vents above and below the lens which is made of two layers of plastic (double-glazed if you like). These facts help cut fogging, though the goggles suffer this more than the Oakley glasses. A wide elasticated and adjustable headband plus thick soft foam around the rim make them comfortable to wear. If necessary they can be worn over a hat or hood and pushed down around the neck when not needed, which is safer than pushing them up on the forehead and risking having them fall off. By carrying them along with the Oakleys I also have a back-up in case I lose or break a pair. Ski shops are full of similar goggles, but again beware of cheap imitations. As well as Scott, Bolle, Jones, Cebe and Smith are among the many with good reputations.

Sanitation

The careless deposition of human excrement is now a problem in too many wilderness areas. All too often every rock within a few hundred metres of a popular campsite sprouts ragged pink and white toilet paper from round its edges. As well as turning beautiful places into sordid outdoor privies there is a danger to health as faeces pollute watercourses and lead to a greater prevalence of giardia and other harmful organisms. Sheer numbers is the biggest cause of the problem, but so is the unthinking siting of toilets and disposal of waste.

One answer, adopted by many land management agencies in North America, is to provide outhouses and deep toilet pits at popular destinations, usually but not always backcountry campgrounds; there is one on top of Mount Whitney in California, the highest peak in the 48 contiguous states and therefore a magnet for walkers. Where such facilities are provided they must be used, and used properly, which is to say not as dumping grounds for rubbish such as empty food packets and empty butane cartridges.

Outhouses are obtrusive and detract from the feeling of wilderness, and taking care with sanitation can ensure that no more need to be built. In any case, in most European and many North American wildernesses there are no such facilities so other methods have to be used. (The following discussion is based on the arguments outlined in *Soft Paths* by Bruce Hampton and David Cole (Stackpole Books) which is recommended reading for all concerned in minimising their impact on the wilderness.) There is no best method, but rather a number of options. Which one you adopt depends on the area. The aims are to prevent water contamination, speed decomposition and shield waste from contact with humans and animals. The first can be done by always defecating at least 200 metres/220 yards from any water. Heading uphill is usually a good way to achieve this. The second and third aims unfortunately conflict as the best way to achieve rapid decomposition is to leave waste on the surface where the sun and air soon break it down. The idea, prevalent until very recently, that burial a few centimetres down was the best way to hasten decomposition has been shown to be wrong. Buried faeces can last a very long time.

Current recommendations are to use surface deposition in little-used areas, well away from anywhere likely to be visited by the few other people who do come, and to smear faeces around with a rock or stick to maximise exposure to the sun and air. In popular areas small individual catholes should be dug around 10cm/4in deep, as the microorganisms that break up organic waste are most numerous here. After you've finished, faeces should be broken up with a stick and mixed with the soil. The hole should then be filled in and camouflaged. A small plastic trowel is useful for this and I carry an orange Coughlans one that weighs 42g/1½oz in a pack pocket. Even if you are travelling in a large group, big latrines shouldn't

Repair kit clockwise from top left, nylon patches, cord, tent pole repair sections, sticky-backed ripstop nylon tape, zipped stuffsack, Whisperlite stove repair kit, Therm-A-Rest repair kit.

be dug unless there are limited cathole sites or the group is staying on a site for a long period (not in itself a good idea for minimising impact). The idea is to disperse not concentrate waste.

There remains the problem of toilet paper. I use a standard white roll with the cardboard tube removed, weighing 100g/3½oz when new. Coloured paper should not be used, as the dyes pollute water. Disposal is difficult as this apparently fragile substance is amazingly resilient, lasting far longer than faeces, and it shouldn't be left to decorate the wilderness. There are two options. The one preferred by most people is to burn the paper and I keep a box of matches in the same plastic bag as my toilet paper for this purpose. Great care must be taken in doing this though, and if there is any fire risk it's better not to. If you have a camp fire, paper should be brought back from your toilet trip and burnt in this. If you can't burn it then, unpleasant though it may seem, you should pack it out in a sealed plastic bag to be deposited in a waste bin or a fire if and when you have one. Women backpackers should pack out used tampons too unless they can be burnt, which requires a very hot fire. If they are buried, animals will dig them up. More specific advice for women, plus a lot of good general advice on backcountry toilet practices can be found in Kathleen Meyer's humorous book *How to Shit in the Woods* (Ten Speed Press).

For those prepared to try there are many natural alternatives to toilet paper including sand, grass, large leaves and even snow. The last, I can assure you, is far less unpleasant than it sounds.

Finally a note that I'm afraid applies to men only. I wouldn't presume to advise women on this topic, but would simply refer them to Kathleen Meyer's book. The topic is urination—simple usually but not when you wake in the middle of a cold and stormy night and are faced with crawling out of your sleeping bag, donning clothes and venturing out into the wet and wind. The answer is to kneel up in the tent and urinate into a wide-mouthed plastic bottle instead. Once you become practised this can be done in a very short space of time. Indeed you need only half wake up. I use a cheap ½-litre plastic bottle with a green screw top, which distinguishes it clearly from my water bottle. Its weight is 56g/2oz. I carry it mainly in winter and spring when blizzards may rage and leaving the tent at night is to be avoided at all costs, but some people carry one year round. Outside of winter I usually just kneel in the vestibule and pee out of the tent or if sleeping out I stand up at the end of the sleeping bag. A pee-bottle could also be useful when biting insects are around however, as then you would have to get dressed before leaving the tent. Not to do so is to invite disaster. Despite warnings, a student on a course I was leading in the Scottish Highlands left the tent for a pee one night clad in just a tee-shirt. He was out of the tent less than a minute but in the morning he emerged totally covered with midge bites from the waist down.

EQUIPMENT MAINTENANCE AND REPAIR

It's an unusual trip when some item of gear doesn't need repairing or at least tinkering with so I always carry a small stuffsac of assorted items, designated the repair bag, for this purpose. Although the contents vary from trip to trip the weight rarely goes above 225g/8oz. Repair kits for specific items live in this bag but have been dealt with elsewhere. Certain back-up items such as Lifeboat Matches live here too, for want of anywhere better.

The most used of the general repair items is the waterproof sticky-backed ripstop nylon tape that patches holes and tears in everything from clothing to tent flysheets. Four strips of different colours stapled together, stuck on card and measuring $22\frac{1}{2}$ by $7\frac{1}{2}$cm/9 x 3in, from companies such as Coughlans, weigh just a few grams. It's best to round the edges of patches to stop them peeling off and I apply a patch to both sides of a hole where possible. These patches may be adequate in the long term by themselves but large holes and tears should be reinforced with stitching round the edges or even a bigger patch. Stitch holes can be coated with glue to stop them fraying and on down-filled items to stop the fill escaping. I either carry a small tube of tent seamseal or something similar for this purpose or else use the one that is part of the Therm-A-Rest Repair Kit.

I also carry non-sticky pieces of nylon in case a major repair too big for the ripstop tape is needed. As such material is often provided with tents and packs in case a repair is needed I've built up a collection of it over the years of which I usually carry two or three sheets of different weights, the biggest measuring 30 x 45 cm/12 x 18in, including a non-proofed one for inner tent repair. The total weight is 28g/1oz. For sewing such patches and any other stitching repairs, I carry a couple of large-eyed sewing needles (you may have to thread them in poor light with numb fingers), plus a roll of polyester or nylon thread (cotton breaks easily and rots). These I keep in an old film canister along with a few spare buttons for any clothing that requires them. Again the weight is only a few grams. Also in the repair bag goes a selection of different-sized rubber bands which have many uses, including resealing opened food bags, keeping the book I'm reading open at the right page, doing the same for my notebook, replacing rubber tent-pegging points or inner tent connectors (though even the biggest rubber bands will only do this for a very short time before snapping) and holding together any items I need held together. A length of shockcord enables me to make more permanent replacements for broken tent-pegging points. Tied into a loop it makes an extra-strong rubber band. Any detachable pack straps that are not in use end up in the repair bag too—although perhaps oddments bag would be a better name.

Nylon Cord

The final item in the repair bag, nylon cord, deserves a section of its own as it's by far and a way the most important. Indeed I find it essential. The type I use is Survival Aids' Paracord which comes in 15-metre/50-ft lengths with a breaking strain of 160kg/350lb at a weight per hank of 115g/4oz. I always carry one length, two on long walks and in bear country. Uses I've put it to include: ridgelines and guylines for a tarp, extra tent guyline, bearbagging food, spare boot laces, clothes line, strap for attaching items to pack (wet socks, crampons, ice axe), swami belt for use with a karabiner and rope for river crossings, lashing for temporary repair to broken pack frame (something I used it for to repair a companion's frame on the Pacific Crest Trail), lowering pack down or pulling it up short steep cliffs or slopes (with cord fed round back or tree or rock, not hand over hand), underfoot gaiter cords, and hat chin strap. Every so often when my cord has been cut up and retied so often there seem to be more knots than cord I replace it, often carrying a few of the shorter lengths as well. Whenever you cut nylon cord, by the way, fuse the ends with heat or they'll fray. I'm not an expert on knots and so simply use half-remembered ones when I use the cord, retying them if they slip—not the safest or best method. Mountaineering textbooks always have a section on knots if you want to learn some properly.

KNIFE

Some form of knife is necessary. I use one for opening food packets, spreading margarine and other foods on biscuits or bread, cutting cord, making 'feather' sticks for starting fires and sundry other minor chores. What isn't needed is a large and heavy sheath or 'survival' knife. Swiss Army knives have become the standard for backpacking and rightly so. This success has led to inferior imitations though—the only genuine brands are Wenger and Victorinox. These are small tool-kits rather than just knives, with the largest having a large number of different features (blades is hardly the right word), many serving several functions. The more complex ones I find too heavy and bulky, as I like to carry my knife in a trouser pocket. For years

I've used the Victorinox Spartan which weighs 70g/2½oz and has two blades, a can opener/screwdriver, a bottle opener/screwdriver a corkscrew and a reamer. What the last is meant to do I'm not sure. The most useful features, used often enough to make me glad I don't carry the most basic version, are the can opener and the screwdrivers. The latter are useful when repairing items such as stoves or packs. Some people like to have one with scissors on it but as the Gregson First Aid Pack has scissors in it, I don't have a need for them. The distinctive red plastic handle makes these knives less easy to lose.

My only complaint with Swiss Army knives is that the blades don't lock and it is possible for them to snap shut on your fingers. For that reason I sometimes carry a 19-cm/7½-in folding French Opinel knife with wooden handle and carbon-steel locking single blade. The weight is just 50g/1¾oz and the blade holds an edge better than the stainless steel Swiss Army ones, though it does eventually discolour. On long walks though I take the Spartan as I may want the other features as well as the blade.

Now, though, I see that lock-blade Swiss Army knives are available and I may just change to one of these. They have larger blades and so weigh more, the basic Adventurer with knife blade, can opener/screwdriver, bottle opener/screwdriver, Phillips screwdriver and reamer plus tweezers and toothpick weighing 128g/4½oz. However as that's more than the weight of the Spartan and Opinel knives combined I might instead carry them both. There are other small knives and folding tool kits around. Gerber, Tekna and Leatherman are some of the quality ones, but the choice of Swiss Army models is so great that there should be one of those to suit everyone's needs.

Keeping your knife sharp is important. I find the best place to do this is at home however, and I don't carry a sharpener in the field. The one that does the household knives can also do your pocket knife.

IN CASE OF EMERGENCY

You need to consider how to deal with possible emergencies on every trip, and certain ventures require specialist items. In particular, walks in really remote country, in snowbound mountains and where rivers or steep rocky terrain may have to be crossed present dangers that can be reduced by carrying one or other of the items listed below. There are many pre-packaged survival kits available, but like the first-aid kits these always seem to contain some items I don't want and others that I carry anyway. The idea is that these compact units go everywhere with you. They might be useful for day walkers but for backpacking I'd rather select and carry items separately. If I make short side trips away from my pack or camp I always take items such as whistle, compass, map, headlamp, water bottle, first-aid kit and a few snacks in my bumbag with me, and on longer ones, perhaps lasting all day, I take the pack itself along with spare clothing, bivi bag and more food.

Signalling: Whistles, Flares & Strobe Lights

If you are injured or taken seriously ill in the wilderness you need to be able to alert other people and would-be rescuers to your whereabouts. Having a bright item of clothing or gear to display is one way of doing this. At night your headlamp or torch can be used for sending signals. Six regular flashes followed by a pause then six more flashes is the international distress signal. Making a noise can bring help too and I always carry a plastic whistle (weighing a few grams) for this purpose, keeping it in a pocket or my bumbag rather than anywhere inaccessible. One comes with the Gregson Pack. I've never used it to signal distress, but it has come in useful for warning bears of my presence on a number of occasions. Again six blasts, pause, six blasts should be used when calling for help.

In most really remote areas any search made for you will probably initially be by air so you need to be seen from above and afar. Smoke is a sure way to attract attention and a fire, especially with wet vegetation added to increase the smoke, could be lit. Quicker and simpler would be to use a flare, and there are various packs of these available. I've never carried flares but there were times during the Canadian Rockies and Yukon walks when having them would have been a reassurance and I intend taking some on my next remote wilderness walk. Taking several small ones seems to make more sense than one big one, and packs of six to eight waterproof miniflares plus projector pen for one-handed operation weigh only 225g/8oz or so and reach a height of around 80 metres/260ft and last six seconds. Larger flares may last longer but unless you carry several of them there's only one chance to draw attention to your plight.

The alternative to flares is a strobe light, which I'd always thought of as big and heavy until my attention was brought to a very light one by arctic wanderer Dick Sale. The waterproof Medik C.I. emergency strobe sends out a light flash every second that is visible for 5km/3 miles. It weighs 225g/8oz, including the D-size battery that powers it and is another likely addition to my pack for my next walk in remote country.

Mirrors can be used for signalling, though only in sunlight, but I don't think it's worth carrying one for this purpose, as anything shiny such as aluminium foil (as used in stove windscreens), a polished pan base, a watchface, a camera lens, even a knife blade, can be used as a substitute, and anyway smoke and flares are more likely to be effective.

In open terrain if you have none of the above, spreading out light- and bright-coloured clothing and items of gear could help rescuers locate you, and I always carry at least one yellow or orange item for this purpose.

Rescue Procedures

If you are alone and suffer an immobilising injury all you can do is make yourself as comfortable as possible, send out signals and hope and pray someone will respond to them. In popular areas and on trails attracting attention shouldn't be too difficult, but in less frequented places and when travelling cross-country you may be totally dependent on those you've left details of your route with to report you missing when you don't check in as arranged. If there's a group of you someone can be sent for help if self-rescue isn't possible. It is important that whoever goes has all the necessary information: the location of the injured person(s), relevant compass bearings, details of local features that may help in finding the place, the nature of the terrain, the time of the accident, a description of the injuries and the size and experience of the group. This should be written down so that important details aren't forgotten or distorted because of stress and hurry. The Gregson Pack has a waterproof call-out card in it and a pencil for recording this information. Making up your own card if you don't have one of these packs would be a good idea even if you travel alone. It could then be handed to anyone who finds

you and goes for help. Once out of the wilderness the messenger should contact the police, national park or forest service office or other body who can arrange a rescue.

In Britain and North America there are volunteer mountain rescue teams who make no charge for coming out. They are made up of local outdoors people who give their time to come out and help people, often at great risk to themselves. If you need their services a generous donation should be made afterwards as they are not government funded. In other areas such as the Alps and the Pyrenees there are professional rescue teams and costs are high. For trips to such regions mountain rescue insurance should be taken out. For more on mountain rescue see *Mountaineering: The Freedom of the Hills*, chapter 20, and *Mountaincraft and Leadership*, chapter 10.

Rope

Roped climbing is for mountaineers and is a different pursuit to backpacking. However there are situations when a short length of rope may be necessary, in particular when crossing deep, fast flowing rivers or scrambling up or down steep rocky slopes. A full weight climbing rope isn't necessary. I've found 7 or 8-mm thick line, with a breaking strain of 1000–1550kg/2200–3400lb, perfectly adequate. An 18–20-metre/60–65-ft length, the shortest that's much use, will weigh 550–750g/20–26oz.

Ropes need to be properly looked after. One day your life might depend on one. They should be stored out of direct sunlight and away from chemicals, so cars are not a good place to keep ropes whether they are on a seat or in the boot. Even with minimum usage and careful storage ropes deteriorate and should be replaced every four or five years.

Snow Shovel

In deep snow a shovel is both an emergency and a functional item. The emergency uses are for digging a shelter in bad weather and for digging out avalanche victims. The functional ones are for levelling out tent platforms, digging out buried tents, clearing snow from doorways in order to gain entrance to mountain huts, digging through snow to running water or collecting snow to be melted for water, standing a stove on when cooking on snow and many other purposes. All in all I find a snow shovel essential in snowbound terrain. Both plastic and metal ones are available but I don't recommend plastic as the blades won't cut through hard-packed snow or ice. I use a Camp model with aluminium blade and detachable wood handle that measures 71cm/28in in length. At 570g/20oz it's the lightest I've found. I usually carry it assembled on the back of the pack. There are many models available, most usually with folding blades and weights between 595 and 710g/21–25oz. Shovel blades that attach to ice axes are lighter but can't be used unless you carry an axe, which I don't always do.

Fishing tackle

Despite my rather negative comments on 'living off the land' in the section on food, I did once carry a length of fishing line and a few hooks and weights in case I ran out of food on a deep-in-the-wilderness trip. I duly ran short of food and on several nights put out a line of baited hooks and on each successive morning pulled it in empty. Experienced anglers would probably have more success, and for them I'm sure it would be worthwhile to take some lightweight fishing tackle.

Threats from Animals

There is a danger—in most areas slight—of attack or threat of attack by animals. How to deal with this problem will be discussed in the next chapter. Here it is sufficient to say that the only difference it is likely to make to your load is if you are going into bear country, when you might want to carry the 400-g/14-oz Counter Assault spray can.

Navigation

Route-finding as a skill belongs in the next chapter, and it therefore makes sense to leave any detailed discussion of equipment until then. Here it's enough to say that on any trip a compass and a map weighing between 28 and 110g/1–4oz will be the minimum gear you'll need. On most trips though more than one map will be needed and you may well carry a trail guide as well. On trips of a fortnight and longer I usually end up with 700–1000g/25–35oz of maps and guides.

OFFICE

I carry enough writing materials and papers to make it necessary to have somewhere to keep them, both for protection and convenience.

There are many different pouches available, most made of nylon, containing several compartments and intended to be fastened to pack hipbelts or shoulder straps. I've tried several but have settled on two, both called Pocket Offices, that fit my needs. On really long trips, when I have more paper and a larger notebook, I use the Baggins Pocket Office, a zip-round Cordura nylon case with small handle measuring 17 x 25cm/6¾ x 9in (near enough Personal Organiser size) and weighing 115g/4oz. Inside there are two large and two small compartments plus two pen slots. It easily holds passport, travel documents, insurance documents, wallet, trail permits, writing paper and envelopes, a large notebook, pens, a paperback book and any other bits and pieces of literature I may collect along the way.

On shorter trips I carry the nylon Gregory Pocket Office which also weighs 115 grams/4 oz but which unfolds to reveal two swing-out pockets for pens and other small items, two transparent pockets for trail permits, passport, a small notebook etc. and two inner pockets, one velcro-closed for tickets, money, credit cards etc. It's smaller and neater than the Baggins one so it can be carried in a pocket but it isn't big enough for lots of papers and a large notebook.

Writing Paper and Notebooks

On trips of more than a week I send postcards to family and friends, buying them at supply points during the walk and often carrying a few grams of them between post boxes, writing them in camp at night. I find that many other backpackers do the same on trips of similar length. On longer trips I also carry airmail paper and envelopes so that I can pen longer missives. The total weight of this is never more than 100g/3½oz.

Keeping a journal on a walk is a way—perhaps the best way—of keeping a reminder of what it was like. I've kept them for all my walks since long before I began writing for anyone other than myself, and I can spend hours reliving a trip I'd almost forgotten by reading them. In order to record as much as possible I try to write up my journal every day, often making a few notes over breakfast and rather more during the evening. I find this difficult enough to do on solo trips; when I'm with companions I'm lucky if I write anything every other day. There are many lightweight notebooks around, many with tear-out leaves, but I prefer something more durable. Since the 1970s I've used the very similar and highly durable Alwych All Weather Cover and Challenge Oilskin Note Books, both with easily identifiable matt black covers. For my annual notebook, in which I keep records of all the trips of a fortnight or less, I use a 162 x 102 mm/6¾ x 4-in size with 80 leaves that weighs 125g/4½oz. On long treks though, when I know I'd fill at least two of those (on the Pacific Crest Trail I filled two plus a smaller notebook bought *en route*) I now use the 203 x 127-mm/8 x 5-in and 140-leaf size despite its weight of 325g/11½oz. In this I also keep my route plan, addresses of people at home and people I meet along the way, lists of how far I go each day and where I camp, reminders of bus and train times and any other information I may need or collect along the way. Looking at my Canadian Rockies journal I see I kept records of my resting pulse rate (which ranged between 44 and 56) and how much fuel my stove used (10–14 days per litre). I also made shopping lists and towards the end even a calendar on which I crossed off the days. (There was an ulterior motive for this as buses at the finish only ran three times a week.) These trivia may not seem worth recording but for me it brings back the reality of a trip very strongly and I wouldn't be without it.

Pens

I always carry at least two pens, a standard biro and a long-lasting and robust Space Pen which will write on greasy paper and when held upside down. Their weight is a mere 25g/1oz. I used to carry a pencil in the office but as there's one in the Gregson First Aid Pack, I no longer bother.

Papers

The number of papers you need to carry can amount to quite a collection, though they never weigh more than a few dozen grams. On trips close to home you may need none, but the further afield I go the more I seem to carry. On any trip abroad you'll need your passport and insurance documents and you'll probably end up carrying your airline or other tickets as well. It's useful to carry some form of identity anyway in case of emergency. In Britain I usually take my driver's licence. Whilst walking I keep my papers sealed in a plastic bag in the recesses of

my 'office'. Trail permits, if required, also go in a plastic bag but often in a pocket or my bumbag rather than the 'office'.

WALLET AND MONEY

Small Cordura wallets weigh so little (around 20g/¾oz) that I carry mine with me, after removing the clutter it somehow fills up with. In the wilderness money serves no purpose and on short trips, when I am never far from home, I carry very little—no more than I need for the return journey. On long trips it's useful, indeed essential, to have money to spend at town stops, particularly on food but also perhaps on accommodation, the launderette and postage. I try not to carry loose change, which is relatively heavy, except for a few coins for the phone. Notes in small denominations are the best form of cash to carry, as in remote and small places there may be nowhere to change large notes. I also carry a credit card as I find one usable in more places than traveller's cheques, which I no longer bother with.

WATCH

Some people leave their watches at home, wanting to escape all ties with organised hours. I'm often tempted to do so but unfortunately a watch does have its uses, even in the wilderness. In particular, knowing how many daylight hours are left can be important in determining whether you pass by a good campsite or push on hoping to find another. When the sun's visible you can estimate this fairly accurately but on dull, overcast days doing so can be almost impossible. A watch with a built-in calendar also helps keep track of the days, something I find can be confusing on long trips. Checking your watch when you stop for a break may also help get you moving again when you suddenly realise that the intended couple of minutes has somehow become half an hour. If it has an alarm you could even set that to wake you up for early morning starts.

PHOTOGRAPHY

Taking photographs is probably the most popular non-essential backpacking activity. People like to have a visual record of their trips. There is an argument that doing so distances you from truly seeing, truly experiencing the wilderness. Instead you just take a quick picture and turn away. When I was learning about photography

I used to agree with this view, as concern about the mechanics of camera use very much interfered with my direct involvement in the scenery. Now however I find the opposite to be true. By taking photography seriously I've learnt to respond quickly to subtle nuances of light, to watch intently the changing position of cloud shadows and the movement of the sun. I follow light, chasing the sun's last rays up mountains at dusk, waking in the dark to leap out of the tent to observe the first golden shafts of light splitting the thick mist on the surface of a lake. There is much I would have missed if it weren't for photography.

The difference I think lies in the type of photographer you are. Those who take only snapshots, simply pointing the camera and shooting at every pretty scene regardless of the light or the viewpoint, may well miss any deeper connection with the wilderness and reduce it to a quick picture-postcard view. But if that is the level of appreciation they are happy with, who is to say it's wrong? Even so, those who take time and care over their photography, slowly absorbing the details of a place in order to make the best picture, the one that most reflects how they see it, may feel, as I do, that this process helps them achieve a deeper appreciation of the wilderness.

Anyone wanting to pursue the subject of wilderness photography further will probably learn a lot from Galen Rowell's marvellous *Mountain Light: In Search of the Dynamic Landscape* (Sierra Club Books/ Century Hutchinson) and from the American magazine *Outdoor Photographer* the only photography magazine of real use to the backpacker.

Equipment

Photography is about seeing not equipment. No amount of expensive gear will make someone a good photographer. That said, the more ambitious you become the more gear you end up carrying. On the Canadian Rockies and Yukon walks I carried 4kg/9lb of cameras and accessories, which will seem an enormous amount to the non-photographer, less than the bare minimum to the enthusiast. I have, however, become something of a professional photographer over the years in that I go on most walks knowing that I have to come back with a set of pictures. Most people should be able to get by with less gear than I carry, most easily by leaving behind

the second camera I always carry in case my main one breaks.

Cameras: There are two choices here. Either a small, lightweight compact or a single lens reflex (SLR) with interchangeable lenses. The first now come with twin and zoom lenses as well as single ones and are usually fully automatic, which means you can literally point and shoot, without even having to focus the lens. Weights run from 185g/6½oz all the way up to 630g/22oz, which is heavier than some SLRs. For someone with no interest in photography but who would like pictures of their walks, the most basic of these are ideal. The more sophisticated ones, which allow the photographer to override the automatic settings, are capable of good results and one of the smaller ones makes a good back-up for an SLR. I have an old manual focus Olympus XA (no longer available, weight 225g/8oz) with a 35-mm lens that I use for this. With it I've taken pictures that have appeared on magazine covers, so it's not a toy. The nearest current equivalent is probably one of the even tinier Minox models.

However even the best zoom-lens compacts cannot match an SLR for versatility. There are two reasons for this. The first and main one is that SLRs take interchangeable lenses so you can use whatever range of focal lengths you want as long as you can carry them. Secondly, with an SLR you look directly through the lens, which helps with composition. With compacts what you see in the viewfinder is not exactly what is reflected in the lens.

My main camera for more than a decade has been an SLR. On long walks I carry a second one as a back-up, on shorter trips I take the little Olympus. There is a wide choice of SLRs, most of them of high quality. Choosing one is really a question of picking the features you want and looking at prices and weights. Top names are Canon, Nikon, Pentax, Minolta, Olympus, Yashica and, if you have enough money, Leica.

After using other makes, I've ended up with two Nikons, the favourite brand of professional photographers. I picked them, as no doubt others have, because of their reputation for durability and reliability, as I've had a number of other cameras fail on me over the years. The cameras are the FM2 and the F801 (called the N8008 in the USA), carefully selected from Nikon's range as they fulfil a number of functions I require for outdoor photography. The

FM2 is a fully manual camera which means it's not reliant on batteries except to operate the light meter. To use it you need to understand how cameras work as you have to adjust the controls yourself, something anyone who wants to take good—as opposed to adequate—pictures needs to know. It also means that the camera will work in very cold conditions when batteries are unreliable. The chances of a mechanical camera going wrong are remote. The FM2 is also very light at 575grams/20oz (without lens).

The F801 is everything the FM2 is not; heavy (825g/29oz with four AA batteries), totally dependent on batteries and with optional auto-focus and auto-exposure. It also has a built-in motorwind and a self-timer that is variable from 2 to 30 seconds. This last rather than any of the fancy electronics was one of the main reasons I chose this camera. Landscapes often need a figure in them to set the scale. When you walk alone, as I habitually do, that figure has to be yourself which means setting the self-timer and running into position. Most cameras have only 10- or 12-second timers which is barely enough. I have many blurred pictures of myself in the act of turning round or of my legs running away from the camera! Thirty seconds is a luxury and allows much more scope with composition. I also wanted the F801's auto-focus capability, though I don't use it often. During the Canadian Rockies walk I often had brief encounters with animals when there was barely time to point the camera and shoot, never mind focus. Many of the results, unsurprisingly, show blurred, out-of-focus animals. Having auto-focus will, I hope, help me gain better results in similar situations in the future.

Spare batteries should always be carried, which for me means another 100g/3½oz of weight with the F801 though only a few grams for the button batteries of the FM2.

Lenses: There is no point in having an SLR unless you also have a selection of lenses. I carry a Nikon 35-70 zoom, Nikon 24mm, and a Sigma UC 70-210 zoom. The last I chose for its low weight of 475g/16¾oz, the Nikon equivalent being much heavier. The 24mm (weighing 225g/8oz) is for landscapes where I want a wide angle to encompass a wide area. The 35-70 zoom is my most useful lens as it runs from moderate wide angle to moderate tele-photo and so is good for landscapes, portraits and detail.

The big zoom is for distant detail, portraits and animal shots. I'd like a longer lens but the weights are just too much. I use zooms because they are lighter than the three or four fixed focal length lenses they replace and also because they aid composition, pictures in the wilderness often being taken from positions you can't change like the edge of cliffs and the sides of mountains.

Filters: These are the most over-used items in photography in my opinion and I carry very few of them. I want the light and colours in my pictures to look natural. For protection and to cut out a smidgeon of ultraviolet light I keep skylight filters fitted to every lens. The only other filter I regularly use is a polariser to cut haze and glare and darken blue skies and I'm spartan with my use of that. If the sky is bright and the land dark I may use a graduated grey filter in a filter holder to cut the contrast and on the rare occasions I take black and white film I sometimes use an orange filter to bring out clouds. Each filter weighs about 20g/¾oz with case.

Films: I nearly always take colour transparency (slide) film because this reproduces best in books and magazines and is needed for slide shows. The ISO number of the film, which gives its speed, is important. For fine detail and the best colours slow speeds are needed; 100 is the highest I use. Kodachrome, Ektachrome, Agfachrome and Fujichrome are the main brands. I mostly use ISO 50 and 100 Fujichrome with pre-paid mailers, so that I can send film home to be developed during a long walk and have the results waiting for me when I get back. Agfachrome RS 50 and 100 are my second choices.

If you want pictures to display and hand round rather than project then colour print film is the one to go for. Kodak, Agfa and Fuji are all good brands. I only use this film when I'm taking pictures for a book or magazine article that may be run in colour or black-and-white. For this I use Kodak Ektar film in 25 and 125 speeds as I've found it is the sharpest and reproduces best.

I take actual black-and-white film so rarely that I can offer no meaningful advice except to say that as well as the companies mentioned above Ilford film has a good reputation.

Individual films don't weigh much but half a dozen 36 exposure ones with canisters weighs around 200g/7oz. I average a film a day so I am often carrying that number and more.

Supports: In low-light and with slow speed film (ISO 25 and 50) support is needed for the camera as you will be shooting at a shutter speed too slow for you to hold the camera steady with your hands alone. As a rough guide, for hand-held shooting the shutter speed should approximate or be faster than the focal length of the lens. Thus a 28-mm lens shouldn't be hand-held at lower than 1/30 second, a 200-mm lens no lower than 1/250. Hand-holding at too slow a shutter speed results in blurred pictures. For really sharp pictures that can be blown up large without starting to show fuzzy edges it is necessary to use a support at higher shutter speeds. This can mean simply propping your arms on a rock, bracing yourself against a tree or even lying down.

The problem is that the required objects will often not be in the right position for the best composition. There are three answers to this, monopods, mini tripods and clamps, and full-size tripods. I use all of them. My walking staff has a screw hidden under the handle to which a ball-and-socket tripod head can be mounted. I use this for animal photography when there is no time to remove my pack and set up the tripod. There are many small table-top tripods and clamps around but the lightest I've seen is the REI Ultrapod at 56g/2oz, an ingenious little device that can be used as a tripod and also by means of a velcro strap as a clamp. I use it on ski trips, strapping it to a pole rammed in the snow for self portraits and to steady the camera. It's too light for long lenses but with wide angle ones it works well.

Even with a monopod and clamp I still need a tripod, both for self-portraits and for low-light photography. I've spent too much time balancing the camera carefully on a pile of stones only to see it slip sideways just as I've run into position, or looking at beautifully lit scenes knowing I can't take pictures because it's too dark. So I feel that having a tripod is worth the extra weight. The problem is in finding a lightweight one that doesn't develop the shakes after minimal use. On the Canadian Rockies walk I took a Slik 500 G (weight 500g/17½oz, which lasted the trip but whose centre column wouldn't tighten fully by the end. I now have a rather more robust though, at 600g/21oz, slightly heavier Cullman 2101 model (sold by REI as the Cullman Backpack Tripod) which I took on the Yukon walk and found much

tougher than the Slik. It looks as though it should last for a few more walks yet. No light-weight tripod will provide the stability of a real heavyweight though and they're useless in a strong wind unless you attach a weight to the base of the centre column (a stuffsac of rocks works wonders). More stable models are too heavy for backpacking however so a lightweight has to do.

Protection and Carrying

Cameras need to be accessible but also, because of their fragile nature, well-protected. They can, of course, be protected by keeping them in the pack but you don't take many pictures that way. I like to carry a camera slung across my body so that I can use it quickly when a picture presents itself. This is a vulnerable position however so I always keep it in a foam padded waterproof case. There are many of these available, from Tamrac, Lowe and Karrimor amongst others, but I've always used the thickly padded Camera Care Systems ones, which I find very hardwearing and very protective. Even when I let a camera fall hundreds of metres down Glen Pass in the High Sierras it was undamaged in its CCS case. There are cases to fit all makes and sizes of camera. I currently use four different ones; a standard Warthog (200g/7oz) for the FM2 with 24 mm lens, a medium Tusker AF (330g/11½oz) for the F801 with 35-70 zoom, a medium Lens Pouch (120g/4oz) for the 70-210 zoom and a small Lens Pouch (90 grams/3oz) for the 24mm lens. The Warthog either lives in the pack or is attached to the side compression strap; the Lens Pouches I carry in the bumbag. To both the

Camera Care Systems padded cases, the one on right with Op-Tech strap and folded Cullman 2101 tripod. 8.31

166

Tusker case and the F801 camera I've attached broad Op-Tech stretch neoprene rubber straps (75g/2½oz) as I find that they really do make the camera feel lighter. Filters and films live in a small stuffsac that resides either in the bumbag or the top pocket of the pack.

Cleaning

For removing greasy marks from lenses I carry a lens-cleaning cloth in a plastic bag. For the inside of the camera I use a blower brush. The combined weight is only a few grams. I only use either if items clearly need cleaning as there is always the chance of causing damage when you tamper with fragile machinery far from any repair shop.

Recording

It's easy to imagine each time you take a picture that you'll remember the details later. You won't—not unless you either take very few pictures or have a phenomenal memory. Some method of recording what you've photographed is essential if you're not to return home to hundreds of pictures which you cannot exactly place. I keep a tiny notebook (15g/½oz) and pen in a plastic bag in my bumbag and note down when and where I start and finish each film plus any particular details I want to retain about the pictures I take. To relate the film to the notes, I photograph this page on the last few frames. I still get the occasional baffling picture but by using this notebook in conjunction with my journal and the maps I can usually work out what everything is. Recording the details of every single shot would be better but I find I simply don't get round to doing this.

ENTERTAINMENT

Reading Matter

As I'm a book addict I always carry at least one paperback on every walk. Too often I end up with several. There are three types of book that might find their way into your pack: trail guides obviously; natural history guides if you're interested in knowing more about the country you're passing through and its plants and animals; and books for entertainment to while away long stormbound evenings in the tent and the hours you may spend marching on tarmac and gravel roads, something that seems inevitable at some point on long walks. The last

category can be about any subject you like. On my 124-day Canadian Rockies walk I read 36 books, an average of one every three and a half days. Of those, 24 were fiction and 12 non-fiction. (How do I know? I kept a list in my journal). And this was apart from an area guide that I carried all the way, parts of which I read several times, and a trail guide I carried on the first half of the walk.

Natural history guides are a problem because you usually need to carry several if you are to identify trees, flowers, mammals, birds etc. In a group you can each carry a different volume but the solo walker has to be selective. I usually carry the smallest bird and tree guides I can find with perhaps a flower guide as well if the weight can be kept down. What I always look for though is a guide that covers everything. There are sadly very few of these. The best I've found is Ben Gadd's *Handbook of the Canadian Rockies* which as well as being a complete natural history field guide covers geology, history, weather and much more, making it worth its 700g/25oz. I wish other areas had such a comprehensive single-volume guide.

Star Watching: The Planisphere

A map of the night sky that can be rotated to show the stars in position for each month is well worth carrying as it only weighs a few grams and takes up no space. I don't use mine often but when I do I'm very glad I remembered to bring it.

Radios and Cassette Players

Tiny radios weighing in the 200–400g/7–14oz range could be worth carrying if you grow bored with reading. Himalayan mountaineers now regularly take portable stereos for use on the climb as well as in camp. I have in the past occasionally carried a radio, on the pretext that it was for weather forecasts, but I found I rarely used it because even in the tent it cut me off from the world I'd come to be part of. Proponents of radios point out that books do the same. But to my mind they do not have the same effect, as all your senses are still available to respond to the world around whereas with a radio sounds from outside are blocked. The faintest rustle or a change in the sound of the wind in the grasses can jerk my attention away from a book and have me alert and listening intently to what is going on, peering into the night to see what animal is abroad or whether the new wind is clearing the clouds and allowing the stars to shine through. With a radio you are enclosed in another world, the one you left behind when you took your first step into the wilderness. But that's only my opinion and not a reason not to carry a radio or portable stereo if you find it worthwhile. My only plea if you do would be to use earphones, as sounds carry in the quietness of the wilderness and we may not all share your tastes. I remember well coming off a high Pyrenean peak, my eyes set on a necklace of mountain tarns far below with green sward ideal for camping stretching out on either side, only to be greeted whilst still a kilometre and more away by the tinkling sounds of music coming from the one tent I could see in the whole vast basin. Once down there I found the sound permeated the whole area so I pushed on, down into the next valley bottom to camp much later than I'd wanted to, but at least somewhere quiet.

Cards and Games

There are various lightweight games groups can take along for entertainment, and of course you can make up your own. A pack of cards is the obvious thing to take and you can buy miniature ones, though a standard sized pack only weighs 100g/3½oz. I've never carried cards but a companion did on the ski crossing of the Columbia Icefield in the Canadian Rockies and we played many games during the four days we spent stormbound in the tents. They could also be carried on solo trips for playing patience, though I can't imagine ever wanting to do so. A hill walking book I read many years ago did recommend carrying a pack in case you became lost. Don't panic if this happens, the author recommended, just sit down and start playing patience because some damn fool is then bound to pop up behind you and tell you which card to play next!

Thermometer

Few people carry these but I've done so for years and find the data collected fascinating. My immediate finding, reinforced whenever I camp with others, was that it's never as cold as people think. Also I've noted that you really do feel warmer when the temperature drops a few degrees below freezing and the humidity falls than when it's a few degrees above. On the Canadian Rockies walk I recorded no temperatures below freezing during July and August and only three nights when they occurred in September, yet by the middle of October it was freezing hard every night. During the four days spent stormbound on the Columbia Icefield the temperature in the tent ranged, astonishingly, from −2°C to 24°C/28°F to 75°F depending on whether we were cooking and whether the doors were open. Having such data serves a more useful purpose too. When I revisit an area I know what temperatures to expect, which helps with planning.

To entertain myself with such detail I carry a circular bi-metallic strip Brannan Maximum/Minimum Thermometer bought from Field & Trek. It weighs 56g/2oz and has a range from −30°C/−20°F to 60°C/140°F. Whether it's as accurate as a mercury one I don't know. It's certainly far more durable. I may buy one of the latter to make a comparison one day. REI do a metal-clad Minimum-Register one with an aluminium case, which weighs 28g/1oz. There are also tiny mercury thermometers attached to split rings for hanging off jacket and pack zippers, with windchill charts on the reverse. These come under a variety of labels (mine is Survival Aids) and weigh a fraction of a gram. They're useful for gaining an idea of the temperature but not for precise readings.

On the Move: Skills and Hazards

Walking in itself is very easy; walking in the wilderness with a pack isn't quite so simple. Whilst on the move you have to find your way, perhaps in dense mist or thick forest, cope with terrain which may mean negotiating steep cliffs, loose scree and snow as well as manicured trails, and deal with hazards ranging from extremes of weather to wild animals in some areas. Mostly, though, walking in the wilderness is relatively straightforward as long as you are reasonably fit and have a few basic skills and a little knowledge about weather and terrain.

FITNESS

There are two aspects to being fit for backpacking. First you need aerobic, that is cardiovascular, fitness to enable you to walk all day and get up the hills without your heart pounding and your lungs gasping for air after only a short distance. Secondly you need muscular fitness, particularly in the legs, to achieve the same ends without waking on the second morning out stiff as a board and aching all over. Achieving fitness takes time. I know people who only make one long backpacking trip a year who always say they'll get fit in the first few days. They then suffer for most of the walk, yet with a little preparation they could enjoy every day. Also, if you're unfit the likelihood of injury from strains and muscle tears is much higher.

The best way to train for carrying heavy loads over rough terrain is to carry heavy loads over rough terrain—what sports trainers call 'specific training'. This isn't practical for most people however, though it's surprising what you can do if you really want to even if you live and work in a city. John Hillaby trained for his 1700-km/1100-mile Land's End–John O'Groats walk by spending the three months prior to the trip walking 'from Hampstead to the City each day and further at the weekends. On these jaunts I carried weight-lifters' weights sewn high up in a flat rucksack that didn't look too odd among people making their way to the office in the morning' (*Journey Through Britain*). At the very least it's wise to try to spend a few weekends getting used to walking with a load before you set off on a longer trip. If during the week you can walk as much as possible, including up and down any stairs, it all helps. Brisk strolls or runs in the evening help too, especially if there are hills to charge up. In fact hill running is probably the best way to improve both your aerobic fitness and your leg muscle power in as short a time as possible.

I've only once trained at a fitness centre and that was before the Canadian Rockies walk. For six months I did hour-long circuit-training sessions three times a week with hour-long runs on the days in between and one day off a week. I found it did help but probably no more than if I'd spent the time walking with a pack and doing some exercises at home. If you want to follow a planned exercise programme you could try looking at *The Outdoor Athlete* by Steve Ilg (Cordillera Press), which includes programmes for 'mountaineering and advanced backpacking' and 'recreational hiking and backpacking', as well as visiting your local fitness centre or gym. One thing I did learn from my fitness centre training was that you need rest days from strenuous exercise. This may seem obvious but I'd never paid much attention to it before, always planning walks on the basis that I'd move on every day. Now on walks of longer than two weeks I aim at having a rest day every week to ten days.

My current regime is to go out for hour-long runs over hilly terrain two or three times a week and to spend at least one full day a week walking or skiing in the mountains. This is apart from the 2–3-day backpacking trips I like to take once a month or so between longer walks, though at the time of writing it's three months since I did so, partly because of the weather but mainly because I've been writing this book!

If you haven't had any exercise for some time it's advisable to return to it gradually, slowly building up the amount you do, especially if you're over 35. Preparing for a walk takes time anyway. You can't go from being unfit to being able to tote a heavy load 25km/15 miles a day in the mountains in a week or even a month.

THE ART OF WALKING

Whilst the simple act of putting one foot in front of the other seems to require no instruction or comment, there are in fact good and bad ways to walk and good and bad walkers. The first can walk effortlessly all day, while the second may be exhausted after a few hours. The way to make walking seem effortless is to walk slowly and steadily, to find a rhythm that lets you glide along and a pace you can keep up for hours. Without such a rhythm every step seems tiring, which is why crossing broken terrain such as boulder fields or brush-choked forest is so exhausting. Inexperienced walkers often start off at a rapid lick, leaving the experienced plodding slowly behind. Aesop's ancient fable of the tortoise and the hare is very applicable here, as the slower walkers often catch up and pass the exhausted novices long before the day's walk is complete.

The ability to keep up a steady pace hour after hour has to be developed gradually however. If you need a rest have one, otherwise you'll become exhausted. The difference between novices and experts was graphically demonstrated to me when I was leading backpacking treks for an Outward Bound school in the Scottish Highlands. I let the students make their own pace, often following them or traversing above the group at a higher level. But one day the course supervisor, a very experienced mountaineer, turned up and said he'd lead the day's walk. And by lead he meant lead, so off he went with the group following in his footsteps, me bringing up the rear. Initially we followed a flat river valley and soon there were mutterings from the students at the supervisor's slow pace. The faint trail we were following began to climb after a while and on we went at the same slow pace with some of the students close to rebellion. Eventually we came to the base of a very steep grassy slope up which there was no path. The supervisor didn't pause but just headed upwards as if the terrain hadn't altered. After a few hundred metres the complaints from the students changed. 'Isn't he ever going to stop?' they said. One or two started to fall behind. Intercepting a path, we turned up it, switchbacking steadily to a high pass. By now some of the students seemed in danger of collapse so I hurried ahead to the supervisor and said they needed a rest. He seemed surprised. 'I'll see you later then,' he said, and started downwards, his pace still unaltered, leaving the students slumped down with relief.

This story also reveals one of the problems of walking in a group; everyone has their own pace. The best way to deal with this is not to walk as a group but for everyone to proceed as they wish, meeting up at rest-stops and in camp. By being split up people will see more as well— large numbers frighten off wildlife much more than small ones. If the group must stay together, perhaps, because of bad weather or difficult route-finding, then the pace has to be that of the slowest. It is often a good idea for this person to lead at least some of the time. If you are the slowest in a party you should object if you're left to fall behind at the back of the group. This is neither fair on you nor safe. I for one find it easier to adapt to a slower pace if I am following someone than if I am in front where it requires great concentration not to speed up to my own normal pace unconsciously. While walking for a long time at a faster pace than you are capable of is impossible, I find walking at a slower one surprisingly tiring, as it is hard to establish a rhythm.

I don't think you can consciously learn to walk economically, using the least energy. It comes with experience. However it may help to try to create a rhythm if one doesn't develop by running one through your head. I sometimes do this on long climbs if finding the right pace is hard and I'm constantly stopping to catch my breath. I repeat rhythmic chants consisting of any words that come to mind (the poems of Robert Service or Longfellow are good—you only need a few lines) and find to my surprise that this often brings about a walking rhythm. If I am tending to speed up I say the chant out loud, which slows me down.

Very occasionally all the aspects of walking come together and I have an hour or a day when I simply glide along, seemingly expending no energy. At these times the distance melts under my feet and I feel as though I could stride on forever and never stop. I can't force such moments and I don't know where they come from, but the more I walk the more often they happen. Not surprisingly perhaps, they occur most often on really long treks. On such days I've walked for five hours and 20km/12 miles and more without a break, yet with such little effort that I only realise how long and how far I've travelled when I do eventually stop. I never feel any effects afterwards either except, perhaps, for a greater feeling of well-being and contentment.

DISTANCE

How far can you walk in a day is a perennial question asked by walkers and non-walkers alike. It's a difficult one to answer as it depends on many factors including fitness, the length of your stride, how many hours are spent walking, the weight carried and the nature and steepness of the terrain. There are formulae for making calculations, the most famous being that proposed last century by W. Naismith, a luminary of the Scottish Mountaineering Club. Naismith's Formula allows an hour for every 5km/3 miles plus an extra half-hour for every 300metres/1000ft of ascent. I've used this as a rough basis for calculations for years and it seems to work; a 25-km/15-mile day with 1250 metres/4100ft of ascent takes me on average eight hours including stops.

The time I spend between leaving one camp and setting up the next is usually 8–10 hours though not all of that time is spent walking. On a flat, paved road in the Great Divide Basin during the Continental Divide walk I measured my pace, whilst carrying a 25-kg/55-lb pack, against the distance posts. It was a little over 6km/3¾ miles per hour. At that rate I should be able to cover 60km/37 miles in ten hours if I did nothing but walk. But I guess that during a ten-hour day I probably spend no more than seven hours walking and average around 4km/2½ miles per hour if the terrain isn't too rugged. And that, for me, is enough. Backpacking is about living in the wilderness not speeding through it, and I want the time to absorb what is around me. I cover distance most quickly on roads, whether tarmac, gravel or dirt, as I always want to leave them behind.

What is important though is not how far you can walk in a day if you push yourself but how far you are happy to walk in a day. This varies from person to person but can soon be worked out if you keep records of your trips. For myself I plan walks on the basis of being able to do 25km/15 miles per day if much of the walking will be on trails or over easy terrain. If difficult cross-country travel will be the norm, I reduce my estimate to 20km/12 miles a day.

As well as how far you can walk in a day there is the question of how far you can walk during a complete trip. This isn't easy to work out as on a long walk you become fitter as time goes on. One way to gain an idea though is to analyse previous walks. On my longest walks, I find that I averaged 26km/16 miles per day on the 4025-km/2600-mile Pacific Crest Trail, 27km/16¾ miles per day on the 4825-km/3000-mile Continental Divide and 26km/16 miles per day on the 2575 km/1600 mile Canadian Rockies walk, which seems amazingly consistent. On looking closer though, I see that individual days vary from 10 to 48km/6–30 miles in length and the time spent between camps from 3 to 15 hours. The shortest distances sometimes took the longest time as well. It certainly gives me some figures to work from however.

One problem with the standard summer fortnight's backpacking is that many people spend the first week struggling to get fit and the second week turning the efforts of the first week into hard muscle and greater lung power, so that by the time they're ready to go home they're at the peak of fitness. The solution is to temper your desires to your fitness. It's easy in the enthusiasm of winter to make ambitious plans that fall apart the first day out as you struggle to carry your pack half the distance you intended. On all walks I aim to take it easy at first until I feel comfortable with being on the move again. This breaking-in period may last only a few hours on a weekend trip but as long as a couple of weeks on a long summer one. On two-week trips it is a good idea to take the first two or three days gently by walking less distance than you hope to later in the trip, especially if you're not as fit as you intended to be.

Pedometers

In theory, with one of these neat little devices you should be able to measure exactly how far you walk in a given amount of time. The trouble is, whether you use the modern quartz digital variety or the old mechanical pendulum type, they work by counting the number of steps you take and converting this into distance. This only works if you have a regular stride, as you probably do on firm, flat surfaces. But in the wilderness, with its ups and downs, boggy terrain, scree, boulders, logs and more, keeping up a regular stride hour after hour is difficult, at least for me. I've tried pedometers but never produced any meaningful figures from them. If you try them, I wish you better luck.

GOING ALONE

It is customary for books like this to advise readers never to go alone but I can hardly do so as I travel solo more often than not and I feel it is the best way to experience the wilderness. Only when I go alone do I achieve that feeling I seek of blending in with and being part of the natural world. The heightened awareness that often comes with solo walking never does so when I'm with others. Solitude is immeasurably rewarding.

Going alone also gives me the freedom to make decisions as and when I want so that I can choose to walk for twelve hours one day but only three the next and to spend half a day watching beavers or otters or lying in the tent wondering if the rain will ever stop without having to consult anyone else.

Of course solo walking has its dangers and it is up to the individual to calculate what risks they are prepared to take. I'm always aware when crossing steep boulder fields or fording streams that if I slip there is no-one to go for help. When there's no one else to depend on, every action has to be weighed carefully, every risk assessed. Off trail in particular, you are very much on your own. I spent eight days struggling cross-country through rugged terrain in the foothills of the Canadian Rockies at one point on my walk along that range. I was acutely aware that even a minor accident could have serious consequences, especially as I was also way off route. Greater care is needed in such situations than during trail travel, where a twisted ankle may mean no more than a painful limp out to the road and potential rescuers are usually not too far away.

LEAVING WORD

You should always leave word with somebody as to where you are going and when you will be back, especially if you are going alone. The route details you leave may be precise, or they may be very vague. On some trips I don't know exactly where I'll end up going so I can hardly tell others. But some sort of indication of your plans must be left. If you're leaving a car anywhere you should tell someone when you'll be back for it. Where you have to pick up a trail permit, there's no problem but in other places a car left empty for days can cause concern and could even lead to an unnecessary rescue attempt being launched. (Indeed a few days after writing this a television programme on helicopter rescue carried an interview with a walker who'd been surprised to find a rescue helicopter landing outside the remote mountain hut he was using, as he'd been reported missing after his car was noticed at a forest roadhead. This was despite the fact that he had left detailed plans of his ten-day trek with his wife and family.) The old practice of leaving a note on your car is no longer advisable unfortunately, as it is too obvious an invitation to thieves.

Whenever you've said you'll let someone know you're safe you must do so. Too many hours have been spent by rescue teams searching for someone who was back home or sitting in a café relaxing because they didn't bother to do so.

FINDING THE WAY

Maps

Knowing how to read a map is a key wilderness skill, yet there are many walkers who can barely do so. I have a regular backpacking companion who has little understanding of maps and is quite happy to allow me to plan and lead routes, never looking at the map from one day to the next. The only solo backpacking he's ever done was on a coastal footpath where route-finding consisted merely of keeping the sea on the same side! There are also some inland areas where trails are so well signposted and trail guides so accurate that a map isn't really needed, though one should be carried just in case you turn blithely down an unmarked or unmaintained trail, only starting to wonder where you are when you realise it's been rather a long time since you saw a trail marker.

Generally though you always need a map for planning walks, for following your route on the ground and for locating the whereabouts of water sources and possible campsites. But maps are far more than just functional tools. They can open up a whole inspiring world of dreams, some of which may well come true. I can spend hours poring over a map, tracing possible routes, wondering how to connect a delectable looking mountain tarn with a narrow notch of a pass and whether it's possible to follow a mountain ridge or whether it will turn out to be a rocky knife edge that forces me to choose another route. Often these fireside schemes become reality months later and I gain great pleasure when an idea hatched at home turns out to be feasible high in the mountains. A few months before writing this I tried out a plan in the Pyrénées to link two regions, between which the maps showed no paths, via a high mountain pass and was delighted when, despite a day of thick mist and rain, my route turned out to be possible, the untracked slopes of steep scree and small crags on the far side of the pass being crossable with care on foot.

Map reading is mostly obvious. Every map has a key. Once you interpret the symbols on a map from this you can build up a picture of what the terrain it delineates will be like. There are two types of map: planimetric and topographic. The first simply represents features on the ground, the second, the topography or shape of the ground itself. Topographic maps do this by means of contour lines which join together points of equal height starting from sea level. Contour lines occur at given intervals which can be anything from 5 to 150 metres/16–500ft. On most maps every fifth contour line is thicker and

has the height marked on it, though you may have to trace it for some distance to locate this. These heights are always marked so that as you read them you are looking up the slope, so they may be at any angle on the map. The closer together the contour lines, the steeper the slope. Note though that cliffs of less height than that between contour lines won't show up on the map. Some maps mark cliffs, others don't. Check the key to see if you may encounter cliffs not shown on the map. The patterns contour lines form represent the three-dimensional shapes of features so once you can interpret them you can tell what the hills, valleys and ridges of an area are like and make your plans accordingly. Studying maps at home is the best way to learn how to read them. Once you become good at it you will find maps come alive, almost becoming the country they represent. Like other skills, map-reading soon becomes something you do automatically.

The scale tells you how much ground is represented by a given distance on the map. Thus on a 1:50,000 map, 1cm on the map equals 50,000cm on the ground, which converts to 1cm = 500 metres or 2cm = 1km (approximately $1\frac{1}{4}$ inches to the mile). For most of the world metric scales are standard with 1:25,000, 1:50,000, 1:100,000 and 1:250,000 the most useful for walkers. The first two give the most detail but the second two cover wider areas, making them good for planning. In countries like Canada, where the 1:50,000 sheets only cover a small area, carrying a smaller-scale map means you can identify features not on the more detailed one. Although the greater detail of large scale maps is best for walking it is possible to use smaller-scale ones in the wilderness. I've used 1:100,000 maps in Iceland and Norway and 1:250,000 and even 1:600,000 in the Canadian Rockies. In the USA the scales of topographic maps are slightly different, being 1:24,000, 1:62,500 and 1:250,000. The first are replacing the second and for practical purposes are close enough to 1:25,000 ($2\frac{1}{2}$in to the mile) to make little difference.

Many topographic maps (those covering Britain, Canada and Norway for example) have a grid superimposed on them. Each line in the grid is numbered and by reading these off you can give the grid reference for precise locations, which can be very useful. Also, counting the number of squares (each side of which usually represents a kilometre on the ground) that a route crosses is a quick way to estimate the distance (diagonals are 1½km). For the non-metric, 8km equals 5 miles.

To work out distances on maps without grids (such as those covering the Alps, the Pyrénées, Iceland and some of the USA) a map-measurer is useful. This is a calibrated wheel which you set to the scale of the map and run along your route. You can then read off the distance. They weigh only a few grams but I've never carried one in the pack. You could of course easily draw a grid on a map without one but I've never done this either.

Whilst large-scale topographic maps are the best for accurate navigation other maps may contain information useful to the walker. Land-management bodies like national parks often issue their own maps showing trails and wilderness facilities that are more up to date than the topo ones covering the same area. In the USA planimetric Forest Service maps at various scales show roads and trails that are often not on the topo maps at all. You can use them for walking as long as you don't mind not knowing how much ascent and descent there is over a particular distance and how steep the terrain is. The 1:600,000 map I used in the northern Canadian Rockies was a planimetric one. I worked out when I would be going uphill and when down by studying the drainage patterns of streams, but of course I had no way of knowing whether an ascent meant 100 or 1000 metres of climbing. Some planimetric maps are shaded to show where the higher ground lies, but this only gives a rough idea of what to expect.

It is possible to do virtually all your navigating just using a map and I am a firm believer in doing so. As long as you can see features around you and relate them to the map, you know where you are. The easiest way to do this is by setting or orienting the map, which involves turning it until the features you can see are in their correct positions relative to where you are. If you walk with the map set it is easier to relate visible features to it. Many people automatically use a compass for navigating (see below), ignoring what they can actually see around them, yet even at night you can navigate solely with the map. I once did a night-navigation exercise on a mountain leadership training course and was the only person to travel their stretch of the route without relying on the compass, even though it was a clear night and the distinctive peaks above the valley were easily identifiable from the map, whilst the location of streams showed me where I was on the valley floor. All the others navigated as though we were in total darkness, relying on compass bearings and pace counting (measuring how far you travel by counting your steps, a tedious and mostly unnecessary practice). If you always rely on such methods you cut yourself off from the world around, substituting figures and measurements for a close understanding of the nature of the terrain you are walking through. I don't like my walking to be reduced to mathematical calculations.

When following a trail all you need do is check the map occasionally to see how far along your route you are. When going cross-country however the map should be studied carefully, both beforehand and while on the move. Apart from working out a rough route, note features such as rivers, cliffs, lakes and in particular contour lines. But don't expect always to find what you expect. The lack of contour lines round a lake may mean you'll find a nice, flat, dry area for a camp when you arrive or it may mean, as happened to me a few times on the Canadian Rockies walk, acres of marsh. Close-grouped contour lines at the head of a valley may mean an impassable cliff or a steep but climbable grass slope. You have to accept that sometimes you'll have to turn back and find another route, that sometimes it will take you twice as long and you'll have to walk twice as far to reach your destination as you'd planned. The map will not tell you everything. When you work out a cross-country route on a map it's always advisable to plan alternatives, especially if the area is one you've not visited before and you don't know what sort of terrain to expect. It may be that when you get there you will find that following the open treeless ridge above the valley is easier than slogging through the dense brush or swamps that lie on your intended lower-level route. Flexibility in adapting your plans to the terrain is important.

The map should always be kept handy even if the route-finding seems easy or you are on a clear trail. A garment pocket or a bumbag is the obvious storage place. It is essential to protect maps from the weather and there are map cases available for doing this, but all the ones I've tried are bulky and awkward to fold and fit into a pocket or my bumbag, so I prefer a simple plastic bag. You can also cover the map with special clear plastic film, though this has to be done before the map is folded. Easier to use are various waterproofing sprays like Texnik or Granger's Map Dry which I'm told are very effective. I've never bothered waterproofing maps, and although some of mine look very disreputable I've never had one totally disintegrate on me. If or when I do I'll probably pay more attention to protecting them.

Maps can be bought at outdoor stores, bookshops, land-management agency offices and direct from the producers. Local guidebooks and tourist offices can provide information on which maps you need for a particular area. Those who wander widely may be interested in R.B. Parry and C.R.Perkins's *World Mapping Today* (Butterworths) which describes the maps available for each country.

The Compass
Despite my preference for using just the map for navigation I always carry a compass. For trail travel it's hardly ever needed, except perhaps when you arrive at an unsigned junction in thick mist or dense forest and aren't sure which branch to follow. Once you strike out cross-country, though, a compass may prove essential, especially when visibility is poor and you can see no features to relate to the map.

The standard compass for backpacking is the orienteering type with liquid damped needle and transparent plastic base plate. Silva is the best known brand. Suunto and Brunton are others. I use the Silva Type 3 model which weighs 30g/1oz and is one of the simpler versions. For backpacking models with sighting mirrors and other refinements are unnecessary. The heart of the compass is the magnetic needle, the red end of which points, not to the north pole or true north but to a moveable point nearby called magnetic north. The needle is housed in a rotatable fluid-filled transparent circular mount marked with north, south, east and west, plus the degrees of the circle with north as 360/0. The base of the dial is marked with an orienting arrow fixed towards north on the dial and a series of parallel lines. The rest of the compass consists of the base plate on which is engraved a large direction-of-travel arrow and a set of scales for measuring distances on a map. Some base plates, like that on the Silva Type

3, also have a small magnifying glass built in to help read detail on maps.

The basic use of the compass is to enable you to walk towards your destination, even if you can't see it, with no reference to the surrounding terrain. If you try to do this without a compass you'll find that in a very short distance you'll start to veer away from the correct line. The direction you walk in is called a bearing. This can be quoted as the number of degrees or angle, reading clockwise, between north and your direction. To set a bearing you use the compass base plate as a protractor, first pointing the direction-of-travel arrow towards your destination, then turning the compass housing until the red end of the magnetic needle and the orienting arrow are aligned. As long as you keep these two arrows pointing to the north and follow the direction-of-travel arrow you will reach your destination even if it is blanked out by mist or hidden by other features. However you can rarely take a bearing on something several hours' walk away and then walk straight to it (although it's possible in desert and wide-open moorland terrain). It's better to locate a much nearer and visible feature that lies on your line of travel like a boulder or a tree (try not to use a sheep or other animal—they tend to move!), and walk to that. Even if you have to leave the exact bearing to reach this point, to avoid a swamp or small cliff say, it doesn't matter as long as you keep it in your sights, as once there you can check your compass again and find another object to head for. In poor visibility you may have to walk on your bearing by holding the compass in your hand and following the arrow if you are on your own. If there are two or more of you one person can go ahead to the limit of visibility then stop while you check their position with the compass and have them move left or right until they are in line with the bearing. Then the rest of the party can join them, and you repeat the process. It's a slow but very accurate method of navigation, particularly useful in white-out conditions in snow covered terrain. I've used it when skiing many times.

If you know where you are but not which way you need to go to reach your destination, then you need to take a bearing off the map. To do this you place an edge of the base plate on the spot where you are, then line the edge up with your destination. You then rotate the compass housing until the orienting arrow is aligned with north on the map (ignore the magnetic needle for the moment). Now remove the compass from the map and turn it, without rotating the housing, until the magnetic needle and orienting arrow are aligned. The direction-of-travel arrow now points in the direction you want to go. The number on the compass housing at this point is your bearing. This is quite simple but unfortunately there is the matter of magnetic variation to be taken into account.

Marked somewhere on the margins of most topographic maps are three arrows showing three norths. True north, that is the direction in which the north pole lies, can be ignored (unless you're walking to the north pole, in which case you have navigational problems beyond the scope of this book). The other two are very important. One is magnetic north, the direction in which the compass needle points. The other is grid north, the direction the grid of the map points (the top of the map is always grid north, so if your map has no grid marked on it the margins can be used). This differs slightly from true north because the latter is a point at the top of a three dimensional globe, the earth. Lines on a model globe leading to it are curved. Maps however are two-dimensional and the grid lines parallel to each other. Clearly they can't lead to a single point. Hence the hypothetical grid north which would exist if the world were rectangular. Because compasses point to magnetic north and maps are aligned to grid north the difference between them has to be taken into account when using the two in conjunction. This angle is measured in degrees and minutes (sixty of which make up a degree) and is called the magnetic variation or declination.

As magnetic north lies in the far north of Canada, in Europe grid north is always west of it. In parts of the states of Michigan, Indiana, Ohio, Kentucky, Tennessee and North and South Carolina in the USA, however, magnetic north and true north coincide, so in areas of North America east of those states grid north is west of magnetic north but in areas west of them it is east of it. The actual difference between grid and magnetic north is often marked on maps. Here though there lies more cause for confusion; magnetic north isn't static but moves, thankfully in a predictable pattern. On an old map the declination won't be cor-rect. Many maps also list the rate of change so you can work out the current figure. For example my 1974 1.25,000 High Tops of the Cairngorms map states: 'Magnetic North—About $8\frac{1}{2}°$W of Grid North in 1972 decreasing by about $\frac{1}{2}°$ in five years'. If your map isn't new and doesn't show the rate of change you may be able to find it in a trail guide or else you can calculate the magnetic variation yourself by taking a bearing from one known feature to another, recording the bearing (without taking any declination into account) then taking the same bearing from the map. The difference between the two is the current declination. A piece of tape stuck on the compass can be used as a declination mark to avoid having to add or subtract it each time you use the compass, though you'll have to move it if you visit different areas.

In Europe and eastern North America, because magnetic north lies west of grid north, when you take a bearing from the map you have to add the declination figure. However if your bearing is taken from the ground, you subtract the declination. A mnemonic for remembering this is empty sea addwater—MTC (map to compass)—add. Of course, in western North America you must reverse this and subtract declination when taking a bearing from the map and add it when taking one from the ground.

One of the few compass techniques I use, other than straightforward bearings, especially in poor visibility whether due to mist or trees, is aiming off. There's always an element of error in any compass work. If your bearing is 5° out then you'll be 100 metres/335ft off the correct line of travel after walking 1km/0.6 mile, 200 metres/650ft after 2km/1.2 miles, a whole kilometre/0.6 miles after 10km/6.2 miles. Because of this it can be difficult to find a precise spot that lies some distance from your starting point if there are no intermediate features to take bearings on. If it lies on or near an easy-to-find line such as a stream however, you can deliberately make an error and aim to hit this line one side or the other of your destination. That way when you reach it you know which way to turn to reach your destination. I used aiming off on a large scale in the Canadian Rockies. I became 'temporarily mislaid', but I knew that hundreds of kilometres somewhere to the north-west lay the little town of Tumbler Ridge which I wanted to reach and that a road ran roughly east–west to the town. By heading north rather than north-west I knew I'd hit the road to the east of Tumbler Ridge, which after several days' walking I did and found myself 75km/46 miles away! But I knew where both I and the town were.

The compass has other more complex uses, for which I would suggest you consult the books recommended below. I rarely use any other than straight compass and map-to-compass bearings and aiming off. Don't rely on your compass blindly though. There are areas high in iron ore where it doesn't work. The Cuillin Hills on the Isle of Skye are one such area. At spots on the main ridge it's possible to have the compass needle turn in a full circle in the space of just a few metres, something Outward Bound students to whom I demonstrated this found rather unnerving, especially in thick mist!

You should keep your compass where you can reach it easily. If it's in your pack you might be tempted not to bother checking it if you're a little unsure that you're going in the right direction. The result, as I have learnt to my cost, can be having to retrace your steps a considerable distance or even alter your route to take account of your error. Like most people, I have a loop of cord attached to my compass (most come with small holes in the base plate for this purpose) though I don't often hang it round my neck. I may tie the loop to a zip puller on a jacket pocket or my bumbag so that I don't lose the compass but can refer to it quickly whenever I want to.

Navigating by Natural Phenomena
There are many ways to navigate without a map or compass but I habitually use only two, the sun and the wind, and then only as back-ups. Knowing where they should be in relation to my route means I usually notice very quickly if they shift. In case I've veered off my intended line of travel—easy to do in featureless terrain like rolling grasslands or continuous forest—I stop and check where I am immediately. (I also check that the wind hasn't itself shifted and what the time is so that I know where the sun should be.)

Learning More
If you want to go into navigational techniques in more detail there are a number of books that can help. These include *Be Expert with Map &* *Compass* by Bjorn Kjellstrom (Charles Scribner), *Land Navigation: Routefinding with Map & Compass* by Wally Keay, (Duke of Edinburgh's Award), *Mountain Navigation* by Peter Cliff (Diadem), *Mountain Navigation Techniques* by Kevin Walker, (Constable) and *Practical Moorland Navigation* by Don Bain (Bivvybug). If you can't learn what you want from them I suggest you take a course at an outdoor centre or else join a local orienteering club.

Waymarks and Signposts
Paint splashes, piles of stones (cairns or ducks), blazes on trees, lines of posts and other methods are used for marking trails and routes throughout the world. In Norway even wilderness ski routes are marked out with lines of birch sticks. Along with signposts at path junctions these waymarks make route-finding very easy. I have mixed feelings about them. Part of me dislikes them intensely as unnecessary intrusions into the wilderness, but part of me is glad enough to follow them when they loom up on a misty day, pleased to be relieved of the task of finding the route for myself. Therein however lies a catch. They may lure novice and inexperienced walkers deep into the wilderness only to vanish, leaving their would-be followers worriedly searching for the next red mark, the next slashed tree. The waymarking of routes doesn't mean you can do without map and compass or the skill to use them.

Useful though it is, I would not like to see an increase in waymarking. I'd rather find my own way through the wilderness than follow markers. So I don't build cairns or cut blazes, let alone paint rocks. In fact I often knock down cairns that have appeared where there were none before, knowing that if they are left a trail will soon follow as people are drawn along the line they mark. The painting of waymarks in hitherto unspoilt terrain is simply an act of wanton vandalism. I was horrified on a recent week-long trek in the Western Highlands of Scotland to discover a series of large red paint splashes daubed on boulders all the way down a 1000-metre/3300-ft mountain spur that is narrow enough for the way to be clear. There wasn't even a path on this ridge before. Now it has been defiled with glaring red paint that leaps out of the subtle colours of heather, mist and lichen covered rock to affront the eye. May the culprit wander for ever lost in a howling

Highland wind, never able to locate a single spot of paint!

Guidebooks

There are two types of wilderness guidebook: area guides and trail guides. The first give a general overview of an area, providing information on possible routes, weather, seasons, hazards, natural history etc. Often lavishly illustrated they are usually far too heavy to carry in the pack and anyway aren't designed for that purpose. I find such books most interesting when I return from an area and want to find out about some of the places I've visited and things I've seen. They're also nice to daydream over.

Trail guides are designed as adjuncts to maps. Indeed some of them have all the topographic maps you need included in them. If you want to follow a trail precisely they are very useful, though they often take some of the sense of discovery out of walking by telling you in advance about everything you'll see along the way. Some cover specific trails only, others are really miniature area guides, full of route suggestions and general information. There are few popular destinations or routes without a trail guide, and many have several. As they frequently contain up-to-date information not to be found on the maps I often carry a trail guide, especially if I'm visiting an area for the first time.

Altimeters

Knowing the altitude is an aid to navigation, especially in high mountains and on routes with great variations in height, and the surest way to find this out is by using an altimeter. I've never myself used one in earnest, however. One of my companions on the High Sierra section of the Pacific Crest Trail had one with him, but I don't recollect that we used it much. There are several on the market, and Thommen is a well-known brand. As they function by recording change in atmospheric pressure, being really barometers with height scales, they can also be used for weather forecasting. I don't think, though, that altimeters are much real use for most backpacking.

On Being 'Lost'

What constitutes being lost is a moot point. Some people feel they are lost if they don't know to the square metre exactly where they are, even if they know which side of which mountain they're on or which valley they're in. It's possible to 'lose' a trail you're following, but that doesn't mean you are lost. I actually think it's very hard to become totally lost when travelling on foot. I've never managed it. Although I was 'unsure of my whereabouts' during the week I spent in thick forest in the foothills of the Canadian Rockies, I knew where I was in terms of my general position and I knew which direction to walk in to get to where I wanted to go. But I couldn't so pinpoint my position on a map, indeed I couldn't locate myself to within 50 or more kilometres in any direction and I've never been able to retrace my route on a map. I wasn't lost though, because I didn't allow myself to think I was, and this I think is the point. Being lost is a state of mind.

The state of mind to avoid is panic. Terrified hikers have been known to abandon their packs in order to run faster in search of somewhere they recognise, only to be found later having died of hypothermia or from a fall. As long as you have your pack you have food and shelter and can survive comfortably, so there is no need to be worried. I've spent many nights out when I didn't know precisely where I was. But as I had the equipment to survive comfortably this didn't matter. A camp in the wilderness is a camp in the wilderness whether it's at a well-used, well-signposted site or on the banks of a river you can't identify from the map.

The first thing to do if you start to suspect that you are not on the course you thought you were is to stop and think. Where might you have gone wrong? Next check the map. Then, if you think you can, try to retrace your steps to a point you recognise or can identify. If you don't think you can do that, work out from the map how to get from the area you are in (you always know the area you are in, even if it's a huge area) to where you want to be. It may be that it's easiest to head directly for a major destination such as a road or town, as I did in the foothills of the Canadian Rockies, rather than trying to find trails or smaller features. Often it's a question of heading in the right direction knowing that eventually you'll reach somewhere you want to be.

On the Pacific Crest Trail two of us mislaid the trail itself in the northern Sierra Nevada after taking a 'short cut' that took us off our map. The evening this happened we *camped above a river we think may lead to Blue Lake'* (journal entry, 22 June 1982), the said lake being the next feature we expected to recognise. My rather confused journal entry for 23 June describes what happened next:

'Took three hours before we were back on the trail and even then we weren't sure where. We must have been further north and east than we thought. The hill we thought was The Nipple wasn't and when we'd finally given up trying to reach it we found ourselves traversing the real Nipple just after I'd been talking about Alice in Through the Looking Glass *only reaching the hill top by walking away from it.'* We only knew we were back on the Pacific Coast Trail when we found a trail marker telling us so. Once we knew exactly where on the trail we were, all the other features fell into place and the terrain we'd been crossing suddenly made sense. That's when we realised we couldn't reach the peak we were seeking because we were already on it.

I have to say that I don't mind not knowing exactly where I am. In fact at times I quite enjoy it. There is a sense of freedom in not being able to predict what lies over the next ridge, where the next lake is and where the next valley leads. I enjoy the release of wandering through what is as far as I'm concerned uncharted territory. This is not to say that I set out to lose myself. Rather I view it when it occurs as an opportunity rather than a problem.

COPING WITH TERRAIN

On and Off Trail

As long as you stick to good regularly used trails and paths you should have no problems with terrain except perhaps for the occasional badly eroded section. Don't assume though that because a trail is marked boldly on a map there will be a clear well-maintained one on the ground. Sometimes there will be no visible route at all; at other times there may be one that starts off clearly only to fade away and become harder to follow as you go deeper into the wilderness. Trail guides and local information offices or ranger/warden stations are the best places to find out about the conditions of an area's footpaths, though even their information can be inaccurate.

Many people never leave well-marked trails, feeling that cross-country travel is simply too difficult and too slow. They are missing a great deal. Going cross-country is different to trail walking and so requires a different approach.

The joys of off-trail travel lie in the direct contact it gives you with the country you pass through. The 40–50cm/15–20in dirt strip that constitutes a trail holds the raw, untouched wilderness a little at bay. Once you step off that line you are truly in the backcountry and you should leave any preconceptions you have about wilderness walking behind. The difficulties you will encounter are part of off-trail walking and should be accepted as belonging to that experience, so don't expect to walk the same distance each day as on a trail or always to arrive at a campsite five minutes before dark. Some days you might do well to walk half as far as you would on a trail and there may be few if any obvious campsites. This shouldn't be alarming though. Uncertainty is one of the joys of off-trail travel, part of the escape from straight lines and the prison of the known.

Learning about the nature of the country you're in is very important. Once you've spent a little time in an area, maybe no more than a few hours, you should be able to start interpreting the terrain and modifying your plans accordingly. In the northern Canadian Rockies I soon learnt that black spruce forest meant muskeg swamps that were so difficult to cross that it was worth any length of detour to avoid them. If the map showed a narrow valley I knew it would be swampy so I would climb the hillside and contour above the swamps. If it showed a wide one I would head for the creek as there would probably be shingle banks I could walk on by the forest edge. It's useful to be able to survey the ground ahead from a hillside or ridge where possible and for this a pair of mini-binoculars are well worth their weight. I often plan out the route for the next day or so from a hilltop using the binoculars to check for ways round cliffs or dense brush.

Most important of all though is your mental attitude. The main reason for leaving trails behind is to experience the wilderness directly with no human artefacts between you and it. Compared with walking on trails cross-country travel is real exploration, of both the world around and yourself. To appreciate it fully you need to be open to whatever may happen. Perhaps you spend half a day finding a way across a river, perhaps you have to backtrack for hours through dense forest because a route couldn't be found up the unseen, unexpected cliffs at the head of the valley. Don't worry.

These are not problems. They are what you are there for. This is what direct contact with the wilderness is all about. Distances and time matter far less once the trail network has been shrugged off. Being there is what matters.

The Steep and the Rough

Steep slopes can seem unnerving, especially if you have to descend them. If you're not comfortable going straight down and there is no trail, make your own switchbacking route, cutting back and forth across the slopes. Look for small flatter areas where you can rest and work out the next part of the descent. A careful survey of the slope before you start down is always a good idea. Look in particular for small cliffs and drop-offs and work out a route between them.

Slopes of stones and boulders occur on mountainsides the world over. Trails across them are usually cleared and flattened, though you may still find your feet sliding from under you at times and have to step from boulder to boulder. When crossing large boulder fields it's best to travel slowly and carefully, testing each step and trying not to slip. Be wary of unstable boulders which can easily tip you over as they move when your weight comes on to them. Balance is the key to crossing rough terrain and a staff is a great help in maintaining this. The key to good balance is to keep your weight over your feet, which means not leaning back when descending and not leaning into the slope when traversing. Both of these will see your feet slip away beneath you. On steep loose scree though, trying to avoid slipping at all will drive you crazy so you just have to accept that you will and move fast enough to overcome the negative effects. Scree-running is a fast way to descend but it erodes slopes so quickly that it should no longer be practised. Many continuous scree slopes in the British hills are now slippery, dangerous ribbons of dirt embedded with rocks due to too much scree running. Also be very careful if you can't see the bottom of a scree slope—it may finish at the edge of a cliff. Because climbing, descending or crossing a scree slope without dislodging scree is impossible, a party should move at an angle or in an arrowhead formation so that no one is directly underneath anyone else. As there may be other parties below you, if a stone does start rolling you should shout a warning—'below' is the standard call.

Traversing steep trail-less slopes is tiring and puts great strain on the feet, ankles and hips. It is preferable to climb to a ridge or flat terrace or else descend to the valley below rather than traverse for any distance. It is very tempting on mountain-ridge walks to traverse round minor summits and bumps on the basis that less effort will be involved. In my extensive experience it won't, yet I'm still frequently drawn into traversing. I advise you to heed my words, not follow my practice!

In general, steep slopes should be treated with caution. If you feel unhappy with the angle or the ground under your feet retreat and find a safer way round. Backpacking isn't rock-climbing, though it's surprising what you can get up and down with a heavy pack if you have a good head for heights and a little skill. Don't climb what you can't descend though unless you can see your way is clear beyond the obstacle. And remember that you can use your cord for pulling up or lowering your pack if necessary, or pass packs to each other if you are in a group. It's unwise to let packs drop down a slope, as they may go farther than you intend. A bad piece of route-finding once left Scott Steiner and me at the top of a steep loose and broken limestone cliff in Glacier National Park in the Rocky Mountains of Montana. Foolishly we decided to descend it rather than turn back, and it took us several hours of heart-stopping scrambling to reach the base. Although we had a rope with us we could find nowhere solid enough to attach it to and so frequently handed the packs down to each other. At one point, though, Scott decided he could safely lower his pack to the next ledge, even though he would have to let go before it reached it. Instead of stopping, the pack bounced off that ledge and then a few more before coming to a halt by a stunted tree 60–70 metres/200–230ft below. Amazingly nothing was broken—not even Scott's skis which were strapped to the pack. If we'd lost it or the contents had been destroyed we'd have had serious problems.

Snow

Travel on snow has been dealt with in the sections on the equipment required and in terms of steepness the above comments apply. However, small but steep and icy snow fields may be encountered in summer when specialist equipment is not being carried. Again, having a staff makes a huge difference. It is much easier to balance across snow on small holds kicked with the edge of your boots if you have a third leg for balance. If you don't, take great care and if possible look for a way round, even if it involves a loss of height or a steep climb.

Bushwhacking

Bushwhacking is the apt word for thrashing through thick brush and scrambling over fallen trees whilst thorny bushes tear at your clothes and pack. It's the hardest form of 'walking' I know and to be avoided whenever possible. All too often though you have no choice and just have to plunge in and fight your way through by whatever is the easiest route.

The main thing to accept when bushwhacking is that it will take a long time and a lot of energy, with very little distance to show for it. A speed of 1km/0.6 miles an hour can be good progress. Climbing high above dense vegetation or wading up rivers are both preferable to prolonged bushwhacking. But if you like to strike across country and leave behind cut trails and prepared paths, then bushwhacking will eventually be essential. It certainly gives you head-to-foot contact with the environment!

Bushwhacking can even become necessary during ski tours. I can remember one occasion in the Allgau Alps when four of us descended from a high pass into a valley where the snow wasn't deep enough to cover fully the dense willow scrub spread over the lower slopes, which rose a metre or two high. Luckily the scrub didn't spread very far, but it was a desperate struggle skiing through it as the springy branches constantly knocked us over and caught at our poles and bindings. And after escaping from the Columbia Icefield, our party was faced with half a day of 'skiing' through dense forest laced with fallen trees on steep slopes above a deep river canyon. Balancing on skis on top of a 2-metre/6-ft high fallen tree trunk whilst carrying a 30-kg/66-lb pack is one of the more difficult things I've done in the wilderness.

MINIMISING THE IMPACT ON TERRAIN

As well as learning how to travel through different types of country we also need to learn to do so with as little impact as possible. A trail is a scar in itself, albeit a minor one. Where they exist though, trails should be used and not wandered away from. Most damage is caused when walkers walk along the edges or just off a trail, widening it and destroying the vegetation along its sides. One should always stick to the trail. Even when it is muddy, the main line of the trail should be followed. On steep slopes in particular switchbacks should always be used in their entirety. All too many hillsides have been badly eroded by people short-cutting switchbacks and creating new, steeper routes that quickly become water channels. In meadows and alpine terrain where it's easy to walk anywhere, multiple trails often appear where people have walked several abreast. Again, you should follow the main one, if you can work out which it is. If snow blocks part of a trail try to follow the line of where it would be. In particular don't create a new path by walking round the edge of a snow patch, as all too often happens.

In many areas, land-management bodies are maintaining and repairing trails, often with controversial methods that some people see as destroying any wilderness feeling. However wide eroded scars made by thousands of boots (and often horses, but that is beyond the scope of this book) hardly create such a feeling either. Sadly some popular paths can only be saved by drastic methods. What walkers can do is to follow trail-restorers' instructions, staying off closed sections and accepting artificial surfaces as necessary in places, and by avoiding the most popular trails, they can reduce the need for further such rebuilding.

When you walk cross-country your aim must be to leave no sign of your passing. That means no marking of your route with blazes or cairns or more subtle signs like broken twigs. It also means avoiding fragile surfaces where possible, edging round damp meadows and not descending soft ground into which you have to stamp your boot soles. Rock, snow and non-vegetated surfaces are best able to resist being walked on. The gravel banks of rivers and streams are regularly washed clean by floods and snowmelt. Walking on them causes no harm.

Solo walkers can easily ensure that no one but a skilled tracker could follow their route cross-country. Groups have more of a problem. For large ones (more than four or five) it can be all but impossible. The answer is to keep groups small. Even then, four sets of boots can leave the beginnings of a trail that others may follow in fragile terrain such as meadows and tundra. To avoid this spread out and don't follow in each others' boot prints. Also, where new trails have started to appear don't use them but walk well away so that you don't help in their creation.

Generally when walking cross-country you should always consider what your impact will be on the terrain you cross and always pick the route that will cause least damage.

WILDERNESS HAZARDS

The Weather

The cause of most hazards is the weather. Wind, rain, snow, thunderstorms, freezing temperatures, heatwaves and thaws all bring hazards in their wake. Much of this book is about coping with weather—that is the reason backpackers need tents, sleeping bags and other specialist equipment.

Learning about weather is useful but don't believe, as some books imply, that your attempts at forecasting can be as accurate as those of expert meteorologists. The weather is a highly complex subject, not fully understood. Its patterns are constantly changing. At present it seems likely that human activities are having a major effect on the weather in heating up the atmosphere—the so-called greenhouse effect. Although many predictions have been made no one can tell for certain what might happen to the world's weather, which has never been stable for long, in the future.

Global changes aside, knowing what weather to expect on a wilderness trip is obviously useful. Area guides and local information offices are the places to look for details of general weather patterns for a region, and radio, television and newspaper forecasts for what might happen on a specific day. In many mountain areas there are special telephone forecasts which include information on the conditions of trails, freezing levels, wind speeds high up, avalanche risk and other useful pointers. Monitoring forecasts for any area you visit regularly will soon enable you to build up an annual weather overview.

However the only certainty about the weather is that it is changeable. Even the most detailed, up-to-date forecast can be wrong. Regional variations can mean that whilst it's raining in one valley, it's sunny in another just over the hill. Mountains in particular are notorious for creating their own weather, their summits swathed in swirling cloud whilst their flanks bask in sunlight. The weather need not affect low-level and below-timberline routes too much. If it rains you don waterproofs, if it's windy you keep an eye out for falling trees but otherwise you plod on. High up, however, a strong wind can make walking impossible and the rain may be falling as snow. On any mountain walk you should be prepared to descend early or take a lower route if the weather worsens. Struggling on into the teeth of a blizzard when you don't have to is foolish and risky. It may even be necessary to sit out bad weather for a day or more. I've done so on a few occasions and have been surprised at how fast the time passes.

Altitude

As you go higher the air pressure grows less so it is harder for your body to extract oxygen from the air. This may result in acute mountain sickness (AMS), typified by headaches, tiredness, loss of appetite and generally feeling awful. It rarely occurs at altitudes below 2500 metres/8000ft, so many backpackers never need worry about it. If you are going high though and it does occur, the only answer is to descend. To minimise the chances of its occurring the advice is to acclimatise slowly by gaining height gradually. If you're starting out from a high point it's probably best to spend a night out there before setting off to aid acclimatisation. Above 4000 metres/13,000ft it's advisable to ascend no more than 300 metres/1000ft a day and have a rest day every 1000 metres/3000ft. The only time I've suffered from mountain sickness was when I took the cable car up to over 3500 metres/10,600ft on the Aiguille du Midi in the French Alps. The moment I stepped out of the cable car I felt dizzy and a little sick and had a bad headache. However as we'd gone up in order to ski down I was soon feeling fine again.

Much more serious than AMS are cerebral and pulmonary oedema (fluid build-up on the brain or lungs) as these can and do kill. The first rarely occurs below 4000 metres/13,000ft, the second rarely below 3000 metres/9800ft. Lack of coordination and chest noises are some of the symptoms, but the non-medical may not be able to differentiate between AMS and oedema. The only answer is to descend and to do so quickly.

Medicine for Mountaineering by James A. Wilkerson (The Mountaineers) has a detailed discussion of high-altitude illness which is worth studying by those planning treks in the Himalayas or ascents of high mountains.

Avalanches

Avalanches are a threat every snow traveller must take into account though they are more of a hazard for the skier than the walker. In spring the great blocks of snow and gouged terrain stripped of trees that mark avalanche paths show the power of these snow slides. The causes of avalanches are not fully understood but they can to some extent be predicted and in many mountain areas, especially ones with ski resorts, avalanche warnings are available. These should be heeded. There is not the space here to go into detail on the subject (nor do I feel qualified to do so) and a partial discussion is probably worse than useful. Those heading into snow-covered mountains should study one of the many books on the subject. *Avalanche Safety for Skiers & Climbers* by Tony Daffern (Rocky Mountain Books/Alpenbooks/Diadem) is one of the best for study at home whilst *The ABC of Avalanche Safety* by Ed LaChappelle (The Mountaineers) and *Avalanche Awareness* by Martin Epp and Stephen Lee (The Wild Side) are light enough at 56g/2oz and 125g/4½oz respectively to carry in the pack.

Lightning

Lightning is both spectacular and frightening. Thunderstorms can come in so fast that reaching shelter before they break overhead can be impossible. On several occasions when caught in an exposed situation by a storm I have learnt that when you're scared enough you can run very fast with a heavy pack. Places to avoid in thunderstorms are summits, ridge crests, tall trees, small stands of trees, shallow caves, lake shores and open meadows. Places to run to include deep forests, deep caves, the bases of high cliffs, depressions in flat areas and mountain huts (these are earthed with metal lightning cables). Remember though that statistically, being hit by lightning is very unlikely—not that knowing that's much comfort when you're out in the open and the flashes seem to be bouncing all around.

Metal doesn't attract lightning but can burn you after a nearby strike so it's best if you are caught in a storm to move away from metal items such as pack frames and tent poles. Sitting on something that insulates is a good idea too. The most frightening storm I've encountered woke me in the middle of the night at a high and exposed camp in the Scottish Highlands where all I could do was huddle on my foam pad and wait for it to pass whilst lightning flashed all around.

If someone in a group is hit by lightning and knocked unconscious they should be given immediate mouth-to-mouth resuscitation.

Hypothermia

Hypothermia occurs when the body loses heat faster than it can produce it. It is a killer of the unprepared, the person who sets out with no rain gear or warm clothing because the weather is fine, only to be caught in a storm far from shelter. The causes are wet and cold, aided and abetted by hunger, tiredness and low morale. The initial symptoms are shivering, lethargy and irritability, which soon develops into lack of coordination, collapse, coma and death if nothing is done. Because wind whips away heat, especially from wet clothing, it can occur in temperatures well above freezing. If you start to notice any of the symptoms in yourself or any of your party, take immediate action. The best remedy is to stop, set up camp, get into dry clothes and a sleeping bag, start up the stove and have plenty of hot drinks and hot food. Pushing on is stupid unless you've first donned extra clothes and had something to eat. Then further exercise will help warm you up as exercise creates heat. Even then you should stop and camp as soon as possible.

The best solution to hypothermia is to prevent it happening. A properly equipped backpacker should be in no danger from it as long as care is taken to stay warm and dry and well fed and not to become overtired.

Frostbite

Frostbite is the freezing of body tissue due to exposure to severe cold. Backpackers are unlikely to suffer from it but it is something to be aware of. Keeping warm is the way to avoid it. If minor frostbite does occur it'll probably be to extremities like the nose, ears, fingertips and toes. If any of these feel numb and look colourless, frostbite may be present. Rewarming in the sleeping bag is probably the best solution whilst in the wilderness. Frostbitten areas shouldn't be rubbed, as this can damage the frozen tissue.

Heat Exhaustion

The cold is what most walkers are afraid of but too much heat is a danger as well. The opposite of hypothermia, heat exhaustion occurs when the body cannot shed excess heat. This can be caused by high temperatures, especially if accompanied by high humidity, but also by wearing too many clothes whilst walking. Typical symptoms are faintness, a rapid heart rate, nausea and a cold, clammy skin. Heat is removed via the skin in the form of moisture and if you are severely dehydrated you cannot sweat, so the main way to prevent heat exhaustion is to drink plenty of water, more than you think you need on hot days. If you still start to suffer then stop and rest somewhere shady, as exercise produces heat. If you feel dizzy or weak you should lie down out of direct sunlight and drink copiously.

Fording Rivers and Streams

In many areas the major hazards you will encounter will be unbridged rivers and streams. Water is more powerful than many people think and hikers are drowned every year. If you don't think you can cross safely, don't try. It's better to turn back or seek another route than to be swept away. But when you come upon a river that can't be forded easily you should search along its banks for a safe crossing place before you give up and go elsewhere. With luck you may find a log-jam that you can crawl or clamber across or a series of boulders you can, with great care, use as stepping stones.

Often though, wading is the only option. Whether you prospect upstream or downstream for a potential ford depends on the terrain. Check the map for wide areas where the river may be braided and also slower-flowing. Several shallow channels are easier to cross than one deep one and wide sections are usually shallower and slower than narrow ones. Overall though only experience can tell you whether it's possible to cross or not. If you decide a ford is feasible study your crossing point carefully before plunging in, and in particular check that the far side isn't deeper or the bank undercut. Then cross carefully and slowly with your pack hip-belt undone so that you can jettison it if you are washed away (though try to hang on to it

by a shoulder strap if you can, as you'll need it when you get out and it will help with buoyancy). You should cross at an angle facing upstream so that the current cannot cause your knees to buckle. Feel ahead with your leading foot and don't commit your weight to it until the river bed beneath it feels secure. A third leg, either your staff or ice axe or, if you are carrying neither, a stout stick, is essential in rough water. If the water is fast-flowing and starts to boil up much above your knees you should turn back, as the force of it could easily knock you over, and being swept down a boulder-filled rushing stream is not good for the health. Once on a week-long trip in Iceland at the height of the spring snow melt (June in that part of the world) my route was almost totally determined by which rivers I could cross and which I couldn't (most of them). In the northern Canadian Rockies during my walk along that range I spent many hours searching for safe fords across the many big rivers found there.

I don my training shoes for river fords, although if there are many to do in a day I usually let my boots get wet and keep the shoes for dry campwear, as constantly changing footwear takes too much time. If I can see that the bottom is flat and sandy or gravelly rather than rocky I sometimes cross just wearing socks. What clothing you wear depends on the weather but mountain water is very cold and you will often reach the far side feeling quite shivery. I find that the best way to warm up is by gulping down some carbohydrates, like a few granola bars, then hiking hard and fast. The best clothes for fording are shorts and a warm top.

If you are in a group there are a number of ways you can make river fords safer. Three people can cross in a stable tripod formation or a group can line up along a pole held at chest level. If the crossing is really dangerous then a rope should be used, the forder being belayed from upstream so that if they slip they pendulum into the near bank. Once the first person in a group of more than two is across, all the others bar the last can use the rope as a handline, crossing on the downstream side of it so that they are facing the current. When doing this it's a good idea to be attached to the rope so that you can't be swept away if you let go under the force of the water. I've used the cord I always carry for this, wrapping it a dozen and more times round my waist to make a swami-type belt, then attaching this to the rope with a carabiner (a climber's snap-link, carried for this purpose) which I slid along as I crossed. My experience of roped crossings is limited however and I'd suggest consulting a mountaineering textbook if you want to know about the rope techniques involved.

I have no experience of swimming across rivers, as those in the areas I frequent are generally too cold, too fast and too full of boulders for this to be a practical proposition. Bigger, warmer and slower rivers can be swum however. For a detailed look at how to do it, see Colin Fletcher's *The Complete Walker* (Knopf).

If you can't find a safe crossing there is one final option before you turn back, and that is to wait. In areas where mountain streams are rain-fed, as in the Scottish Highlands, they go down very quickly once the rain stops, a raging torrent turning into a docile trickle in a matter of hours. (The opposite happens as well of course, so it's best to camp on the far side of a river or you may wake to a nasty shock.) Glacier- and snow-fed rivers are at their lowest at dawn, after their sources have frozen overnight, so if you camp on the banks you may be able to cross then. I did this a couple of times in the Canadian Rockies and although I had to stop early I did manage to cross safely the next day. In other respects though, meltwater streams are the worst to ford as you can't see their beds through the swirling mass of rock silt and therefore can't pick out the boulders or see how deep they are.

Poisonous Plants

Unless you are intent on relying on plants for food—in which case you need to be very sure you know what you're eating, especially with fungi—you don't generally have to worry about poisonous plants when backpacking. There are few that can harm you by external contact. The only one in Europe that can is the stinging nettle, whose sting, although painful, is nothing to worry about unless you dive naked into a clump. At low elevations in much of North America the rather nastier poison oak, poison ivy and poison sumac are found. These closely related small shrubs can cause severe allergic reactions, resulting in rashes and blisters in many people. If you brush against this stuff you should immediately scrub the affected area well with

water and soap if you have any as the oil that causes the problems is water-soluble. It's also tenacious and long-lived so you should also wash any clothing or equipment that has come into contact with the plants. If you still start to itch after washing the affected area, calamine lotion and cool salt-water compresses can help, as can some cortisone creams. Over-the-counter preparations for poison oak and ivy rashes apparently make matters worse if taken while suffering an attack.

Forest service, national park and tourist information offices in areas where these plants are to be found can usually provide identification leaflets, which are worth studying and carrying, and you may find warning notices at trailheads.

A final plant to watch out for is devil's club, whose stems are covered with poisonous spines that cause inflammation on contact. It's found in forests in British Columbia and possibly elsewhere (the source of my information is Ben Gadd's *The Handbook of the Canadian Rockies* (Corax)). I came across large stands of this head-high large-leaved shrub in the Canadian Rockies just south of the Peace River, mixed in with equally tall stinging nettles. I normally try to avoid any unnecessary damage to plants but on this occasion I used my staff to beat a way through the overhanging foliage.

DEALING WITH ANIMALS

Encountering animals in the wilderness, even potentially hazardous ones, is not in itself a cause for alarm, though some walkers act as if it were. For me, observing wildlife at close quarters is one of the joys and privileges of wilderness wandering, something to be wished for and remembered long afterwards.

Animals shouldn't be approached too closely though or disturbed in any way, for their own sake as well as your safety. It is their world you are in and they should be left at peace therein. At times though you will come across animals unexpectedly and at close quarters. When you do, move away quietly and without rapid movements so as to cause as little disturbance as possible. With most animals you only need fear attack if you startle a mother with young and even then, as long as you back off quickly, the chances are that nothing will happen.

A few animals pose more of a threat and need special care, and these are dealt with below. Insects of course are also animals and the ones most likely to be a threat, to your sanity if not your bodily health. The items and techniques needed for keeping them at bay are dealt with in chapter 8.

Snakes

The humble serpent is probably more feared than any other animal, yet most species are harmless and the chances of being bitten by one are remote. In the main wilderness areas of Europe and North America only three poisonous snakes are to be found—adders in Europe and rattlesnakes and copperheads in North America—and they don't live everywhere; they are not found above the timberline or in areas as far apart and dissimilar as Alaska and Ireland. None of them have venom likely to cause serious harm to a fit, healthy person. In tropical countries in Asia and Africa and also Australasia more poisonous species exist and those intending walking there should obtain relevant advice.

Snake bites rarely occur above the ankle, so wearing boots and thick socks in snake country minimises the chances of being bitten. Snakes anyway will do everything possible to stay out of your way; the vibrations of your boots are usually enough to send them slithering off before you even see them. As they are creatures of the night, padding round a campsite in snake country barefoot or in sandals or light shoes is inadvisable. Walking at night can present difficulties too. On my Pacific Crest Trail walk I travelled through the Mohave Desert with three others. Battered by the heat of the day we decided to seize the opportunity of a full moon and hike at night. However we quickly found that rattlesnakes, which abound in the Mohave, come out at night and we couldn't tell them from sticks and other debris. Several times we stopped and cast round anxiously with our torches for the source of a loud rattle. Once, the snake, a tiny sidewinder, was found between someone's feet. We didn't hike at night again.

On that trip I carried a Coughlan's Snake Bite Kit (56g/2oz) containing suction cups, antiseptic ampule and swab, scalpel blade, lymph constrictor and instructions in my shorts pocket. The current advice though is not to use such kits as there is a considerable risk that someone who is not medically trained will cause more harm than the bite itself. Instead Peter Steele in his *Medical Handbook for Mountaineers*

(Constable) suggests the following: 'Wash the bite thoroughly with soap and water. Do not suck or slash the skin over the bite, or pee on it. Bandage firmly and tightly over the bite around the entire limb, splint it, and keep it hanging down in order to reduce venom entering the blood-stream.' The victim should stay still and rest whilst someone goes for assistance. If you're on your own you may have to sit out two days of feeling unbelievably awful unless you're close enough to a habitation or road to walk out quickly.

Rattlesnakes seem to strike more fear into people than other snakes, though I don't understand why. By rattling they at least warn you of their presence so that you can avoid them, unlike adders. If you're interested in knowing more, there is a detailed and interesting discourse on them and the legends surrounding them in Colin Fletcher's *The Complete Walker* (Knopf). And for those who want to know more about snake bite and its treatment I recommend James A. Wilkerson's *Medicine for Mountaineering* (The Mountaineers).

Bears

In many mountain and wilderness areas of North America black and grizzly bears roam, powerful and independent. Knowing that they are out there gives an edge to one's walking. You know this is real wilderness. Bears live here. In many areas though, bears no longer roam. Grizzlies in particular have been exterminated in most of the USA apart from Alaska; there are now just tiny numbers in small parts of Montana, Idaho and Wyoming (mainly in Glacier and Yellowstone National Parks). They are only found in any numbers in Alaska and in Western Canada (the Yukon, North West Territories, British Columbia and western Alberta). Without the presence of bears, wildernesses shrink and become tamer and less wild, less elemental. I like knowing they're there, lords of the forests and mountains as they have been for millennia.

But for too many people bears are no more than a potential threat, a bogey to fear. Yet the chances of even seeing a bear, let alone being attacked or injured by one, are remote. In 12,850km/8100 miles of walking in bear country, most of it alone, I've only seen ten black bears and three grizzlies, and none of them has threatened me—most have run away. You are far more likely to be injured in a road accident getting to the wilderness than attacked by a bear, as I found out at the end of the Yukon walk. The truck in which I had obtained a ride spun off the highway and turned over twice, so that I arrived back in Dawson City in an ambulance. I'll take the wilderness, bears and all, any time!

There are ways to minimise the chances of encountering a bear though, which should be followed. The following discussion is based on the advice given in Stephen Herrero's *Bear Attacks: Their Causes and Avoidance* (Nick Lyons Books) which is recommended reading for anyone venturing into bear country. When camping, food may attract bears. How to deal with this is dealt with in the food section of chapter 7. When you're on the move you want bears to know you're there so they'll give you a wide berth. Most of the time this isn't a problem. Their acute sense of smell and hearing will alert them to your presence long before you're aware of them. However a wind blowing in your face, a noisy stream and thick brush can all mask your signals. Then you should make a noise to let any bears know you're around. Many people wear small bells on their packs for this purpose but these aren't really loud enough. It's better to shout and sing or even clap your hands or blow your safety whistle. And whilst doing so use your eyesight as well. In the Canadian Rockies I once came across another hiker sitting on a log eating his lunch and calling out to warn bears he was there as he did so. I walked towards him for five or more minutes without his seeing me, and finally startled him by calling out a greeting when I was a few steps away.

In open terrain and on trails you should scan ahead for bears. A pair of binoculars helps greatly with this. Is that a tree stump ahead or a grizzly bear sitting by the trail? Binoculars will tell you. As well as actual bears, look for evidence of them in the area too. Pawprints and piles of dung are the obvious signs, but also look for scratch marks on trees and mounds of freshly dug earth in alpine meadows, where grizzlies have been digging for rodents.

If you see a bear before it sees you detour quietly and quickly away from it. Be particularly wary of female grizzlies with cubs as 70 per cent of known attacks are by mothers defending their cubs. If the bear is aware of you again move away from it, perhaps waving your arms or talking to help it identify what you are. Don't stare at it or act aggressively. You don't want to be seen as a threat. The only grizzly I've met at fairly close quarters moved slowly away from me once I'd made a noise and let it know I was there. The nearest it came was about 50 metres.

In wooded country look for a tree to climb as you move away in case the bear comes after you. Black bears can climb trees but may not follow you up one, and the more dangerous grizzly can't climb. Indeed one bear-country saying is that the way to tell the difference between black and grizzly bears is to climb a tree; the first will climb up after you, the second will knock the tree down! If the bear keeps coming and you do climb a tree you need to get at least 10 metres/32ft up to be safe.

Very occasionally, a grizzly will charge. The advice as to what to do if one does is mixed. It's only worth trying to climb a tree if one is very close—you can't outrun a bear. Dropping an object such as a camera or item of clothing in front of it may serve as a distraction and allow you to escape. It is better not to drop your pack. If it eats your food the bear may learn to regard future walkers it meets as food sources, and your pack will also help protect your body if it actually attacks. If dropping something doesn't work, the choices are between trying to frighten the bear by yelling, banging objects together (metal on metal may be effective), hitting it whilst standing your ground or backing slowly away, acting in a non-threatening manner by talking quietly to the bear (the option Herrero says he would choose himself), dropping to the ground and playing dead, and running away. The last isn't advised as the bear may chase you.

You could also use a repellent spray that is available called Counter Assault. This is a strong version of the cayenne-pepper-based anti-dog sprays and has been shown both in the field and in controlled tests to repel bears. In one case a grizzly that had already knocked a man down and was biting him ran off when sprayed in the face with Counter Assault. The makers stress that it isn't a substitute for knowing about bear behaviour and taking the usual precautions: 'At best, it is very slim protection. But it's better than no protection at all.' It's non-toxic (the bears aren't harmed) and available in 400-g/14-oz canisters. There's also a holster for carrying it on your belt. It's probably available elsewhere but my information on Counter Assault came courtesy of Ecomarine Ocean Kayak Centre, 1668 Duranleau St, Vancouver, BC, V6H 3S4, Canada. I've never even seen it myself but the literature is impressive enough to make me decide to carry a canister next time I head into grizzly territory. Doug Peacock, in his book *Grizzly Years*, however, doesn't recommend repellents.

In bear country ranger stations and information offices have up-to-date information on areas that bears are using and whether any have caused trouble. Trails and backcountry campsites may be closed if necessary. For your own safety and that of the bears, obey any regulations that are in force.

Hunters

In many areas the late summer and autumn sees wildernesses fill up with hunters carrying high-powered rifles and looking for something to shoot. Make sure it isn't you by wearing something bright like an orange hat or jacket. In areas where hunting is highly organised such as the Scottish Highlands, stay away from areas where it is taking place. Estate offices will let you know when this is and may request you to restrict where you go to avoid disturbing the deer or grouse.

BACKPACKING WITH CHILDREN

I'm afraid I can give no personal advice on this, as I have had no experience of taking children backpacking. But there are books on this subject. Two that are well regarded are *Starting Small in the Wilderness: The Sierra Club Outdoors Guide for Families* by Marlyn Doan (Sierra Club Books) and *Take 'Em Along: Sharing the Wilderness with Your Children* by Barbara J. Euser (Cordillera Press).

A Final Word

As I finish this book, I am surprised at how it has grown, each chapter doubling in size before my eyes or rather my fingertips. I didn't know I had so much to say. I hope you have found my thoughts of interest, perhaps even of use. Let me know what you think. I will undoubtedly have got some things wrong and will have omitted ways of doing others. To know what these are will help make any future edition a better book.

As I write these last words spring is coming to the hills, the first flowers are appearing and every dawn brings new birdsong. The familiar feelings of wanting to see what lies over the next hill, to head into the sanctuary of the wilderness, are stirring within me.

It is time to put down my pen and go backpacking. See you out there, in spirit at least.

Appendix One
Equipment Checklist

This is a list of every item you might take on a backpacking trip. No-one would ever carry everything listed below. From it I select what I need for each particular trip for which I make specific lists.

Carriage
Pack
Bumbag
Daypack

Footwear and Walking Aids
Boots/walking shoes
Running shoes
Insoles
Wax
Socks
Liner socks
Pile socks
Insulated booties
Gaiters
Staff
Ice axe
Crampons
Snowshoes
Skis
Ski poles
Ski boots
Climbing skins
Ski wax

Shelter
Tent with poles and pegs
Tarp
Bivouac bag
Groundsheet
Sleeping bag
Sleeping bag liner
Insulating mat

Kitchen
Stove
Fuel
Fuel bottles
Pouring spout
Windshield
Pan(s)
Mug
Plate/bowl
Spoon(s)

Kitchen continued:
Potgrab
Pot scrub
Water container—large
Thermos flask
Water bottle(s)
Thermos flask
Water purification
   tablets
Water filter
Matches/lighter
Plastic bags
Food

Clothing
Inner Layer:
Tee-shirt
Shirt
Long-johns
Underpants
Warmwear:
Shirt—synthetic
Shirt—wool
Shirt—cotton
Wool sweater
Pile/fleece top
Insulated top
Vapour Barrier suit
Shell:
Windproof jacket
Windshirt
Waterproof jacket
Waterproof
overtrousers
Legwear:
Shorts
Walking trousers
Fleece/pile trousers
Breeches
Salopettes
Headwear:
Sun hat
Bob hat
Thick balaclava
Thin balaclava

Clothing continued:
Headover
Pile-lined cap
Bandanna
Hands:
Liner gloves
Thick wool/pile mitts
Overmitts
Insulated gloves

Miscellaneous: Essential
Head lamp and spare
   bulb/batteries
Candles
Pressure lantern
First-aid kit
Compass and whistle
Map
Map-case
Altimeter
Pedometer
Map measurer
Guidebook
Repair kit:
ripstop nylon patches
needles and thread
tube of glue
stove maintenance
   kit/pricker
rubber bands
Waterproof matches
Washkit
Dark glasses
Goggles
Sunscreen
Lip salve
Insect repellent
Mosquito coils
Head net
Snake-bite kit
Bear-repellent spray
Flares
Strobe flasher

Miscellaneous: Essential continued:
Emergency fishing
   tackle
Cord
Knife
'Office', notebook, pen
   and documents
Watch
Toilet trowel
Toilet paper
Rope
Plastic bags

Miscellaneous: Optional
Binoculars
Photography:
cameras
lenses
tripod
mini tripod/clamp
filters
cable release
lens tissue
film
padded camera cases
Books
Cards
Games
Radio
Personal stereo
Thermometer

Appendix Two
Suggested Reading

This is not a comprehensive list but rather one of books that I have found inspirational, helpful or at least interesting. Many of them are not backpacking books as such but all of them are about or have relevance to wilderness travel. Many are referred to in the text.

Techniques and Equipment

Bain, Don: *Practical Moorland Navigation*, Bivvybug
Barton, Bob & Wright, Blyth: *A Chance In A Million: Scottish Avalanches*, SMT
Barry, John: *Alpine Climbing*, The Crowood Press
Birkett, Bill: *Modern Rock and Ice Climbing*, A & C Black
Brady, Michael: *Cross-Country Ski Gear*, The Mountaineers
Cliff, Peter: *Ski Mountaineering*, Unwin Hyman
Cliff, Peter: *Mountain Navigation*, Diadem
Collister, Rob: *Lightweight Expeditions*, The Crowood Press
Cross, Margaret & Fiske, Jean: *Backpacker's Cookbook*, Ten Speed Press
Daffern, Tony: *Avalanche Safety for Skiers & Climbers*, Diadem
Doan, Marlyn: *Starting Small in the Wilderness: The Sierra Club Outdoors Guide For Families*, Sierra Club Books
Epp, Martin & Lee, Stephen: *Avalanche Awareness*, The Wild Side
Euser, Barbara J.: *Take 'Em Along: Sharing the Wilderness with Your Children*, Cordillera Press
Fleming, June: *The Well Fed Backpacker*, Random House
Fletcher, Colin: *The Complete Walker III*, Knopf
Greenspan, Rick & Kahn, Hal: *Backpacking: A Hedonist's Guide*, Moon Publications
Gillette, Ned & Dorstal, John: *Cross-Country Skiing*, Diadem/The Mountaineers
Hampton, Bruce & Cole, David: *Soft Paths: How to Enjoy the Wilderness Without Harming It*, NOLS
Hart, John: *Walking Softly in The Wilderness*, Sierra Club Books
Herrero, Stephen: *Bear Attacks: Their Causes and Avoidance*, Nick Lyons Books
Ilg, Steve: *The Outdoor Athlete*, Cordillera Press
Keay, Wally: *Land Navigation: Routefinding with Map & Compass*, D of E
Kinmont, Vikki & Axcell, Claudia: *Simple Foods for the Pack*, Sierra Club Books
Kjellstrom, Bjorn: *Be Expert with Map & Compass*, Charles Scribner
LaChapelle, Ed: *The ABC of Avalanche Safety*, The Mountaineers
Langmuir, Eric: *Mountaincraft & Leadership* Scottish Sports Council/Mountainwalking Leader Training Board
March, Bill: *Modern Rope Techniques in Mountaineering*, Cicerone
Manning, Harvey: *Backpacking One Step at a Time*, Vintage
McHugh, Gretchen: *The Hungry Hiker's Book of Good Cooking*, Knopf
Meyer, Kathleen: *How to Shit in the Woods*, Ten Speed Press
Moran, Martin: *Scotland's Winter Mountains*, David & Charles
Parker, Paul: *Free-Heel Skiing*, Diadem/Chelsea Green
Pedgley, David: *Mountain Weather*, Cicerone
Peters, Ed, ed.: *Mountaineering: The Freedom of the Hills*, The Mountaineers
Prater, Gene: *Snowshoeing*, The Mountaineers
Reifsnyder, William F.: *Weathering the Wilderness*, Sierra Club Books
Rowell, Galen: *Mountain Light*, Century/Sierra Club Books
Steele, Peter: *Medical Handbook for Mountaineers*, Constable
Tejada-Flores, Lito: *Backcountry Skiing*, Sierra Club Books
Walker, Kevin: *Mountain Navigation Techniques*, Constable
Watters, Ron: *Ski Camping*, Chronicle
Westacott, Hugh: *The Walker's Handbook*, Oxford Illustrated Press
Wilkerson, James A.: *Medicine for Mountaineering*, The Mountaineers
Winnett, Thomas & Findling, Melanie: *Backpacking Basics*, Wilderness Press
Wood, Robert S.: *Pleasure Packing*, Ten Speed Press

Backpacking Stories and Tales of Adventure

Abbey, Edward: *Desert Solitaire: A Season in the Wilderness*, Ballantine. Essays and anger about the deserts of the South-West USA.

Berton, Pierre: *The Arctic Grail*, Penguin. Story of the quest for the North-west Passage and the North Pole, 1818–1909.

Brown, Hamish: *Hamish's Mountain Walk*, Gollancz. The first continuous traverse of all the Munros

Brown, Hamish: *Hamish's Groats End Walk*, Gollancz. Britain end to end.

Cudahy, Mike: *Wild Trails to Far Horizons*, Unwin Hyman. Ultra-distance multi-day hill runs.

Fletcher, Colin: *The Thousand-Mile Summer*, Knopf. Walking the length of California through desert and mountain.

Fletcher, Colin: *The Man Who Walked Through Time*, Knopf. First trek through the whole of the Grand Canyon.

Fletcher, Colin: *The Secret Worlds of Colin Fletcher*, Knopf. Backpacking stories and philosophy.

Hillaby, John: *Journey Through Britain*, Constable. Britain end to end.

Hillaby, John: *Journey Through Europe*, Constable. Europe north–south.

Huntford, Roland: *Scott & Amundsen*, Hodder & Stoughton.
Huntford, Roland: *Shackleton*, Hodder & Stoughton. The stories of three of the great polar explorers.

Lopez, Barry: *Arctic Dreams*, Scribner's Sons/Macmillan. Will inspire you to visit the Far North.

Maxtone-Graham, John: *Safe Return Doubtful*, Scribner/PSL. A history of polar exploration.

Mikkelsen, Ejnar: *Two Against the Ice*, Rupert Hart Davis. Sledge journeys and survival in Greenland early this century.

Moran, Martin: *The Munros in Winter*, David & Charles. The first winter traverse.

Muir, John: *The Mountains of California*, Doubleday. A classic from a pioneer of wilderness preservation.

Murray W.H.: *Mountaineering in Scotland/Undiscovered Scotland*, Diadem. Classic tales of the Scottish hills

Newby, Eric: *A Short Walk in the Hindu Kush*, Secker & Warburg. Hilarious story of a mountaineering misadventure.

Peacock, Doug: *Grizzly Years*, Henry Holt. Two decades of wilderness bear-watching.

Rice, Larry: *Gathering Paradise: Alaska Wilderness Journeys*, Fulcrum. Wilderness backpacking and canoe touring tales.

Rowell, Galen: *In the Throne Room of the Mountain Gods*, Sierra Club Books. One of the best Himalayan mountaineering expedition accounts.

Rowell, Galen: *High and Wild*, Lexicos. Essays on wilderness adventure.

Schaller, George: *Stones of Silence*, Andre Deutsch. Wanderings of a wildlife expert and mountain-lover in the Himalaya.

Sheridan, Guy: *Tales of a Cross Country Skier*, Oxford Illustrated Press. Ski tours in the Himalayas, the Yukon, the Pyrenees and more.

Shipton, Eric: *The Six Mountain-Travel Books*, Diadem/The Mountaineers. Classic tales.

Simpson, Joe: *Touching the Void*, Jonathan Cape. Intense, almost unbelievable tale of survival after a mountain accident.

Smith, Roger, ed.: *The Winding Trail*, Diadem. Anthology of walking and backpacking articles.

Steger, Will: *North to the Pole*, Ballantine. Story of successful unsupported dog-sled journey to the North Pole with much interesting detail on camping techniques at -60°C.

Styles, Showell: *Backpacking in the Alps & Pyrenees*, Gollancz. Accounts of three long walks.

Tilman, H.W.: *The Seven Mountain-Travel Books*, Diadem/The Mountaineers

Tilman, H.W.: *The Eight Sailing/Mountain Exploration Books*, Diadem/The Mountaineers
Classic tales.

Townsend, Chris: *The Great Backpacking Adventure*, Oxford Illustrated Press. Includes accounts of Pacific Crest Trail and Continental Divide walks.

Townsend, Chris: *High Summer: Backpacking the Canadian Rockies*, Oxford Illustrated Press. First continuous walk along the whole range.

Venables, Stephen: *Everest Kangshung Face*, Hodder & Stoughton. Another of the best Himalayan expedition books.

Selected General & Regional Guidebooks

Bradt, George & Hilary: *Backpacking in North America*, Bradt
Butterfield, Irvine: *The High Mountains of Britain & Ireland*, Diadem
Clear, John, ed.: *Trekking: Great Walks of the World*, Unwin Hyman
Gadd, Ben: *The Handbook of the Canadian Rockies*, Corax
Hargrove, Penny & Liebrenz, Noelle: *Backpacker's Sourcebook: A Book of Lists*, Wilderness Press
O'Connor, Bill: *Adventure Treks: Nepal*, The Crowood Press
Reynolds, Kev: *Classic Walks in the Pyrenees*, Oxford Illustrated Press
Schmidt, Jeremy: *Adventuring in the Rockies*, Sierra Club Books
Simmerman, Nancy Lange: *Alaska's Parklands*, The Mountaineers
Swift, Hugh: *Trekking in Nepal, West Tibet & Bhutan*, Hodder & Stoughton
Townsend, Chris: *Adventure Treks: Western North America*, The Crowood Press
Townsend, Chris: *Long Distance Walks in The Pyrenees*, The Crowood Press
Unsworth, Walt, ed.: *Classic Walks of the World*, Oxford Illustrated Press
Wayburn, Peggy: *Adventuring in Alaska*, Sierra Club Books
Williams, David: *Iceland: The Visitor's Guide*, Stacey International
Wilson, Ken & Gilbert, Richard: *Big Walks*, Diadem
Wilson, Ken & Gilbert, Richard: *Classic Walks*, Diadem
Wilson, Ken & Gilbert, Richard: *Wild Walks*, Diadem

Appendix Three
Useful Addresses

1: Walking and Backpacking Clubs

These are bodies which organise backpacking and walking ventures and also campaign on behalf of walkers. They have journals and newsletters and regular meetings at which members can swap information on equipment, techniques and places to visit.

UK

The Backpackers Club,
P.O.Box 381,
Reading,
RG3 4RL

The Survival Club,
The Square,
Morland,
Cumbria,
CA10 3AZ

The Ramblers' Association,
1/5 Wandsworth Road,
London,
SW8 2XX

Long Distance Walkers
Association,
Wayfarers,
9 Tainters Brook,
Uckfield,
East Sussex,
TN22 1UQ

USA

The American Hiking
Society,
1701 18th St. NW,
Washington,
DC 20009

Appalachian Trail
Conference,
Box 807,
Harpers Ferry,
WV 25425

The Sierra Club,
730 Polk Street,
San Francisco,
CA 94109

Continental Divide Trail
Society,
P.O.Box 30002,
Bethesda,
MD 20814

Pacific Crest Club,
P.O.Box 1907,
Santa Ana,
CA 92702

2: CONSERVATION BODIES

These are environmental organisations which place an emphasis on wilderness preservation.

UK

The John Muir Trust,
Edinburgh,
EH9 0LX

Scottish Wild Land Group,
1/3 Kilgraston Court,
Kilgraston Road,
Edinburgh,
EH9 2ES

USA

The Sierra Club,
730 Polk St,
San Francisco,
CA 94109

The Wilderness Society,
1400 Eye Street,
10th Floor,
Washington,
DC 20037

3: MAGAZINES

UK

The Great Outdoors
The Plaza Tower,
East Kilbride,
Glasgow,
G74 1LW,
Scotland

Climber & Hillwalker
(address as above)

High Magazine
164 Barkby Rd.,
Leicester
LE4 7LF

Trail Walker
EMAP Pursuit Publishing,
Bretton Court,
Bretton,
Peterborough,
PE3 8DZ

USA

Backpacker
Rodale Press,
33 E Minor St,
Emmaus
PA 18098

Outside
1165 N Clark St,
Chicago,
IL 60610

Outdoor Photographer
16000 Ventura Blvd,
Suite 800,
Encino,
CA 91436

Canada

Explore
Suite 410,
310-14 St N.W.
Calgary,
Alberta T2N 2A1

4: MAIL-ORDER CATALOGUES

UK

Field & Trek
3 Wates Way,
Brentwood,
Essex,
CM15 9TB

Survival Aids
Morland,
Penrith,
Cumbria,
CA10 3AZ

Cotswold Camping
Broadway Lane,
South Cerney,
Cirencester,
Glos
GL7 5UQ

USA

REI
PO Box 88125,
Seattle,
WA 98138 0125

5: BOOTMAKERS

Lundhags
PO Box 29,
5 - 8 30 05
Jarpen, Sweden

Peter Limmer & Sons,
PO Box 88,
Rte 16A,
Intervale
NH 03845
USA

6: BOOT REPAIRERS

Shoecare
33 St. Mary's St,
Preston,
Lancashire,
PR1 5LN

7: SLEEPING BAG CLEANING AND RECONSTRUCTION

W.E. Franklin,
116–120 Onslow Road,
Sheffield,
S11 7AH

Duvet Designs,
Dunkleywood Farm,
Falstone,
Hexham,
Northumberland,
NE47 1AQ

Mountaineering Designs,
PO Box 5,
Bramhall,
Stockport,
SK7 3AX

8: FOOD BY MAIL ORDER

Alpineaire,
PO Box 926,
Nevada City,
CA 95959, USA

Trail Foods
PO Box 9309-B,
N. Hollywood,
CA 91609- 1309, USA